# Against All Odds

*Back to Front*

AN AUTOBIOGRAPHY

---

ADOLPH A. C. OKORO

All rights reserved. No part of this publication may be reproduced, stored in a retrieval system or transmitted, in any form or by any means electronic mechanical, Photocopying, recording or otherwise, without the prior permission only of the Author Mr Adolph A. Okoro, or his heirs or his agents as expressly permitted by law.

British Library Cataloguing in Publication Data.
1st Edition 2024
Copyright © 2024
ISBN: 978-1-9996642-0-6 First Published by:

KINGSLEY BOOKS SERVICES LTD
Email: kingsleynonye@yahoo.com
Website: https://www.kingsleybooks.online

# Table of Contents

FOREWORD ................................................................... xi

WHY I WRITE THIS BOOK? ........................ xiii

CHAPTER ONE ............................................................ 1

   Précis Of My Guiding Ethos - My Religious and Philosophical Beliefs .................................................................. 1

CHAPTER TWO ......................................................... 14

   My Genesis – Nigeria - Imo State - Abba, my Hometown - Okoroha Family .................................................................. 14

      BRIEF POLITICAL HISTORY OF NIGERIA ............... 14

      NIGERIA: PLACE IN AFRICA ............................................. 16

CHAPTER THREE ..................................................... 19

   Imo State of Nigeria: Abba Town: Okoroha (Ezeala) Family .................................................................. 19

      ABBA TOWN, ABBA CITY ................................................. 20

      NDI IGBO – IBO PEOPLE .................................................. 22

      ABBA ............................................................................................ 23

      OKOROHA EZEALA ............................................................ 28

      OZIGBU OKOROHA ........................................................... 30

      IJEZIE, OSUAGWU OKOROHA ....................................... 30

      NWAOKORO AHUMIBE OKOROHA ........................... 31

      OFOHA THOMAS OKOROHA ....................................... 31

- PRINCE JACOB OGAMBA OZIGBU .................................. 32
- THE CHILDREN OF THE FOUR SONS OF OKOROHA ......... 32
- OKOROHA DAY ................................................................ 33
- MY FATHER: AZUNNAH DAVID OSUAGWU OKOROHA .... 33
- MY MOTHER ELIZABETH EJIMOLEKE OKOROHA ............. 36
- GRANDMOTHER DAADA IGBEDIE ..................................... 37
- STEPMOTHER CYRINA NKECHINYERE OKOROHA ............ 38
- UDARA FRUIT .................................................................. 41

# CHAPTER FOUR .................................................................. 45
## From Birth ........................................................................... 45
- EARLY LIFE ..................................................................... 46
- MY FIRST SCHOOL ......................................................... 56
- MY GRANDFATHER ......................................................... 65
- MY GRANDMOTHER ........................................................ 72
- MY EARLY SCHOOL ........................................................ 77
- CHRISTIAN UPBRINGING ................................................ 82
- QUEEN ELIZABETH II'S VISIT TO NIGERIA ....................... 86
- DEAD AND MIRACULOUS RESURRECTION ...................... 87
- NIGERIA INDEPENDENCE - 1960 ..................................... 90
- LEAVING SCHOOL AND THE VILLAGE: ARRIVING IN PORT HARCOURT ..................................................................... 91

# CHAPTER FIVE .................................................................. 96

Dampened Hopes...................................................................96
   THE SURVIVAL SPIRIT...................................................100
   LEARNING TRADES AS AN APPRENTICE: AUTOMECHANIC, WELDING, ELECTRICIAN, RADIOMECHANIC................102
   THE DREAM: ALTAR BOY AND BOY SCOUT..................102
   IRISH PRIESTS – REV. FR. PATRICK FLYNN .....................107

# CHAPTER SIX .......................................................................114
Seminary: The Priesthood...............................................114
   LEAVING THE SEMINARY ..................................................122
   BISHOP GODFREY OKOYE ................................................128
   THE NEW SCHOOL .............................................................132
   THE BIAFRAN WAR: 1967 - 1970......................................136
   AS A MILITIA – PLATOON COMMANDER........................138
   THE BIAFRAN AIR FORCE (BAF) OFFICER........................142
   THE BATTLE OF OKIRIKA/ELEME REFINERY ...................145
   THE FALL OF PORT HARCOURT (PH)...............................149
   AIR FORCE BASE IHIALA (ABI) .........................................152
   PATIENCE ............................................................................152
   AIR FORCE BASE IKENANZIZI, OBOWU (ABO) ..............156
   AIR FORCE BASE UGAH (ABU).........................................158

END OF THE WAR ................................................................ 161

HOME AND SAFE ............................................................... 163

## CHAPTER SEVEN .............................................................. 170

What Caused The Bloody War? ............................................ 170

POST WAR SURVIVAL ..................................................... 178

PATIENCE LEAVES .......................................................... 182

CAPTAIN IBRAHIM ......................................................... 184

## CHAPTER EIGHT ............................................................... 188

Back to School: St Augustine's Grammar School, (Sags), Nkwerre ................................................................................ 188

SCOUTMASTER 1ST ORLU TROOP ................................ 191

PATIENCE REMARRIED ................................................... 192

## CHAPTER NINE ................................................................. 196

My Friend, Christopher (Rogers) Oguamanam leaves for St.Paul/Minneapolis, USA ................................................... 196

DUPED: AN EARLY FORM OF "419" IN LAGOS, NIGERIA 198

HSC AND A' LEVEL GCE EXAMS ..................................... 203

SEND OFF PARTY: FAMILY/ABBA .................................... 208

THE BISHOP AND THE SEMINARY .................................. 212

PARTING FOREVER WITH MOTHER: DEPARTING HOME ................................................................................................ 214

PARTING WITH MY FATHER ............................................. 217

MY COUSIN EDDY ............................................................ 220

## CHAPTER TEN ........................................................... 223
### Departure from Nigeria ............................................ 223
#### ARRIVAL IN ZURICH, SWITZERLAND ............................ 224
#### HAMBURG (GERMANY) MAY DAY 1972 ....................... 226
#### ADENIJI – SENT BY GOD ........................................... 230
#### HOCHRAD STRASSE, HAMBURG ................................. 234
#### INNOCENT ONYEJIAKA ............................................. 235
#### HANS PETER HAUSCHILD ......................................... 239
#### EFFECT OF EUROPE ON MY FAITH ............................. 244
#### PASTOR ROTH AND THE UHLIG FAMILY ...................... 248

## CHAPTER ELEVEN ..................................................... 254
### Arriving In USA – St. Paul/ Minneapolis: Twin Cities 254
#### TERRY ROBINSON ................................................... 254
#### MISS MARILETA WANTOCK ...................................... 256
#### MY FIRST CAR ........................................................ 258
#### GRADUATION IN 1975 ............................................. 265
#### JOHN HANCOCK INSURANCE OF BOSTON, MASS ......... 266
#### MY SISTER PAT VISITED USA .................................... 267
#### CAROLYN WALKER .................................................. 267
#### DAUGHTER CHICHI .................................................. 269

- AZUKA UCHE ..................................................................271
- ANNUS HORRIBILIS ........................................................275
- PATRICIA RETURNS TO NIGERIA FROM GERMANY ........285

## CHAPTER TWELVE ..............................................................287
### Cletus, My Baby Brother Admitted to The University of Nebraska, USA ..................................................................287
- U.S. OFFUTT AFB BELLEVUE, NEBRASKA ......................288
- UCHE MY FIANCÉ WENT OFF TO MEDICAL SCHOOL ......291

## CHAPTER THIRTEEN ..........................................................312
### Abandoning Pharmacy and Law for MBA and PhD ....312
- CLETUS ARRIVES USA ....................................................315
- TIME WITH JOHN HANCOCK INSURANCE COMPANY ....319
- SOLACE IN THE UNRAVELLING UPHEAVAL ....................319
- LULAMA CAME ALONG FROM SOUTH AFRICA ..............320
- THE DEATH OF MY MOTHER ..........................................321
- BIRTH OF MY SECOND DAUGHTER ................................327

## CHAPTER FOURTEEN ........................................................331
### Military Avenue Dry Cleaners and My First Home ......331
- THE MILITARY AVENUE LAUNDERETTE IN NEBRASKA ...335
- SHERRY SMITH AND OUR SON MONSO ........................337
- DEATH OF CAROLYN CONNIEGENE WALKER OKOROHA 342
- LEAVING AMERICA – RETURNING HOME TO NIGERIA ..342
- ARRIVING IN NIGERIA 1984 ..........................................345

## CHAPTER FIFTEEN ............................................. 351
### New Wives and Children ........................................... 351
#### NYSC ............................................................. 352
#### BUSINESS ........................................................ 353
#### VISIT TO USA FROM NIGERIA — SHERRY AND MONSO 358

## CHAPTER SIXTEEN ............................................. 361
### Diagnosed with Diabetes in Houston, Texas ............. 361
#### RELOCATION TO LAGOS ................................... 368

## CHAPTER SEVENTEEN ........................................ 377
### Migration To London, United Kingdom ..................... 377
### (UK) ................................................................ 377
#### PATRICIA, MY EX - WIFE .................................. 380
#### GREENWICH, LONDON BOROUGH ...................... 382
#### LYNN OKORO .................................................. 385

## CHAPTER EIGHTEEN ........................................... 390
### Becoming a London Lawyer in England ..................... 390
#### ESTABLISHING AND MANAGING A LAW FIRM ........ 392
#### LING ZHANG AND OUR SON, AMARA, GUAI GUAI .... 398
#### VISITS TO NIGERIA AND OPENING OF MY ANCESTRAL HOME AT ABBA ............................... 400
#### LUNG CANCER IN 2012 ..................................... 402

## CHAPTER NINETEEN .................................................. 421
Visit to USA in 2014 ............................................................ 421
### VISITING BEIJING, CHINA ................................................ 427

## CHAPTER TWENTY .............................................. 447
Acute Or Chronic Sinusitis, (Rhinosinusitis) .................. 447
### EYE PROBLEM ................................................................. 450
### PROSTATE CANCER ....................................................... 451
### CORONA VIRUS (COVID 19) ......................................... 464

## CHAPTER TWENTY-ONE ................................... 473
Government Palliative Schemes to Assist UK Residents
.................................................................................................. 473
### AKARAKA ......................................................................... 475

## CHAPTER TWENTY-TWO ................................... 479
Use of WhatsApp During The Corona Virus Pandemic
.................................................................................................. 479
### THE YEAR 2022 ............................................................... 517

## CHAPTER TWENTY-THREE ................................ 537
Our Surprise Caribbean Cruise Holidays booked by My Wife, Lynn Okoro ................................................................. 537

## CHAPTER TWENTY-FOUR .................................. 549
What Is Nze Na Ozo Title? .................................................. 549
### THE LAST LEG OF LIFE!!! ............................................... 552
### YOU MAY THINK: ............................................................ 554
### OLD IS GOOD .................................................................. 555

# FOREWORD

It is an honour to write the foreword to this exciting and exacting tome 'Life is not a rehearsal' says an aphorism, and "it is not life that matters, but the courage you put into it'. These sayings capture the gravamen of this book about a living doyen and oracle – a transcendental being, who is undeterred or delimited by circumstances of birth, place, origin, time, space, age, culture or religion.

The centrality of the author's life is the abiding grace and providence of God, upon which all human aspirations and goals are attainable, and all obstacles are conquerable. With these canons as the spiritual and philosophical shibboleths of his existence, the author anchors his undertakings on perspiration, diligence, determination, guile, gut feeling and ambition, catholic devotion, spartan courage and native intelligence.

The admixture of these virtues and adroitness pitches to us the intrinsic qualities of an avatar – the subject of this treatise whose life is admirable, remarkable, novel, distinguishable, irrepressible, commendable, enviable, worthy, and imitable.

I commend this book as a clinical and canonical reminiscence of an alpha male who has been undeterred by the turbulence of life. Indeed, a candid and beautiful human story that is rich in anecdotes, proverbs, biblical injunctions, logic, philosophy, and simple common sense. This piece is pungent, no holds barred, truthful and unusually insightful.

It is a blend of the clash of civilisations, and the challenges of inhabiting a global village that is diverse and vast.

This book is a testimony to the 'never say die' spirit of a progenitor and the acknowledgement of the uncommon grace our creator bestows on everyone, despite the vicissitudes of life.

**Sope Adeeko, Ph.D., LL.M (Int'l Econ Law) (Warwick), LL.M (Lagos), LL. B(OOU), BL, MCIarb.**

**Solicitor, Senior Court of England and Wales; Solicitor and Barrister of the Supreme Court of Nigeria.**

**Aare Adimula, Oke-Odan**
**London 2024.**

## WHY I WRITE THIS BOOK?

I have come to terms with the fact of my mortality. I have therefore decided, among other things, to leave some legacies, including building a school, assisting, and empowering people, and above all writing an autobiography. It is my wish to put my story in black and white, before I go to join my ancestors, my father, and forefathers, in perpetual and everlasting rest.

It is my wish to leave behind in written form, some of my life experiences, my struggles, my beliefs, and views about life. This book is not a blueprint or guidebook for everyone to follow, it is simply unique. However, my story may encourage, uplift, teach, or motivate some who read it.

I believe a positive character is everything in life. We are all born of woman. Whether one believes in creation or evolution, it is certain living things live for uncertain, indefinite, but relatively short periods and must, inescapably die. We open our eyes and find ourselves in this spaceship called mother earth, in which we are doomed together. None of us is getting out of here alive! Life is what we do and what happens to us in the short period we are here. It is good to leave a footprint as you pass through this life.

Personally, at almost eighty years of age, I look back and shudder. I have had a somewhat eventful life, so I felt I should publish my life story and my views on life events generally. I have dazzled, baffled, and confounded many.

I believe my story is interesting, breath-taking, at times humorous and shockingly extraordinary!

**Barrister, Chief, Dr, Nze, Sir Adolph A.C Okoro Abba Town, Nigeria, 2024.**

*My enrolment as a solicitor in United Kingdom in 2006.*

*Myself in my chieftaincy regalia.*

**CHAPTER ONE**

------------------------

# Précis Of My Guiding Ethos - My Religious and Philosophical Beliefs.

I came to terms with the fact I will one day pass away. Therefore, I decided, among other things, to author a story of my life. I just want to leave behind a written form of my life experiences, struggles, beliefs, opinions, every situation, and experience of my life.

It is not a blueprint or guidebook for everyone to follow. It is simply unique. It is my belief that all present-day living things are born, or are products, or off-springs, of other living things. Therefore, the very first living species must have been made or created by whom? The unanimous answer remains GOD, who is described in many ways by different people with varied beliefs. The age-old questions of who God is and the purpose of life will rage for ever. The answers to these questions vary, and the debate will continue evermore. Even those who say living things evolved, have failed to say what started X before it evolved to Y? Anyway, whether born, created, or evolved, living things live for uncertain, indefinite but relatively short periods, and must inescapably die. We open our eyes and find ourselves in this spaceship called mother earth, in which we are doomed together. Life is what we do and what happens to us, in the brief period that we are here.

Later in life, certain eternal truths became clearer to me, that just like those before me and those after me, no one gets out of this world alive. The same fate awaits poor and rich, sinners and saints, short and tall, thin, and fat, super stars and hobos, presidents and prisoners, blacks, whites, Asians, Northerners, Southerners and so on. There is no blueprint on how to live a long life, get rich and so on. No one knows yet which of today's one year old children will live a long or a short life. My mother once told me 'Tomorrow is like a pregnant woman; no-one knows yet what it will deliver' (Echi di ime).

There are no guarantees in life, except the inevitability of death for all. How long we live is potluck. Sometimes, I cannot help but wonder what life is all about? One is born, and starts learning the ropes –how to crawl, how to eat, walk, run, go to school, learn a trade, marry or not, raise children or not, make mistakes, make money or not, store wealth or not and so on, then one day, one is found belly up. We came with nothing to this earth, and we leave with nothing. By the time one seems to be mastering the modus operandi of life and survival skills, it is then sadly, time to go. Where? Some say they go to meet their maker, who alone - he or she was not made and does not die - universally called God in different languages.

God could be a mere figment of our imagination, who knows? But it's very logical to have God, otherwise no one could explain the origins of the universe, or humanity. Having said this, I then quickly wonder if God create us in his own image and likeness, or did we humans, out of stupidity, naivety, or desperation, think and create God, to exist in our own human image and likeness. Some people do not believe that God exists, whilst others are agnostic about the qualities of God.

Thus, life on earth appears, or science informs us, to have been here for over six billion years and it will go on 'per Omnia circula circulorum' forever and ever. Unless we selfdestruct, or another star comes to destroy us, no one knows.

In my genealogy, from hand down stories, I know only up to my great grandfather (Okoroha) in my family tree, and I have no idea or certainty who were his own grand or great grandparents. One day, those of us alive today will become a very distant memory, perhaps mythical names. In my small way, I have tried to be legendry and leave a footprint in the sands of time.

Things are not what they seem, because what appears to be your advantage today, can become your downfall tomorrow, and your suffering today may become your strength later. Though, I do not see suffering as something to boast about, or to be proud of. The reality of life is that when one thinks he has found the answers, the questions change. It is my belief that one owes it to oneself, for the time here on earth, to do what makes one happy. If it makes you feel good, aspire to it, and do it, so long as your actions are not intended to harm others. Happiness, I have found to be relative, depending on what makes one happy. One man's meat is another man's poison. For some people, happiness may come from not having to go to work, for another it may be the thrill of jumping off a cliff. We came with nothing, and we leave with nothing, except our reputation, in some cases, if you are fortunate, like me in authoring this book, you leave some legacy or footprints in the sands of time.

For me, legacy could include one or more of these examples: having children, authoring a book, building a lasting family business and family home, In the end a book you have written, a company or charity you have started or gifted, which employs and helps others. A legacy could mean virtuous deeds done, a decent family home in your own homeland, as in Nigeria, for example, if you are a Nigerian. Legacy could be the testimony people give that you changed theirs, or other people's lives for the better.

Getting rich is ninety nine percent sheer luck unless you are lucky and inherit wealth. I also say that people become successful by ninety-nine per cent inspiration and one per cent perspiration. Unless you are destined to succeed, all your arduous work may still come to nought. Some of us may work little and be hugely successful, while others may work hard and yet have nothing to show for their efforts. For life on earth, some work hard, whilst others hardly work. One must work hard, then hope and pray that God blesses one's efforts. Unless you scoop the lottery, wealth will not drop through the letterbox whilst you are watching TV or sleeping.

At the end of the day, there are no guarantees in life. A medical doctor who lives a healthy lifestyle can drop dead at a noticeably early age, whilst a chain smoking, drug addict, hobo, tramp, hooligan, or alcoholic may live to be eighty or a hundred years. A super rich person may be childless, or have a disabled, or unintelligent child, whilst the poorest of the poor can have beautiful, handsome, intelligent children, or vice versa. A preacher or cleric's child can turn out to be a vagabond, wayward or a prostitute, whilst a prostitute's child may become a cleric, a nun or even president of a nation. A short person may have tall children, whilst a tall person could have short offspring.

I believe in predestination to some extent, that is, each one of us comes into this world with our fate inscribed on our palm or forehead. We also become who we are by nature and nurture. In my hometown, we call the belief in predestination: AKARAKA. We are who we are, mostly by Grace if you are religious, or luck if you are not. Why are some people born with good health, long life, or a knack for success in every endeavour?. This is what is called undeserved blessing, good nature, good luck, or providence.

There is a God, or what some call Higher Power. To me, God is the being to whom we ascribe as the maker of the universe and this world, its contents and inhabitants and planets. It's God only, who Himself was not made by anyone or anything else. Whether we profess it or not, we are all in some degree Agnostic. God is beyond our imagination. God cannot be conceptualized nor compartmentalized. God is not an old white or black man with a long beard, who lived in the sky. We all, at one time or another, have our doubts, disbeliefs, and unanswered questions. We are not sure of it all. Faith, they say, is belief in what you have not seen, or cannot prove. I personally do not think that our existence, the organization, the order in the universe and on earth, the intricacies of our human bodies and organs, came about by sheer accident, or by a big bang, or out of our own self will, wishes or efforts, as proponents of Charles Darwin seemed to say. They claim animals and birds for example, developed long beaks or sharp teeth and so on to be efficient or effective in hunting or otherwise. If Darwin is right, we would by now have developed wings and become airborne. All people, over six billion years on earth, would have developed or evolved into having bigger and longer private parts. The monkeys and apes we see in zoos, would have evolved and become human beings. If Darwin is correct, among other things many people would have changed their height, looks, build or the original colour of their skins, maybe to be more brown, black, or white. Human beings are more similar than they are different. There is good and bad in every race, colour, creed, or gender. Your best mate, or the one who helps or saves you in life may not necessarily come from same town, country or continent as you. Though charity they say should begin at home, your own brother or sister, someone close may also end up being your worst foe.

For luck to kick-in, you must be at the right place at the right time. You must do your necessary one per cent perspiration before God the Almighty can assist you. You must buy a lottery ticket before you may luckily win the lottery. You must be in the game to win it. You must be able to enroll in a school or college, study hard before you may luckily pass exams, graduate, and perhaps qualify as a professor, doctor, lawyer, engineer, or butcher. We must firstly do our absolute best before providence can do the rest for us. We must be able to recognize opportunities and take advantage of them when they present themselves. Funnily enough, we all pray to succeed, ironically even thieves, robbers, and all others engaging in amoral, immoral, or illegal activities. Prayers in my opinion are fervent wishes. No matter how much we pray God does not do for the individual what the individual can do for himself or herself.

Indiscriminately, all prayers are answered in the affirmative or negative. All prayers are answered which makes everything look like a 'random world of Riley' for all of us. Is anyone, or God really in control? Deciding on which prayers are answered, or what actions or events are allowed to occur.

This brings to my mind the axiom that many of us are born great whilst others achieve greatness. This book gives special salute to the people who recognized the bondage in their lives, limitations they were born into and did something to change their lot. I agree with St Benedict's monastic saying that 'to work is to pray' 'laborare est orare.' Every positive thought is a silent prayer. Prayer itself is a fervent wish or dream. No venture, no success! If you do not dream, a dream never comes through unless you act on it. You may never know any success if you do not venture. The higher the risk, the more the reward or the harder the fall. No pain, no gain!

By God's special grace, I belong to the group who were born to struggle. At times, I sit down and ponder, wildly sometimes, as I wonder whether I could be able to put my life story in black and white and how long and daunting that would be ? I have luckily lived a quite simple and contented life. My best qualities being that I have always appreciated every inch of progress I make. I am grateful for each day I wake up alive. The world is a big camera which is snapping every second, day and night. Even when people have not seen us for many years, their impression of us is picture of us in their mind's eyes, of when they last saw us. Every new day comes with its own blessings. I therefore believe I should wear a smile daily, even after a disappointment and even on the day of my transition. I am not sure if 'this is it' or are we going elsewhere from here? It is better to be positive and be prepared, in case there is an afterlife. Every child born has a role to play, an impact to make, and work to do on this earth. A person's destined role, their mission on earth, may take a long time, or a brief period, to accomplish before they depart.

I have lived with many of these perplexing and paradoxical thoughts, some of which are eternal truths, I have no clear answers, and finally decided that the life of a man is arguably incomplete, if he has failed to put down on paper, his travails, and thoughts as a legacy for future generations and posterity. Some may disagree with my thoughts, some may say 'Huh! I think that way too!' whilst others may be inspired. I say 'to God be the glory' as I write for posterity and humanity.

I have concluded that one of the admirable qualities of civilisation is the documentation of things and events. Unlike in most parts of developing nations, where wealth of knowledge, discoveries and events were never documented or preserved, thus they have been lost, to the disadvantage of posterity. Today there are no pictures of my great - grandparents, let alone documentation as to how they lived or their ingenuities. Paradoxically, much as I have certain unmitigating niggling doubts about the form of God and the hereafter, I am a special child of God, He loves me, He is in-charge and in control of my life. From the age of seven to twenty, I assumed the name "Nwachinemere" which means a child favoured by God. As an adult I took Nze title of "Akaraka and Akarauga" which means that from birth I'm blessed. When I depart this earth, I will be pleased to have left various legacies and footprints, namely my twelve children and their descendants, and their mothers, that I have changed their lives, all the people that I have assisted one way or another, or the houses I left behind in London and in Nigeria. The businesses I had and bequeathed to my family, the school I built in Nigeria and the houses I built for other families. The pride and joy my family derive from my academic prowess and qualifications, my cultural titles: Nze Na Ozo . All these achievements are written in the book of my life story forever!

*My Late Mother Elizabeth Ejimoleke (Fanny)Okoroha and sister, (Patricia).*

*My Late Mother Elizabeth Ejimoleke (Fanny) Okoroha*

St Augustine's Grammar School group photos in Nkwerre Nigeria.

**CHAPTER TWO**

--------------------------

# My Genesis – Nigeria - Imo State - Abba, my Hometown - Okoroha Family

## BRIEF POLITICAL HISTORY OF NIGERIA

I was born in the south-eastern part of Nigeria, my home country. The name Nigeria is coined from River Niger which runs through the area. The British invaded Lagos and the vast areas and annexed it as their own in 1861. They colonised Nigeria, calling it a British protectorate, from 1901. As a British protectorate, there was southern and Northern Protectorates which were (amalgamated), joined together as one Nigeria in 1914. The colonisation of Nigeria continued from 1901 to 1960 when the people of Nigeria gained independence from Britain. Nigeria became a republic of three regions (northern, western, and eastern regions) in 1963. Due to the coalition of North and East, Sir Balewa (Hausa-Fulani) of NPC was the first Prime Minister, whilst Dr Azikiwe (Ibo) of NCNC was first Governor General, President 1963-1966. Chief Awolowo (Yoruba) of AG was in opposition. In the first republic, it is possible that the Westerners (Yorubas) felt that the Ibo and Hausas out manoeuvred them. The first republic ended in January1966 by a military coup d'état. The new military head, General Ironsi was assassinated in July 1966, in addition to this, many Ibos were massacred in the Northern region. As a result of these events, the Eastern Region of mostly Igbos formed a Republic of Biafra and tried to break away and ceased from Nigeria. Biafra/Nigeria civil war ensued from 1967 to January 1971. General Gowan led from 1966 until July 1975. He was ousted by General Murtala, who ruled until he was gunned down in February 1976.

General Obasanjo took over and ruled from 1976-1979 when he peacefully handed over to Alhaji Shagari for the second republic, which ended 1979-1983, when the military led by General Buhari then took over until 1985. General Babangida staged a palace coup d'état and led until 1993. Mr Shonekan briefly ruled 1993-1993. General Abacha then led until 1998 when he died in office. General Abubakar as interim head led until 1999 and Obasanjo came back as a civilian leader from 1999 to 2007. The Yar'Adua civil rule ended in 2010 (20072010) when he died in office. Mr Goodluck Jonathan, led from 20102015, Buhari came back as a civilian ruler in the fourth Republic. Part of the tragedy of Nigeria is that you cannot remove a bad leader by the ballot boxes, and they won't resign, corruption is endemic from top to bottom.

6th May 2015 to present. Elections in 2019 were won by All Progressives Congress party (APC) and Mohammadu Buhari, a Muslim, was returned to power.

I am apolitical. I have never voted in any Nigeria election. Maybe, because I have never been home in Nigeria during the elections. People vote only for candidates from their town, state, or tribe. People also vote for those who have given more money as a bribe to them. This is regardless of the name of their party, or what they state as their aim or goal. Manifestos are not worth the paper they are written on. People can say anything, promise heaven on earth to be elected, after election, they renege on their promises. I do not like discussing Nigerian politics. It does not matter who wins, the regime is the same. Most Nigerians believe that politicians are there to feather their own nests. The February 2023, general election was anything but free and fair. Mr Peter Obi who was the most popular choice of the people was said to have lost to Tinubu of ruling party APC.

## NIGERIA: PLACE IN AFRICA

My home country, Nigeria is the largest Black African country. It lies on the west coast of Africa. It is situated at a latitude approximately 10 degrees north of the Equator and stretches to latitude of approximately 140 degrees North. The width starts from longitude approximately thirty degrees East of the Greenwich meridian, to longitude approximately 130 degrees east. Altogether, Nigeria has an area of about one million square kilometres. The population is an estimated 120 million peoples. Nigeria has boundaries with five other African countries, namely the Republic of Benin, on the west side, in the north, the Republic of Niger and in the east is the Republic of Cameroun. In the northeast is Lake Chad, which connects to Niger Republic and Chad. In the south is the coastline awash by the bight of Biafra and Atlantic Ocean.

Nigeria has two main climates, rainy season, and dry season. It also has two main vegetations - Tropical Rain Forest in the southern half of the country and the Tropical Savannah in the northern half. The average temperature all year long is around 30 degrees centigrade, 80 degrees Fahrenheit. Generally, it is extremely, often unbearably, hot. The copious sunshine is a mixed bag. It is fun, but it can be torture. Lagos beaches filled with sun lovers, bikinis, shorts, bare bodies. The warmth is a fertile land for pestilence, such as flies, mosquitoes, and snakes. Nigeria still has over two hundred ethnic groups and languages, but the three main ethnic groups are the Ibos (NdiIgbo) of Ibo land in the east, Yoruba of Yoruba land (Ndi- Yoruba) in the west and Hausas of Hausa land (Ndi-Hausa) in the majority north. There are many small or minority tribes including the Fulanis, Gwaris,Tivs, Idomas and Kanuris in the north, the Nupes, Urhobos, Itsekeris and Ijaws in the west, the Ibibios, Ijaws, Efiks, Kalabaris and Ogonis in the east.

Nigeria used to have three main regions Eastern, Western and Northern regions, naturally divided by the Rivers Niger and Benue, but now has 36 United States of Nigeria, including the Federal Capital Territory (FCT) Abuja, created in 1991, which forms the Federal Republic of Nigeria. Before then, Lagos was the Capital of Nigeria from the outset.

*Another Family Group Photo.*

**CHAPTER THREE**

------------------------

# Imo State of Nigeria: Abba Town: Okoroha (Ezeala) Family

I am an ibo man (Onye – Ibo), so I am not Onye-Yoruba nor Onye - Hausa. I was born in 1944 into the Okoroha family of Ogwuaga, Abba, Nwangele LGA, Imo State, Nigeria. Okoroha family is sometimes referred to as the family of Ozigbu - "Okoro-Ozigbu," Ozigbu family, and Okoroha family. This dichotomy has caused some people to erroneously think Okoroha is the brother of Ozigbu. The eternal truth is that Okoroha is the father of Ozigbu. Since other kindred in Ogwuaga refer to our family, also as Umuazeala, we have changed our name to Okoro Ezeala, or Ezeala Family, to cure the dichotomy in nomenclature, though to achieve this aim, we must advertise and officially inform all and sundry never to refer to us anymore as Okoroha or Ozigbu family, rather only by Ezeala family.

Presently, we have over 250 living persons – men, women, and children. Thus, Okoroha family is the most populous and successful single family in Abba town, which we fondly call 'Abba City'. There are over forty storey buildings and ten bungalows in the Ezeala family compound. There are over a hundred money making and productive adults in our family with the same surnames. We boast over Fifty University graduates.

We have about eight Doctorate Degree holders, six Barristers and Lawyers, six Engineers, four Accountants and Auditors, ten Nurses and allied medical professions, many Businessmen and women of national and international repute. We have over fifty family members and their own families living in European countries, United States of America and South Africa, and other African countries. We continue to be united and act in unison under one family Prince, and one family Chairman under our respected elders. We bury our dead together; we speak with one voice as far as possible. Every family member is a representative of the entire family, both at home and abroad.

## ABBA TOWN, ABBA CITY

My hometown, Abba is in the South-eastern part of Nigeria. Abba is in the former Eastern Region of Nigeria, (formerly East Central State of Nigeria) and in the present-day Imo State of Nigeria.

Abba town is in the equatorial rain forest and has plenty of vegetation. The roads have dusty red soil, the farms have rich black soil and there are sandy compounds. Thus, Abba is blessed and enjoys fertile land of red and black soil. It enjoys two main seasons, rainy and dry, which are characterised by monsoon rainfall and copious sunshine, alternating every six months of the year. The Rains fall long and hard between April and September with a two- week break in August. The dry season brings relentless, fierce sunshine. The beauty is that sometimes the sun shines whilst rain is falling. Rainbows are usual and frequent sights. Within this period, there are also approx. three months November to January, of a not so hot period, called Harmattan. During this period, it is winter in the northern hemisphere – including Europe, China, Russia, Canada, and North America. Thus, the Harmattan is a result of the northeast, trading dry and freezing winds, blowing from Europe, across North Africa and the Sahara Desert to West Africa and to the Gulf of Guinea. If anything, it is a dry cold period. Our old men used to say that Harmattan was the best time to find a nice girl to marry, because the best girls are the ones whose lips and heels are not so dried-up and cracked from the dry cold climate.

Abba is in the former Nkwerre, and present Nwangele Isu Local Government of Imo State, Nigeria. Abba has four villages namely: Umuopara or Umuokwara, Umudrunna, Ekitiafor and Ogwuaga. Now, as I write, the four villages have disintegrated into four autonomous communities. The population of Abba is perhaps less than five thousand persons.

The breakup of this small town can hardly be said to be the best-case scenario, or in best interest, or accepted by most of the indigenes of Abba.

The present-day Abba-elite have founded an Association of Abba Autonomous Communities which aim to achieve, at least, cooperation and harmony amongst the communities. My Parents are Mrs Fanny Ejimoleke and Chief David Azunnah Osuagwu Okoroha.

## NDI IGBO – IBO PEOPLE

The IBO TRIBE is said to be descendants of Gad, one of the lost tribes of Israel - the Jewish Nation. Gad, the seventh son of Jacob, (the patriarch of Judaism), left his homeland in the Middle East, wandered off to this part of West Africa and had children with a local lady. The first son named Eri, begot Aguleri, whose children gave birth to the progenitors of the entire Igbo race. The word "Igbu" or "Igbo," is "Hebrew" which bastardised or mispronounced in vernacular as Ibo.

If one goes through the Old Testament of the Bible, one can see and appreciate the culture and customs of the Ibos mirror that of the Jews. There are similarities in things like circumcision (Ibeugwu) on the eighth day of birth, regards for first son (Okwara) and first daughter (Ada), the first fruits, weddings (Igbankwu) and births (Ibioro) ceremonies, burial and mourning of the dead for 8 days (Iliozu, Ikwaozu, and Igbankpe), inheriting of the dead brother's wife (Ikuchinwanyi).

Due to the Jewish origins of the Ibos, they are generally fairer in complexion when compared with other ethnic groups into the present-day Nigeria, such as the ndibini, ndi-Yoruba, ndiIjaws, Itshekiris, Tiv, and ndi-Hausa. The Ibos, like the Jews, are deeply religious, highly superstitious, they love money and are shrewd and astute businesspeople. Notably, the "Onyx" stone of Gad was discovered by Jewish missionaries in Aguleri in year 1995.

## ABBA

Hand down stories had it that a man called UBURU came to this area of Igboland about four hundred years ago. He was a heavy weight warrior from Abam town, Abiriba/Ohafia, which is in the present-day Abia State of Nigeria. He came with his wives, sons, daughters, and loyal followers. The sons of Uburu included Okwara, Durunna, Afor, Ogwunaga, and Osuama. Uburu pitched his tent and occupied the land he named Abba, which lay inbetween the existing villages of Isu, Owerri-Nkwoji, Okwelle, Umudi and Dikenafia (then known as Umuawobe). The four villages of Abba were named after the sons; thus, the children of Okwara became Umupara; Children of Duru became Umudrunna, Afor and his family occupied a midland/centre, which became known as Ekitiafor and the fourth son took the smallest but most fertile part of Abba, called Ogwuaga, and the fifth son lived at Osuh present day Eziama and Umunume parts of Mbano.

Note that:

1. It is probably a coincidence that in the Bible, Abba is said to mean "father."
2. There is also a disbanded Swedish musical band known as Abba.
3. There is another town called Abba in Anambra State.

Aba the capital of Abia State which spelt with a single letter "B"!

Abba and Osuh ama people used to be together and belonged to Okigwe Province, but re-designation in the 1920s, made our Abba town to be reassigned under Orlu province. To this day persons from Abba and people from parts of Mbano cannot engage in fights with each other, because they are said to be siblings – of same mother and father. The seventh son of Uburu was said to have wandered off with his own children and established new towns called Abagana and Abba, both in Anambra State. Up till the present time, the people of Abagana always state that their ancestors came from Abba Orlu. Until about 1965, before the Nigerian civil war, people from the said parts of Mbano did have a special day in every year when they marched and trooped, decorated in cam wood, chalk, and crimson, to the "ikpa" Abba, to pay respect and homage to their ancestors and ancestral home. At about the same time, some other group decamped from Arochukwu and arrived in a nearby land and decided "kwerre" or agreed to settle there and the town became known as Nkwerre town in Orlu.

The newly created Abba town was attacked from many fronts by its neighbours, namely Isu, Owerri Nkwoji and Umuawobe. Their reasons being that Abba people took their farmland. Abba fought back and vanquished their enemies on all fronts and survived. Abba is said to have fought the most prolonged war with Umuawobe and Abba was said to have killed them mercilessly. In the end, Abba became so good at warfare, that Abba people became reputed as warmongers and mercenaries. Long ago, Abba people were often hired and paid by other towns to come and fight their various inter clannish wars, thus to this day Abba is called "Abba nwauruogu" and "Abba huruogu-ju-ri" which Abba people who have tactical superiority and who rather fight than eat. Neighbouring townspeople, always quipped 'why do you want to fight, unless you are from Abba?' Anyways, Abba people of today are illustrious and peace loving.

Uburu gave his respective sons the Ofor, staff of office and authority to rule over the respective villages of Abba. Dim Ogwuaga was the first autonomous head of Ogwuaga village of Abba. Dim was the first to settle in the fertile land known as Ogwuaga Abba, as head of all settlers in Ogwuaga, Abba. He was given the Ofor and staff of office of Ogwuaga people. Ogwuaga means fertile land, where crop yield and harvest are huge and plentiful. At the demise of Dim Ogwuaga, power automatically was handed over to his first son Dim Agu. The name Agu means Lion.

Dim Agu was so named because legend has it that at the death of every son of the Dim lineage, the dead man would more likely than not, turn into a lion and roam visibly in Ogwuaga. Dim

Agu's children included Okoro Ezeala, those living at Okoro-Okwareke, Ukwu Ubengba or Umunne Ato and Ofegu. The Uriabia kindred later were allowed to settle among the DimAgu clan. Mbara-Ukwu and Mbara-nta (also called Mbara Uhuala) were called Mbara because at the time they lived at the outskirts of Dim Agu's compound. At the death of Dim Agu, his son Ezeala, took over as custodian of the "Ofor-ukwu" Ogwuaga.

## OGWUAGA HAS TWO SECTIONS DIM AGU (FIRST SON) AND DIM UZIE (SECOND SON)

In the Dim Agu section, we have three sub sections, namely Dim Agu, Dim Ukwu Ubengba and Uriabia.

In the small Dim Agu are Okoro Ezeala (Ezeala Family) which is my family, Dim Anorue (ofe egu) and Okoro Okwaraeke (Okwaraeke family).

The Dim Ukwu Ubengba, also called Umunne Ato has Akwaraku, Ugwuegbu and Duruchukwu. Uriabia is so called because their forebears migrated to our land and have become part of us. Uriabia has two sections, Nduhu and Ndiulo.

Dim Uzie has two main sections namely Mbara Ukwu and Mbara Uhuala. Mbara Ukwu is known as Amato (three stools) namely Dim Uzie, Umu Onyeka and Umuogbu. The Mbara Uhuala does not have a clear origin, but has three sections Umudike, Obom and Duru Oshishie. In my days, all kindred did everything together as one people. It was fun because 'the more the merrier,' especially during weddings, burials and moonlight nights.

Ezeala brought greater unification and progress in Ogwuaga, somewhat like a "king" among the people of Ogwuaga. He oversaw construction of wider roads in Ogwuaga. During his time, there arose further land disputes with Ogwuaga and Isu people. Ezeala rallied Ogwuaga to extend and dig more trench networks "nkoroh" all around Ogwuaga. He commissioned construction of trenches around Ogwuaga to ward off outside aggression. The deep and wide trenches made it difficult for the enemy to secretly come and attack our people. Today, the nkoroh network has almost disappeared in toto. They are either levelled or built over.

Ezeala like his fathers, before him, also continued to double as the chief priest for all Ogwuaga people. As chief priest, he offered sacrifices to God, or gods, on behalf of his people and generally mediated between God and his people.

His authority or consent or blessing was required by any inhabitant of Ogwuaga to conduct certain rites: marriages, burials, the building of houses, construction of trenches, or when going to war. Ogwuaga has one and only shrine "IHUALA" or face/ front of our land. The Ihuala is a bushy and virgin patch of land. It is the altar where all sacrifices and offerings are made to God.

At that time our people were not Christians, but they still worshiped the one and only almighty God
the Chikwuabiama, the "okakaa" (almighty) "Chineke" (creator) "chinenye ndu" (giver of life), "chinenye-nwa" (the giver of children "chinenye aku na uba" (giver wealth), "chinenye

amamihe" (giver of knowledge and wisdom). These are various praise names for God, the Almighty. At the death of Ezeala, his sons Durugwonenye and then Okoroha took-over the stool of his father and was known as Mazi Okoroha Ezeala. People still refer to our family as Umu Ezeala, The children of Ezeala.

## OKOROHA EZEALA

In the history of Abba, Okoroha my great grandfather was the head and the Ofor title holder in Ogwuaga, Abba community. Okoroha lived around 1825-1900. He inherited his stool and title from his lineage of Dim Ogwuaga, who begot Dim Agu, who begot Ezeala, who begot Duru-Ugwunonye, the father of Okoroha. His family is the head and first family in the entire Ogwuaga. The headship is sometimes contested by OkoroOkwaraeke.

From here on, one half of Ogwuaga called or referred to our family, interchangeably as "Umudim," "Umu DimAgu." Exclusively, Okoroha family, to this day is referred to as or "Umu Ezeala." Okoroha duly inherited his father's stool and the Ofor-Ukwu-Ogwuaga (the staff of office) of Ogwuaga and all the land, titles and rights that came with the position. He had four half- brothers. His mother hailed from Adam Family of Ezimoha Mbano. The Adam family is said also to be inlaws to our late King, Eze Justice Ojiako and Akwuiwu families of Ogwuaga Abba. The significance is that these two families rank highest and in pari-pasu with Okoroha/Ozigbu Family in Ogwuaga and in Abba.

Okoroha bought more land and expanded his wealth and compound. He started his own family and married three wives. He had four sons. The sons and their father bonded together inseparably. He carefully chose the names of his four sons.

1. Nwaugwo Okoroha, called Ozigbu-dimpka, Ozigbu.

2. Ijezie Osuagwu Okoroha, called BikuBiku and Yeye

3. Nwaokoro Okoroha, called Ahumibe

4. Ofoha Okoroha, called Iheanagwam and Thomas.

Every member of this family hails from one of the four sons of Okoroha. The descendants of Okoroha Ezeala to this day hold and retain the all-powerful Ofor- Ukwu Ogwuaga, and we proudly remain the head family of Ogwuaga Abba. Okoroha was a farmer and itinerant herbalist and fortune teller, who travelled to different villages and places.
His second wife had only one offspring named Ijezie Okoroha, who later was named Osuagwu (and BIKKU BIKKU), because he carried his father's herbal bag and went everywhere with his father.
Okoroha then married a third wife. who gave birth to two more boys – Nwaokoro Ahumibe Okoroha and Ofoha Iheanagwam Okoroha. Today we do not know how many daughters he had, but I recollect that one matriarch Akukwah married Okoro

Chukwu or Chukwu family in Eziama, Osuh, Mbano is one of Okoroha's daughter.

## OZIGBU OKOROHA

Ozigbu Okoroha, may have lived around (1860 -1930). The first son of Okoroha, Ozigbu was an extraordinarily strong and popular leader. He married four wives namely Nwannedie, Onyiridie, Chiagorom, and Onudie. When he died in the early 1930s, he was survived by his above named four wives, and fourteen children, namely: Ekerionye, Ogamba Jacob, Olueze, Benson, Francis, Obiakpolam, Onyegbule, Augustin, Ezihe, Lawence, Nwaefere, Nwaubani, Hilary and Nneduru when Ozigbu died, Osuagwu looked after the Ofor and family, on behalf of his young nephew, Prince Jacob Ozigbu, the first son of Ozigbu , until he Osuagwu died in 1962.

## IJEZIE, OSUAGWU OKOROHA

Ijezie Okoroha also known as Osuagwu and Biku-Biku lived around 1862 -1962. He was the second son of OkorohaOsuagwu was a wealthy farmer with many livestock, farmland, and a big barn. Osuagwu married seven wives and had nineteen children. He was born Ijezie but because his father was fond of him and travelled everywhere with him, he was nicknamed Osuagwu. In the later part of his life, he took the personal title or chose to be known as BIKU- BIKU, meaning "I am a confident self-made man." I am the king in my household, just as you are king of your own household. He has many children David Azunnah, Urewuchi, Gilbert Emenike, Fidelis Nwaechefu,

Titus Ikeokwuadim, Adanma, Ogonnaya, Michael Anelechi, Emmanuel Igboeruche, Diana Theodora, Nnembu Maria Gorrati, Irene Egojiuka, Theresa Esinonu, Livinus, Ndubueze, Josephat, Oluchi and Pepetua.

Osuagwu held the family together for over thirty years as one until his demise at the old age of 102 years, in 1962. He lived the longest of the four brothers.

## NWAOKORO AHUMIBE OKOROHA

Nwaokoro Okoroha also known as Ahumibe Okoroha lived around 1865- 1940. The third son, Mazi Nwaokoro Okoroha had one wife and at his death left behind his wife Mrs Onudie and four sons and a daughter namely: Nwaoja, Ekechi, Nwamadi, William and Romanus.

## OFOHA THOMAS OKOROHA

The fourth and youngest son, Ofoha Okoroha was the first person to become a Christian in Okoroha family. He was christened Thomas, and later wedded in Church to his only wife, Mrs Ugadie Cecelia. Ofoha Okoroha, also known as Iheanagwam lived from about 1870 to 1956. He was converted and became a Christian. When he was baptised, he chose the name Thomas after St Thomas Aquinas, and he wedded in the Catholic Church. Mazi Ofoha was a devout Christian, along with his wife. He was survived by his wife and four sons and a daughter. His children are Godwin, Benedict, Rose, Cyprian, and Charles.

## PRINCE JACOB OGAMBA OZIGBU

After the death of Osuagwu Okoroha, Prince Jacob Ogamba Ozigbu as the first son of Ozigbu Okoroha took over as head and leader in the footstep of his forebears. He was a great unifier and mentor to his younger brothers. He had long a career as a Police Officer. Prince Jacob Ozigbu took a personal Chieftaincy and a title from the King of Abba town, Uburu1 as Duruemezue 1 of Abba. In effect, Duruemezue means 'one who has done everything' and met all conditions. At his death, his first son Prince Reuben became Duruemezue 11, and the holder of the Ofor. When Prince Reuben Ozigbu passed away in 2016, his first son, Prince Kingsley became Prince Duruemezue 111 and holder of the Ofor Ukwu, Okoroha and of Ogwuaga Abba. He had a personal chieftaincy title as Idejimba. Prince Jacob attempted to make every person bear the surname of Okoroha. He always called us Umu-Okoroha also he referred to the family as children of one man.

## THE CHILDREN OF THE FOUR SONS OF OKOROHA

Okoroha's four sons, had twenty-six (26) sons (excluding daughters), to name them by their first or Christian names and in order of seniority are: Jacob Ozigbu, David Okoroha, Benson Ozigbu, Francis Ozigbu, Gilbert Okoroha, Augustine

Ozigbu, Fidelis Okoroha, Onyegbule Ozigbu, Obiakpolam Ozigbu, Lawrence Ozigbu, Titus Okoroha, Ekechi Okoroha, Hilary Ozigbu, Nwamadi Okoroha, William Okoroha, Godwin Okoroha, Michael Okoroha, Romanus Okoroha, Benedict Okoroha, Emmanuel Okoroha, Cyprian Okoroha, Charles Okoroha, Livinus Okoroha, Josephat Okoroha, Jonathan Okoroha and Ndubueze Okoroha. The children and wives of these twenty-six men now number over two hundred persons.

## OKOROHA DAY

In 2012 and 2015 the entire family celebrated Okoroha family day. It was a fantastic and fun-filled day, attended by dignitaries and well-wishers. All our children from all over the world came home to Abba with their own families.
We are the EZEALA family. Now, with the aim of amicable coexistence and family unity, we are all working towards this goal. Despite the differences, family will always be family no matter what.

## MY FATHER: AZUNNAH DAVID OSUAGWU OKOROHA

My grandfather, Ijezie Osuagwu Okoroha's children, both male and female in their order of birth are David Azunnah, Urewuchi, Gilbert Emenike, Fidelis Nwaechefu, Titus Ikeokwuadim, Adanma, Ogonnaya, Michael Anelechi,

Emmanuel Igboeruche, Diana, Nnembu Maria Gorrati, Irene Egojiuka, Theresa Esinonu, Livinus, Ndubueze, Josephat, Oluchi and Pepetua.

My father, Mr David Azunnah Osuagwu Okoroha is the first son of Ijezie Osuagwu Okoroha. I was born first son of David, by his first wife Mrs Elizabeth Fanny Ejimoleke. I was thus born in the "house of David." David in the bible was said to be the man after the heart of God.

My parents saw my birth in 1944 as God's blessing. If the saying is true that some people were born with 'a silver spoon in their mouth', then the aphorism, or maxim, applies only partially to me. I was told that I arrived amidst relative pomp and pageantry, as my grandfather was so happy that he called me Anyiam, meaning his taproot, indicating that his genealogy will endure. By my birth, my parents and grandparents felt that the Osuagwu Okoroha lineage became doubly secured and they had triumphed. My grandfather, Ijezie Osuagwu was a single child of the second wife of his father Okoroha and that is the reason my birth meant so much to him. He was still alive and had a living son and a grandson. In those days, our grandfather had the privilege of giving names to all his grandchildren. He called my cousin Edmund 'Obasi', called my cousin Samuel 'Ihezue' and myself, 'Anyiam'.

My mother called me Chibuzor, God is first. She felt like God did not forsake her, instead, that God answered her prayers. At my baptism, my Godfather was Romanus Okoroha. I became known as Adolphus. My full name became Adolphus Anyiam

Chibuzor Okoroha. Later, I shortened my name to Adolph A.C Okoro. I have this for the sake of simplicity and the convenience of my western, American, and European associates. I have lived, studied, worked, married, had children, divorced, widowed, remarried, been afflicted with sicknesses, in Europe, USA and England since 1972 when I left Nigeria. In search of the proverbial 'Golden fleece' to this day, and the writing of this book, in 2023.

The first sons of the first twelve grandsons 'Opara' of Okoroha, referred to as second generation cousins are in order of seniority Reuben, Christian, Innocent, Edmund, Adolph, Samuel, Petercan, Benjamin, Paul, Edwin, Isaac and Anayo.

My father, David was a Sergeant Major in the British colonial Army. He went and fought around Southeast Asia and Myanmar, Indian and Japan warfronts in the Second World War. He returned from the front due to injury, in 1943, before the end of the war. He was a training Sergeant Major, Warrant Officer 11, (WO11) Major and a Warrant Officer. He wore a military armband and a big belt across his chest. He commanded parades and blew the bugle.

My father was born around 1900 and he was also the first son of Ijezie. The young David joined the Nigerian Colonial Army with little or no basic education. Originally, he was training recruits in Zaria, Kaduna, and Port Harcourt. At a later stage he was shipped to Myanmar and the Southeast as an infantry soldier. He rose through the ranks to the rank of Sergeant. He spoke fluent Hausa language. He also learned a trade in the Army and by the time he was honourably discharged, he was already a Grade 1 carpenter. That was his profession for the rest of his life.

My father David was a brave, honest, self-respecting, and hardworking gentle man. He was not rich in the material sense, but rich in integrity, descendants, and the legacy he left behind. On his death in 1975 three wives and ten children survived him, namely Adolph (author), late Patricia, late Patrick Friday (Ufele), Cecilia, Jude (Pope), Cletus Chidex, Peterlaz, Iyke Damian, Charlie James and late Eugene Chinedu; and today, there are over thirty great grandchildren.

## MY MOTHER ELIZABETH EJIMOLEKE OKOROHA

My mother, Elizabeth Fannie Ejimoleke was born in about 1930 and she was orphaned at the age of 10 years. The young Ejimoleke also had no formal education. Her aunt, Obiaraure Igbedie, the second wife of my grandfather, took her young niece to live with her, to help run errands, do chores and above all to baby-sit Igbedie children. Her light complexion was so fair and solid that local men and women nicknamed her nwanyibekee, a white woman with short lips. She was also described by some as an Indian woman. As a poor, little girl, my mum grew up in her new home and her beauty, fair complexion and industry landed her into an arranged marriage to my dad, the son of Igbedie's husband. The family and elders deemed it fit to have her remain in the family as a wife, rather than having her married off outside the family.

# GRANDMOTHER DAADA IGBEDIE

It is very sad and a great pity that Igbedie had twelve children, none of whom lived beyond a month, or two. It is now speculated that the children were born and died of diabetes, because eyewitness said that the children were born with a big head and eyeballs. So it happened that where my mother was brought up and raised from the age of 10 years, became where she found her husband at 15 years of age.

My father was the prince and heir apparent in the Osuagwu Okoroha lineage or sub clan. The events of her arranged marriage were possible because of her good behaviour. My father and his siblings lost their mother Nwanyieke, the first wife of Ijezie, whilst they were young; hence Igbedie (second wife) was given custody of my father David and his siblings, Gilbert and Urewuchi. My father and his siblings thus regarded Igbedie as their mother and fondly, they called her Daada even though she was in fact their step mum. Indeed, my mother, my father and his siblings and myself and all other members of Okoroha family addressed Igbedie as Daada.

A few years after my birth in August 1947 my younger sister was born and nicknamed "Baby Fannie" because we had an older cousin called "Baby Egbedie". My sister's full name being Patricia Ekeoma. Okoroha.

## STEPMOTHER CYRINA NKECHINYERE OKOROHA

Our father then married his second wife Nkechiyere Cyrina in 1951. My mother was the happy go-lucky type. She was always happy and ready to laugh. She had no time to worship the rich. She spoke her mind and was ever ready to laugh, sing or whistle a song. I was the centre of my mum's world. My mum always exclaimed with my name 'Adol'.

The year of my birth was still among the primitive and dark days in rural Nigeria. My mother was barely fifteen years of age, I was told that her labour for my birth lasted two days, behind our hut. The delivery native doctor and matron was my uncle's wife Onyiridie Ozigbu. Eight days after my birth, the matron and my adopted grandmother were sent to the native doctor, along with the fallen stub of my umbilical cord. The soothsayer without hesitation pronounced me to be the re-incarnation of the late first son of Okoroha, Ozigbu, who was also known as Ozigbu Dimpka.

In those days, at the naming ceremony of a boy, a goat was usually slaughtered to mark the great occasion and to celebrate the birth of the first son of the family. Everyone proclaimed that the long-awaited baby boy had arrived, the crown prince in the Ijezie linage. A goat was slaughtered at Abba and another goat was slaughtered at the township, the garden city, Port Harcourt, as a sign of boundless joy amid celebrations. The naming ceremony was full of merriment with assorted food, including foo-foo, garri, akpu and pounded yam, plenty of rice and stew, with stock fish, lama, and goat meats. The name Adolphus is my Christian baptismal name, chosen after the Swedish Bishop Gustav Adolphus.

The name was probably chosen for me because at that time of my birth, during the Second World War, the most powerful man on earth was the German Adolf Hitler. He was thought to have shaken the four corners of the earth to its very foundation. The truth is Adolf was a bad man who believed in 'Deutschland uber ales' - 'Germans above others.' The Nazi's ideology that any person, who was not white, tall, blonde, with blue eyes was sub-human and did not deserve to live. So, the world united against Hitler, led by the United Kingdom and the United States of America, crushing Adolf Hitler. He finally committed suicide, killing himself in a bunker.

Perhaps it was naively hoped that I would somehow, someday also be an immensely powerful or important figure. My experience is that life is not easy for anyone. In the game or battle of life, some people are players in the thick of it, while others watch the players. Whenever I could, I loved to play rather than watch. Though, you see the funniest side of life when you watch others. I can safely say that at times I have taken the bull by the horns. I can say that the rest of my life has been an uphill task but has seemed relatively easy. I battled with the forces of the world, not just to improve my lot in life, but that I may someday leave this world a better place than I met it. Early on in life, I told myself that I will always do my best and leave the rest to God.

I was told that the local women who brought baby gifts at my birth, predicted various occupations for me, the new-born, such as a doctor to heal people, soldier to fight great wars for our land, engineer to build big houses and bridges. Some said I would go to the white man's land overseas and become a lawyer. My mother said I was nicknamed 'oyibo' meaning
'white' because I was so fair in complexion, just like my mother. My mother told me how she always simply replied that her son was wonderful gift, given to her by the grace of God. If someone said to her how is your son Adol or that they saw her son Adol, she would immediately say - "Adol is not my son, he is God's son." I was fully breastfed and weaned at seven months old. My father banned any of his children from being nursed with animal (cow) milk. He believed that children nursed with cow milk are usually docile, weak, and lacking in practical common sense. One could easily see his point of view especially when city children come to the village and display total dependency, overt ignorance of nature and lack basic survival skills.

Those were the olden days, sometimes nostalgically called 'the good old days' There were no roads in Abba town but a maze of age-old, foot trodden tracks. There were also gullies of trenches around entire Abba Town. The trenches were dug by two generations of people before my time. The trenches were used during inter-tribal or clan wars to keep out invaders. Life was rural, and agrarian. There were less than five homes in Abba, roofed with zinc or corrugated iron sheets. The rest of the homes in Abba were built of red mud and thatch roofs. Our house was like most other people's homes, made of mud walls and raffia thatched roofs. They were good homes. They kept us warm during cold rainy seasons and kept us cool during the scorching sunny, dry seasons. Near each home was a big "Olu" or deep trench where the mud was dug to build the house. The trenches were then used for cultivation of huge yam and cassava mounds. Some people use it for banana and plantain trees cultivation. As a kid, I used to be scared at night when I walked past trenches alone. It was worst on very dark nights when the moon did not appear in the sky. It would even be more terrifying on dark, rainy, windy, and thunderous nights.

**UDARA FRUIT**

In the heart of the family compound stands an Udara tree, a timeless presence intertwined with our family's history. This tree predates even our grandfathers, holding a legacy that is both precious and rare. When its matured fruits descend and rest upon the ground, whoever retrieves them is granted the privilege of consuming them.
The Udara tree holds a revered status as a symbol of fertility. It is enveloped in superstitions, regarded as a sanctuary for the

spirits of our departed ancestors and the souls of our yet-to beborn offspring.

Climbing the Udara tree and plucking its fruits is strictly prohibited. This sacred tree is reputed for dispelling untimely demise and the Specter of barrenness from its surroundings. It is not a tree that is intentionally cultivated, for severing it from the earth without proper consultation and appeasement of the divine forces is considered an affront.

The Udara tree bears a powerful aura of reverence and trepidation across the expanse of Igbo land. Its nocturnal visits are sparse, as the veil between the mortal world and the ethereal realm is believed to thin during the night hours, allowing the spirits to emerge.

Our specific Udara tree is referred to as Nwannu, which translates to "salty." A pivotal custom restricts the harvesting of its seeds for commercial purposes, as this act would be tantamount to trading our potential offspring in the market square.

Moreover, the medicinal value of the Udara tree extends beyond its symbolism. The bark and leaves hold remedies that address afflictions such as infertility, barrenness, and various other ailments, offering a glimpse into its profound connection to life and well-being.

On such rainy days or nights, we sat around beaming fire logs, roasting corn, yam, and pears and listened to 'Ifo' thoughtprovoking and eye-opening, sometimes mythical, tales from the elders. Everyone knew everyone in my hometown. One could go out for an entire day and had only to close their front door, without a lock and key, and yet no one would steal from them. Everyone watched over one another and looked after each other's welfare, children, and livestock, such as chickens, goats, sheep, cows, and pigs. We were each other's brother's keeper.

Most ingredients for daily foods were gathered from our gardens. Little money was spent on salt which was imported and occasional fish and meat. All carbohydrates such "Ji," known as yam / pounded yam; "Akpu," known as cassava / garri; cocoyam (ede), plantain, banana came plentifully from our farms. The vegetables and various edible leaves, melons, uha and peppers (ose) were grown around our homes. Some edible wild vegetables such as Ukazi and mushrooms were gathered from big bushes and forests or ikpa. Drinking water was collected from spring streams, Onuala. Four other streams in my town, Nwangele Ebu, Okwaraeleke and Otuakwu were for washing clothes, bathing, and fishing. Men and boys set traps in the bushes daily and overnight, and could catch rabbit, squirrel, deer, bush meats, wild bush-pigs and even snakes, as sources of protein in our meals. Other sources of protein included certain ants, grasshoppers, and raffia-palm maggots. Men drank wine produced from palm trees and raffia palm trees.

People came together to help each other, to rejoice and celebrate, or to mourn and cry with one another. The villagers took turns, got together to cultivate one another's land, or build/rebuild his hut and do same for the next person. People contributed small pots of money for members of the meeting in the form of communal association and at the first appearance of every new moon, the money in the pot was given to individual members in turn, until all members had collected, and the cycle continued. The member whose turn it was to take the pot, would cook a big meal for all members to eat and drink together. The money collected could be a windfall that enabled the person to build a home, buy a new farm, more seeds, seedling for planting, build a barn, or bigger barn, or even marry a new wife. It was normal for a wife to marry another woman for her husband as her co-wife, if the former was barren, or produced only girls.

**CHAPTER FOUR**

------------------------

# From Birth

My survival was not merely attributed to the efforts of my folks and myself, but mostly led by my intuition, sheer luck, and destiny. Later, as an adolescent, my ardent determination, enabled by luck or grace propelled me to make my life perhaps better than it could have been. This determination to succeed also made the rest of my life a restless struggle to improve my lot. Progress made has been by inspiration, arduous work, prayer, and luck. My Zodiac sign being Sagittarius, I am naturally a hunter, an enterprising person, an achiever, and a pioneer. I am a child of God, a dual citizen of the world and the universe. I have the same rights as everyone else, the moon, the stars, and the grasses, to exist on this planet and in the universe. I have the right to be here and the responsibility to leave it a better place than I found it.

When I transit from earth, I do not know where I will go, I hope to be in heaven, but I am happy to leave the footprints that I, Adolph A. C. Okoro walked on this earth. I believe that success should be measured not by where you get to, but by where you started.

## EARLY LIFE

A million and one things made it necessary to write my life story. A flash back in time reminds me of incidences that buttress the fact my journey on earth has been guided by some divine or mythical power. From my early days, I have believed there is God, who some people, cultures, religions may refer to as Chi, Oluwa, Allah, Higher Power and so on. I believe that no human being has ever seen God physically. Some of us vividly experience God's existence spiritually and in desperation we ascribe human attributes to God. God is much larger than our human minds and imagination can ever possibly describe. We are best described as agnostic, believing that there is a God. By nature, we are not competent to describe the attributes of God, nor are we able to discern all his will, or the role he plays in our day to day lives. Some of his will for us is unquestionably clear, such as the need for male and female to copulate and produce new offspring and to breath, eat, drink, rest, sleep, hunt for food and to help each other. The opinions of various clerics and religious guru and leaders are, at best, guesswork of what God is or wants.
Yet every religious group preaches its own version of God with passion, authority, and persuasive authenticity. Some have died,

been willing to die, or to kill others, for what they believe about God's will. It is even, sometimes as a mark of respectability in every society, that people follow others to church, mosque, synagogue, and other places of worship, in the hope they are not seen as unreligious, amoral, or evil.

Many people go to places of worship mechanically, without honestly believing in what is preached, but simply wanting to appear upstanding in the eyes of their neighbours, friends, and relations.

It seems to me, Darwin and Wallace's theories of evolution are bunkum, they do not in any way contradict the religious doctrine that God created the world and all that is in it. The fact that a living thing can mutate, learn, change, improve through wilful or forced evolution does not extinguish creation as origin of the very first living species. For example, the God given instinct in all living things to breath, eat, expel waste from body, to procreate and look after our young off springs are naturally ordered by God or nature for all to obey.

I have no doubts whatsoever that providence or inexplicable divine powers have controlled most of my own life from birth up till now. I believe that God the Almighty carved me in the palm of his hand. His power has been my faithful and palpable companion. How else could I have single-handedly, humanly survived all my travails and arrive at where I am today, on my own life's pilgrimage, as I write this my humble biography.

From the early days of my childhood, I noticed strange miracles around me. From childhood to the present time, I have premonitions of some things before they happen. I may not have won the lottery, or become the president of my country, but by any stretch of the imagination I consider myself to have been a lucky child. For instance, I remember a day in Port Harcourt, at about 10 years of age, when some boys and I strayed into the compound of a white European expatriate, in search of ripe fruits (guava and mango) to eat. Back then, the main reason for any family keeping a dog as a pet was purely for protection. They function as guard dogs. It was well known that white foreigners, whenever they saw an intruder in their compounds, all they needed to do was whistle to their obedient dogs to 'catch am.' Then the intruder was done for, the dog would be at the intruder's heels in a minute and bite the hell out of them.

In this incident, we went into a Port Harcourt government reserved area, (GRA as they were called in those days) in search of mangoes, sup-sops, pawpaw, and guavas. We were able to pick or pluck some and our pockets were full. We picked some fallen fruit and aimed sticks and cudgels, throwing them to the top of mango trees, to drop the ripened fruit. I was the weakest of the three boys. My attempts could not even reach the top of the mango tree, let alone hit or bring down any mango. After several attempts, I was fed-up and resorted to helping the stronger boy's pick up their fallen fruits, in the hope and believe that out of mercy they would give me some.

Suddenly, a Caucasian male and a female appeared from the back of the bungalow with their big dog. They instructed the dog to "catch them." The beast appeared very happy to obey. A hot chase ensued. I had never run so fast in my whole life, yet I was the slowest of the three boys.

The dog appeared to have caught up with me first and I surrendered myself to be eaten alive. Much to my surprise the dog powered past me in hot pursuit of the faster runners. The dog floored one of them, giving him multiple bites on his buttocks and ankles. It taught us an unforgettable lesson - never to trespass onto a white man's compound, never to go plucking mangoes ever again in such a place!

God is full of surprises. To this day, I do not know why the dog ignored me, the slowest runner. Many such incidents in my life thought me never to beat my chest when I succeeded or survived, our apparent conquests are for most parts by sheer grace of God, or luck. Our successes, at best, are ninetynine per-cent inspiration and luck, while only one per-cent is challenging work or perspiration.

Another baffling incident that remains vivid in my mind to this day was when we went coconut hunting. The four of us were out in the jungle to pluck ripe coconuts, by throwing stones and sticks at them. I tried my hardest without any success. Each of my three friends succeeded by knocking down a coconut each. At the end of the day, when each of the boys gave me a third of their own coconut, I ended up with one full coconut, which was more than any of them had. These things never cease to baffle and dazzle me. The rest of my life followed a similar pattern. When I, or others, think that I am through, providence often dictates otherwise, seemingly not through with Adolph Okoro yet. It is funny that he, who laughs last, always laughs the best.

I am putting my story on paper, in the hope that it might entertain, enlighten, motivate, and inspire future generations. I do tell people to trust their God, think positively and do their best in life. It is important to do any 'good' we can do today, while we can do it. There is no better time for anything. It is a fact that it is only those who dare to win. One must buy a lottery ticket before God can use the opportunity to help one to win. If I am honest, sometimes man created God in man's image and likeness. I am a Catholic Christian by sheer accident of my birthplace. If Muslim parents bore me, or I was born in a different part of the world, I could have easily been a Muslim or Hindu or even a protestant Christian. I do not believe any longer that God has any favourite religion, so long as people do not harm, hurt or kill other people for Him, or in his name.

The native doctor had decreed I was, without question, the reincarnation of my grandpa's deceased brother who was powerful but died in his prime. The dead man's surviving wives preferred to call me by his name. Now, African traditional belief, Buddhist and Hindus theories of reincarnation contradict the Christian theory of resurrection on the last day. Christianity does not believe in re-incarnation. But my Christian parents believed in reincarnation and my wider Christian family still hold the same belief. It is therefore safe to conclude that our African Christians' beliefs to this day are rooted in what one can call half-Christian and half-pagan ideas. Even most of the present-day pastors are more of 419duppers, magicians and self-acclaimed exorcists, fortunetellers, and money doublers. They declare that the more money you give to them, the more money God will give back to you.

They are quick to dig up from the Old Testament that you must give to the church and its pastors a "tithe" which is a tenth of your total weekly, monthly, and yearly income, otherwise you are eating poison to your detriment. One pastor told me that if I do not pay a tenth of my income, then the devil is taking ninety per cent from me.

My adopted grandmother, Mrs Igbedie Obiaraure Osuagwu Okoroha, was my mother's aunt. Her maiden or name at birth was Enyiaka. The family hailed from Ezike, Mbano. Her name Obiaraure, meaning she 'was born to enjoy'. Igbedie was the name given to her by her husband, meaning that she was the husband's "safe box" which is more than a "piggybank." Igbedie also raised my father and his siblings, brother Gilbert and sister, Urewuji, because their mother, my grandpa's first wife, Nwanyieke from Umuolu Isu died after a brief illness whilst her children were toddlers. My younger sister was said to be the re-incarnation of Nwanyieke, our father's natural mother.

My mother often likened her union with my dad, David the carpenter to that of the biblical betrothal of Mary to Joseph the carpenter. Their son was born in the lineage of David as my father was also David. My deeply religious mother used to liken me in some religious-superstitious way to the biblical stories of Jesus. I have not been a holy man like Jesus, so whether there is any sense or meaning to my mother's belief, I believe that, for one thing, the story of my life from birth to this day has been of wonderment. I have dazzled some of the people who knew me, and I have baffled some others to this day. I used to ponder how it is that my life has biblical connotations, such as 'son of David' the first male child of a carpenter.

At the end of the second World War (WW2), the soldiers of the other commonwealth countries such as Nigeria were demobilised. The Nigerian battalion was constituted as the 82nd (West African) Division of British Colonial Army. After the war, the Division disbanded. They were used and discarded.

My father had a small special box full of medals of bravery awarded by the British Army. Unfortunately, we lost this box with all our earthly possession during the Biafra-Nigeria Civil war. We fled from Port Harcourt in 1968, as the enemy shelled and captured Port Harcourt. My father and I were at the war front. My mother and her co-wife gathered all their things together with my siblings and left through the bushes, to Abba. Our House and all that was left were declared abandoned properties by the enemies.

My father was honourably discharged from the British Colonial Army. He later entered the Nigerian civil service. He became employed as a Grade one carpenter with the Colonial Public Works Department (P.W.D), now known as Nigerian Federal Ministry of Works and Housing.

In 1955, when Queen Elizabeth the Second visited Nigeria, all the Second World War Veterans reassembled to form a second tier of the Nigerian Police Force (NPF), deployed in all the cities throughout the federation. My Dad was again prominent, as the Sergeant Major at the Mile 1 Diobu, Port Harcourt Police station. I used to take delight in polishing his boots and leather belts with black Kiwi polish, as well as shine the NPF uniform, shirt buttons, and raincoat buttons with Brasso. I was so proud to watch him with my friends and other spectators, as he commanded the platoon of police officers in the open field at Diobu Police Station. His rank was the same as he had whilst in the British Colonial Army, Sergeant Major, and warrant officer1. My Dad was so proud to wear his rank ensign and the medals of honour. He also blew the bugle 'Ta-ta-tra-taaa'... lasting for over five minutes. Those ex-military men turned police constables were fondly called "Eliza Police" Force or special constabularies.

When the Nigerian civil war, also termed by some as Nigeria Biafra war broke out in 1967, Dad was over 60 years of age. He was again called upon to serve the nation, to either remain a special police constable, or serve in the Biafran Army as a warrant officer one. He chose to join the Biafran Army. He trained battalion upon battalion of the new recruits, who passed out in three weeks, followed by immediate shipment and deployment to various war fronts. He was based initially at Port Harcourt, Stella Maris College Depot. After the fall of the city in 1968, he was relocated to Ogwa Depot and Mbano where he was on duty the day the war ended on 15th January 1970. He strolled home as if he had not been to war. Everyone was so happy that Dad, 'Uke' the bow, the old war horse, the colonial Warrant Officer survived the war. People kept saying 'old soldiers never die'.

After the war, Dad re-joined the Nigerian Ports Authority, where he remained until he unfortunately passed away in 1975 at the age of 75 years. It was said that he ate contaminated rice from a ship at the Lagos Marina harbour.

His death was an accidental misadventure and sadly so untimely considering that he was very fit and as 'strong as an ox' to the last day.

As a child, I lived with my parents in Port Harcourt, the city at the South-eastern part of Nigeria named after the first British Administrator and Mayor, Mr Harcourt. The city boasted of its busy Marine activities, Port and Harbour, schools and colleges, factories and businesses, numerous trees and coastal swamps, among others. Port Harcourt was also known as the 'Garden City'. It was a beautiful and boisterous city, with multicultural and multi-ethnic representations. It was a home for people from all levels of society. Its richness in oil, modern buildings, and its aquatic gains were among the city's pulling power. One of its striking major features was the football team named Pitakwa 'Red Devils' which featured superstar players of those days like, Onyeador, Onyeawuna, Nwaturuocha, Ibiam, and Uwalaka to mention but a few. The superstar footballers of those days sadly had the glory, but not the money. Football was a pastime activity. The players lived low in single "face me and I face you" rooms, or lived with their parents and earned a living from employment with any of the following companies: UAC, Railway, GBO, Leventis, Taylor Woodrow, PWD, ECN, NPC, NPF, Prisons, Ports Authority to name a few. One of the popular musicians who was resident in "Port high life" was the king of high life music, Cardinal Rex Jim Lawson, who was an Mbanmiri-man himself as he hailed from Kalabari, with mixed parentage of a Kalabari father and Ibo mother.

The Ibos come from upland, and fondly referred to the people from Port Harcourt and riverine areas as "Mbanmiri" people. In between the riverine people and Ibos are the Ikweres who speak adulterated Igbo language. The Mbanmiri women of those days were rather notoriously hot, popular or had a reputation. Some of the popular Riverine towns of those days included Okirika, Abonema, Buguma, Kalabari, Ogoni, and Bonny. The Ikweres, from Diobu, Igirita, Ahoda, Mbiama Umumasi and Umukoroshe people were not real Mbanmiri, they were more of Ibo in their dressing, speech, and behaviour.

A popular fish was the 'Atabara' and those who bought and sold the fishes from sea were nicknamed 'Atabara Women' usually with huge round breasts and bottoms.

Every year on Empire Days, schools in Port Harcourt Province assembled at Bernard Carr Field, and had a march past, and sports competitions. My cousin, Cosmas was the one to watch as he came first in the one hundred yards, 220- and 440-yard races. His older brother Innocent was known as the "local kid Bassey" in the boxing ring. I joined the boxing club but after I knocked down one, Basil, who had to be revived with icy water, I hung up my gloves and ended my boxing career. Though the poor child first gave me a fat lip, had he not woken up I would have been done for murder. I would not have been able to escape his family's reprisal and vendetta.

# MY FIRST SCHOOL

My very first day at school was in 1950 when I was 6 years old. It was at the Christ the King Catholic (CKC) School, Diobu, a suburban part of the Garden City, Port Harcourt. I had to go over the railway line from Mile One, Diobu to Dline, Diobu which was also the Aba roadside of the town, where the school and Mission were situated in one and same hall. Academic wise, we were taught the ABCD ...., the Ibo / vernacular counterpart. ABCDEFGH were pronounced in Ibo language as Aa -Bee Chii-De-Eei-Ffii-Ggei-Hhei.... We were taught also 123, 1 to 100, in both Ibo and English languages. Some of my best memories of those early school days were the recess (short break), and recreation times, when we spent our pocket money on roasted groundnuts, now called monkey nuts, hot Akara bean cakes, Agidi (solid pap), Abijiokpo (marshed kidney beans), and Moimoi.

Another highlight of those early school days was the physical education (PE) period, where we clapped our hands over our heads, or with arms outstretched, hovered round and round, singing 'akpakoro-kpankoro' I liked to play the game of 'fire on the mountain' when we must run round the circle of pupils. When the teacher says 'fire is out' you must grab a seat and sit on it, otherwise you are out of the next round of the game. This went on until there was one last person who was said to have won the game. I do not remember much else about my early school days at CKS, Ikot Ekpene Street, Aba Road, Diobu, Port Harcourt.

After two years of ABC, Pre- infant 1 and 2, or kindergarten or nursery, my parents pulled me out of the school and sent me home to our village, to live with my grandfather and grandmother at Abba. It was my parents' belief that if I were raised in the village rather than the city, I would grow up to be more sensible and self-reliant.

I enjoyed 'recess' periods, we left classrooms and ran outside to do whatever we liked. Usually many ran together to the urinary, and the boys could urinate together, even looking at each other. Unfortunately for the few girls, they had to queue up and take turns to enter a urination room for girls, one at a time. Some used recess time to answer nature's long calls in the latrines. After you had eased yourself, you then got to play with the other kids. Looking back now, I do not recollect seeing any hand washing facilities after using the toilets.

I looked forward to recess times, because that's when you spent your one or two pennies on bean cakes (akara) sweets, and such nice delicacies and your recess period was also spent playing with other kids. The games included chasing each other, onye lere anya na azu, afugom oyim onye gab u oyim, itu okwe, itu uga, chiringa kpumkpumkpu ogene ogene ogene, oga na ga nye, oso elu and so many others. I remember in those days I sometimes sat under a big flower tree and sang old war songs, which I learnt from my grandfather and many students would gather around me to listen. I do not know why some nicknamed me Okenwe, meaning 'male monkey'. Then some differentiated me as the male monkey from Ogwuaga, as opposed to the male monkey from another part of

Abba, Umudurunna Abba. In appreciation of my songs, some people gave me chewing gum or sweets, or any gift at all. I used to enjoy the popularity. One of my favourite songs was "Okenwe na ra udara na mbara ikpa" meaning that an old male monkey that went out to an open space must be careful, watchful, and vigilant, in case a hunter caught him off guard. Recess was usually shorter than the midday recreation period, which lasted an hour, rather than thirty minutes. Some could go home and come back to school within an hour, some chose players and played football games. Such teams did not have to be eleven on each side, it could be four, five, six, seven, or any number on each side.

My grandparents also requested I should be brought to live with Igbedie, my adopted grandmother who was childless. I was eight years old in 1952 when I went to the village. I remember vividly how Igbedie treated me with such profound love and care as though I was her natural son.

At school, I soon realised I had completed 'ABC-nta' or 'small Abc' class in Port Harcourt, so my new class was the 'ABC Ukwu' or the 'big ABC' class, which was at St Theresa Nursery School, Abba, before progressing to standard one and two (STD1 & STD2).

I spent the years 1955 and 1956 in junior primary school. Senior primary school was from standard three to standard six, after which I attained the First School Leaving Certificate in 1960, at 16 years of age.

My 8 years of schooling at St Theresa's Primary School, Abba, from January 1953 to December 1960 was initially painful, but by the end of second year, I was quite settled and happy. At the end of every academic year, results were called in the school assembly, because there were no written school reports. I always heard my name called among those who passed, progressed, and promoted to the next class in the new year. It was a great feeling. Those who failed had to repeat the class and I was fortunate not to have repeated any class.

Many of the teachers liked me fondly and petted me. Every year there was a teacher or two who took me as their 'boy,' either to carry their bags, files or submit exercise books for marking to their houses, before I headed home. In return, I was hardly ever punished, and I obtained favours. Every year and in every new class, I was always either the class monitor or the prefect 'head boy' or the school bell ringer, also called the regulator. Every pupil came to school barefoot, locally referred to as going 'tentoes' My Parents bought two pairs of Bata made shoes for me, but I was forbidden to wear my shoes to school, so I wore them only on Sundays to church and Mass services, or during other big social occasions such as weddings.

Attending the same school but different classes were a few of my cousins, namely Godwin, Martin, Michael, Romanus, Benedict, Emmanuel, Louis, Cyprian, Ukaonu and Canisius.

As a big family, we protected each other. The older members of the family looked after the younger ones.

The junior primary school days were notably full of fun memories, for me, because every Monday at assembly the teachers would go round and check our fingernails, toenails, hair, teeth, and school uniform. If you were found to not meet the hygiene standard, you were flogged with six strokes of the Cane, on the buttocks, for each offence, in front of the rest of the pupils. From std1 to Std6, I was twice put at the top of the table, in the assembly hall and in front all the pupils, as a model pupil.

Those were moments of fame, as I was shown as a proud example of how neat a pupil should look and appear. Also, twice, or so, I stood in front of the entire school pupils, to present poetry recitations. On one occasion, I memorised, crammed, and recited the entire poem 'Tell me not in mournful numbers, Life is but an empty dream' written by an English man Mr Longfellow. On another occasion, I recited 'United we stand, divided we fall'.

Living and attending school in the village, rather than in the Garden city, was both fun and beneficial. Especially, in my case, I had the best of both worlds, because I spent almost every holiday with my parents in Port Harcourt, or with my maternal uncles, Damian and Uzoukwu at Aba and Enugu or at Onitsha with my uncle and godfather, Romanus, who was also known as Monday. Even as an adult, my Godfather was called 'Monday' simply because he was born on a Monday. He lived at Onitsha, and I loved the Otu market and Ochanga market and I loved the Olugbu vegetable soup with mangala fish.

In those days, many people were called such names as Friday and Sunday. I did not know why no-one was ever called Saturday, or Tuesday, Wednesday, or Thursday. Anyway, no matter where I spent the holidays, I always returned home to Abba with a fresh haircut. Also, a new metal school box, new set of clothes, school uniform, a pair of shoes, singlet, under wear (called 'drawers,') handkerchief, sunglasses, a sharp cutlass for school grass cutting and other types of wooden toys, or gadgets in vogue, at the time. I even had a suit, trousers, vest and coat. Other kids teased and envied me, saying I wore an 'Adam Coat.' Even to this day, I do not know why waist coat or vest was termed 'Adam Coat.'

Most of my classmates and schoolmates were those whose parents were living in the village as petty farmers, animal farmers and petty traders. I learnt to survive as they did, by learning the art and skill of clearing bushes, tilling the soil, making single and ridge mounds, sowing seeds and cash crops, weeding the farms, so real crops were not smothered by useless wild weeds, harvesting and stocking cash-crops into barns for subsistence and for the next farming year.

I could set iron traps to catch squirrels both "Uze" and "Usa," rabbits, rats and even snakes. I learnt to gather Maggots "eruru" from dead raffia palm trees, locust insects "aku," caterpillars "egu," crickets "nte" and other edible insects and grasshoppers. I could catch bats "ekwikwi" and bring down owls "ohuru." I was able to weave baskets "ekite" and mats" ute" from raffia palm "ngwo" leaves. I learnt to climb palm trees "nkwu" and other trees with my two bare hands and feet, without a ladder. I sold some of my handiwork at local markets, for my pocket money. I could make raffia thatches to fix thatched houses. Sometimes, I was hired or requested to do pro-bono work by some old ladies. It could be to repair their leaky thatched huts, or climb at some height to pluck fruits, trim the trees or pluck the "uha" leaves, which are an unbelievably delicious vegetable. I went to the stream "onuala" daily, at the first cock crow, to fetch clean water for our cooking and drinking. After school and after my afternoon meal, I roamed the bushes, to fetch firewood "nku" to make fire for all our cooking.

At night if the moon shone, I participated in the moonlit nights 'fun and games', telling the mythical, legendary and folklore stories "Ifo," participating in hide-and-seek games. These mythical "Ifo" stories would make many a child wise, canny, and shrewd, as they did to me. I often wondered why the tortoise "mbe" was always the hero and star, outwitting all other animals. I learnt the deep Igbo vernacular phrases, proverbs, adages, idioms, riddles, and words of wisdom. Looking back at that point in my life, I felt strongly that growing up in the village was one of the best things that ever happened to me. The experience made me a man, a resilient man, with loads of common sense. As a result, I made sure that my three children and granddaughter born in the USA experienced part of their formative years in Nigeria. My first daughter, with an American mother, continues to say, 'I thank you daddy, for taking me to grow up in Africa, I now have the best of both worlds'.

When I went to townships or cities, such as Port Harcourt on holidays, I was quick to adjust and became a city child even as a holiday maker. I could speak the broken or pigeon English "pidgin English" which was and still is the 'lingua franca' for all the township peoples, who hailed from various ethnic groups of Nigeria. I was streetwise and went out with the lads to the big public fields, to play football or tennis. I often took a part time job as ball-boy at European tennis clubs or caddied at European Golf Clubs. I was good at games of draughts, cards and ludo.

During nights in the city, the young boys in our street would congregate at a particular lamppost, to yap, shoot the moon, gossip and tell-tales. 'Kiss and tell' was rife. I quickly discovered a small business opportunity, whereby I bought one or two dozen guinea fowl "Ogazi" eggs at a time, boiled and retailed them under the lamppost, at almost the double the cost price. Soon my younger sister Pat joined me in the business, but she sold only peeled oranges. She peeled off the orange–skins in different shapes and patterns, including the "sweetheart" and the "hausa-girl-hairdo" or "Yoruba hairdo" styles. During holiday periods, such as Easter and Christmas festivals, the city streets turned into carnivals. I bought my own masquerade mask, gear, and paraphernalia. With two to four other lads, we danced on the day, collecting money 'dashes and tips from spectators. We literally and politely asked, urged, or hounded people to give us money in support and in the spirit of the festivities. Often, we made enough profit from these various endeavours to use as pocket money, without bothering our poor parents for our spending money, other than for our school fees. Sometimes, I was able to give loans to my father and my mother, to put into her petty trading business. My Dad occasionally nicked a penny or two from me for his cigarettes. My masquerades "ekpo" started with a simple costume, then I progressed to fancy dress "Ulaga," and later I graduated to the horrendous looking mask called "ojuju-kalabar." Much later as a teenager I formed a Fancy Dress Dance Club which was inspired by the culture of Lagos people. Though, I had never been to Lagos, but the songs were all in Yoruba language which we memorised without really knowing their meaning.

The drums and samba were fashioned after the juju drumbeats of leading Yoruba musicians such as I K Dairo, Victor Olaiya, and Bobby Bensen.

Once schools re opened I went back to my village, Abba. I regarded Igbedie as my grandmother. I learnt grandma and grandpa had emphatically requested I should be brought home to them, to be looked after by them and to be 'raised properly' as grandpa's heir apparent. I also needed to help them with household chores, in respect of livestock rearing and farming generally. I was an errand boy at their disposal. Among other things, I soon began to accompany my grandfather, Ijezie, whom everyone called "yeye" in his herbal and spiritual healing works as his apprentice.

It was made clear to me that I had no say in the decisions taken about my young life. The rule then was 'spared the rod and spoil the child.' All children were beaten, both at home and at school, to make them better men and women of the future. I just had to obey and keep quiet. I did not have any grudges or begrudge anyone. I obeyed and respected my elders. I was completely contented and happy. The powers that be had spoken. The modern-day psychologists would say that one became separated from one's biological parents at the tender age of 8yrs, and as such they used it wrongly to explain dysfunctional behaviour among the youth of today. Such was never the case with me, or with children in my village raised in this way during the period.

Though one could say I was somewhat separated from my immediate parental closeness in early life, it did not turn me into a person with deviant behaviour or into a real, or potential, mass murderer. I think for Africans, these situations make us rather to become better, as we overcome tricky situations. I did not feel abandoned or neglected, rather the situation taught me to develop acute common sense, selfreliance and independence early on in life. Initially I hated being caned or flogged, but soon developed 'a very tough skin'. When other children would shed tears, I would take a flogging of six strokes, even on my bare bottom and not bat an eyelid. Older boys taught me that if one ate copious quantities of red-hot pepper, they made your skin tough as those of a crocodile. And Boy, did I eat all kinds of paprika and red-hot peppers and intentionally I pretended that I felt no pains.

## MY GRANDFATHER

Grandfather, Ijezie 'Bikku Bikku' (yeye) was the second son of his father OKOROHA, who was said to be a lone child. My great grandfather Okoroha was said to be hardworking, visionary, and prosperous. In a certain twist of history, Okoroha as first son, felt alienated by his two junior brothers, hence he swore and intently married three wives to propagate a large family. Today his living descendants – are numbered over two hundred men and women. The number of storey buildings in our family compound is now over fifty. Okoroha arguably may have lived from 1830 to 1900 AD, he left behind four sons, namely: Nwaugwo also known as Ozigbu, Ijezie also known as Osuagwu, Nwaokoro also known as Ahumibe and Ofoha, 'ihenagwam' the youngest, who was later converted and baptised into the catholic church and took the name Thomas. He also wedded in the church.

In respect of Okoroha's sons:

The first son, Ozigbu had three wives and the following sons: Jacob, Benson, Francis, Obiakpolam, Augustin, Lawrence, Hilary and Oyegbule.

The second son Ijezie had five wives and the following sons David, Gilbert, Fidelis, Titus, Michael, Emmanuel, Livinus, Josephat, Ndubueze, and Cajetan.

The third son, Nwaokoro had a wife and the following sons: Leonard, Nwamadi, William, and Romanus.

The fourth son, Thomas, also had a wife and the following sons: Godwin, Benedict, Cyprian, and Charles.

My granddad, Ijezie 'Biku Biku' lived from about 1880 to 1963. He was a renowned native religious priest - an art he had learnt from his own father. He was a Seer, a Soothsayer, an Herbalist and in general, a Native Doctor. He practised the best fortune telling in our town, Abba and beyond. He could make goodluck charms. He gave treatment to barren women for pregnancy and cured infertility. He cured impotence in men, insanity, and broken bones. He cured people who were possessed with devilish spirit of "Ogbanje" or "Icharius" which comes back to hunt people from their previous life or (re-incarnated lives).

He used native voodoo "onumonu" to heal those who were poisoned by snake bite or poisoned by their fellow human beings. He would make them throw up the poison inside their bodies. One of his sons instructed an Artist and Sign writer to produce four signboards which were mounted at strategic junctions in our town and roads leading into our town. These gave maximum publicity to his works and skills.

My grandfather had a juju/voodoo placed strategically at the front gate to our compound. I remembered vividly on one occasion a thief raided our house at night, gathering some sheep and other items to be stolen and taken away. However incredible as it may sound, the thief became morose, disoriented and was unable to leave our compound. He was rather seen perambulating, pacing up and down our large compound until daybreak, through sunrise, after everybody had seen and identified him as a local person, he was shamed and released from his bondage by my grandpa.

I helped in the shrine and traveled the length and width of our village with him. We went to anywhere or place where his services were needed. My duty was to carry his medicine bags, and we walked the long and tortured dirty, narrow pathways and footpaths, to wherever duty called. We sometimes entered the thick bushes of the rainforest in our village and neighbouring ones, in search of herbs, tree barks, roots and leaves of medicinal plants with potent values, that were needed to complete a medicinal concoction for his numerous clients, or patients. At times, my job was to prepare the pepper soup with the he-goat meats, chicken, roosters, and turtles or even mutton offered as animal sacrifices for the efficacy of the rituals. Often, I ate a whole lot of the meat either alone, or with him, because women, girls and Christian's relatives were either forbidden to eat them, or voluntarily abstained from eating any part of such sacrificial meat due to their Christian beliefs. Grandpa was the Chairman of the Abba Development Union (ADU) Home Branch for four consecutive years in the 1950s.

I learnt a few of the trivial things from my grandpa including the incantation of "Haa!" – which means 'Amen' to his libations and prayers. He was not a Christian, but he always prayed to the same one and only God. He requested blessings from God the Almighty when he prayed. He invoked the Chukwuokikeabiama"Obasi" (Heavenly father) or the Ahiajioku. He caused rain to fall if there were episodes of abrupt dry seasons. On special days, his clients paid him to ensure that there was no rainfall on such days. He could literally do and undo. He also went about curing people with various infirmities. He mediated between men and their gods. He also had the responsibility to initiate or ordain new pagan or native converts as priests. That is those who had been trained, tried and tested in the various acts of paganism, incantation, herbal and spiritual healings, among others. It's noteworthy that the universal God of surprises answered my grandfather's prayers just as the Supreme Being answers prayers from the priests of all other religions and denomination, as well as prayers from atheists – those who do not believe in the existence of God.

One of his acts that baffled me to this day was the 'NWAEBE' - a Hollow round gadget of about two inches in length and diameter, with a string that was in the middle of a hole. The Nwaebe could come down at his command in a fast or slow motion or in any number of stops to prove its point. It was used to confirm or find stolen items, or locate lost items, or to discover what was done, or said, in secret. He prepared charms aimed against thieves and robbers. The Nwaebe was used also to confirm or deny controversial issues or arguments or find culprits. Nwaebe was full of mysteries, and it was a product of my grandpa's ingenuity, which unfortunately we have unwisely abandoned.

For some reason, at first it never bothered me, as I became known at school as a 'pagan-bag carrier.' The bag usually contained feathers, white chalks (Nzu) finely grounded to powder form, yellow chalk (Edo), a statue of his god, representing his staff of office or shrine among various other paraphernalia. Every morning grandpa would bring out the Ofor (staff of authority) to dedicate himself, and his family.

He invoked protection from Obasi, God the giver of all life. My grandpa believed that with God, nothing is impossible. To me that is a true faith, though in its crude and lowest form. Jesus also preached that with 'faith you can move mountains.' Today, I honestly regret the fact that none of us, his children and grandchildren learned the art or mystery of the Nwaebe and his religion. We abandoned all interest in our African beliefs in favour of Christian or Muslim religions from the European or the Arabs.

My grandfather also owned large barns of yams and many livestock such as goats, sheep, and fowls, at a point, I was the only male child left in the village with him, I collaborated hard with him and his six wives on the farms. Exclusively, grandpa and I were the shepherds, after Michael and Emmanuel left the village. Daily we took the herd of about twenty sheep to shrubbushes to graze. We would also cut fresh leaves (fodder) to feed about ten goats on leashes behind the barn. The goats were tied to their goat-stakes in the huts. I often wondered why goats could not be taken to the fields like the sheep or vice versa. Our town elders usually decreed a yearly ban on goats and sheep being left to roam freely, during cultivation periods of the year, because they ate the vegetables and tender sprouting leaves of cash crops such as cassava, yam, and cocoyam. He goats were exceptions to the rule. Hegoats were free to roam and eat whatever they liked to eat. Throughout the ages, he-goats have resisted being put on a leash or restrained from wandering freely in pursuit of shegoats. The he-goat would rather kill itself, hitting its head on a wall, tree, or whatever around him. A hegoat will never freely or willingly follow, if it is being dragged or pulled by a female.

Male goats, called he-goats, always had an awful smell about them. Occasionally at night, Grandma told me to go and check that the 'diabolical and evil one' had come back into the livestock shed. I once mustered courage and asked Grandma why she referred to the he-goat as 'the despicable and evil one.' She told me that the he-goat ran out of the barn early, every morning, strutting around the entire village in double quick step, bleating 'baababaaaba,' calling and searching for female goats to mate with.

Mating is its primary preoccupation. That is what it does all day long. He sticks his mouth up, puts his nose up the ass of every female goat, investigating if they are on heat and ready to mate. He mounts and mates with them, even with his own mother, grandmother, and sisters. He-goats could never be put on leashes, they would kill themselves. A he-goat would commit suicide if he could not see a she-goat around. If you are taking a he-goat to the market, he would never walk freely if a woman were pulling him. I observed a he-goat's mating takes a few seconds, but dogs could mate for over an hour, oblivious of how many people are watching them.

I helped with other boyish and manly duties, such as climbing trees to pluck the fruit, leaves, vegetables or even to cut off branches, to trim trees, repair leaky thatch roofs and so on. I learnt the ropes from my grandfather's two young sons Michael (Anelechi) and Emmanuel, before they left primary school and left the village. They were two of the six children of my grandfather's third wife, Nwanyidie. I could weave baskets and mats. I owned my own iron traps to catch rabbits and squirrels. I learnt how to climb palm and coconut trees with my bare hands, or with "Ete" - special climbing ropes. I earned pocket money for sweets and "Akara" bean cakes from weaving baskets and selling them at our Eke-Ezeala, Nkwommiri, Nkwo-ebu and Nkwo-orji local market days. I also earned a few coins here and there doing odd jobs, such as clearing bushes, mound and ridge making for the sowing of crops and tubers during the cultivation season. I assisted in tedious ploughing of the farm soil with hoes, rather than with oxen or tractors as they do in some parts of the world.

## MY GRANDMOTHER

Grandmother Igbedie was, arguably, my grandpa's favourite among his six wives. She was very generous and soft-hearted, and she was a successful market trader. Although, I called her my grandmother as tradition demanded and she functioned as a grandmother, indeed, she was really my step grandmother or adopted grandmother in the modern context. My father's mother, who hail from Umuorlu Isu, was my grandfather's first wife. Sadly, my father lost his own mother, Nwanyieke during his infancy. Thus, my father and his younger sister and brother were nurtured to adulthood by my grandfather's second wife Igbedie, and she became my grandmother.

She slaughtered goats and rams for retail sales at the local markets. She was the only female butcher in our town in the male dominated trade. On every market day, she went and bought a goat or two, had them slaughtered, cut up into joints and retailed. She usually made her profit, and she retained certain cuts of meat for the family meal. She also sold live fowl. Unlike grandpa who had big farms and barns full of yams, Igbedie was rich with cocoyam, cassava, beans, cucumbers, peppers and various forms of tubers and vegetables. She owned dwarf bananas trees, plantain trees, pineapples, coconut, cola nut, oil bean trees, palm trees, breadfruit trees and many 'feminine crops', the men considered would undermine their masculinity, if they included these into their cultivation.

Igbedie always stated 'Chi', God the giver, was too harsh on her. Even before I came to live with her, she was already in menopause and in her late fifties, well past childbearing age. Incredibly, she had had fourteen live childbirths, but none survived beyond six months to one year of age. It was said that each of her babies was extra-large and with a noticeably big head. Her experience was quite pathetic. However, she never looked at other women's children with malice. Instead, she took every child as her own. It may have been the reason I was sent home to live with her. It must have been truly heart breaking to have buried fourteen children, one after another. In 1957, she married her own wife, Felicia, and gave her to grandpa, as a new wife, a new beginning, to have children in her own, Igbedie's name. She always regarded me as though I was her own natural son.

Since I was the only child for a long time in the house, I received all the love she had to give. I had to do all the house chores too, including walking two miles to and from the village stream "Onuala" before going to school, or after school. It was my duty daily to go into the bushes to fetch firewood for our cooking. Sometimes, I would fetch enough to distribute a bundle of firewood to each of my grandfather's other wives. In return, they always brought gifts from the markets for me and gave me meals, whether I had eaten at grandmother's house, or not, or gave me a haircut when my hair became long and bushy.

The Grannies were getting old when I came to live with them. I lived with them for eight years, up to 1960, when I was aged sixteen. With two or three other kids in our compound, as cousins, we usually went to the village stream around five thirty in the morning, or during moonlit nights. It was best to go either early in the morning, or late at night, as at these times one could be sure of fetching clean, clear, undisturbed water.

During rush hour, water from the spring/ stream often turned muddy, unclear and dirty. When we went to the stream early, or late, we were taught to cough or clear our throats at the top of the hill, before descending to the mouth of the spring/ stream. This was to alarm the stream ghosts and spirits to take shelter, so we humans would not see them and jeopardise our human lives. Stories told that a few people in the past who went to stream unannounced, had fainted and some even died from the shock of what they saw. Onuala stream had a twin sister stream, the "Okwaraeleke," where we went to swim, fish and to wash clothes, but the stream water was not drinkable. It was cluttered with so much rubbish and water reeds and weeds.

During school term, after school at 1 pm, the pupils walked home barefoot. Some days on our way home we would revert to climbing other people's mango, pear or coconut trees to pick the fruits, without the tree owner's permission. Having gotten home from school, after eating our lunch, the usual agenda was to go to the bush to fetch firewood for cooking. We cooked over the tripod stands inside the house during rainy season. We also cooked on tripods made of cast iron, or moulded mud or clay outside the house, during the dry seasons (November- March).

While looking for firewood invariably, we would hunt and kill rabbits, squirrels, guinea fowl or any other local wild animal for food.

I sometimes stumbled upon a cluster of edible mushrooms or wild vegetable leaves such as "Ukazi." These were a windfall for my grandma, as she did not have to pay money for such ingredients, for our meals.

One day, when we were digging a rabbit's hole, a seven-foot snake slithered out from the hole. We pursued it all over the bush, it slithered up a tree, we threw objects at it, until it fell to the ground, coiled up in anger and stood erect, ready to attack. However, we overpowered the cursed serpent with a barrage of stones and sticks. The boys made a good pepper soup with it. We even found eggs inside the snake. I learnt from the older boys that a Snake bites only by accident, or in self-defence. They do not usually seek to pursue humans, to bite them. Often, we went fishing and swimming into the late evening.

At night, after dinner, if it were a clear moonlit night, children would indicate their interest by raising their shrieking voices from their homes or huts. We then assembled at wherever was a spacious area. We sang, danced, and played games, such as hide and seek and 'poppy', where a blind-folded child tries to locate and touch another blind-folded boy or girl, who answers 'o-yes' to the call. Then we would tell stories of folklore, where the tortoise 'Mbe' was mostly the smartest or most cunning hero of all animals. The lion was often depicted as a fearsome, but silly animal. Some days, I was happy to be referred to as 'Mbe', but sometimes I resented such a nickname.

Rainy seasons are from May to July each year. These were dull and scary nights. Night came so early, and the moon was hidden behind the clouds. It was pitch dark by early evening. Dry season was glorious. The sun appeared early each day and the birds sang happily.

A moonlit night afforded young men unforgettable opportunities, to mingle, touch and 'play' with the girls. And this was usually the starting point for immoral and dirty jokes and behaviour. Every generation goes through that 'golden period.' It becomes a forum to learn good and bad behaviour from one's peers. Boys begin to touch the backside, breasts, and private areas of the girls. My grandpa once said that mothers who remember how they behaved during the moonlit nights, do not allow their daughters to participate at such a time. However, moonlit nights were not always like this, often there would be a schoolteacher in the neighbourhood, or even a good Christian mother, who would assemble the kids and tell them stories of Jesus Christ and the bible. There were nights when 'the moon refused dinner', meaning the moon no longer appeared early in the evening. On such nights everywhere was pitch dark and fearsome. Even a banana tree would appear as if it was a moving monster. Since there was no electricity, the entire village was covered with a thick blanket of darkness and deathly silence. Families stayed indoors from 6pm when darkness set in and spoke or whispered to each other in low voices.

From the surrounding bushes one could hear the nocturnal insects, animals, and birds. The one that always frightened me the most was the owl, because any time an owl did one of her numbers: 'o-o-o-o-wooh,' 'o-o-o- grooh' near a house, nine times out of ten somebody would die on the same night. This was the case when my uncle Onyegbule died. The dark night became more awesome if it was during rainy season.

The heavy downpours would come with terrible winds which upturned trees, blew down branches and at times scattered the raffia thatches and rafters off the tops of houses. On these nights, it would be almost impossible for another family in a different home, to hear a person's cry for help, if they were in danger. On dry dark nights, one could hear the groan of large animals and murmuring of the trees and tall elephant grasses. Sometimes, people would wake in the morning to find thieves had visited the compound and stolen yams from the barn, or a few goats or chicken, which were usually kept outside, behind the huts.
The night-time taboo and belief in those days was that no one dared to mention the names of certain animals, especially 'snake' at night. The mere mention of its name at night invariably conjured the cursed creature to suddenly appear. If you must mention it and escape repercussion, the nickname of "rope" or "string" was carefully used.

## MY EARLY SCHOOL

My infant and elementary schooling continued in the village at St. Theresa's Catholic School, from 1952-1960. At school, I was a keen and average pupil. I was a bit of a rascal, and I had several friends. The teachers and principals liked me, I was popular. They nicknamed me 'baby face.' I was appointed either as class monitor or regulator, year after year, from standard one, through to standard six. I was always 'teacher's pet'.

During the rainy season, it could be 'raining cats and dogs' for days and nights at a stretch. Those were dark, gloomy, chilly days, with puddles on the roads. Most people did not own an umbrella, so pupils ran to school, ran errands, with banana leaves or cocoyam leaves over their heads, the same as the adults who went to market, or to meetings, or to funerals. After school, everyone clustered around beaming log fires at the "Obi," roasting and eating sweet corn and pears, warming up, almost roasting themselves. We told stories and cracked jokes. My grandfather's hunting dog, "Ogidiga" competed with children for strategic position nearest to the fire. Obi is usually a small hut at the centre of the family compound, where the head of the family normally sits and meets family members and receives visitors.

Each morning at assembly before classes resumed, pupils took turns to recite any memorized recitation. In the six years of my primary education, I recited a few poems. One was 'United we stand, divided we fall' another 'when I was at high school of Edinburgh,' and another 'Tell me not in mournful number, life is but an empty dream.'

On a few occasions, I was made to stand up on top of the teacher's table at Assembly, to show myself off to the rest of the pupils, as an example of how to dress neatly. I also showed clean teeth, clean toes, and fingernails. Growing up and schooling in the village influenced my future life and adulthood, relationships with men, women, people in general. It made me modest and very appreciative of any achievement or progress I made, however small.

Grandad had a number of domestic animals, such as sheep, goats, and fowl. I cast my mind back and I can remember my life in the village with grandpa. Those were the good old days! Soon after my arrival in the village, I was dedicated to serve at the shrine. It was full of carved gods and goddesses with dried or fresh blood dripping on their wooden, mud or clay bodies. Some of the gods were represented by creeping stems, perennial live-sticks, stumps, and stunted shrubs. My grandfather's crystal ball was a wooden bowl, but you could bet on his pronouncements. Most of the sacrificed animals were taboo, not to be eaten by women of any age. While self- professed Christian members of the family also abstained on Christian grounds, grandpa and I feasted endlessly on the meat. It ranged from snake, chicken, turtle, ram, goat, sheep, pig, pigeon, and guineafowl to cow and bull. I had to always wear protective and good luck fetish charms and talisman around my waist and neck.

I was also a young shepherd; I tended the flock of sheep and herd of goats. I was keen on working alongside the men, fixing the thatched huts, climbing trees, hunting, chasing squirrels, digging rabbits, trap-setting, and fishing. I owned my own cutlass for bush-clearing and a hoe for tilling and ploughing the farm.

Grandpa told us a story: 'One day begins a story' they always say and that 'one day' was in the year 1810. The men of Abba were in a half peaceful, half fearful mood. The breeze was hot, the sun as strong as if it were making the kill of a lifetime, or as though there were to be no more sunrises.

There had been a terrible rumour circulating in the village for some days. It was a sort of 'open secret,' which no one wished to acknowledge who, or where they heard it, in case it was not true. Apparently, it was imminent, the small, quiet, and peaceful town was on the brink of invasion by aliens.

Azubuike, a terrified one-eyed witness, described what he saw with his naked eye, as 'nightmarish!' He confided that it was 'unthinkable! Unimaginable!' He was supposed to have been captured, along with several others, by the so-called 'aliens,' gigantic men. The middle-aged Azubuike had gone to the distant town of Aro in his year-long search for a second wife. He luckily escaped through the bush, nevertheless, he lost an eye in the process. This was nothing compared to what would have befallen him, had the foreign intruders succeeded in chaining him up.
He gave an unintelligible description of them. No one could imagine the type of men he talked about, who were said to be neither charcoal black, as our northern neighbours, nor brown like us, nor white as the gulls, but 'plain ghostlike, without toes, with sapphire eyes and riding on iron horses.' The usual peace and quiet of Abba was badly affected. No one knew what to expect, or what not to expect.

Each morning, we assembled for inspection of school uniform, our teeth, toes and fingers nails, hair cut (Kojak style) or brushed hair and whether one had taken a bath before coming to school. A failure mark on each category merited six strokes of the cane on the bare buttocks or on the palms of hands. Any form of stealing, or any pupil caught exhibiting or practising sexual acts of any type, was brought before the headmaster and such pupils were named, shamed, whipped, and booed publicly. I will never forget the case of one child, Chukwudi. He was reported to have stolen at night, by dipping his fingers into a pot of soup, eating up the snails and cod stockfish in the soup. Later he broke into the school building and stole a goat at the Nkworji market. An angry market woman saw Chukwudi walking past at the market and instantly smashed a coconut on his head. Chukwudi still managed to scramble away, as though nothing happened. The town elders later went to his house, apprehended him with the cooperation of his parents and he was paraded around town, before being lashed forty-eight strokes of the cane. In those days corporal punishment was effective.

Every Monday at school, roll calls were made and those who were not seen at church on the previous Sunday also received punishment. Though I assisted my grandpa in his pagan rituals, rarely did I fail to accompany other children to the Catholic Church, for mass on Sunday. I attended church regularly for two reasons: Firstly, I did not want to be whipped at school the next day for being absent, secondly, we were taught that those who missed church, or sinned, would be condemned to eternal hellfire. It was also fun to wear our beautiful, smart Sundayclothes and show off to one's schoolmates, or to impress the girls.
The local church in my village had a priest, Rev. Father Hacket. He lived in the neighbouring village Amaigbo Parish. The town Amaigbo was famous in those days for two main reasons. One is

the hometown of the famous slave boy, who became King Jaja of Opobo. Two, Amaigbo was also the birthplace of the first Nigerian World boxing Champion, Dick Tiger.

Rev. father Hacket attended our church for mass, only once a month. The Irish priest had to cover well over twenty churches in his parish. So, it was a rotational deal. He rode a huge motor bike, a Triumph, and one could hear the booming sound almost a mile away. When we did not get a priest on a Sunday, one of the schoolteachers who was also the Catechist performed an ordinary church service. He read the day's Epistle and the Gospel and led in prayers and Rosary. We normally had Mass and Holy Communion only when the priest visited.

## CHRISTIAN UPBRINGING

By the end of 1957, I was thirteen and neither baptised, nor receiving the Holy Communion. I became aware that if I died without baptism, I would be doomed to the dreaded eternal hellfire. I was told the original sin from Adam and Eve was still hanging over my head. This fact gave me the creeps. I felt even worse when the Catechist explained to me that I was not eligible and would not be baptised, since my mother and father were 'living in sin; so long as my father was a polygamist.

As I could have been baptised and had my original sin 'washed away,' as a week-old toddler, now, as a grown up my only way out was to attend catechism classes, pass the exams, after which I would then be baptised.

I dutifully embarked on the programme on my own initiative, and by the end of the year I was baptised. I later qualified through similar exams and received my first Holy Communion. To receive communion, one had to attend Confession, whereby one tells the priest his sins, such as confessing that one had 'lied, committed fornication, missed church service etc,' after which the priest gives you absolution or forgiveness. The priest also gives the penitent some punishment which must be completed before forgiveness is full and final. Punishment ranged from saying one Hail Mary, to a full chaplet, or Rosary. The recipients of Holy Communion, in those days, must fast for at least 12 hours and on receiving the blessed sacrament, one must not allow it to touch one's teeth, body, or hands. Otherwise, myth had it that the whole place or vicinity of the church will be covered in a pool of blood!

Next, becoming confirmed was the next target on my
Christian religious path. I had to wait for a bishop to visit, as only a Bishop could administer the Sacrament of Confirmation.
It took two more years before such an opportunity arose and I became confirmed.

On 1st January 1958, my mother gave birth to a baby boy at Port Harcourt, when I was there on holidays. I personally named him Cletus (Chukwudi) meaning 'indeed there is God'.

Life in our village was simple and pure. Everyone went about their normal life without a fuss. Schoolchildren played football, or soccer, bare-footed. All the bushes served as a toilet, be it around home or on the way to school, or to the market. If one was pressed in the depths of the night by a natural call, one still had to go into the bush. I hated to go outside of my room at night. I used to be a bedwetter as a little boy. Every morning, I was ridiculed for urinating on myself in bed. I was cured by eating roasted wall geckos. At school, only the teachers wore shoes. Often the heels of their shoes were slanting, with holes in the soles. The shoes were usually incredibly old and old fashioned. In those days rice, milk, eggs, and tea were the preserves of the rich, eaten by the poor only rarely, such as on Christmas day, Easter day or on other special occasions.

In my grandmother's mud and raffia thatched house, there were no clocks, television (TV), radios, or telephone. We guessed the time of day by observation of natural signs, such as cock crow, or with the position of shadows, or the sun, illness and injuries were cured with certain leaves, roots, or tree barks. If anyone was taken to the distant hospital, then the case was referred to as 'very serious in other words the odds where they would not survive. Patients usually arrived at hospital with 'one leg in the grave.' If someone died, they were buried on the same day, without any medical (Coroners) report and no certificate of death was required. I have since wondered if sometimes a person may have been buried 'half alive.'

The elders and chiefs in the village were 'a law unto themselves.' The police were rarely called for any crime.

Judgements were often pronounced, and punishments meted out by the chiefs, Nze's and elders of the village. There was no female representative among the elders. Men ruled the day and made all the vital decisions, which the womenfolk must accept whether they liked it or not. Women and children were to obey their husbands and fathers. They were to be 'seen and not heard.' A woman's role was simple, to look after the home, while the men were mostly the breadwinners who owned a large barn of yams and were respected as good hunters who provided meat for food. An adage stated that any bad occurrence in villages created an advantageous opportunity for the Nze's, chiefs and elders, big meal merriment and sometimes gratification in the form of bribes and kickbacks. Although I was a child, I witnessed instances which could be classified or deciphered as 'subtle influences.'

Any matter requiring someone to appear at the Whiteman's District officer (DO) Court would been seen as a profoundly serious and grievous matter, a crime such as murder, manslaughter, or grievous bodily harm (GBH). Invariably, some land disputes ended up with the parties lashing out with a machete and inflicting deep cuts on each other.

In those days, most journeys within the village and its environs were made on foot. There were limited means of transportation, from A to B. However, very few men of means owned Hercules or Raleigh Bicycles. There were also a couple of lorries that plied between the village and the cities. The journey from my village to Port Harcourt, was sixty miles away and it would take almost an entire day to arrive. A journey to Lagos, which was then the capital of Nigeria, was about three hundred miles away and would take some two to three days. On the back of the lorries was clearly written: 35 MPH. (miles per hour). The lorry and bus owners always inscribed mottos or philosophy on their vehicles. A typical inscription was either in English or the vernacular, such as 'Why

Worry?' 'Who made you a judge over others?' 'Vanity upon Vanity' 'Mind your own business' 'Agana doga!' – We must continue to try' 'The struggle continues' 'one with God is a majority' 'Thank God, the Almighty' 'I shall Return' 'Safe Journey' 'Jehovah Jire!' 'Oh Jesu' referring to Jesus.

## QUEEN ELIZABETH II'S VISIT TO NIGERIA

I was in elementary school when Queen Elizabeth 11 of England visited Nigeria in 1956. She travelled with her two children, Charles, and Anne. One of my teachers told me her son Prince Charles would be the next King of England, on the death of his mother. We were taught to sing 'God save the Queen.' Schools were closed and students were lined along the streets with the British Union Jack flags flying at full mast.

Each person waved the small or miniature British flag and the Queen's motorcade drove past.

My mother was baptised that year and took the name Elizabeth as her Christian name. A name that was both biblical and royal. One of my uncles had a baby girl the same year and she too was named Elizabeth. My mother bought one of the Queen's pictures and it was hung in our living room.

A legend in those days stated that during the Native's first encounter with the Europeans, our people were baffled and bewildered at the ghostlike, pale human beings they saw. For them, it was an astonishing and unbelievable sight, when a white man removed his entire upper set of teeth, showed them around. then put them back in his mouth and was able to chew coconut with same set of teeth!

However, any remote association with a white person in those days was regarded as a thing of honour. A man was arrested for killing another man over an adulterous affair with his wife. The colonial police officer or 'courtma' (Court messenger) took him away in hand cuffs, in a police van. Unbelievably, villagers who saw him started waving their hands admiringly towards him, as a mark of honour, for riding in a van with a white man, although the man kept shouting, 'Aka jim! Aka jim' meaning 'Am under arrest, Am under arrest'! However, passers-by could not make out a word of what he was babbling due to the speed of the van, his words were lost in a rush of the blowing wind as the van sped away to prison, for the man to await trial in a colonial court.

## DEAD AND MIRACULOUS RESURRECTION

In 1960, I went to Okigwe for an Entrance Examination into Okigwe National Grammar School, Umuna. After the examinations, the transportation I took to go home arrived extremely late in the evening. I was heading to Anara. The vehicle was also carrying the foul-smelling body of a dead man. Rows of plank benches were removed nearer the tail board of the lorry, to make room for the corpse, who was stretched out on a mat, on the floor. I sat on the remaining bench at the rear end of the lorry, the only passenger. I could not avoid looking at the dead man's uncovered eyes and face and I had never been so scared in my life. I left the lorry at Okwelle at around eleven o'clock, in the dead of night and in total darkness. I walked through bush tracks for three miles to Abba, my hometown. I met no living human being on my way. I had nightmares, my head became swollen, and I fell very ill. The next day my grandfather sent me to Port Harcourt, for my parents to arrange treatment for me.

It was possibly a malaria attack. My mother went to a drug company and bought some herbal tea and epsom salts, a mixture for laxative, and she must have given me an overdose. It was said that I was breathless for twelve hours. To the extent that a coffin was brought, and a lorry chartered to transport my body home for burial. Since our village home was about sixty miles from Port Harcourt, it was suggested that to avoid, 'wetin you carry' and 'how manage' questions by the police, bureaucratic and regulatory hitches on the way, it was advisable to take the body first to the city general hospital for a death certificate. And that was God speaking. Fortunately, a doctor was available at the hospital to take a quick look at me. While he was doing all he could to revive me, he asked the nurse to place a phone call to the bishop's house. Bishop Okoye sent Monsignor Cyriacus Mbah (Then Fr. C.S. Mbah) on the sick call. I was unconscious and unable to speak or confess my sins. He was said to have administered the last orders or 'Extreme Unction' by putting the holy oil into my mouth. Thirty minutes later, I miraculously opened my eyes and immediately demanded food, followed by my then asking to use the toilet.

As far as I was concerned, I recalled that when I was so close to death, I was transported in a big lorry. The lorry drove past church after church in an atmosphere of dazzling sunshine and drizzling rain. Naked children were playing in the rain. I saw rainbow after rainbow. When the lorry finally reached its destination, I came down to face about twelve wise old men. They looked like the biblical Moses. I figured I was brought for some judgement but was not so sure. They motioned a seat to me and offered me a kolanut and in my culture, kolanut is the first thing one offers to a visitor as a sign of heartfelt welcome. The eldest man breaks it into pieces invoking God's blessing and protection on everyone.

When I received the kola nut, I then asked 'mama, E-sim taa oji' that is 'mum, should I eat the kola?' The words said in the dream, in my subconscious mind, came out alive, in my conscious life. There were over twenty family members by my hospital bedside. As they heard me speak, people started shaking me, shouting 'No, don't eat!' 'Do not eat, come back! come back!' 'No don't eat!' It must have been at that point I opened my eyes. When I awoke, I was amazed at where I was. I wondered how I had got there. I was surprised at the number of our people who gathered around me. So it happened that in 1960 I literally died and was miraculously resurrected. I missed a month of schooling due to illness. When I returned to school, I joined the St. Jude Society. St Jude began to intercede in all my prayers, and to date St Jude is my patron saint. St Jude novenas worked miracles in my life from then on.
By this single act, I felt that truly God had much interest and love for me. Out of His mercy for me and/or my parents, out of love

for me, God mercifully extended my life "Quid Retribuam": - what shall I give back to God? I shall give my life. It was no longer doubtful in my mind that God had called me to serve Him as a good Christian. Somehow, I began to believe that I would not die until I attained old age – the biblical 'three score years and ten'. I came to believe that no person, or devil, or witch, can ever hurt me again. It became clear to me that truly I am a special child of God. Some may say it was a foolish belief, but it worked for me, as it gave me enormous, fearless confidence, from then on.

## NIGERIA INDEPENDENCE - 1960

On 1st October 1960, Nigeria obtained independence from Britain, and became self- governing. I was two months away from finishing standard six, my last year at elementary school. I believe, as a gift to Nigerian school children, the government, or the Queen of England, brought loads of powdered milk for us. That was the one and only time we were given milk at school. Our joy was dampened when rumours started circulating that many pupils from other schools had died after drinking the free milk. As a result of these rumours, most of the school children in our area ran away from school or abstained from drinking the milk. I listened to the benefits of drinking milk, such as it being good for my body and bones. I was also aware that in my family we only used a few drops of condensed peak milk with our cups of tea. In the village, I did not have any opportunity to drink tea. When I went on holiday to Port Harcourt, my parents made tea for us perhaps on Sundays only and drank with sugar, milk, bread and akara (bean cakes). With some hesitation, I cautiously drank the free cups of government powdered milk for the entire week. I remember waking up every day, to tell people 'See, I am still alive'!

## LEAVING SCHOOL AND THE VILLAGE: ARRIVING IN PORT HARCOURT

In those days no one talked of 'three-square meals', as one must be rich, or very lucky to have it. Maybe three-square meals were the exclusive right of the extraordinarily rich. In my family, we were far from rich. We took each day as it came. We ate when we saw food, be it 'square or oblong!' Anything edible was food. I certainly never went to school or bed feeling hungry. It could be a proper meal of foo-foo with soup or roasted yam, cocoyam, corn or plantain with ground fresh green peppers and fresh red palm oil. We were taught to wash hands before our meals because everyone ate with the five fingers and the palm, normally of the right hand. Up to ten people could wash their hands in the same bowl of water, even after the water looked black and murky.

In my final year, at the age of 15 years, I learnt a sophisticated poem and recited it from memory in the assembly hall, before the entire pupils and teachers. Today, I may not remember where I left my car keys a few minutes ago, but amazingly, I can still recite the same poem that I memorised over 50 years ago. I will quote it below because some of the lines still guide my life to this day. Henry Longfellow authored the poem titled: **"Life is but an Empty Dream"**.

*Tell me not in mournful numbers, Life is but an empty dream!*

*For the soul is dead that slumbers, and things are not what they seem.*

*Life is real! Life is earnest! And the grave is not its goal.*
*Dust thou art, to dust thou returnest, was not spoken of the soul.*

*Not enjoyment, and not sorrow, Is our destined end or way. But to act, that each tomorrow, Find us farther than today.*

*Art is long, and Time is fleeting, and our hearts, though stout and brave, Still, like muffled drums, are beating Funeral marches to the grave.*

*In the world's broad field of battle, In the bivouac of life, Be not dumb, driven cattle! Be a hero in the strife!*
*Trust no Future, however pleasant! Let the dead Past bury its dead.*

*Act, -act in the living present! Heart within, and God overhead!*

*Lives of great men all remind us, we can make our lives sublime,*

*And, departing, leave behind us, Footprints on the sands of time.*

*Footprints, the perhaps another, Sailing over life's solemn main,*

*A forlorn and shipwrecked brother, Seeing, shall take heart again.*

*Let us then be up and doing, With a heart for any fate.*

*Still achieving, still pursuing, learn to labour and to wait.*

In Summary, I took to heart the poem telling us not to waste life; to live it now, to be the best we can be. That yesterday is gone, tomorrow is uncertain.

We should not let fear stop us aiming high, to be a hero, enthusiastic, optimistic, positive and to live as a shining example to others. We should pursue our hopes, thrills, and goals. I add to this, one of my favourable lines in the constitution of the USA, about everyone having an inalienable right to pursue happiness.

In that final year, I passed three common entrance examinations to the top catholic secondary schools of choice, which in those days were called Colleges. That made me happy. My grandpa and grandma were sort of sad that I was leaving them in December 1960. On the contrary, I was more enthusiastic at leaving the village; I was looking forward to entering the college (secondary school) the following year, January 1961. I assured my grannies that I would come home every holiday to be with them. I took their minds ten years further on, telling them to imagine what joy it would be when, by that time I would be well educated, maybe become a doctor, a lawyer, or an engineer, have a senior service job, own a car, build a storey zinc roofed house etc. They gave me their blessings into the "palm of my hands." I gave them hope that after I attained a sound education, I would be able to assist many people, perhaps the entire family, village, and our town. I would buy them things, all they ever wanted, by the grace of God. The night before I left home, we had a big meal.

Grandpa told me to catch one of the big fowl and kill it, for grandma to cook for dinner. I was given a full leg of chicken with my meal.

In the morning, at 5 am, they woke me, and we walked for half an hour to Anara Motor Park, where I caught the lorry and travelled to Port Harcourt, to join my father, mother, brothers, and sisters. I was always fascinated by Port Harcourt, Pitakwa or Port as the city was colloquially called. I loved electricity in homes and the streetlights in some main streets. The pump (pipe borne water) which was found in certain parts of the city. Our room in Port Harcourt was full of people. My father, with two wives and eleven children, lived in one room and parlour, in a 'face me, I face-you yard.' The room measured no more than ten feet by twelve feet. Two beds occupied adjacent positions in the bedroom. All our other belongings, including the sleeping mats, cooked and uncooked food were put away under the beds. The parlour was where eleven of us, the children, slept. More than half of the children engaged in chronic bed wetting. Such that, in the mornings, the stench in the house was corrosive.

I knew all along that my parents were poor compared to some of my friends' parents. However, my parents were still better off than some other families. We were not the worst or poorest. So, our financial, economic, or social position never really made me feel sad or emotional. I was a self-contented kid. Instead, I felt sorry for my dad who had to share out the entire contents of his pay packet to his wives and children on every payday. I noticed the family lacked some basic and essentials things of life that we ought to have. I kept telling my mother and father that when I grew up and completed my college and university education, I would work and buy them all their needs, the things that they never had, such as a good house, radio, furniture, nice clothes, shoes and so on. Our neighbours and relations regarded me as a good, smart, and intelligent lad for having so much love and respect for my parents. As often as my parents or other people gave me such compliments it made me proud and encouraged me much more, to be more exemplary. Such remarks made me keener and eager.

I often wished I could really fast forward in my life, so that I could start to do the things I promised. I enjoyed and craved the praise. Sometimes, I wished that I could find a bundle of money on the road, so I could do more to overturn my parents' situation overnight. I knew at that time several relatives had pinned their hopes on me.

**CHAPTER FIVE**

---

# Dampened Hopes

In January 1961, however, my joy of the city environment was quickly damped, when my father informed me, he could not afford to pay the twenty pounds a term for my college education. I was initially numbed and shell-shocked! What a shattered dream. I had informed my schoolmates and others I would be starting college soon. I thought of my future, and I thought of the shame. It hit me terribly, beyond my imagination. I was devastated but did not rebel. I remained humble and loyal. If they had the money surely, they would do it for me. I put my hope in God to solve my problems. My life and thinking started moving towards the Almighty, who gives and takes, according to his will. When I looked around, I noticed my parents worked tirelessly, every day. Dad worked at PWD while mum was a petty trader at the Diobu main market. I concluded their poverty had nothing to do with laziness, more likely it was with life's wheel of fortune. The mysterious ways of creation. Dad was recalled, serving part time as a police officer, since the time when Queen Elizabeth visited in 1956. His rank was sergeant major in the "Queen Eliza Police force." They earned little or nothing for their service. Dad was such an honest man that he could never accept a bribe no matter the difficulties at home. Sometimes mum would nag that he was a coward. He always replied that 'a good name is better than riches.' I was proud of my dad. I used to go alone, or with friends to the Police Barracks' field, to watch him command and inspect police parades.

It was obvious that my folks were poor as the proverbial church rat, but it had never crossed my mind that my dad could not pay twenty pounds a term for my school tuition and boarding fees. He said he could not even pay ten pounds a term if I attended as a day student. Financially, it was clear that dad was one of the less fortunate of his siblings and half-brothers. Some of our wealthy friends and relations were desperately praying for a child, or two, and incredibly, others such as my dad, had the gift of many clever children, but did not have enough money to pay for their further education. This is one of those mysteries of this world. It shows that no one has everything they want in life. Why was it, I wondered, some people seemed to be well-off financially, owned rental properties, owned homes, commercial and private cars and could sponsor their wards conveniently.

I boldly went to some of my father's friends and relations for financial help to enable me to enter college, but none obliged me. The hard facts and realities of life began to form and crystallise in my mind, that in life, 'ours is ours' but 'mine is mine' As a matter fact, some people I went to for help were already sponsoring two or three of their own children, or siblings. in colleges, so the scenario seemed a plausible excuse not to help me. Some suggested I go to learn taxicab driving or welding, become an electrician, or car mechanic. My inner spirit and intuition did not accept any of these occupations as good options for me.

I considered that although my father was not paying college fees for anybody, truly his burdens such as paying rent, feeding two wives and twelve children was too much for his monthly wage of ten pounds per month. It was not a bad pay cheque at that time, considering that college leavers working for big companies earned roughly fifteen pounds per month. My Dad's monthly rent alone was in the region of three pounds, before the cost of medical bills, bus fares, schoolbooks, school uniform for six children in elementary schools, dues and contributions in the village and kindred meetings. His two wives, my mother, and her co-wife, provided food from their profits.
There was no glimmer of hope that my father, or anybody else, would pay my way through secondary school at any time!

On one occasion, the reality that I would not go to college caused me to shed tears openly. When I cried my father said, 'look at it!

I will not kill myself!' He declared he could not help me if I stubbornly refused to learn a trade as an occupation.

I was convinced by my inner soul, that if I did not attend secondary school, I would be a poor man for life and the cycle of poverty would continue in my family. I also told myself that I would never marry more than one wife, because I considered polygamy contributed to my father's parlous financial status. I made up my mind, even at that age, that my future wife must also be educated and have an excellent job and income to supplement mine. I would also have only two, at most four children, two boys and two girls! On the other hand, it was joyful to have siblings and relations around you. At school, church, streets and at home, family members provided protection, good company, and camaraderie. Sibling rivalries and family expectations were challenging, motivating, and
inspiring. Now, with hindsight, I believe in the axiom
'Man proposes, and God disposes.'

My life was in turmoil at that stage. I would, in turn, laugh and weep at myself and for my future. Somehow, I began to shelve the idea of going to college. Nonetheless, I hated to imagine the prospect of poverty, illiteracy and hopelessness that would perpetuate in our household. When my classmates left for various colleges, I wept for the last time over my predicament. I told myself that I will do my best in this life and leave the rest to God. After about a week of recrimination, I sobered up, to face facts squarely. It was 1961 and I had left elementary school.

I was now sixteen years old. Sometimes I got horny, I ejaculated during wet dreams, at night. My nipples had swollen. I had pubic hair and some duding moustache and goatee. I had suddenly become a man. Inspiration told me that certainly, I was now on my own. I must take control of my own destiny. I would no longer depend on other people, but on myself and my own God. What you will be, you will be. Be sure to put in your best struggle and leave the rest to God. God creates all men, but not the same fate, each to his own destiny. I began to search for mine.

## THE SURVIVAL SPIRIT

There was a two-room commercial institute (typing and shorthand) down the block from our house. The signboard said the owner was a London trained stenographer and advertised for those with the standard six qualifications to enrol for the Royal Society of Art (R.S.A) certificate in a two-year course.

To raise the two pounds a term school fees for the commercial institute, I decided to become a public porter at the market and at the nearby bus stops. I reported daily with coil-rolled rags, forming a pad on my head. Thus, I carried, on my head, any load, or wares to the owner's destination, for an agreed tip, or fee. It was like running my own business for the first time in my life. The harder I worked the more money I made. On an exceptionally good day, I went home with two or more shillings, all profit. Some days I was even luckier and was hired as an on-the-spot labourer, on building sites. I filled drums with water, or worked with a head-pan, shovelled sand, gravel/ chippings, mixed cement, and sand, or loaded and unloaded bags of cement, planks, etc from vehicles, lorries, and tippers.

I bought a piggy bank, where I saved two shillings per day towards my education. I was happy I became a source of help to my mum, providing some money for her grocery bills. Also, I could buy my own clothes and shoes. Frankly, to date, I still do not know why those used or second-hand clothing items were called 'Okirika wake-up' when it is Abiriba people who specialised in the dealership of second-hand clothes. The bales of used clothes were usually brought in from our neighbouring country Cotonou, Benin Republic. Even to date, used clothes and other accessories are very handy to people seeking help to make ends meet.

My new self-employed status did not last. In only a few months I became bankrupt, as I was sadly incapacitated with severe neck pain. Therefore, my only source of capital ceased abruptly. To be honest, my physical build was entirely unsuitable for heavy, laborious work. I was not rugged, muscular, and stocky, rather I was slightly frail, skinny, and slender. When I recovered, I went to the typing school and paid the school fees of two pounds. By half term, I had the opportunity to use the typewriter twice a week, for forty-five minutes each. I was still doing 'ASDF' semi-colon LKJ by the end of the term. I had no money for the second term and went back to square one. I was down but not out. All I had to do was 'keep looking up.' If the creator never sleeps, my turn shall someday come, I consoled my poor self, though I thought in such a heavenly way, putting my trust in God. In those days, there was nothing like being 'born again' or 'seeing the light' as some people claim to do nowadays.

## LEARNING TRADES AS AN APPRENTICE: AUTOMECHANIC, WELDING, ELECTRICIAN, RADIOMECHANIC

At this point in my life today, the truth seems obvious, that I could not study or learn anything where fees had to be paid, no matter how paltry the amount. So, my father again started talking to some semi-skilled and self-employed tradesmen, asking them to take me on as an apprentice. I swallowed my pride and started with 'Ike welding shop' and after a week I moved to 'Luke's Car Mechanic workshop.' Two weeks later I went from there to 'Good Luck Electrician' and eventually I ended up at 'Joe's Radio Repairs' None of these worked out for me. It just did not 'click'. Often, I stopped going to a place due to lack of bus fares, or pocket money for food at lunch time. The year 1961 was a restless and embattled year for me. My hopes of entering secondary school were hopelessly shattered. I floundered around aimlessly, helplessly. I was now a Christian by baptism, I trusted God, but that's as far as it went. There was nothing else to gain 'til after death, for all I knew, at the time.

# THE DREAM: ALTAR BOY AND BOY SCOUT

In 1962, my cousin who is only a year older, proudly emerged with Grade 1 in Cambridge examinations, from Stella Maris College, Port Harcourt. The entire members of the family gathered to celebrate Edmund's success, at his father's house at King Jaja Street.

Sadly, another son of the family, who was many years older than Edmund, was unsuccessful that year in the same examination. There were discussions about Edmund's brilliance and the prospects of his proceeding overseas for further studies. Our uncles ruled out sending Edmund overseas. It was said that studying overseas was too expensive and caused too much suffering for foreign students. By special arrangement through our kinsman, Honourable Barrister E.C. Akwuiwu who was a member of the Federal House of Representatives, Eddy soon started work as a Customs Officer in Lagos. Though Eddy's father was well to do by the standards of those days and Eddy could be said to have been born with the proverbial silver spoon in his mouth, I just wanted to emulate his academic prowess at that stage.

One night after this, I had a dream, which today could be referred to as a vision. I awoke with two decisions in mind. One, was to become a Server at Mass and the second was to join the Boy Scouts in a personal way. I awoke feeling fresh and could not express why I was so ecstatically happy. In this state, I went to the catholic mission and straight to the Rev. Fathers' house at Christ the King Church, Diobu, to talk to any priest there. I knew none of them by name and one of them knew me only as a parishioner.

I had been baptised and confirmed but I considered that as a type of insurance benefit, to be reaped after death, but which had nothing to do with my fate, or my life, here on earth. As a practising Catholic I went to church regularly, though most of the time many of us were unable to get into the church building during holy mass. The young ones, like me, took delight in playing outside, watching people and cars till 'ite, missaest' Latin, which translates as 'go, the mass has ended.' The congregation usually responded with the chorus 'Deo Gratias' meaning 'Glory be to God' and everyone dispersed to their various homes.

Church attendance for many Christians at that time was purely a routinely mechanical act, people believed their mere appearance at a church service fulfilled their religious obligation.

In any event, at the mission I met with Rev Fr. Patrick Flynn C. S. S. P. (a Holy Ghost father). He was a tall, white, huge, and handsome Irish priest. I went to him cautiously, as although he was a priest, I was not sure if he owned a vicious dog, like other white people in Nigeria in those days. Once bitten, twice shy! After my earlier experience with dogs, I dreaded any further encounter with any ferocious, pugnacious hound dog. They would run crazy at the slightest provocation, until they were satisfied that they had defeated their human opponent.

Fr. Flynn listened as I explained to him, blushing as I did so, 'Father, I want to be a Mass Servant.' His big blue eyes, pierced through me, as a hot bread knife slicing through butter. He had never seen me before, I did not even attend the Christ the King

school, which was under his supervision. He appeared unconcerned by my newness and the fact that my father was a polygamist, and my mother was not a member of The Christian mother's Association, because she was unwed in the Catholic Church. Not even minding that I was born out of wedlock by the church's standard, the Priest accepted and directed me to the man in charge, the Sacristan, Mr Eze. That was the day the Lord called me. As He said,
'You have not chosen me, but I have chosen you.'

Within a week, I had served my first mass as an acolyte, pouring water over the priest's fingers, an act of ablution, a symbolic washing away of sins, before offering. This was followed by my carrying the wine and water to the priestcelebrant, to offer and consecrate into the body and blood of Christ. I felt I was in Heaven, transformed into a happy, holy child of God, from that day onwards. The transformation was real and palpable. I became new, more cheerful, thoughtful, relaxed, confident, even in cleanliness, personal appearance, and body stature. Humbleness to my parents and my elders radiated a remarkable Christ likeness. The day after my acceptance as an altar server, I went to the St Andrew's Anglican mission, Diobu. I met Mr Ogbokuma, an Okirika one-eyed man, the scout leader. He enlisted me into the Eagle patrol of the Scout Troop. The Scout honour and promise; 'On my honour I promise to do my best, to do my duty to God and my country, to help other people at all times and to obey the scout law' was the most touching vow I had ever taken. The Scout laws of obedience, honesty, trustworthiness, thriftiness, cheerfulness, cleanliness and so on, were the best formative instruction any young child could get. I was forever in the public eye, from that time onwards. Surely, it was because nobody expected less than honesty and truthfulness from an Altar boy, or a Boy Scout. If I said 'on my honour, this is the truth' that was it. I became genuinely determined not to fail. I resolved to do my best to succeed where my dad had been held back. A passage in our Scout book said, 'what you are tomorrow, you are already becoming today.' Also, the children of today will become the fathers and leaders of tomorrow. I took each one of those statements to heart, and it soothed me.

The star, or light, that appeared at the end of the dark tunnel of my life was Fr. Patrick. Flynn. The Irish priest showed interest and concern in me and my future. Indeed, he was a Godsend to me. In most cases providence uses fellow men to express the Godhead.

I went to the mission every evening after whatever spot job, pottering or scavenging, I did. Somedays I even went to water side at Abonema wharf and provided woodcutters with clean water in exchange for firewood, which I resold to roadside batcher, kiosks, hoteliers and "bukas." I also carried enough firewood to our home for my sweet, dear mum and her cowife. I served at the daily six o'clock morning masses. I joined the St. Jude Society.

In many instances, St. Jude my patron saint (the miracle worker, helper of the helpless and despairing people) helped answer my prayers. As a member of society, every week we had to do pastoral job such as helping old people, visiting the sick in their homes, or hospital. My prayer book also showed how many years of indulgences attached to each prayer and each day. I strove to accumulate as many years of plenary indulgence as possible. I even kept a record like a bank statement, on how much treasure I had banked away in heaven, where there is no moth, rot, or thieves. The bank of heaven, though it pays the interest here on earth, a hundredfold, yet the principal sum is safe. Decent work is the legal tender, measure for measure.

## IRISH PRIESTS – REV. FR. PATRICK FLYNN

Later, Fr. Flynn found out that I was a victim of certain crippling financial circumstances, and he asked me to come and live with the Parish Priests at the mission. I moved into the boys' quarters with the steward, one Donatus Eke, from Mbaise. His uncle, Mr Eke was the mission catechist. It did not take long after I moved in, when Rev, Fr. Charles Ohaeri, a native circular priest was posted to the parish. He was a tall, neat, decent and impeccable man, whose black priesthood was an embodiment of holiness, but also the essence of the presence of God in this world. He became my mentor. Meanwhile my cousin, who is a year younger, successfully completed the standard six education and passed the entrance examinations to New Era Technical College, Port Harcourt, but he was unable to attend. His own father, like mine, was not financially well off enough to pay for his education. He learned to drive and soon my cousin became a licensed taxi driver. At times I envied his economic independence. However, I did not waiver in my quest to find a way to go to a secondary school.

My duties at the mission included serving mass and doubling as a cook and steward for the priests. Some days I served at more than two or three masses. Whenever we had some out of-town priests visiting and staying overnight, each had to celebrate his own mass. On some Sundays we went out of station to say masse or make sick calls to the dying. I washed the priests' cars. I swept, dusted, made up the priests' beds, bedrooms, washed dishes, set and cleared dining tables or just accompanied priests to their various personal outings. After siesta (the afternoon sleep) the foreign priests usually drank tea, no matter how hot the weather. That never ceased to surprise me. I was always around at 3 p.m.to serve tea. I also helped count Sunday collections before it went to the bank. To examine and count large sums of money had a way of giving me joy, even though the money was not mine. From the stipends, dash, and gifts which I received, I gave my parents a little help and saved towards my future education. By the new year of 1962, I was still hoping and preparing to enter secondary school. I had even bought all my class one books, a uniform, canvas shoes and sandals. To my disappointment, once again, the main school fee of twenty pounds was nowhere to be found. Two weeks after school commenced, Fr. Flynn summoned me and upon discovering my predicament, he asked me one question 'would you like to become a priest?' 'Yes father' I replied. Immediately, he produced a handwritten note for me to take to St. Peter Claver Seminary, Okpuala to begin my training for the priesthood. I was accepted automatically, without further question. I was now a Seminarian.

The Rector gave me an acceptance letter and a prospectus. I was expected to return with my kit and the fees of seven pounds a term (subsidised), one third of the cost of a regular secondary school per term. In ten good days, I could not raise seven pounds from anybody I knew. I was frustrated and despondent. The shame of returning without such a paltry sum would be so embarrassing, so I simply stayed away. I was smart enough to write to the school explaining how I hadn't foreseen the difficult financial circumstances for my parents and as such could only resume the following September. A few days later, the news came that my grandfather Biku Biku had died in his sleep, in the village. He had been sick for over a year; he was 105 years old.

The day before his death, I had a premonition. First, I picked up a moving snail on the main road, on a hot and sunny afternoon. Secondly, as twilight came, a big bird almost perched on my head, singing single monotonous short notes. As I pondered over these two unusual signs, a further sign occurred, in that the 'requiem song' (Latin funeral song) tumbled out of my mouth. The song for the dead made me spit-out in denouncement of any evil thing, or sad news coming my way, but it was too late. Before the dawn of the new day, a messenger arrived from the village, with the sad news that my grandfather, Ijezie Okoroha had died during the night. I felt as if in a trance when the story was narrated.

The messenger told us that before he died the only name and the only word that he was able to say and keep repeating was my name 'Anyiam, Anyiam, Anyiam.' That is the name my grandfather had given to me at birth (Anyiam means a joyful proclamation that his lineage will stand forever, Anyiam also means a taproot). I have always wondered what he would have told me if I had been present at his death bed. However, he meant well. I still believe that his spirit hovers over me, guiding, guarding, protecting, and directing me like an angel.

With my grandfather's death, my years' life savings up until that day, were wiped out. I had saved about two pounds in total. A pound was twenty shillings. I handed it over to my father, to help him with the funeral expenses, as he groaned that although he had money, he would only be paid in about two weeks, yet every member of the family had to return to the village immediately, for the sizeable funeral. My father, being first born son, was required to shoulder most of the expenses and responsibilities. All the in-laws and extended family members: uncles, cousins, nieces, nephews, and friends were expected to be in attendance. His burial turned out to be a carnival. The various dancers, masquerades, magicians, acrobats turned out and performed. Loads of cannon gun shots were fired. These gun powder shots were called "mkponala" and "ogbondu" One group of masquerades the "Oshe" has remained ever in my memory since that day. Any person, who stepped into the ring to dance the oshe dance, first gestured to announce and show graphically how many people he had beheaded or killed in his lifetime. The next terrifying dancer came from Abiriba, our inlaws. There were four big muscular, strong, half naked men with bulging biceps. Each was carrying a long basket on their heads. On each basket were three to four human skulls. The men had fresh palm fronds around their necks, waist and in between their lips. They danced majestically to the heavy drumbeats. My father, the chief mourner, found time to proudly walked into the arena, bend down and grab a handful of sand, which he threw up in the air, thereby indicating to the crowd, that as a veteran soldier of World

War 11 in Myanmar, formerly Burma, the number of enemies vanquished by him was uncountable.
The crowd and drummers understood his message and went into a berserk, tumultuous, wild frenzy.

The burial took place on the next day after his demise. Prior to his burial, a messenger was sent to Amaraku to procure a coffin and the messenger came with a wooden coffin which he ferried on his bicycle. There was a heated debate about the burial site. Some believed, as a titled man, he should be buried in his bedroom, sitting on his favourite reclining chair, with his traditional-medicine handbag hanging on his shoulder. Eventually, due to Christian beliefs, the suggestion of burying him inside his bedroom was shelved, in favour of burial outside, in the forecourt of his main house. The funeral and associated funfair lasted for four days and nights, in celebration of his life. After all, he lived to the ripe old age of 105 years, with six wives, eighteen children and many grandchildren. After my grandfather's burial, my family returned to Port Harcourt, and I resumed my quest for education and a better future. Perhaps it was the childhood deprivation and poverty, or possibly my unreasonable pride, that gave me earnest resolve to excel in my lifetime. It seemed I was desperate to bring some hope and light into our family. My only weapons to emerge victorious in these goals, were prayers, church attendance, hope and sheer trust in God, for his mercies. I had to be transparent, humble, honest, and hardworking.

For a while, I lived at the mission serving the priests. Often, priests from other parishes would take me on loan for a few days or a week to help in their respective parishes, St Philip's, St Mary's, Bishop's House, and at Stella Maris College. I remember such other good Irish priests as Fathers, Darcy, Mahoney, Kilbride, Mullen, Murphy, Flynn, and O' Flynn.

Occasionally, a Rev. Fr. Slaven or Rev. Fr. Fraser would be kind enough to take me in their car to visit my parents' house to visit them, or drop off a message. Whenever the children saw the white priest, from the beginning of the street to the end, there were tumultuous shouts of 'Father! Father!' On the same basis when I returned to our street on foot, everyone called me "Nwa-father," meaning the Rev. Father's son. Some people at that stage believed that I was already becoming a priest, while I had not even entered the seminary. I hardly fooled around with other boys. The girls liked me a lot, but I had no time for them. When I showed interest in any girl, there was no 'hanky-panky.' It was purely platonic. In most cases the girls who gathered around me were daughters of Christian mothers or were themselves aspirants to sisterhood. Anyone who did not take a closer look, might have concluded otherwise of our friendship. Also, younger kids were drawn to me. They sang and danced "Adol enato ka sugar" which translates: Adol, you are as sweet as sugar. My mother was so proud of me.

At seventeen, I was shy and embarrassed by my breasts. My nipples were almost like that of a girl's. An older girl lured me into her sister's matrimonial bed and defiled me. She lived with her older married sister in the same yard with us. She was not a

Catholic, but a member of Cherubim and Seraphim sect. We were caught and word got round and reached my mother's ear. My mother nagged me, slapped me, and threatened to come to the missions to report me to the Rev. Fathers. The girl's sister had the nerve to address me as her 'in-law'. That brought me more shame and anguish. My worst dilemma was how and where to confess the mortal sin of fornication. All the priests knew me. They also knew that I was preparing to enter the junior seminary the following year.

It was one of those sins classified as a mortal sin. I could no longer receive Holy Communion. If I died in such a state, I would surely go straight to the dreaded hellfire. I finally solved my problem by journeying to a distant parish, confessing and receiving absolution (forgiveness) for the sin. This incident reinforced the bible story about women, just as Eve was to blame for Adam's fall.

In the same year, my mother gave birth to a baby boy. I named the new baby Damian, after St. Damian. My mother called him Ikechuckwu (by power of God). Unfortunately, the older boy to Damian died. His name was Christopher, aged two.

**CHAPTER SIX**

# Seminary: The Priesthood

In January 1963, I happily enrolled into the Sacred Heart Seminary at Port Harcourt. My financial position remained precarious to say the least. Rev.Fr. Kilbride had known me from the parishes. He immediately appointed me as Head Boy or Senior Prefect. Even after Kilbride left, the succeeding Priests and Rector followed in his footsteps, in dealing with me. Year after year I was a topmost functionary. Year after year I maintained either the 1st or 2nd position in academics. I maintained a strong standing out of a class of seventy students. Throughout term my Rector's remarks in my report cards were either 'promising' or 'very promising'.

I was a good all-rounder. I played in the school first eleven and I was good in sports. I started the Boy Scout troop, and I was the Scout Master. I led in the chapel morning and evening and for refectory prayers or the Angelus (the Mid-day prayer). I was given a 'Black Book' where I recorded names of other seminarians who broke the rules and regulations. Offenders included latecomers to chapel, classes, refectory/dining, labour, sport, siesta, and those missing classes.

I recorded noise makers, anywhere on the campus. Also, those who forgot table manners, or sat two on a bed, holding hands (Noli mea tangere) never touching others (vir soli, nun quam duo) It was prohibited for two people to always do things together, or for one person to always be by himself, a lover of solitude. Any form of insubordination, headiness, rough behaviour, committing any of the seven deadly sins: pride, covetousness, sloth, envy, lust, gluttony, anger, failure to show any of the four cardinal virtues: Prudence, justice, self-control, and temperance: Any seminarian whose name appeared in the senior prefect's (my) black book, up to three times in a term, was expelled. He had lost his vocation (calling.) A Seminarian who broke any of the ten commandments of God, was punished with automatic or summary dismissal.

The way of the Lord is always mysterious. The wisdom of men is the foolishness of God. My life was never happier, confident, or fuller of hope. The future was bright. I figured that for the present, I was getting the best of everything, an all-round education for my age. I had high prospects of becoming a priest at the end of my studies, which were progressing well. If I did not become a priest, I would still be properly equipped to go out into the world, well trained to succeed. As St. Paul I said, 'To die was gain and to live was joy.' Even if I dropped dead then and there, I sincerely believed I would be heaven bound.

At our Ahoada campus, one Theophilus was reported to have had 'something to do with a harlot' and he had to pack and leave school immediately, as the story infiltrated the campus. The incident usually called for extra-rosary and meditation for that single act of threat, an invasion of God's breeding ground by the son of darkness. We lived in love, chastity, diligence, modesty, joy, charity, and peace. Above all, faith and hope, wisdom and knowledge were very equally commended and those who failed to measure up academically were expelled irrespective of their faith, hope, charity, and chastity.

Bishop Okoye explained to us, during one of his visits, that a priest must have two strong wings to soar like an eagle: chastity and knowledge. Letters posted to or sent by seminarians, were read and vetted. Often some students just got up and left on their own personal conviction. I was a part of the institution. I was leader of ceremonies; the choir could not go on without me. I supervised the cook, the stores, and the food. I paid my school fees. I prayed hardest and played hardest.
On one occasion I returned home on holiday and my parents noticed that although I had originally gone to the seminary unsure of becoming a priest, they now observed deep commitment and spirit within me. They began to ask me repeatedly 'so, you will not be married? So, you will not have children? So, you cannot earn money or help your family, brothers, and sisters?' And I told

them not to worry about tomorrow; God will take care of it. I told them all they had to say to God was 'This is our first son, first fruit and we give him to you,' and that they should sit back and wait for their reward, a hundred times and over. I would also quote a biblical verse 'First attain the kingdom of God and every other thing will be given to you'. They were both shy and terrified to question the Lord any further.

During the holidays, every seminarian had to do pastoral work at his parish and obtain the parish priest's recommendation and reference, to take back to the school upon resumption of the new term. I practically lived wholly and entirely in my parish and always returned with good remarks. Each holiday I became Baptismal Godfather to several boys and other little children, whose parents had observed and liked my ways and wished their wards to emulate me and follow in my footsteps.

In my second year in the seminary, my junior sister Patricia graduated from standard six. She followed in my footsteps, used my connections with the priests and the bishop and started at Presentation Girls College as a novitiate, or aspirant to nun hood. She was on Bishop Okoye's scholarship and became their all-round leader too. That is another of God's graces. People who knew our parents marvelled at how they had managed to put two of their children into secondary schools.

While Patricia was in elementary school, more than five suitors had come wanting to marry her. Each would entice our mum with gifts and money. Our mother and father accepted each man who showed up to marry the thirteen-year-old daughter, but the poor girl would write to me or come to my school in tears. I would either give her a note, or rush home, if permitted, and insist she must not be married until she had finished her secondary school education. My parents had started to respect my opinion in family decisions. Some people argued that if she had got married, as the first son, I would have been paid the dowry. The dowry would be mine to do with whatever I wished. I could use it to pay my school fees, go into business, marry, or save it in a bank, provided I allowed her to marry. I knew that I would personally gain on her marriage, but to be fair to my sister, I chose to let her have the opportunity of furthering her education and to allow her to mature. I resented the idea of 'selling' her away too early, to any taxi driver, for just fifty to hundred pounds dowry. She was so dear to me. She emulated every step I took. After my baptism, Holy Communion and Confirmation, she followed suit and achieved those life passages. When I became a Mass Server at CKC Diobu Port Harcourt, she became a member of the Church Choristers. When I joined the Boys Scout, she joined the Girls Guide. So, it was a joy to me, when Patricia attained the bishop's scholarship and continued her studies. For me, it was another victory. It was another sign from God, that 'whatever we ask in His name, He will do it'. In fact, with a white chalk, I wrote on the front of our door 'with faith you can move mountains.' Then in Latin underneath I wrote "Adjutorium nostrum in nomine Domini" meaning our help is in the name of the Lord. Not only were my sister and I able to attend secondary schools with little or no money, but we were also placed above many other students, who came with plenty of money, from wealthy parents.

Often those kids from rich families lacked drive, commons sense and leadership. Most times such students were spoilt brats, with wavering faith; they just had to be led and protected.

In the seminary the rising bell went at 5:30am, by the regulator. I would shout 'Benedicamus Domino' the rest of the students in the dormitory would respond 'Deo gratias.' Next was wash up, morning mass, breakfast, classes, lunch, labour/sports, dinner, prep, night prayers, 9:30pm - lights off. Students who tried to 'cockroach,' meaning those who tried to read with camouflaged lanterns or torchlight, were disciplined severely, if caught.

Seminary food was a rich and balanced diet. Self-service, but you could only take what you were sure of finishing, there should be nothing left on your plate. Nobody was allowed to eat any food left on another student's plate. Correct use of cutlery was enforced, fork in your left hand, knife in your right hand. A spoon was used for soup or pap, but a fork was required for rice and beans. A student was expected to be always courteous: 'Salt, please!' 'please', 'sorry', 'thanks' There was no talking between mouthfuls of food, or across the table. One should never chew or churn food noisily. One should never lick one's plate. Most of the time I said the grace before and after meals in Latin: The "Benedicte...."

Unlike a regular secondary school, fagging, chumming, petting of younger students, or such acts, were not allowed; every student washed his own plate and clothes.

Now, they say that power corrupts, and absolute power corrupts absolutely. Every new student wanted to curry favours from me. I was weak to such temptations.

I always obliged fragile kids, or those whose parents had personally handed them over to me for exceptional care and supervision. I had a chain of younger students serving me, colloquially referred to as 'fags.' One pupil washed my clothes, another carried and washed my plates, and so-on. I was the scout leader, and half the students were scouts, and consequently, my fans. I could grant certain privileges and cover it up nicely, to ensure the Rector would not find out. The tutors were meant to supervise me, but often turned a blind eye on my fagging business. One staff member, late Rev Dr Obiukwu was my friend, we had common interests. He was popularly known as the 'game man' His was a late vocation, because he attended a regular secondary school before deciding to try the priesthood. Mr Nwanna was the organ and choir wizard. I heard he committed suicide, a few years later. My closest friends also included Messrs Obiajulu and Rev. Dr. Omenka.

During one of the school holidays, I stupidly got in a joke fight with one of my cousins; the dumb kid busted my head open with a dwarf shovel, used for the disposal of children's faeces. I had fifteen stitches. The frontal head bones were shattered. On reflection, I realized the head injury may have altered the wiring of my brain. Ever since that unfortunate incident, I experienced drastic behavioural changes. Despite my calm demeanour and external posture, I became an impetuous and risk-taking avatar, undeterred by any immediate danger, risks, or challenges. I was led more by instinct than reason. I became a product of sheer will, force, and destiny, with unqualified faith in the Supreme Being. It is incredible, however, that despite my impetuosity, in most cases, success was always the product of my ostensibly unusual sojourns, blind steps or sometimes irrational actions.

Rev. Okafor, (now Rev. Dr. Festus Okafor) took over Rector ship from Fr. Kilbride and later left for the USA for further studies. He attended Washington University in Maryland, USA. Next came Fr. C.S. Mbah (later Monsignor), who was the last Rector during my time at the Sacred Heart Seminary. Fr. Mbah incidentally happened to be the same priest from Bishop's House, who had administered the last sacraments to me, a few years previously, before I entered the seminary. During that holiday, my mother had her last baby boy. I personally named him Eugene (Chinedu) which means God leads.
One evening, towards the end of my final year, after the GCE examinations, we were in the classrooms; Some were studying, others completing their homework, or assignments. At 8.00pm, the bell rang, this was unusual.

I looked at my schedule, the bell should have rung at 9.30pm, not 8.00pm. If there was any emergency assembly, the Rector should have first informed me, as a senior prefect, and I would have instructed the regulator about any change in the regular schedule. I was somewhat upset therefore, and in fact would have replaced the bell ringer. There were occasions when regulators overslept or dozed off and woke up in confusion and rang erratic bells. I assumed it was one of those occasions. I went to the prep room and called out to the regulator. 'Why did you ring the bell?' He was trembling as he told me the Rector had asked him to ring and everyone should assemble in the chapel. With foreboding, I assumed something must be very wrong. Otherwise, surmised that, whatever had happened must involve me personally, otherwise why was I not aware of the situation?

## LEAVING THE SEMINARY

The Father-Rector, late Fr. Mbah (later Monsignor) cleared his throat and began to speak as if he were about to deliver a homily, in a somewhat sorry and disappointed tone. He used words like, and I quote, 'Today will go down as a sad and memorable day in the history of this seminary. Today five of you have lost their calling to the priesthood. There is a rule here that nobody 'touches another', or 'sits two on a bed.' There are also rules against 'fagging' and 'favouritism.' These rules have been broken by one who has been trusted with the responsibilities of supervising and enforcing them. This house is a house of God, where seeds are sown to grow into a future, for Christ. When a tall tree falls in the forest, it usually also knocks down several other, smaller trees. So it is, that the senior Prefect, OKOROHA will leave the seminary with the following four students.' The Rectors named the students and gave a final instruction that we should leave the campus at first light, the following morning. He said that I had chosen to have the students as my servants, and they had been happy to serve me. They all broke the rules.

It was like a bolt from the blue. It was a matter of grave silence and concern. The night prayers were said in a rather low tone and rather too early. Everyone dispersed and headed singularly in different directions, to their respective dormitories. It was like the end of an era, like a breeze that blows, no-one knows where it comes from, nor withers it goes. No one knows when it will come his way. The standard bearer was sniped, and the remnants were left dumbfounded, bewildered, and confused. No one spoke a word, nor had any nerve left to even whisper to fellow seminarians, let alone come to me to sympathise, or discuss the calamity. One could hear a pin drop. The villains, as well as the victors said nothing. The darkness of the night portrayed the fear and uncertainty that emanated. If the Senior Prefect, Okoroha of all people, could lose his vocation and be expelled, then no one else could be sure of his stay or vocation in the school.

My role in the school, only yesterday, seemed indispensable, unmistakeable, and solid. I had started the Scout Brigade, registered, and remained the life scout leader. The school had even paid for the one-week scoutmaster's course. which I attended in Enugu earlier that year. The school had also paid for the General Certificate of Education (GCE) Level Examinations, which I sat a couple of months earlier.

I left the chapel, headed straight to the bathroom, and emptied my bladder. This catastrophic event seemed unreal. Nevertheless, somehow, I found inner strength to guide me. Whatever happened to me in life, was the will of God, part of His grand design. As when Galileans were crushed in a collapsed building, by an accident, Jesus told the crowd that those who were spared the tragedy, should never think that they are more righteous in the eyes of the Lord. Also, in the case of a certain man born blind from birth, Jesus explained that neither the man, nor his parents sinned, but that the works of God might be displayed. Surely, it was unfair to punish me simply for being too good. Surely it was unfair to punish me so severely, but perhaps I deserved it because 'what goes around comes around'. To God, be the glory!

I began to look inwards and indeed, examined my conscience. I felt sorry, repentant, and descended into self-pity, deliberating over what I had done wrong, albeit inadvertently. Often, I sprung up in self-righteousness and began to question why the priest failed to 'call me in', to discuss the matter, or give me the opportunity to defend or explain myself. I thought it was too autocratic, theocratic, and not democratic. It was the house and there was no appeal to God's decisions.

As suspected, some jealous students had ganged up and reported to me, alleging favouritism. They may have claimed that I had a harem of servants, who did my laundry and dishes, whilst I in return petted, protected, and favoured them. The false accusers might have also claimed I was recording in my 'black book' only the names of those who refused to do my personal chores. Or that I was partial, selective, unfair, and harsh in the manner of meting out punishment to students who broke the rules. It may have been that they reported how my boys gathered around my dormitory corner, sat on my bed, and even enjoyed senior jokes. I examined every single rule and imagined every conceivable violation. It bothered me more, that Father Rector had not been fair to me. After all, every other senior student had a fag or two. Why me? Why such drastic action? Father Rector had displayed so much confidence in me. Could it be the evidence was so overwhelmingly convincing, that he himself was so hurt, he could not face me? I was chilled to the bone, by this thought. Then I considered the innocent children, who had sought refuge in me. Children, whose parents had personally handed over to me, for their care and direction. How and what would I tell their parents? I felt angry, empty, and humiliated. It was a long night. Self-conviction made matters worse.

I began to consider how I would face my own family, relatives, acquaintances, neighbours, and fellow parishioners. How would I break the news? What conceivable story could any lay person understand or believe, as the reason for my leaving the seminary and for no longer becoming a man of God. To say that 'I quit' was as heinous as to say that I was expelled. Some persons, even pious people, would not give it a second thought, before they drew their own conclusions. I had either committed an outrageous sin, or I had merely entered with the dubious intention of obtaining a desperately needed, cheaply funded, quality education. Besides, the most circulated misconception was that the only reason any person leaves the seminary or catholic priesthood, was due to women related issues. They may speculate that it was either that I had fallen in love, or wanted to marry, or that I had put some woman in the family way. Anyway, you looked at it, the stigma was gruesome and painful.

It was a long, dark, stormy night. I prayed, reflected, and pondered on my past, present and future. I didn't sleep at all that night. Several times I deliberated over whether a way could be found to leave the seminary campus invisibly, or park up and leave during the night, just to avoid eye contact with the lads, when morning dawned.

There was no thought to pull closed the mosquito net, which hung over my six-spring Vono bed, in the long dormitory. The two holy pictures, which I had always stuck with Sellotape on my dormitory locker, were removed and at the bottom of one, the Sacred heart of Jesus, I wrote 'Father, not my will, but Thine' On the other, Immaculate heart of Mary, I had written 'Regina Ceali ora pro nobis' (Queen of Heaven pray for us). Finally, I placed the pictures into my shirt pocket and packed, haphazardly, as the first morning light appeared. The time had come to kill Ali Baba.

Cocks crowed and birds began singing. A new day dawned. I lifted my chin and told myself 'If you do not look on the sunny side in your trials, you add to your problems and misery. What cannot be helped, must be endured'.

Early that morning I mustered courage and for the last time as the senior prefect I shouted the "Benedicamus Domino" others responded "Deo Gratias ". I thought of stopping over at Mr. Obiukwu's corner to seek his advice, but figured that would count as a further breach, since no one was supposed to talk until after morning mass. Instead, I went along to the chapel. As
I moved up to the altar at Holy Communion to receive the Holy Eucharist, I wondered what the priest's reaction would be. There was no incident, or any hint of embarrassment, I was given the Communion. The Priest said, 'Body of Christ' and with my eyes closed and mouth open, the priest placed the Eucharist on my tongue, and I said 'Amen.' After Holy Mass, I followed Father

Rector to his residence. Our meeting lasted just a couple of minutes. I handed over my black book and some money I had collected. He had no objection to my going to see His Lordship, Bishop Okoye, in Port Harcourt.

It took significant courage and determination to move around the buildings to gather my books, bucket and possessions. The four other lads who had also been dismissed, were packed and ready to leave. A handful of students and staff members managed to have a few words with me. I promised to write soon and to keep in touch. The five of us left together, moving towards the school main gate. The first commercial vehicle pulled up; the conductor indicated he had room for two. I boarded the vehicle with Nnodim, the Volkswagen roared back to life and pulled away. The remaining three ex-seminarians had to wait for other vehicles to come by. We never saw each other again. The world is so vast, yet so small, depending on your standpoint and observation post.

You cannot cheat nature, they say, and since I had not slept the previous night, I quickly dozed off in the noisy, rocking vehicle, temporarily untroubled, my head dangling from left to right. The motion of the vehicle woke me repeatedly and a while later, a lady vomited all over me. She said that she could not stand the smell of petrol. The driver seemed to stop every five minutes to either drop-off or pick-up passengers. He bought gas at every other filling station, a few bottles at a time.

The estimated journey of one hour from Ahoada to P.H. took two hours. Nnodim continued his journey as I got off at Diobu main market bus stop. I hired two porters to help carry my luggage to my parent's new rented residence. I paid the boys handsomely, one shilling, as that had been my job before entering college. At that time, my parents' residence consisted of four separate rooms, one room and parlour for each wife and her offspring. At the time, each had five surviving children. Their husband slept in whichever side of the house he chose. My boxes and cartons of books were dropped in my mother's room, I told her I had a terrible problem at the seminary and promised to tell her everything when I came back from the bishop's house. She rushed after me to the bus stop, ready to jump onto the bus with me. I assured her there was no need and things would be fine. She reluctantly went back to the house, where she waited restlessly for my return.

## BISHOP GODFREY OKOYE

Next, I caught a bus to Township and got off at Harbour Road, near St. Mary's Cathedral. I walked the remaining two miles to the Bishop's House, which was situated opposite Stella Maris College. I met Fr. Fraser and explained why I had come. I was told there would be an hour to wait, before I could talk to His Lordship. Fr. Fraser, cool and calm, as always, took me to the cooks who fed me. An hour passed, then I was told the bishop was ready to see me.

After pouring my heart out to the bishop, lamenting on all that had gone wrong at the Seminary and seeking his sympathy, I hoped he might reinstate me. I explained how I had gone to the seminary believing God had called me and chosen me to 'follow

Him.' I told him it was denigrating to just 'let me go'. His Lordship spoke like a loving father, with a calm and comforting voice and with spiritual logic. Of course, he already had an idea, if not complete knowledge, of what had happened to me in the seminary. He must have been put in the picture by the Rector. He went on to explain to me that it was never intended that everyone who went through the seminary would become a priest. 'God may prepare some of the students, as now in your case, for distinct roles, such as in the laity, or on the outside church ministry, or His ministries in the government, hospitals, schools and so on. He will call good Christians and prepare them in different ways, towards the long paths of His highest benefit and glory. Whatever decision God takes, is always for our own good. God might even be thinking of making you a government minister one day, to work for Him on a certain level in the government, or to work in any company, to bring the workers to Light and to the knowledge of their Creator. The seminary was a place where the Lord sows the seeds and trains His labourers, before sending them to His Vineyard.' It was therefore considered I had received sufficient grace and training to relocate and become his witness and ambassador, anywhere else I may go, even if it meant starting at a new school. He advised me to take my studies seriously and sit my West African School Certificate and more O level exams in two months' time. After listening to him, everything became clearer to me and made more sense. I pondered on this for some time, then handed it all over to God. The battle has always been His, the past, present, and future. Then I asked His Lordship how I should go about completing my schooling. I must be attached to a school, in order to sit for the exams. I explained my financial predicament, as having little or no prospects. He knew I was progressing well at school, I was diligent and possessed certain traits of leadership, so he sent me home to return with my father. This was to assess my very real financial predicament, my fears and my needs.

I went straight to the Wharf, the Nigerian Ports Authority, where my father was working at the time. After leaving P.W.D, he worked for Taylor Woodrow, and the Costain, before he started with the Ports Authority. He was made redundant quite often, but somehow readily found new employment within days.

My father was shocked to see me. I was supposed to be in school and school was not out yet. He asked if something terrible had happened, alluding to a death in the family, house fire, fatal accident; otherwise, why was I not at school? I told him I had a problem at school and had been expelled from the seminary. I said that I might continue my studies at Stella Maris College. If I must continue, the bishop wanted to see him first. I assured him I had enough money for our bus fares. He had come to work not expecting such incidental expenses. So, we left as soon as he clocked out at five p.m. and went to meet with His Lordship.

The bishop soon understood my father was on a tight budget. So, it was agreed he could pay the sum of ten pounds, half the usual cost of twenty pounds, for my board and lodging, thereby granting me a partial scholarship. We expressed our gratefulness and left. On the way home, my dad, deep in thought and with an air of disbelief, said to me 'Do you mean to tell me that Bishop has no wife and children?' I calmly replied 'No, he is a celibate priest' With a touch of finality, my dad stated that the bishop's family genealogy must have 'ended' tragically with his birth, and that was a disaster.

This exchange with my dad was a classic example of trying to describe heavenly things with a worldly mind. The impossibility of understanding these circumstances is what is called 'mystery'. Some have chosen to become eunuchs to give their undivided attention to God. The greatest mystery being that in denying himself, he still lived in such an obvious embodiment of serenity, happiness and contentment.

I was relieved that Jesus still loved me. The fact that I did not have to stay idly at home for even one week was quite a solace, a graceful consolation indeed. It reinforced the bishop's advice to me on the divine purpose in everything and in all things, the assurance of divine providence. Above all, I developed a special spiritual feeling: as God always referred to Israelites as His chosen people, He made me, and He marked me apart as His chosen child. I knew that not everyone got the chosen favour, or the luck I had received. I began to feel invincible again and my hopes and ambition grew by leaps and bounds.

I began to believe that with God in your heart, nothing is impossible. The creator had a plan for my life. All I had to do was to keep a cool and level head, work hard, watch, and pray and I would reach the Promised Land, having first laid a good foundation in the kingdom. I realised that rather than frowning at me, the bishop had both consoled and nudged me to new and higher aspirations.

# THE NEW SCHOOL

Throughout the next week, all efforts to raise ten pounds failed miserably. So, I started on a second round of visits to the relations who had earlier declined to help me, on the premise of the hope in the biblical injunction, of perseverance. Remembering that due to the widow's persistence, the judge granted her request to stop her from wearing him out with her persistent coming. That day, one of my father's brothers, Pa Fidelis, gave me the ten pounds privately . I reflected on this but concluded that maybe some people did not let their left hand know what their right hand was doing. Happily, I went to Stella Maris College and waited to see Reverend Father Fraser who was a tutor at the college, in addition to being the Bishop's Orderly. When I finally caught up with him, he said, 'Adolphus where have you been, we've been looking for you.' I hesitated 'Um... Um...I.' Whereupon he interrupted me and told me the bishop decided instead to send me to help Reverend Father
O'Brian at Imiringi Ogbai (near Mbiama)."

Fr. O' Brain had a Land Rover waiting. I threw my boxes in the back of the jeep and we sped off to Mater Dei High School.
On our way, Fr. O' Brain said, 'tell me about yourself, Adolphus' I told him about my grades for the past four years had never gone below second position in class. I also told him that I played the church Organ, sang baritone base in choir, I was the pioneer and scout leader of the school, master of ceremonies, president and secretary of various societies in the seminary. For every term I had been in the seminary, I had either been the senior prefect or

the dining or labour prefect, in addition to my other roles. I intimated to the priest that I had taken GCE 'O' level and passed four papers and that forthwith, I intended to prepare myself and take the West African School Certificate Examinations (WAESCE), which would enable me to be admitted to a Higher School, or to University.

A Pontoon ferried us, with the jeep, over the Mbiama River, from there we continued to drive along the worst road I had ever seen, it's called Jankrama, and then to Imiringi Ogbia. This Riverine area was outlandish to me, because I had come from Ibo heartland which is upland. It gave me a culture shock.

There were barely four weeks of school term left. I had a very frustrating and depressing experience in those few weeks, trying to fit in socially and in other ways too. I felt I was out of my element. I was in an entirely different world, a fish out of water.

The regular Catholic secondary schools were indeed quite different to Seminary life, no matter which way one looked at it. The secondary school students bathed together in one open bathroom hall. The students observed each other's private parts, compared, touched and of course, cracked obscene jokes. In seminary, no seminarian was ever allowed to see the nakedness of another. Hence, for most of the period that I was at the school, I took baths whilst wearing my underwear. The secondary schools' students smoked cigarettes and worse yet; some were regular users of Marijuana (weed or Igboo). The rolled-up cannabis was called a 'joint' The regular cigarettes had been nicknamed 'fag' or 'jot' The slang 'Pass jot' meant one stick of the fag was passed around five or six students, one or two drags or puffs for each person. To my shock and horror, I became aware of students, who went out of campus through the back of the school, via bush tracks to the town, to drink and socialise with women and prostitutes. One's personal effects were not safe, as a considerable amount of stealing or 'tapping' took place. The trivial stealing of other students Bics pens and pencil was even baptised with a new name of 'tapping' Unfortunately, I was a victim on a few occasions. Fagging, chumming, and petting that were banned in the seminary were considered 'the norm' in secondary school. Everyone engaged in it. Some people even jammed their beds together, so that they slept like they were twins, or people in love.

Upon arrival, I was immediately assigned to assist the Chapel Prefect. Morning Mass was supposed to be compulsory, but only a handful students attended, or addressed the confessional and Holy Communion. Class periods and preps were noisy. Fights broke out from time to time in the dining room, sports and games grounds, dormitories, even in the classroom or during study periods. After the regular classes which everyone had to attend, in the yellow and blue school uniform, the students wore all kinds of mufti, depending on what they could afford. As a result, the evenings and weekends became a carnival show parade of Swantex shirts, navy blue trousers, alligator shoes, crepe sole shoes, barleys, supidoes, and suede shoes. Tereguy and woollen trousers meticulously marched with Arrow shirts. Rolex watches and flat caps; name it and they had it. They wore clothes and shoes that I brought from the seminary, which made me a laughingstock. My entire wardrobe was no more than two shirts and two pairs of trousers, my sandals, and a pair of canvas shoes. None of the secondary school's materialistic exhibitions ever occurred in the seminary. Because I could not bath whilst everyone else was looking, nor smoke, fight and execute, one of the 'dudes' Chakadezule, unilaterally gave me a nick name and addressed me as the 'Pope.' It stuck like glue. As a Seminarian, I would have loved to be so called, as it would have signified, I was good, but at the secondary school, the name had a connotation of religious fanaticism, or unreasonable righteousness.

The contrast between the hustle and bustle of secondary school materialism, and the calm and silence of spiritualism in the seminary, in my estimation stretches as far as the east is from the west. Maybe I was being too pious, trying to observe man, the real animal, with the eyes of a godly seminarian.

By the end of the four weeks, a final exam for the term took place and I took a comfortable lead, with second position, out of the sixty students in the class. I gathered all my belongings as the school vacated. I had hoped not to return to school. Though Fr. O'Brian had placed me in charge of several things, I still had misplaced euphoria, believing somehow, I could be reinstated to the seminary. Whilst going home on vacation, instead of using the Jeep, we were made to travel by an Engine boat to Imbiama. In the company of other students, we boarded a bus to Port Harcourt. I was proud to have started a Boy Scout troop, dramatic and debating societies which the school did not have before my arrival. I did all these effortlessly, by my own volition and inclination, mainly due to my personal disposition and natural inspiration. Despite the difficulties I faced, I strived to excel at the top in scholarship, industry, and morality.

After the exams and during the holidays, I went back to the bishop, to be re-instated into the priesthood, so as to proceed to Bigard Memorial Senior Seminary, Enugu, for my Philosophy and Theology courses. I told his Lordship how I could not cope with what I had experienced as a layperson so far, and my awkwardness in the regular school life. I had been living in a community that lacked morality, was devoid of calm, serenity, and order. Every other student seemed to me to have been 'doomed to hell'? The students were worldly and basking in sin and hedonism. I likened myself with the picture of how the angel Lucifer fell from grace to grass. I felt banished. I also returned to the seminary and spoke with the Father Rector Mbah, about my spiritual frustration. In both places, I received only words of blessing and encouragement, to get on with my new life and to shine as an ex-seminarian. God was still using me; thus, I should have no reason to feel rejected or dejected. Therefore, I received the College education I had always wanted, despite everything else.

Thanks to God, no failure in life is final. Besides, man is not judged by how many times he fails, but by how many times he is able to get up. Won't you agree with the adage? The good thing about the future is that it comes one day at a time 'Give us this day our daily bread' a day at a time, we are asked to say in our prayers.

# THE BIAFRAN WAR : 1967 - 1970

In mid-1967, the Biafra War started and progressed with intensity. My only option or viable activity was soldiering. Personally, at this point, I would admit I was still a pious man, full of zeal and zest, full of courage and faith. I could feel the presence of Omnipotence in and around me daily in everything I did. There was no big deal or craze about being 'born again' I was simply confident God's presence was around me. I never missed regular prayers in the morning or evening, before and after meals, plus the occasional ejaculations, which in religious terms means short mental prayers, such as 'Oh God,' 'Lord helps me' and His grace was usually sufficient for the day. Every new day came with its own miracles.

I literally floated along merrily from day to day. By my words, actions, mannerisms, and personal relations with everyone, I considered I was an eloquent testimony and witness to the presence of the great "I AM, WHO I AM" in me.

The future was as bright for me as it could be. I did not have much of anything, however I was quite content, nothing bothered me. My needs were catered for, I lacked for nothing. I was educated. I had forgotten about my early pagan upbringing and subsequent difficult days. I appreciated other people's success, and never had cause for envy, malice, or jealousy. Nothing frustrated me, for even in the face of trials and tribulations, I knew the easiest way to get on my feet was to first get on my knees, and I did just that. Beauty and material wealth in other people merely gave me joy, hope, delight, appreciation, and admiration. I always spoke the truth and acted boldly, I was full of self-confidence. In my subconscious mind, I had a deeply embedded conviction, the sky was the limit, it was all a matter of time.

## AS A MILITIA – PLATOON COMMANDER

As the distant sounds of war began to edge closer and closer to home, the air became ominous and frightening. The Ibos truly were confronted by our neighbours, and they faced annihilation. It had become an Islamic Jihad, a type of 'Holy war' to propagate the Mohammedan or Islamic Religion, at the expense or annihilation of the Christians. I personally saw the events of those days as the Northern Region's attempt to lord Islam, over the Christian populace. Whether it was war propaganda from the top Ibo echelon or pure truism, none of it sounded good. So, once the call for enlistment into the Biafra military was announced, I enlisted with vigour. It was a call to defend not only our lives, but to preserve the faith, religion, and culture of our people. To be honest, I had given very little thought to the potential magnitude of the war and the effect it would have on me. The notion of war was equally vague, and I often thought of it as propaganda, a war of words. I guess when you go to war, you never dwell on the fact you might even be killed. In fairness, I thought the whole exercise might not last long. In July 1967, I joined the Civil Defence (also known as Militia). I was duty bound as a young, red-blooded Christian to 'join' in defence, if necessary to lay down my life for my people and my religion.

I voluntarily went to the Militia camp, located at the Government College, Borokiri, Port Harcourt. One fine evening, after two weeks training, I was in a group chatting with my cousin Alpho and a dear friend Okehie and others. The brigade Commander requested two volunteer school leavers, to be appointed Platoon commanders, to lead two separate platoons, in the defence of certain Riverine areas of Pitakwa. My four comrades disappeared into thin air. They no doubt knew what I did not: that a person could die in warfare. I was the first to volunteer and step forward. Was it all bravery and gallantry? I honestly couldn't tell, it may have been naivety, or had to do with the fact I didn't want to go and lay around back in the house. Besides, I had surmised that should Biafra survive as a sovereign State, those of us who proved heroic would be recognised, rewarded, and compensated with job appointments and other privileges. It had not been long since I was Scout Master at the schools I attended, that surely qualified as a type of paramilitary training. I did the camping, hiking, pathfinding, forest walking, and swimming and so on.

Therefore, I could not run away. How could I sit at home with the women and children, when men, real men, were out in the battle fields? I must be counted among the real men, who not only went to war to prove their manhood, but who lay down their lives to defend their homeland, for the sake of Christ. In any case, there was nothing else to do apart from soldiering. Being 'one of the lads', I chose to be known by a new nickname "Sir Fabro Dudu" rather than "Astral Billy" which was my nickname at the Seminary.

My father, a World War two Veteran, Sergeant Major David Azunnah Osuagwu had even been recalled from the Ports Authority, as a World War two veteran, an old war horse. 'Old soldiers never die', they say. They fade away, one might add. My father was fondly called by his nickname "Ukeh," (tightrope) at the training depots, where he trained army recruits. I figured if he could go once again to war, it was incumbent on me to do the same. Lion begets lion; quite naturally, I wanted to be seen as a 'chip off the old block'.

My platoon leadership at Okirika was eventful. The morning parade, drill, weapons training and cleaning, inspection, and deployment to beasts and trenches. At intervals, there were inspections of the locations and beats, or sentry positions and guard duties. I had a personal bodyguard and bunker sentry guards. Sometimes I used the nearby Okirika Grammar School as my rendezvous (R.V.). Native fishermen fraternised with us, providing loads of fish, crabs, oysters, clams and "isam," fished from both fresh and saltwater creeks.

My platoon numbered one hundred and twenty strong militia. The arsenal and armoury contained one hundred and twenty brand new machetes, equal to one man, one machete. In addition, we had backup weapons of two heavy duty police mark four rifles, five rounds of 'cock and shoot'. The bullets were long and as thick as my middle finger. I retained one of the rifles and rotated the other among my deputies, daily. The few months at Okirika were initially uneventful, except for occasional enemy air raids at the nearby Eleme refinery. With reflection, I cannot help but imagine the ridiculousness of us trying to shoot down MIG Jet fighters with such short distance, low calibre guns. There was only one Anti-Aircraft gun which was well camouflaged. When the enemy planes came, they usually targeted the anti-aircraft gun stand and tried to destroy them. Sometimes the enemy planes would manoeuvre, as they surveyed the entire creek where we had our beats and observation posts (O.P.) Invariably, there were casualties after each air raid. On one occasion we went to the yacht club off Harbour Road and there was a two-jet air raid. Out of pure instinct, I ran towards the area with other Corp members, where I came across the bodies of two lads who had been hit by bullets and another child, Andy, whose right hand had been torn from his body, when he was hit by a rocket. After the raid, we made our way to a damaged building, to pull more of the dead from the rubble. I was so lucky to escape unhurt from that deadly raid. My mother said my God was awake.

'Yea, though I walk through the valley of the shadow of death, I will fear no evil'. Sleeping on beats, bunkers and in open places day and night, slowly began to change my life and my values. I had no opportunity to attend Sunday church services, let alone daily morning mass. The fellowship of Christian encouragement was gone, the reason being all the white priests, or most foreigners, had left the Biafra enclave for their own safety. There were only five Nigerian priests remaining from the original fifty, in the Port Harcourt Diocese, as it was then. My religious attitude began to erode. Certain reevaluations crept in during those boring days and nights, the vigilant watching of the waters and creeks, for enemy amphibious landing, infiltrators, and saboteurs.

All men who were men had gone, engaged in the 'win the war effort' at the war front, or other out of bound's establishments. There were no more open businesses, and it became necessary for people to join any, more permanent branch of the armed forces. To support military boys and to survive the hardship of the war, women paraded themselves before soldiers, in the bushes, camps, depots, and creeks, for their invaluable 'Adam' I may have succumbed to an Eve, and her temptations, on more than one occasion. It was all about winning the war effort. However, as a good Christian, I only parked my boots in Angelina's room when she was not at my windowless military bunker. This period was the first time I was free and unsupervised in my life. There were no parents or grannies, teachers, or priests looking over my shoulder and sometimes it was fun, at other times it felt odd to be 'part of the crowd.'

## THE BIAFRAN AIR FORCE (BAF) OFFICER

In November 1967, there was an announcement about a second batch recruitment into the Biafra Air Force. I was twenty-three years of age and in charge of all major decisions in my life.

The recruitment venue was at my Alma Mater, Sacred Heart Seminary, the new campus at Umokoroshe, Port Harcourt. The BAF was occupying part of the Campus. They had the power to commandeer any building during the war in Biafra Republic. I promptly went to the school early and met with Revered Father Rector Mbah, who lived on one side of the school compound. I told him why I was there and stated my intention of becoming an airman. The connection was made. It was astonishing, I emerged as one of only sixty men, selected from over three thousand applicants. Selected candidates were sent for a medical examination at a centre, located at the Shell BP offices. I was given a blood test, recalled within a couple of hours, and told to submit a further test. The nurse asked me if I had eaten banana or ice cream before the test. I said I had eaten an ice cream cone.

She said it was probably why my sugar level was high and told me to go, I was ok. Much later in my life I was diagnosed with diabetes, this was the first signal I would be diabetic.

The Airforce was the highest of four forces – Airforce, Army, Navy, Police. Airforce personnel wore a neat uniform, red beret, and red muffler (scarf) around the neck and received a good regular salary. Such an officer was the ladies' number one choice. We were fondly referred to as Airforce guys, chaps, or lads. We were the proud eagles. Major Amuchenwa was an idol and a symbol of the Air Force. He was fair in complexion, tall and handsome, and was the first Commander of the Biafra Air Force, having come to Biafra from the Nigerian Air Force.

I went in person to the militia headquarters at Igboukwu street Diobu to notified them of my acceptance as an Airforce recruitment airman. I returned my paper ID and other items issued to me as a militia. I proceeded to the new BAF Barracks for air force training. The training was snappy, rigorous, effective. Six weeks intensive training on drills and combat tactics and the basics: salute, obey orders, fall in line, forward march, left-right, left-right, about turn, horseshoe formation, dismantling, stripping, cleaning, assembling weapons, charging, using the bayonet, moving in the terrain, recognising signs and signals. We were also taught how to mount a sentry or roadblock and then shout 'Halt! Hands up! Advance to be recognised! and so on. Two of our mates at training used to march like gorillas. One, Morah, could only move right left, instead of left-right. Sadly, he was the first casualty of our batch in recruitment and training.

The BAF was well fed, and we were the first to be paid with the new Biafra mint: fresh, crisp notes from the Central Bank of Biafra. My very first pay packet, a raw seven pounds, was sent in its entirety to my sweet mother, with a portion of it to Igbedie whom we fondly called 'Dada' By this time, due to incessant and indiscriminate air raids or sorties in the city of Port Harcourt, the civilian inhabitants had deserted it for safer villages, or other rural areas. My folks were now in our village in my hometown Abba. Port Harcourt was becoming deserted, a ghost city. As enemy shelling moved closer, more of the inhabitants of Port Harcourt abandoned the city. The forces had commandeered all available vehicles, so transportation became exceedingly difficult. People fled with just a handful of possessions, whatever they could carry on their heads, as they trekked hundreds of miles into the hinterland.

When my pay packet arrived home, it made news locally. It was said I was without peers, by the biblical act of giving my first fruits to my parents, in recognition of their toil while rearing me. After that first gift, in subsequent months my mother received a portion of my pay. It astonished her to receive such a substantial sum of two or three pounds, every month. I desperately wanted to ease her burden of feeding my four younger siblings and herself. Apart from Pat, my sister, the three boys Cletus, Damian, and Chinedu were all under ten years of age and my mother had quickly returned home to Abba with them. Pat had followed me and joined the women's wing of the militia. She eventually joined the Army Chaplain, Rev Fr Orji. I reassured myself she must be safe, somewhere at the war front, my father, a Sergent Major (WO2) was safe at the training depot, and later the regiment moved from Port Harcourt to Isiokpo. My mother's co-wives, their children, and the rest of the Okoroha family were safe in our hometown, although most young men over seventeen years had voluntarily joined, or conscripted, into one arm of the military or another.

News of the considerable praise I had received from every mother in our village reached me at the barracks. I experienced a sensational feeling of personal success. At that age, I loved to be praised and appreciated. I would have considered jumping off a cliff if it meant earning more praise!

## THE BATTLE OF OKIRIKA/ELEME REFINERY

On completion of air force military training, it happened that I was again posted to Okirika, where I had been a Militia Platoon Commander. This time, I was to defend Eleme Refinery from air raids and sea invasion. In a matter of a few months, the Nigerian Naval 'Nigeria vandal' troops invaded Bonny, the coastal and foremost oil jetty town, situated near the Atlantic Ocean. Nigerian Federal Navy invaders landed and blockaded the Sea Port with NNS Ogoja. From this vantage point, their thrust inland, into the hinterland, had a domino effect. The towns fell, one after another. In a matter of a few weeks, the enemy headed to Port Harcourt (P.H.) via the Ogoni, Eleme and Okirika axis. The airmen were not trained specifically for ground defence combat, however, in view of the imminent fall of Port Harcourt (Pitakwa), both the airmen and seamen were deployed alongside the infantry and militia, to defend the garden city with the 'mother of all battles.'

The big guns boomed. The nonstop shelling from both sides, however lopsided, made my heart pound. I trembled, as those of us in the Air Force, the air force guys, were now moved to the war front. We were armed with Czech made Madison automatic rifles. Each magazine contained approximately fifty bullets. We were issued with combat boots, caps, steel helmets, trench raincoats, camouflage trousers etc., bayonets, water bottles and dry packs. Four army colour trucks conveyed us to the trenches, at night. Specifically, the aviators were to defend the Eleme Refinery, including surrounding Okirika creeks. It coincided that I was dropped off at the head bridge where I had been when I was a militia. This gave me the initial satisfaction of familiar terrain. I knew the track was around the trenches and bunkers. The enemy artillery airpower, the pounding, and rockets, did not faze us.

We took cover and waited for them to come closer, possibly even to land, on the assumption we were all dead. It took barely a week before we found ourselves face to face with the enemy. One of the first things I noticed about the Nigerian Soldiers was they did not look to be of Yoruba extraction, they were almost all over six feet tall. We called them 'gwodogwodos' meaning 'giants', from the Hausa people and Niger republic. The enemy soldiers were well armed and kitted; however, they were less tactical and seemed careless as to how many of their number were killed. If a Biafran soldier found he had no way out, he endeavoured to killed as many of the enemy as he could before he perished. Fallen enemy soldiers were many and were a valuable morale booster, providing us with arms, ammunition, dry packs, money, uniform, and good boots (compared to our sandals and trainers)

I was undaunted. My Chaplet (rosary) hung around my neck, tucked into the collar of my uniform, a 'breastplate of fortitude.' If necessary, I was prepared to die. What could be sweeter, more honourable and fitting, than to die for one's faith and one's motherland. 'Dulce et Decorum Est pro Patria Mori' translated: 'It is sweet and fitting to die for one's country' One could hear the whistling of many bullets; In the military they say one does not hear the bullet that kills him. I was resigned to the knowledge that each breath may be my last.

The battle continued for two days. Was it fierce? I say it was a fiasco. We were routed. It was petrifying, I thought we were blitzed. We were exchanging fire with the enemy, in all directions, even at the top of the trees above us. Suddenly, the enemy surfaced where we least expected. They outflanked us. We were totally baffled when our boys were shot, from behind us. More confusion was caused by enemy bazookas, raining down from the treetops. The Nigerian gunboats were bringing more reinforcements. No sooner had they arrived, than they climbed the trees, as O.P. Snipers. At this point we were routed and disorganised. It was chaos. Every soldier on his own, to fight or flee, succeed or fail. The military slang was 'use number six' meaning 'save your own life the best way you can'. So, we fought for our lives. Believe me, the situation at that moment was beyond any expertise, or experience in warfare. A matter of fate and faith. Soldiers ran in different directions. Jomo, my close friend, who took control of the big machine gun (artillery), was first to die, near to me. As I ran towards the Jetty, I saw Anefo slumped, his face almost unrecognisable, it was shattered. I ran towards the oil terminal jetty for two reasons, namely, I had been at Okirika before. I knew there was a jetty, and I knew the way. As a former militia Commander, I had patrolled the beat. Very few individuals who ran in that direction were saved. As we ran along the bridge, the enemy soldiers were shooting at us incessantly from the bridge head. They were able to cut off those who lagged. The bullets flew around me, a distinctive 'humming' to my left and right. The soldiers on both sides invariably jumped over their dead, in a quest to attack, retreat, or advance.

As I have stated, in war one does not hear the bullet that kills you, any bullet you do hear has already passed by. The few of us, running towards the end of that bridge, were not even sure of what we might find at the jetty terminal. It terminated in the middle of the wide sea, where large tankers docked, to load oil. Whether by providence, fate, or coincidence, a navy boat was preparing to leave the jetty terminal, when I arrived at the scene. It was not an enemy vessel! It was our own Biafra navy. I flung myself onto the boat. Ojike was limping and unfortunately, was unable to haul himself up as the boat left. He fell onto the bridge and was unable to get up. He may have been taken a prisoner of war or been killed. The latter was probably the case, otherwise he would have returned at the end of the war.

It was after I jumped into the Biafra naval rescue boat, I discovered a bullet, embedded in my forehead, through the front of my helmet. I was lucky. Had it gone deeper, I would have been killed instantly. The bullet was removed at the Port Harcourt naval base and the laceration stitched up.

## THE FALL OF PORT HARCOURT (PH)

Two or three days later, the entire city of Port Harcourt fell, including the air force base, the international airport and the naval base, lost to the enemy troops. There were hordes of people, who abandoned their homes and possessions, with only the clothes on their bodies and whatever they were able to carry on their heads, their only earthly possessions. Some women were pregnant, carrying two or more incredibly young babies, or children. Three, four, five-year-olds crying, as they shuffled along for miles, behind their mothers. There were no young or adult men among those fleeing, only those who were old, infirm, or disabled. Any able-bodied man found among the group was a 'straggler' an able-bodied man, avoiding military service. Such persons were immediately arrested, frog marched and conscripted into the Biafra Army, from where they were moved to the warfront within a few days. For over two weeks, we had no cooked food in the airforce, which we had hitherto enjoyed. We were given rations of dry packs of fried plantains and yams.

Previously, Port Harcourt was the main city and the biggest in Biafra. However, once the enemy broke through the Riverine and creek areas, through Bonny, Ogoni, Eleme and then through Okirika, Buguma, and Degema, the fall of Port Harcourt became imminent. Biafra appeared to be shrinking and sinking. The fall of Enugu preceded the imminent fall of Onitsha thus, Umudike in Umuahia (a small section of the town) became the official headquarters of Biafra after the fall of Enugu. The head of state, Colonel Ojukwu, broadcast daily to the young nation, from his bunker in the town.

The Nigerian forces who invaded Port Harcourt were the Nigerian Marine Commandos, led by the "scopian" late Colonel Benjamin Adekunle. The people of these riverine areas, who in those days the Ibos referred to generally as Mbanmiri people, were said to have heralded the arrival of the Nigerian troops as their liberators, from the clutches of the Ibo people. Many Biafrans saw the actions of these people as sabotage, regarded as saboteurs.

Not so long ago, their people were killed alongside the Ibos, as Easterners or as Southerners, in the Northern parts of Nigeria. Not so long ago, they supported the cause of Biafra, and they had made a U-turn. The Nigerian propaganda promised a separate state of their own, within Nigeria. Most Nigerian oil wells are in these areas. Mr Ken Saro Wiwa, of Ogoni was to be appointed the Administrator of the proposed Rivers State.

As Port Harcourt was shelled, the mass exodus of Ibos was heartbreaking. The Ibos had built Port Harcourt. The mayors, past and present, Ihekwoaba and Nzimiro were Ibos. The Ibos owned about ninety percent of the businesses, including both commercial and residential buildings. Nearly all the residents of Pitakwa spoke Ibo, or Pigeon (Broken) English. A mass of humanity filled the roads out of the city, heading home to the hinterland, with whatever they could carry. I ran to our house, in

Afikpo Street, in my air force uniform, red beret and camouflage jacket. There was no one left in our yard. I entered our rooms and looked around. I couldn't remove any of our possessions, or anything else either. Any military person, especially in uniform, caught with household items, was shot on the spot, either for causing panic, or they were seen as a looter, straggler, or saboteur. I managed to take a few school pictures from my photo album, put them in my shirt pocket, then locked the door behind me, for the last time.

No military person was allowed to leave Port Harcourt, as the city had to be defended to the last man. Colonel Achuzie mounted a roadblock at Igirita, which was ten miles from Port Harcourt city centre. He personally shot in the knee any military personnel who tried to flee from defending the city. It was rumoured a few military men changed into muftis and if discovered were shot, as cowards. When the enemy captured the Air Force base, Naval Base and Army Garrisons, the Nigerian soldiers changed clothes and wore Biafran Military Uniforms. It was chaotic. One could not be sure if the uniformed man coming towards you was the enemy, or not, until it was often too late. Some western and northern Nigerians were caught and burned alive. When it became clear that Port Harcourt had been completely captured by Nigerian troops, a few brave, or lucky, Biafran Airforce persons who survived, were transported to Bishop Lasbery College, Irete, Owerri, our new Air Force Base. It was a secondary school, with neither compound, airstrip, or field, nor any navigational or air support system. We had two helicopters at the base, and it wasn't long before we lost one, with its entire five-man crew. Biafra also had a B52 bomber and two

tiny remote airports at Uli and Uga. The majority of airforce personnel, both officers and other ranks, were deployed to fight alongside the infantry, both Army and Navy in Uguta and Egbema war fronts. Many lost their lives in the trenches and ground warfare in those areas. There was no further recruitment into the Biafra Air Force. I was among the few lucky ones, promoted and deployed to the Air Force Base
(AFB) Uli (Ihiala). Once again, I considered I had landed 'on my feet!

## AIR FORCE BASE IHIALA (ABI)

After the fall of Port Harcourt Airport, Uli became Biafra's main Airport. Biafra was now becoming smaller and smaller, and morale was exceptionally low. Those of us who were based at ABI Uli were considered extremely fortunate, though we suffered more air raids and casualties. Whereas the rest of Biafra was dying of hunger and malnutrition, the Airforce lads at Uli were getting married, buying motorcycles, eating well and comparatively enjoying life. We had access to bales of Stock fish, bags of salt, foreign cigarettes, and other essential commodities, which came by air. These items were not handed out as rations, hence, to get them, you simply had to either steal, or purchase them cheaply from those brave enough to steal, or from those with the right connections.

# PATIENCE

In late 1968, I was deployed to Ihiala junction as a sentry at the check point. I met a young native girl there and quickly befriended her. Patience was beautiful, tall, slim, and darker in complexion. She was endowed with a curvy shape and large firm and voluptuous breasts. When she wore a tight belt around her waist, she imitated the shape of a wasp. She was eighteen years old, while I was a twenty-four-year-old Biafran Airforce guy. From the day after we met, we lived together, basically until the end of the war. After I met Patience, I severed my friendship with Nenne, an Arochukwu girl, who used to live with her parents in the same street as us at Port Harcourt.

Coincidentally, she, her parents, and siblings were refugees in my hometown, Abba, as Orochukwu had by fallen by then, captured by the enemy. In 1969, Patience fell pregnant. She calmly told me we shall have a baby and I hit the roof. I was not ready for marriage, much less becoming a father. I ordered her to 'do something about it' or leave my house. Both of us had a Catholic upbringing and we were in a dilemma, having been taught abortion was a mortal sin. It would also have been shameful for Patience and her family, had she remained pregnant and lived with a man, without marriage. We struck a foolish deal. If she terminated the pregnancy, I agreed to organise a traditional marriage. She played her part of the deal, by drinking local concoctions of herbs and a local alcohol brew called KI-KI. We then sent a message to her parents that I was visiting with my family, to perform the traditional marriage rites.

I chose my close airforce friends as my best men: Ken, Kingdom, Dike, Barclays, Bestman and Sam. We went to Patience' parents and made her proud by performing the traditional wedding rites. By this time, I had become more 'of the world' than the former, pious ex-seminarian I had been. I was popular, and everyone who knew me, including officers and other ranks, fondly addressed me as 'Sir Fabro Dudu.' We bought palm wine, kola nuts, local snuff, a bottle of schnapps hot drink, several tubers of yams and a goat, among other things, for the traditional marriage rites. Everything that was needed for the occasion was provided. Afterwards, Patience and her parents were happy, and we continued to live together as man and wife.

Initially, my parents were not informed of the news of my marriage, neither did they know I was living with a woman in my military quarters in Uli air base. One of my 'so called' best men went home and casually let the cat out of the bag. To our great consternation, my mom got wind of what had happened, and she was furious. She said that what I had done was sinful, shameful, and abominable. She said we should have kept the pregnancy and got married. I told her I didn't want to end up without an education, only to the level of a college degree and to be burdened with a wife and children. I said I had originally only wanted to marry a woman after I had attained a university degree, or similar. I wanted to bring a total change of fortune into my family, I strongly believed the only way I could achieve this was firstly through attainment of a sound education. I was hopeful of travelling to the United States of America someday soon, to further my studies. Optimistic as I was, I hadn't a clue as to how I could ever obtain the money to go to America. Rightly or wrongly, I believed in my mind Patience would be an obstacle to such a dream. If we remained married and started having children, I would end up living from hand to mouth and our children may suffer and may not have the chance of a good education.

While I was at ABI, I forged a friendship with one of the English Mercenary pilots, popularly known as Bruce. Suddenly, the Uguta one (1) warfront went haywire, more airmen were mobilized and sent in for frontal ground offensive, as well as defensive.

I was among the aviators, so was mobilised. Armed with a Madison Automatic rifle, close fighting with the enemy, I used rapid burst action, when necessary. I ducked, dived for cover, crawled, ran, walked, swam, until our task was accomplished. I lived in the trenches, ate, and slept there, whatever the conditions. We pushed the enemy back and advanced, and when it became safe to do so, the air force lads were recalled to base. With a few exceptions, most of the enemy perished in the battle. Our casualties were minimal. Nevertheless, the statistics represented human beings, on both sides. With hindsight, I can assure you my survival was not all about my prowess and gallantry, but the firm belief my time had not come. It was chaotic, dreadful, pitiful. My war experiences, at times, made me yell out that no one should ever have to fight a war! To cause loss of life in this way was clearly barbaric. It was even rumoured that some soldiers roasted and ate captured enemy soldiers.

I lived in a rented bungalow outside the base in a modern house. My customary wife, Patience, lived with me. My cousin Isaac lived with us. My sister and other family members came and stayed for days at a time. On one occasion, my father visited me in his full uniform as a Sergeant Major. Young men who refused to join the military could not freely travel outside the village, because of the fear of being conscripted into the army. I would order Patience to hide away at times, to avoid being seen by my family and visitors.

Maybe people should never push their luck. On the other hand, it is only those who dare that win. I had been promoted from airman to corporal, a non-commissioned officer (NCO) and I was comfortable. I imagined myself in a few months as an air force officer and that suited me. It would bring with it more prestige. After all, the bible advises us to aspire to whatever is noble. Yes, I considered, God wanted me to become an BAF officer and a professional. So, I applied for and was accepted into the Air Traffic Control Officers Cadet course (ATCO). The team was to carry out a highly sophisticated and technical job; we were sent to Ikenanzizi, Obowo for the ATCO training.

## AIR FORCE BASE IKENANZIZI, OBOWU (ABO)

I had my misgivings about leaving the Uli Air Base. However, one cannot be in two places at the same time. I had heard that Ikenanzizi, Obowu was a very dry base in terms of wartime social and economic activities, but I was not the type to dwell on pessimism. I am an eternally eccentric optimist. Also, the last time the war became chaotic and encroached closer, the general duties officers and airmen were, as a matter of course, mobilized overnight. They were despatched to the war front as combat soldiers, alongside the infantry. Therefore, I considered it a move for survival. It was pertinent to turn professional, or technical and to be settled in a permanent job. I reasoned too; it may be a good profession to follow after war ended. At that time, having such an opportunity to specialize was rare, it was also competitive and classy. I went with the hope of being posted back to Uli after the course, firm in the conviction I had always been lucky, and would get my wish.

I agonised over the reality that I was living very well at Uli ABI in a bungalow off base, near the traditional ruler's house, HRH Eze Agbasiere. I was living with my wife and my cousin, who also doubled as my personal batman, though people usually called him my 'back man.' There was a lot of wheeling and dealing in virtually any type of essential and scarce commodity. The money came in, everyone fed well around the air base, in contrast to the abject existence of the soldiers at trenches on the war front, or at other air force bases.

The two-month training at Obowu stripped me of all previous comforts. Food was scarce. The officers' mess, shared with the Cadets, provided inferior quality food. There were no extracurricular or side businesses to carry out. We had no access to the essential commodities. Those of us with contacts at ABI, would hitch rides to Uli at the weekend, to beg for food, or for resale. One got into trouble if tattoos (head count exercise) were called at midnight, or any other time and one was not around to be counted. Punishment for even one night's absence without leave (AWOL) was a day in the cell or guardroom, also called 'the slammer.' The official pay was low, depreciated and irregular. The Biafra money was increasingly becoming worthless. We grinded through it, accepting the situation as one's contribution towards the 'win the war' effort.

The air traffic control course was an enriching and valuable experience. The basic lesson in Morse Code was already familiar to me. It was the same as I had learnt as a boy scout, namely: Alpha, Bravo, Charlie, Delta, Echo, Foxtrot, Golf, Hotel, India, Juliet, Kilo, Lima, Mike, November, Oscar, Papa, Quebec, Romeo, Sierra, Tango, Uniform, Victor, Whisky, Xray, Yankee, Zebra. Air traffic controllers worked from a control tower at every airport. They communicated with the pilots and gave directions on take-off and landing instructions and weather and traffic information. While I was at the training centre, my wife Patience and my affectionate 'boy' went to the village, Abba, to remain until I completed the course, and was posted to an air base. Patience thought it wisest, on her personal conviction and free volition to remain with my mum, irrespective of where I was. It was hoped that at the end of the course I would be redeployed to ABI. On the contrary, I was posted and sent to Biafra Tactical Air Command Base Ugah, ABU, near Aguata and Akaokwa.

## AIR FORCE BASE UGAH (ABU)

The new air base, ABU was totally different to ABI. It was arid and in-active, a remote, scantily populated town. I tried to make the best of a horrible situation with a few close friends such as Pappy J, Nwala and Njoku. We worked day or night shifts at the Control Tower, according to duty rotas. When we were off duty, we used the time to scout for side businesses, buying and selling, scouting for food, fun and otherwise. The Relief planes, carrying materials such as corn meal, ground rice, egg yolk, bales of stock fish, sugar, salt, cigarettes etc, came only once every so often. Usually when there were landing problems at Uli, such as when ABI was under intense enemy bombing. ABU served only as a backup air strip. An enemy air raid at ABU was exceptionally low, so we were relatively safe there. Sometimes the enemy MIG air raids took us with our guard down. The control tower was well camouflaged. The anti-aircraft crew would often start shooting after the enemy planes had completed their bombing mission and left the area, because artillery men did not want to be targets. Some fighter planes unscrupulously and cowardly completed their raids by merely dropping a bomb load in the bush, or in school grounds, churches, and orphanages.

Sad news reached me that my younger sister, Patricia, had become a victim of the indiscriminate Nigerian Military Air Raids, over St Mary's Hospital, Amaigbo. She had gone there to visit our junior bother Patrick, who was hospitalised and awaiting a leg amputation.

Prior to this, my sister oversaw Caritas Charity Relief centre at Ihioma, Orlu. I regarded my sister's position as having given my family multiple blessings. In the first instance, by a stroke of luck, the war did not reach Abba, my hometown, at all, hence my family members lived in their own homes, throughout the war, having fled Port Harcourt at the beginning of the war. Except for those of us who were in the Biafra armed forces, none of my family members left our hometown either as refuges, or war victims. Additionally, my sister's position ensured my mother received from the members of Caritas, regular weekend visits, when they brought assorted relief materials and essential commodities, such as stock fish, corn meal, salt, rice, egg yolk, and sometimes rolls of cigarettes. My mother, as a matriarch, doled out these food items to people, as she pleased. Indeed, during the war, my mum was the envy of her peers and the towns people's eyes. She had a husband who was sergeant major at a nearby training depot, her son was an air force officer and her daughter a Caritas relief officer. In addition, for over a year towards the end of the civil war, the Red Cross head office was based in our compound.

My life by now had changed considerably. You are your own best judge of your physical, social, and spiritual wellbeing. I could always tell when I was no longer my usual self. The change may not have reached a radical or critical stage, but I knew I was on a downward spiral. From being a pre-war teetotaller, I engaged in occasional social drinking, and I had begun smoking four or five cigarettes a day, while sensual cravings were more frequent and I had no strong moral or spiritual restraints, only the occasional niggling regret. Sometimes I remembered to pray; other days prayer escaped my mind completely. Even when I did say my prayers, they were rote, short, no longer ritualistic, or out of a prayer book. Sometimes, making a sign of the cross was my entire prayer. At other times, I became upset and depressed without any apparent reason, other than my inner worries. I was no longer my usual self. I could no longer overcome temptation, such as sex, drinks, and cigarettes.

The Air Force Base, Uga gave me a 'breather, to really try and re-assess the bloody war and my part in it. In the end, I counted my

blessings, thanking Providence for sparing me so far, and on so many occasions, when I could have so easily died. Many times I had cheated death: Numerous 'near miss' bombs and shelling at Okirika, Port Harcourt, Igirita and Uli airport tarmac. At the fall of Port Harcourt, the bizarre pandemonium which ensued as the enemy captured the Biafran Air Force Base supply stock and tactically changed into Biafran BAF uniforms. Many civilians were killed by men in our own forces' uniforms. Word spread that our entire Biafra air force had turned into saboteurs and killed our own people. Many of our genuine lads were thus hacked to pieces, by enraged Biafran Civil Defence. This was how three of my course mates met their death, namely: late
Morah, late Aguma and late Chekwas. I was spared by sheer luck. I had taken a right flanking at Umuomasi while these soldiers were among those who met their death at Leventis Motors Port HarcourtAba Road. So, Ugah Base was a type of haven for me. There were soldiers who suffered injury, lost limbs and had shell shock.

There were soldiers who were stranded and slept rough outside the base. I was an officer and slept comfortably on my bed every night when I was not on duty. Massive conscription into the Army was ongoing. There were many disabled, shellshocked infantry lads, who were also AWOL and became beggars. Whilst able bodied, ragged, and starving soldiers became robbers. On the warfront, many of our soldiers were in rags, some even fought bare bodied, or with tattered shirts and trousers. Many of them fought for days, weeks, on empty stomachs.

# END OF THE WAR

Suddenly we heard rumours the Marine Commando Division of the Nigerian Army, led by Col Olusegun Obasanjo had captured Owerri and Uli ABI fell on the 11 January 1970.

On 13th January 1970, once it was announced that the war had ended, Lt Col Philip Effiong announced that Ojukwu had fled the country (to the Ivory Coast) and all Biafrans were urged to lay down arms. He handed Eastern Nigeria back to Gowon, as the Nigerian Head of State. I was chilled when I realised, we, the Ibos, had become a defeated people. The future was grim and dark again. However, it was also something of a relief war had ended, albeit not in our favour. I calmly took off the Air force Uniform. I hid my automatic Madison and its loaded magazine, in one of my mattresses, and began the lonely trip home to my village, Abba. I hired a push-truck, loaded few vono-iron beds, mattresses, tables, chairs, curtains and so on, because I was intent on living in my own room, as a semi- successful man, when I reached my village. I hired two local men to push the truck to my town, which was about twenty miles away. On foot, we travelled through Uga, Akpuru, Akaokwa, Osina, Uruala, Isiekenesi, Dikenafia, Umudi, Okwelle to Abba. Throughout the journey, I expected to run into the enemy, the victors, Nigerian Army roadblocks. I did not hesitate, dwell on negative thoughts, or allow any perceived hazard to slow me down. What would be, would be. We finally saw the checkpoints at Uruala, and later at Umudi. Thankfully the Nigerian soldiers bought my alibi, that I was a returning trader from a distant town. I was too afraid to mention I had been in any branch of the Biafran Armed Forces. The roads were heavy with various calibres of ex-soldiers heading to different destinations. Most were tattered, dirty, hungry, and rugged. Some were limping on one leg or none, on crutches. Some were suffering from shell shock and permanently shrieking and shouting. My optimism and luck paid off. I respected the power of positive thinking.

## HOME AND SAFE

I observed it was natural for people to continue to walk until they reached their own homes, no matter how many days it took them. No one made the mistake of not knowing their very own home, no matter how far they had to go. My arrival home was greeted with happy cheers. Little children cheered and ran towards me from some distance, as we approached the compound from afar. The older men and women followed suit, with wholehearted excitement and tumultuous jubilation and this continued for some considerable time. There was happy uproar, each time one of our family members arrived home – my dad, my sister, Lieutenants Emma and Eddy, Captain John, Engineer Ike, other ranks, Christian, Innocent, William and so on. Engineer Ike was reputedly one of the inventors of the renowned "OGBUNIGWE" – the Biafran locally invented land mine, which destroyed many enemies in Awka and (ROB) Republic of Bennin Sectors. My father, who was at the training depot, was one of the first to make it home, one of the eighteen other people from the Okoroha family clan, who had joined various arms of the campaign.

Sadly, two of our brothers, Amadi and Ibe never made it home. My brother, Patrick, the first son of my father's second wife limped home with a foot in Plaster of Paris, (POP) as a result of injuries sustained whilst trying to jump into a friendly army truck at Ikot Ekpene sector. As a family, we were grateful to God that our human loss was minimal, compared to some other families who lost many loved ones. Sadly, and regrettably, there is neither any record nor accountability for those who died in the war, nor any burial site.

The Okoroha compound was used as the Red Cross Headquarters towards the last year of the war. As a result, a lot of people were still loitering around our compound for some more 'relief' There were some women and children who were suffering from Kwashiorkor, which was locally named the 'boots' The Symptoms of the illness included the swelling of the legs, enlarged belly and drooping face. It was caused by the absence of essential nutrients in the body especially the table salt. There was an acute food shortage due to the blockade.

At the beginning of the war, to incorporate the Yoruba ethnic group, the Nigerian head of state General Gowan appointed Chief Obafemi Awolowo as the Minister of Finance of the Federal Republic of Nigeria. This was a political manoeuvre as at that time, it was rumoured that Awolowo had stated if the Ibo people move away from Nigeria, then the Yoruba would follow. However, once in office as the finance minister, he promptly imposed a blockade at Bonny, against Biafra, declaring that 'starvation is a legitimate instrument of war' That blockade in fact became the greatest undoing of the young Republic of Biafra, because more people died from starvation than from bombs and bullets.

During war time, Chief Obafemi Awolowo, told Gowon, the then head of state, that it made no sense to allow those you were fighting to have food. From then on, food supplies to the warring Biafra enclave dried up. In desperation, starving soldiers and civilians ate previously untried leaves, roots, tubers, lizards, ants, snakes, rats, dogs, cats and worst of all, human flesh. The amount of International Food Aid was as a drop of water in an ocean of starving masses, the tip of an iceberg. Quite naturally, the sun only shone on those standing, before it ever reached those flat on their stomachs.

*Myself as a young Biafran Air Force Officer with my colleagues during the Nigerian-Biafran War in 1967.*

*Myself as a young Biafran Air Force Cadet Officer during the Nigerian-Biafran Civil War, 1967.*

*Myself in 1964 in Port Harcourt before The Biafra - Nigerian Civil War.*

*With my cousin, Sam Okoroha, 1970.*

**CHAPTER SEVEN**
-------------------------

# What Caused The Bloody War?

The way I understood it is this. When Nigeria gained Independence from Great Britain in 1960, the Ibos mostly Christians, were the most educated. The Ibos quickly assumed posts and positions vacated by colonial masters. The Ibos were mayors and head of various private and public organisations, especially in the northern parts of Nigeria. It was not long before others began to see and resent the Ibos as Indigenous colonialists. The Ibos were also hardnosed businesspeople. Nigeria as a nation, was named after the river Niger and the country was created artificially in 1900 by the British, following the European Powers 'Berlin Conference' of 1884. Approximately three hundred different tribes were put together as one nation. The tribes were different in many ways: language, religion, culture, food, dress, and so on. Three major groups emerged, namely the Ibos in the East, Yorubas in the West, and Hausa-Fulani in the North. The Northerners are Muslims who regarded by their Emirs and Sultans as the Godgiven sources of all political and religious authority. They were barely touched or influenced by the English culture, religion, or education. The masses obeyed their leaders without question. South Westerners were similar, the masses obeyed their Obas (Kings), but unlike the Northerners, the Yoruba king was not Autocratic, individuals could rise to leadership, sometimes kingship, on merit, rather than by birth. The Easterners appointed their leaders democratically and by birthright. Hence, it's said 'Igboamaeze,' meaning the Ibo does not recognise any as their king.

The quest for independence from Britain in 1923, was initially sought by a Yoruba, Herbert Macaulay, the son of an emancipated slave. In the 1940s and 1950s the movement was led by an Ibo, Nnamdi Azikiwe and Yoruba's Obafemi Awolowo. In 1944 Macaulay and Azikiwe formed the NCNC Party, Awolowo formed the Action Group Party, while the Hausa formed the NPC. Therefore, the three parties were respectively regional and tribal. The Ibo and Yoruba leaders also feared northern domination, as the north at that time constituted approximately sixty percent of the nation's sixty million people. However, the Northerners did not want independence from Britain, they feared it would mean Ibos and Yorubas, who were already westernised elites, would dominate the political and economic fabric of the Nation. Thus, as a compromise and to attain Independence, the North wanted the nation to remain as three parts, East, West and

North, allowing the North to remain as the majority and giving them majority seats and votes, in the federal government. The key leaders were Alhaji Tafawa Balewa, who became the first head of Government (the Prime Minister) and Dr Nnamdi Azikiwe, the first President, Chief Awolowo was leader of the opposition, in the federal parliament. Awolowo was concerned about the political shenanigans of the Belawas NPC and Azikiwe NCNC, in addition to the up-and-coming 1963 federal elections. The NCNC and NPC muscled in on Awolowo AG with federal might and Awolowo subsequently cried foul. The NPC and NCNC led Federal government, subsequently arrested Awolowo and some of his party members, for the offence of treasonable felony. They were tried and imprisoned. He remained a prisoner when the coup occurred in 1966.

On 15th January 1966, Major Nzeogwu and other officers mounted a coup d'état, citing electoral fraud, general corruption, and maladministration, as their reasons. They agreed to kill all the civilian leaders, regardless of ethnicity. The coup plotters assigned assassins to the North, the East, and the West. The coup majors sent to kill the leaders from Ibo ethnic group, namely Azikiwe and the Eastern Premier Michael Okpara, for their incompetence. However, they were unsuccessful in killing those whom they were sent to kill in the East. It was rumoured the Ibo leaders who were 'marked men' were tipped off and they vanished. The coup majors sent to the North and West conducted their killing assignments with military precision; Two Hausas – Fulani leaders, the Prime Minister Alhaji Tafawa Balewa and the Northern Premier, Alhaji Ahmadu Bello, the Sardauna of Sokoto, were all killed.

Additionally, Chief S.L. Akintola, the Western Premier and Chief Festus Okotie Eboh, the Federal Minister of Finance were also killed. It must underscore that senior military officer of Hausa and Yoruba extractions such as Brigadiers Mai Malari, Ademulegun and some of their family members were killed.

General Aguiyi Ironsi, an Ibo, then became the first Military Head of State. Riots in the North saw the massacre and pogrom of over 30,000 Ibos. Ironsi naively left himself bare and did all he could to appease the North and allay their fears, assuring them there was no Ibo agenda, but it was to no avail. Northerners were unhappy that the unitary federal government in which they were a majority, had effectively been abolished by the coup and replaced by a unitary military junta government, headed by an Ibo. To the Hausa/Fulani the Nigerian governmental structure at time merely added insult to injury.

In July 1966, a counter coup led by a Hausa man, Murtala Mohammed, killed Ironsi and appointed a Northern Christian, Lt Col Yakubu Gowon: As the head of State. General Aguiyi Ironsi was at the time on a state visit, to the western region of Nigeria, he was guest of the Military Governor of the Western Region, Brigadier Adekunle Fajuyi. It was said that Brigadier Fajuyi sought to protect the Head of State, who was both his boss and his guest. He refused to release General Ironsi to the counter-coupist Danjuma, offering instead, to be taken captive, with Ironsi. In the event, the plotters assassinated both men. It is interesting that in the intriguing Nigeria politics of the time, a Yoruba leader laid down his life to save his Ibo comrade.

On assumption of Office as the Military Head of State, General Gowon made a move to restore a strong central government and released Awolowo from prison to obtain his alliance and support. Lt Colonel Emeka Odumegwu- Ojukwu wanted a loose federation. There was stalemate and because of this impasse, more massacres ensued. Genocide and pogroms against the Ibos, by both northern soldiers and civilians, followed in September 1966, and continued unabated. It was estimated over thirty thousand easterners and southerners were killed, while over two million Ibos and other Easterners were forced to flee the North and the West.

Ojukwu was amongst other qualities, a gifted orator. He proclaimed 'we have crossed the proverbial Rubicon. From the way we have been treated, we can no longer feel safe, or free to go back to live with the Hausa – Fulani people' Our mantra became such slogans as 'We must be on Vanguard, be Vigilant'. Ojukwu asked the people 'If others reject you, will you also reject yourself?' The Answer was a resounding 'NO!' 'This means we have to say let bygones be bygones, breakaway and secede from Nigeria, then as a nation, look after ourselves and indeed mind our own business, paddle our own canoe. A stern warning is that if we are attacked, 'even the grass, will fight.' These ideas and beliefs were later internalised in songs and music, which were sung when soldiers were marching or drilling.

In January 1967, Gowon and Ojukwu met in Aburi, Ghana to discuss and map out the way forward for Nigeria. After they agreed conciliatory measures to appease the Ibos, after what had happened, Gowon returned to Nigeria where he quickly reneged on the guarantees to be given to the Ibos, instead announcing the division of Nigeria into twelve federating states. East had only three, the west had four while the North had five.

Ojukwu felt that reneging on such a life and death agreement was unforgivable, besides, the wealth of the nation was its crude oil, most of which came from the East. The Ibos chanted 'on Aburi we stand' but the chants fell on deaf ears. A compromise could not be reached.

On 30th May 1967, Ojukwu, having obtained a mandate from the Eastern Region Elders, Chiefs, and elite, declared the independence of South-eastern Nigeria as the REPUBLIC OF BIAFRA (from Bight of Biafra). Gowon gave an ultimatum, and on its expiration, he attacked Biafra on 6th July 1967 to 'crush' the rebellion. Biafra mobilised to fight an all-out war for survival as a people. Ojukwu had warned that 'if we are attacked, even the grass will fight.' Awolowo stated that if East goes from Nigeria, the Yorubas will follow, as Oduduwa Republic. However, as soon as Gowon speedily appointed him Finance Minister of the Federal Republic of Nigeria, Chief Awolowo produced his famous policy of 'blockade and starvation' the legitimate instruments of war. Due to that single act of Awolowo, a Biafra militia person told me 'If you see a snake and a Yoruba man, kill the Yoruba man first, you can deal with the snake later.' Ironically, mistrust was mutual, as the Yorubas repeated the same about the Ibos. Those were the politics and political manoeuvres of the time. The mood in Biafra was that Ojukwu was an Orator and Messiah, we were all to fight together or die together.

Initially, the war appeared to be between Hausas and Ibos, until Gowon brought others over to the Hausa cause. Though the Ibos were more like the Yorubas than the Hausas, the Ibos believed that a typical Yoruba man could not be trusted. The Hausas outnumbered the Ibos by a ratio of approximately six to one. If the Yorubas had not teamed up with the Hausas, the Hausa or Yoruba alone could not have defeated the Ibo. Most of the Nigerian Military war front commanders were of Yoruba extraction. The Hausas were the foot soldiers used as pawns. They even imported illiterate "gwodogwodos" from Chad and Niger Republics, as mercenaries. The 'seven footers' were placed in th forefront of the war zones. The first shot of the war was fired at Garkem near Nsukka on 12th July 1967, Colonel Shuwa led the troop. Biafra put up remarkable resistance in places such as Onitsha Niger Bridge, Benin, Abagana, Arochukwu, Umuahia, Uguta, Onne, Ikot-Ekpene and Awka to name a few.

There was an amusing story about three Nigerians; an Ibo, Hausa and Yoruba, who were stranded and very hungry, in a desert. Suddenly they saw an oasis, with ripe fruits on a tall treetop. The Hausa man prostrated and prayed for hours without success, for Allah to cause the fruits to fall so he could eat. The Yoruba man gathered stones and sticks, threw and threw in vain, to bring down the fruits. The Ibo man rolled up his sleeves, climbed the tall tree and with his bare hands plucked all the ripe fruits from top of the tree. All Nigerians agreed the Ibos were prepared to work hard to achieve their goal. The Northerners believed that the Ibo man came begging for water, hence they call us "yammiri," but before long 'he ends up owning a house'.

Similarly, the westerners call the Ibo "kobokobo" meaning hustler for goods and pennies, who come with nothing, but eventually, like Jews, become landlords. Conversely, the Ibos also have pet names for the Hausa as "alakuba" people, referring to how they seem to somersault when they pray. The pet name for Yoruba is "ngbati ngbati" referring to their tendency to proceed, but elongate the discussion with those words and also, we call them 'ofemmanu' people, referring to Yorubas excessive use of oil when cooking stews and soup. The Hausa also refer to the Ibos as "dogoturanchy" people, meaning that the Ibos unnecessarily speak too much grammar.

Biafra had widespread international sympathy such as from Canada and France, but only five countries recognised Biafra as an Independent County. Britain and Russia armed Nigeria, while Biafra had nothing to fight the war with. USA was neutral and only aided Biafra through the Red Cross and Caritas. People were sent to war fronts barehanded or with machetes. Our Engineers invented the renowned land mine "Ogbunigwe" which killed hundreds of Nigerian soldiers in Awka sector. Our troops even managed to capture or liberate the Mid-West region of Nigeria and were less than one hundred miles to Lagos, the then capital of Nigeria. The Biafran Operation was initially led by Lt Colonel Banjo, a Yoruba man himself, but he was later executed as a saboteur, along with Major Ifeajuna.

The war lasted nearly three years, ending in January 1970, claiming over one million lives from both sides. With hindsight, I believe the war should not have been fought.

# POST WAR SURVIVAL

The euphoria at coming home alive, quickly faded and the economic reality of being a member of a defeated ethnic group and people among other Nigerians, set in. As was once said, by the time we a find solution to an inconvenient situation, the question changes. Those of us who had survived the war, had to find a way to move forward; what to do, what to eat, what to wear. Thus, able bodied men and women began afresh, in their search for survival. Highflyers and some middle-class Ibos went to Lagos, Kano, Kaduna, Port Harcourt, Ibadan and other big cities, in search of businesses and subsequent fortune. Locally, we trekked ten or more miles to Owerri, Okigwe, Orlu and wherever there were Nigerian Army Garrisons. These were the nearest economic centres. The Nigerian Army persons were paid in the Nigerian currency that we did not have, as our Biafran currency had been outlawed by decree. The only act of mercy by Gowon in this respect was a policy granting twenty pounds to any Biafran with a bank account prior to the war, regardless of any amount standing to the person's credit.

We gathered our valuables: jewellery, clothes, radios, clocks, watches, briefcases etc., and sold them, to lay our hands on the new Nigerian currency. The previous Nigerian currency had also been replaced. Biafra money was not legal tender and was no longer accepted as currency of trade, even in the local village markets. We sold our personal belongings, even heirlooms of sentimental value, just to earn real money. By so doing, I accumulated a handsome capital of over three pounds and eleven shillings (three guineas). This was enough to buy a bicycle and launch me as a garri and provisions trader. I bought valuable items at 'knock down prices' from the villagers and sold them to the soldiers at their garrisons for 'a bargain price.' I then bought more provisions for resale, such as cigarettes (Flight, Marlboro, Benson & Hedges, Philip Morris, Lucky Strikes and Mars), salt, sugar, milk, biscuits, face and hair creams, pomades, vaseline, soaps for washing the body (Palmolive, Astral) and those for washing clothes (Omo, Surf, Sunlight). Garri is the staple food in Nigeria. It is like farina, semovita, Greis, cornmeal or potato flakes, it's locally produced from cassava tubers, the tubers were cleaned, grinded, fermented, fried, and dried. It looks like dough when hot water is added to it. It is starchy and mostly carbohydrates. Some people eat garri three times a day, as their 'three-square meals.' In such cases, a change of diet meant drinking garri with freezing cold water or eating it with different soups. It is eaten for sustenance of life but has little or no nutritional value at all. Sometimes, I went to distant markets where I bought bags of garri and caught a bus back home. Retailing it locally, I made a shilling or two in profit, plus the family had something to eat. I was also biding my time in the village, just to be sure it was safe to venture outside our hometown. Gradually life appeared to normalize, other than for the lack of money. Our former enemies would chat with us, laugh and joke. They bought and sold with us. They became more and more friendly and married our women, in something of biblical proportion. Our women wanted men with the currency, the liquid cash. Many highranking military officers and other ranks of other ethnic groups abandoned their own local women for Ibo women, to take as trophy wives. Therefore, many of our girls did extremely well.

To be fair, I must salute General Gowon, the then Head of the Nigerian Military Government. He was a practicing Christian, for it was under his auspices that Ibo tribesmen, women and children were spared total annihilation. It is anyone's guess what might have happened if Gowon were a Muslim, or conversely, if the Ibos had won the war. Sometimes, I wonder what my own people would have done if they had the upper hand and had carried the offensive into the Hausa – Fulani 'enemy' heartland. I consider it magnanimous that Gowon did promptly announce that the concluded war ended with no winners or losers 'no Victor, no Vanquished.' He then launched the big 3R's 'Reconciliation, Rehabilitation and Reconstruction'. The implementation process may have been cosmetic and shabby, due to the ever-present greed in all men, especially the helmsmen found in the Nigerian corridors of power.

My sister and I had a thanksgiving Mass offered to glorify God for preserving us and members of our family. It was after the madness of war that sanity returned and the grim reality of the wastefulness of war crystallised. Approximately over a million Nigerians from both sides were killed, dead forever. The Biafran dead were not even accounted for, nor properly buried. There is still no record of our soldiers killed in action, no money paid in compensation to their families, widows and orphans. I always pray that the souls of the dead rest in peace.

Amid the so-called 3Rs, the suffering of the Ibos continued to this day in numerous ways. The first shocking blow was that the Nigerian Government announced that no matter how much Biafran money you had, if you brought it to the bank, by a decree, you could get twenty (£20) Nigerian pounds flat, per head. The next crushing blow was the conspiracy that any properties owned by an Ibo in Port Harcourt and some other big cities, were classed as 'Abandoned Properties' and lost forever. My rich uncles, and others like them were hurting, as most of their properties were 'abandoned' in Garden City, Port Harcourt. To my recollection, no Ibo lost any of the landed property in the western or northern regions. It was a war that perhaps never should have happened. There is no honour in defeat. For the Biafrans, it was like becoming a foreigner in their own homeland. The immediate question was 'where do we go from here?' None of us had a job. At that time, in January 1971, I was twenty-five and I had never been employed, except by the defunct BAF.

The burden of feeding my family (parents and siblings) unofficially rested on my shoulders, until my father fortunately returned to work with the Nigerian Ports Authority (NPA) Lagos. I was always happy to help. I was not the type to go scheming or engage in con-artistry (locally called Onyeoshi, Wayoo, Ole, Akanakpa, or bogi- bogi). I joined millions of honest and lowly, law-abiding Ibos in search of a livelihood. We turned hawkers and petty traders.

The defiant ones went underground and operated nefariously at night. The weak ones amongst us, such the mentally burnt out, amputees, invalids and the disabled became roadside alms beggars. They were equally sad and bitter, as society or government had made no form of social provision to cater for them. A sizeable number of our women and girls were commandeered by the victorious soldiers. Yet many of our girls, even married women, through their own free volition, or in defiance, ran to them and were shackled or cohabited with them. (Kwaringida). A number were used, abused, battered, and discarded like trash, dropped like hot potatoes, while a few lucky ones to this day remain happily married, some even to the highest ranked Nigerian military men.

## PATIENCE LEAVES

Since the war had not ended in favour of Biafra, it became clearly ridiculous to my way of thinking to remain married within the realms of my social and economic situation. I considered it absurd to start making babies with my wife, Patience, while none of us had 'made it' or had a good income. It would have meant raising children, who in turn would suffer deprivation, thus perpetuating the crippling cycle of poverty in the family lineage. I swore to break the pattern, not for my selfish interest, but for brethren and the unborn and for posterity. I vowed to be an institutional family pedigree, a pacesetter. a pioneer, a steppingstone, a type of springboard for others. I have always believed that any new thought or change starts with single-mindedness.

I believed I should only get married and have children, after attaining a respectable social, academic, and economic height and status. Only in such a position could one be sure to at least obliterate illiteracy and socio-economic dwarfism in the family, from generation to generation. The change must start somewhere, by someone. I had no doubts, I had a mission in my life. I wanted to leave a legacy, or footprint, however small, before I died and felt in my bones somehow the hand of God was on my shoulders. I considered my aspirations called for sacrifice and self-denial. My convictions told me nothing could be more gratifying than to do the things posterity would always benefit from, and thereby one would be remembered for ever. It did not bother me, that at the time I had no financial means, or benefactor to help me fulfil my ambitions. Yet I was singularly determined to attain the highest point of academic and social position humanly possible, to end my perceived impecuniosity in my immediate and nuclear family. My critics at the time labelled my avowed aims as 'blind ambition'. My thoughts were that when I did get married, I would have become a university graduate, and my prospective wife would be equally highly educated and professionally minded. Thus, I took a drastic stance and asked my wartime wife, Patience, to leave without further ado, in the interest of everyone. I told her that she was free to re-marry. I explained my reasons, that I was still considering becoming a priest and if that didn't work out, I would find a way to go overseas for further studies.

Ironically, Patience teamed up with my mother. Both pleaded, cried and tried to persuade me to remain married to Patience, to no avail. My mother even implored me to leave Patience in her sole care and custody, to allow me to pursue my dreams. I refused. Patience begged that she was a qualified tailor and owned her Singer sewing machine, which would have enabled her to earn a living without becoming a financial burden to me. I was immovable. They read my lips and reluctantly accepted the verdict. My mother knew I loved the beautiful Patience; however, I was also a person of tough inner convictions and vision. So, she comforted Patience and reassured her everything would turn out right, before long. Having given up my wife, it seemed, like Paul of Tarsus, my rucksack became light.

## CAPTAIN IBRAHIM

My beautiful sister, Patricia, by chance was a friend to one Captain Ibrahim, who was the Paymaster for Okigwe Garrison Nigeria Army. I met him at Okigwe during one of my Garri business trips. He was a young man, two or three years older than me. He was drawn to my charisma and asked if I would like to stay a few days as his guest. I was obliged and was treated like a King. He already had an Ibo cook. We ate fried eggs, fried ripe plantains, sliced bread, pap, Akara and tea with peak milk, for breakfast every day. We had boiled or fried yam, with rice, beans, fresh or dried fish or meat stew for lunch, and in the evenings, we ate pounded yam or garri with either Calabar vegetable soup (edekaiko), or egusi or bitter leaf or ogbono (the draw-soup). I was refreshed and went home after a week, feeling like a new man. Two weeks later, the captain visited our family and was equally treated like royalty. He asked if I would like to travel up north to Kaduna by road with him. I accepted his invitation with no iota of fear or hesitation. It was the first time I had been close to a Muslim, or a Nigerian Army Officer and I was surprised to note that he behaved exceptionally, like a good
Christian. I spent about a month in Kaduna. Schools in the East, or then Biafra, had not reopened. I knew no other person in Kaduna before we set off on the trip. The Ibos were still suffering from the pains inflicted by war. The journey took two days by

road, with a Mercedes Benz flat boot, I was amazed to discover that Kaduna market was already full of Ibos. I met some Ibos that I knew from back home. I ran into an Ex-seminarian named Ogali, and another known acquaintance called Ojile who attended Mater Dei High School Imiringi near Ahoada. I wondered at how quickly they had managed to return to the North, despite the pogrom and the only recently concluded civil war. I thought to myself, the Ibo people are very courageous, indomitable, and resilient. The Ibos are perhaps the Jews of Africa. Captain Ibrahim wanted me to join the Nigerian army and asked me to stay in Kaduna and wait for the army cadet recruitment day. I initially obliged him, however, after a long wait, where nothing seemed to be happening any time soon, coupled with the fact schools were due to open soon in the East, I felt I must return home without further delay. I had decided I would try to go back to the Senior Seminary for priesthood or enrol and complete the Higher Secondary School Certificate (HSC), also called the post-secondary education. Otherwise, I hoped to find a way to travel overseas in search of greener pastures. At the top of my list of dream countries then were the USA, Russia, England (UK), France or western Germany. I was least keen on joining the Nigerian Army. Maybe I should have joined. I could have become important today.

One early morning at the breakfast table, I informed my host I wished to return to the East to continue my education, as school was starting soon. The captain was generous and magnanimous, he gave me many gifts, new clothes, cash and arranged my travel back to the East, by road. That was the first time I ever travelled to the northern parts of Nigeria. I enjoyed the trip, it made me a better and wiser man, both with the knowledge of other Nigerians and with horizons in general. My stay in Kaduna was an interesting eye- opener. I had the shock of my life when I visited the Kaduna market to discover Ibos were already quite settled as store owners, as if they had never been to war at all. I was wrong initially to think I was the first of my kind to venture up North. Some Ibos might have arrived in the Northern Nigerian cities on the day after cessation of hostilities. I had never seen so many Hausas and Fulani together. There were so many Mallams (Hausa men) in long white gowns and lamas (cattle) were everywhere.

I travelled back to the East second-class, in a long semi open top Mercedes Benz (911) truck. About twelve of us were seated on two hard wooden benches in the demarcated portion, just behind the driver.

The driver and two persons sat in the front of the lorry; we sat in second class, while some cattle, bound for the East, stood in third class, some of them peeping out of the tail board of the truck. The journey took two days and we arrived at Enugu, Ogbete market at noon the following day. A further two-hour taxi ride took me home. I proudly distributed gifts of secondhand clothes, and onions, which I brought to every member of my immediate, and larger, extended family. The cynics and critics were astonished at my courage, for they figured that Hausas could have used me in the kind of witchcraft or voodoo, that perpetually multiplied their wealth. I brushed all negativity away as primitive superstition. I did not dwell in such fears. Fear can only limit, hinder and cripple you. You cannot fly with the eagles if you walk with ducks. Caesar once said that what you need to fear in life is fear itself. My trip to Kaduna went exceptionally well.

**CHAPTER EIGHT**
-------------------------

# Back to School: St Augustine's Grammar School, (Sags), Nkwerre

The thought of returning to the priesthood surfaced and became topmost in my mind. I cycled down the thirty miles to Isu-Njaba where the Seminary was temporarily located, since the fall of Port Harcourt. Students, priests, and staff who knew me received me warmly. I approached the Rev. Father Rector, Mbah with the possibility of my returning and being recommended to the Senior, (Biggard Memorial) Seminary, Enugu. His polite answer was 'no', as a matter of policy. I consoled myself, by concluding that there had been no harm in trying. I was not at all surprised. I spent the night there, ate dinner and breakfast with the seminarians and left early the next day.
Since that door had closed, I quickly decided to apply and enrol into the Sixth Form, to complete the higher school certificate (HSC) and Advanced level (G.C.E A-levels), at St Augustine

Grammar School (SAGS) Nkwerre. The school was situated only three miles from my hometown, Abba. I cycled there and was accepted instantly. The ever-present problem of money manifested again. The fee for the day students was ten pounds. Since I had no financial backing from anyone, I turned to my livestock assets of two goats and six fowl, which were sold to pay my school fees and purchase necessary books. I had owned and reared poultry, their sale often came in handy, in times of emergency financial need. My cousin Tony and I were in the Sixth Form for the two-year course, from 1970 to December 1971. We rode daily on our bicycles to and from the school, come rain or shine. Tony was fortunate to be sponsored by one of our wealthy uncles.

During the second semester we moved in and became borders to improve our studies. I was immediately appointed the school Dining Hall Prefect in charge of the Refectory, kitchens, and stores. I couldn't believe my luck, it felt like being appointed Minister of Finance. Every other weekend I would travel to some distant market with the school van and the kitchen staff, to purchase food stuffs for the school. I felt elated to have been found worthy of holding such a sensitive and lucrative position in a school to which I was a relative newcomer. The student population from form one to the lower and upper sixth forms numbered over a thousand.

S.A.G.S is a grand old college which was started by early Anglican Missionaries in 1948. The school has the reputation of excellence, as hundreds of illustrious Nigerians who belong to the nation's cream of the crop had their formative years in this esteemed establishment. S.A.G.S was one of the few schools in the then Eastern Region. with Post Secondary facilities. The school

Motto: 'Ibu Anyi Danda' meaning 'ants accomplish their heavy tasks in unity' and this illustrates the practicality of the diligence, unity, and cooperativeness of the ants, for the purpose of problem solving and progress. It is still a premier institution, first among equals. It has shone in many ways, such as in soccer (football), sports, drama, debate, scouting, quality staff and students and above all, in the final year's student's examination results. Many government ministers and company directors are eminent alumni of SAGS. All former students are proud to tell the world that SAGS is their Alma Mater.

The people of Nkwerre jealously supported the school as the window of their hearts, or the proverbial apple of their eye. During my time there, most of the students were from Nkwerre town and surrounding towns such as Abba, Amiagbo, Isu, Owerre- Nkworji, Umuozu, Umudi, Orlu, Dikenafia, Isiekenesi, Umudi to name a few. There are a sizeable number of students from owerri province, such Mberi, Egbu, Uratta and so on. As well as a handful from Onitsha and Asaba, the then Mid-West. The people of Nkwerre and its environs called "ndi uzo ulo" in Orlu province area, are generally known for their wits, shrewdness, remarkable common sense and sense of humour. As a people, historically they migrated as part of the mass movement of people from Arochukwu and Arondizuogu.

They are generally said to be as cunning as the tortoise (mbe). They are bold, daring, and effusive. And all aspects of these people's culture manifested on the school campus.

## SCOUTMASTER 1ST ORLU TROOP

I reactivated the Boy Scout troop of the school, after the war. The East Central State Scouts Commissioner, Mr. S. S. Anyiam personally settled the Scouts leadership tussle and entrusted me with the Scout Mastership of the school's 1st Orlu Troop. Mr. S. Opara, another sixth former was contesting, as new student I should not be placed above him, he had been at SAGS before the war. However, I had attended more scouting courses and jamborees than he had, even from my priesthood days. I took the Boy Scouts at SAGS to exciting new heights. The fun adventures, camping, hiking, parties and so-on ensured half the entire student population become Baden Powel's Boy Scouts.

The most memorable camping was held at Egbu Girls Secondary School, while one of the hikes took the troop to my family compound in Abba, via Umudi. In my final year in 1971, we pulled off one of the most sensational inter collegiate Jamborees on SAGS campus. It was attended by well over two thousand boys and girls. It was like a circus, scouts and nonscouts had fun, 'a whale of fun' (nkwa), some undoubtedly took it to the limits. My studies continued very well. I was on superbly good terms with the principal, staff, other prefects, and the students. I can humbly say I was an 'all-rounder!'

Some of the other prefects of the day included S. Ekenna, the senior prefect, who later attended the University of Nigeria, Nsukka, and subsequently became honourable member of the Imo State House of Assembly. Mr Nwadike, who after studying in Rome and Chicago, Illinois, became the Honourable Nigerian High Commissioner to Trinidad and Tobago in the West Indies. Mr S. Amadi, the labour prefect, became captain of a ship with the Nigerian Ports Authority. Mr Nwokedinaobi, a former student of the University of Ibadan, later became Managing Director of his Chemical and Pharmaceutical companies. Mr Ihekwazu and Mr Nwagwu went to Houston Texas. Mr Nmezi, Mr. Okolie, and Mr Uzoma became academic doctors and are now professors in the American Universities, including in the state of Maryland, Washington and Virginia, USA. Mr Aniebunwa and Geoffrey attended Universities of Calabar, and Ife respectively and later became teachers. My cousin, Tony Ozigbu later studied at Edinburgh and returned to become a high-ranking collector in Nigerian Custom and Excise. At SAGS, I hustled, wheeling and dealing on and off campus to pay my fees. In addition, I kept up with the needs of my mother and younger brothers, who were all in elementary schools. Like a cat, I always landed on my feet. Each of my prayers was somehow answered. Some people looked at me as though I was a spirit or had a talisman or good luck charms. I was an enigma, whatever I did or said, was good. I continued to be inwardly renewed daily, with my total dependency on the higher power – the almighty God. I did not need drugs or alcohol, I was born naturally 'high,'

## PATIENCE REMARRIED

Sometime during 1971, while I was at SAGS, one of my cousins, Romanus who was then a Nigerian Police Sergeant, (later an Inspector of Police) was looking around for a nice girl to marry.

He spoke to some elders, and they got together. It was agreed I should take him to Patience's family, so Romanus should marry Patience, since I was not prepared to continue as her husband. I accompanied him and we journeyed down to Ihiala, her hometown. The venture was disastrously futile. She did not only refuse to marry him, but cried bitterly because she still wanted me. I was her very first love. I was twenty-six years old, but my mind was far removed from thinking about marriage to Patience, or to any woman for that matter. I was single-minded, focused on achieving greater heights in life. I boldly told her I wanted to go overseas for further studies. It was up to her if she wanted to wait in her father's house until I returned as a graduate. The funny thing is, I didn't even know if, how, or when I could go overseas to study. I could only pray to God to forgive me if I was wrong in the way I treated Patience. Only God knows all things.

Six months later SAGS had a friendly soccer (football) match with Trinity High School, Uguta. Our school van driver, Sokwe, had us heading to Uguta via Ihiala with a bus full of players and intending spectators, like me. The students sang songs merrily, back, and forth.

At Ihiala, I diverted the school van to Patience's family compound. Her father told me that she had just remarried. I was astonished, flabbergasted. I demanded to know who had married my wife. Her father instructed one of his sons to take us over to her new home, in another village in Ihiala. Whilst with the School van and students, we drove over to the new husband's house. As our van pulled up, she came out in utter surprise at the oddness of a school van and multitude of college men. When I stepped out from the front seat of the van, she recognized me. Her husband was standing helpless as she flung herself on me and cried unrestrained, yet again. I was invited into their home. I took a couple of students along wi th me. The new husband and I got acquainted. He offered us some beer and palm wine. I usually didn't drink, but this time I decided to take a sip. I lifted the tumbler full of white palm wine (palmy) and in my very own hands the tumbler shattered to pieces. I even became mystified at myself. As we left the house, I consoled her, announcing I was leaving in a short while, to the United States of America. Again, at that point, I did not have admission to any university in America, or any promise of sponsorship. How, I was to achieve that, I didn't have a clue, but I remained extremely optimistic

Amazingly, Patience had married a local millionaire. The lucky man owned a Petrol Station. It was the biggest filling station after the war, between Onitsha and Owerri roads. I thought such is life. I was happy for her in any event, especially as she appeared to have married well and 'married up'.

We finally made our journey to Uguta. At the final whistle, SAGS had beaten Trinity High School, by three goals to one. One of the upper sixth form lads, Crossman Udom, was the first son of the Proprietor of Trinity High School, Uguta. He took some of us home for light refreshments before we headed back to our school. All the way home the boys chanted and sang merrily and victoriously. The driver was advised not to drive 'furious' meaning he should drive in a slow and steady manner, for the students' comfort and safety.

Until the day I die, I will continue to sometimes regret the fact I sent Patience away. A child born in 1968 would have been 50 years old in 2018. And no one knows what any child will become, or turn out to be, in life. It was a childish mistake and youthful exuberance, to say the least!

**CHAPTER NINE**
------------------------

# My Friend, Christopher (Rogers) Oguamanam leaves for St.Paul/Minneapolis, USA

In 1951, I returned from Port Harcourt to resume schooling at our hometown, Abba. I was a pupil at the age of 7 years when I met Christopher, later known as Rogers, who was one of the pupils in my elementary class 1, then called "ABC Nta" before the "ABC Ukwu", and before being promoted to Primary Standard one (Std 1) in 1955. We were in the same classes, until we both passed and left St Theresa's Primary School Abba, in 1960 after completing standard six (Std 6). Christopher then went to Onitsha to attend Bethel College for secondary education, whilst I went to Port Harcourt where it became clear I could not enter secondary school at once. I heard no more from Rogers until we met again at SAGS in lower sixth form for the HSC, after the civil war in 1971. We embraced each other and exchanged congratulations for surviving the civil war. He was a Biafran Army officer, Captain by rank, whilst I was an Air Force, Air Traffic Control Officer, and Flying Officer by rank. He intimated that he had an elder brother in Minnesota, U.S.A. He told me if his elder brother helped him, as he had promised, to get admission, he would abandon the HSC and proceed to the USA. I was instantly excited for him, though I did not have such an Abraham for a father. Such birth rights came with enormous responsibilities. It is incredibly good to be a first son if the father is rich and eventually leaves wealth to be inherited. But, if the parents are poor, then the first son, like me, faces an uphill struggle, with few benefits, rather with liabilities. In fact, I have never had an elder brother. I am the first son and elder brother to all my numerous siblings.

Early in the second and final year of our post-secondary course in 1970/71, my childhood friend, Rogers received admission to the University of Minnesota. We were studying Chemistry, Botany and Zoology at A-levels. His elder brother Cletus, had been in the USA for many years, including during the war, fulfilled his promise and got admission for Rogers. Rogers was not a popular student. I was one of the most popular students on the campus, and I was popularly known as "Sir Fabro Dudu" the Scout Master, and the Dining Hall Prefect. I volunteered and used my popularity and influence to organise a psychedelic and groovy send-off party for him on the SAGS campus. The party was one of a kind. It was fun and 'wellattended' Rogers was so impressed with the turnout, the music, the speeches, and the whole atmosphere of the party was great fun! At the end of the party, Rogers called me aside and said 'Sir Fabro Dudu, you have done me a great honour, and I promise to get you an admission once I get to the United States of America.' It was a firm promise, and it heightened my anxiety, as my dream of going overseas might come true someday. Well, if you do not dream, dreams will never come true for you! Much as I was glad to know someone might get me an admission to study in the USA, I had not considered how I would find money to get there or pay the school fees. I did not lose sleep over things like that. I was like the mythical dog that was quoted to have said 'just throw out the bone, do not bother about the battle between him and evil spirits, over the bone.'

## DUPED: AN EARLY FORM OF "419" IN LAGOS, NIGERIA

About a month before the end of the year, in November 1971, the school's science master, knowing I was travelling to Lagos, gave me £10 to purchase catfish for the Higher School Zoology laboratory examinations. I went to Lagos hoping to kill three birds with one stone. I intended to see my father who lived in Amukoko, Lagos and collect whatever amount of money he could give me towards my schooling. I also looked forward to visiting my cousin Eddy, who was Customs Officer at the Ikeja Airport and resided at Olatilewa Street in Lawanson, Itire, Lagos

I was also scheduled to take a test in English as a foreign language (TOEFL). Foreigners who wished to study in any of the

American Universities were required to pass such an examination before they could obtain admission. I booked to sit the exam at the American Embassy, in Lagos.

I hit the jackpot. My visit coincided with my father receiving his pay packet from the Nigerian Ports Authority (NPA) the day after my arrival. He joyfully handed me £7 for school fees. He also gave me £3 for my mother and her co-wife. I wrapped the £10 pounds neatly, tucking the bundle away inside my underpants. I was making doubly sure I did not risk losing it or having it stolen, especially in the normally overcrowded Lagos 'molue' buses. I sat the two-hour examination, I passed and the 85% pass result was handed to me.

I left the Custom Quays on Marina Street, where my dad worked and walked across to Tinubu Square, the very heart of Lagos, to catch a bus to Racecourse then to Victoria Island, where I bought the catfish for my school laboratory, Mission accomplished! I then returned to Tinubu Square, waiting for a bus to take me to Lawanson. Then a smart looking man of my age approached me. He stared into my face, with a smile and called out, Emeka! I told him that I was not Emeka. He then said Ikechukwu? Onitsha? I said no and told him that I was not from Onitsha, hoping he would leave me alone. I told him I was from Port Harcourt, and he said 'yeah, that's it, I thought as much!'

He then produced a story that he was driver to a rich Benin Chief and that his boss wanted to buy loads of fertilizer. He asked if I knew where he could get bags of fertilizer at a cheap price. He said his boss was ready to pay the sum of three thousand naira for one hundred bags of fertilizer and that if we could locate a cheaper seller, we could make a fortune. I told him that I didn't know who, or where fertilizers were sold.

He then claimed he knew where we could buy them for a pound each, while his boss would pay us three pounds each. He only wanted me to go with him to see his boss and get the three thousand pounds. I said I would go with him, thinking this man was a Godsend. I considered I would be mad not to accept this wonderful business proposition. If the plan succeeded, I could be going back home to the East with a thousand pounds in my pocket. I told him that I was ready to go with him to his boss. My new friend, Johnny, said we should take a bus to where his boss was staying. As soon as we saw the bus going in the direction, he hopped on, but I could not follow his pace, too fast for me. Observing I continued to miss the buses, he asked me to be faster, like him. Finally, we caught the same bus to Shomolu, Lagos. We walked into an isolated bungalow, and he announced 'This is where my boss lives. We entered a place that looked like a simple two room apartment, with one of the rooms used as a lounge for visitors and the second one was the bedroom. It was a usual room and parlour, in a 'face me and I face you' type of building, which normally had the shared communal kitchen, toilet and bathroom at the rear.

I sat down while he went in to inform his boss of my presence. A heavily bearded man, six foot tall, appeared wearing crimson attire. He appeared unable to speak a word of English. His driver functioned as his interpreter. He launched into some strange Bini language, that I could not make out anything from 'Gbo gbo blab la ri gima sirow.' He asked whether I was the manager of the fertilizer company? The driver advised me to answer 'yes,' so I said 'yes', nodding my head. Then he babbled something that sounded like 'Karma kari babble bla'? He asked whether he could trust me with his own money. The driver interpreted again and advised me to 'Tell him yes', and I responded, 'yes', the boss retorted another gibberish 'pon tap on te Fili fili komba?' He asked again if I had ever managed big money before? The driver said I should reply 'yes' and that I handled big money for the company every day. I replied, going with the flow. The chief responded 'kuruma money'?

The driver asked me if the chief wanted to know how much money I had on me at that time, because he wanted to be sure that he was not dealing with just any poverty-stricken riffraff, that might run away with his money. I proudly told him I had £10 in my pocket. The Chief thundered 'T akum ba' The driver translated that the Chief requested that I should give my ten pounds to him, as a guarantee that I will not run away with his own money. I gave him my money, and he went into the bedroom to bring the big money, £3000 for the purchase of the fertilizer. I had simply and quickly dipped my hands inside my pocket and given out the entire £10, possibly comprising the school fees and feeding money for his wives, my father had given me. For a moment, I regretted I already spent the science teacher's £10 earlier on the purchase of the laboratory catfish. I would have added it to what I had given him to make him think better of me. In fact, I would have given anything for the £2,000 pounds profit that would soon be split between the driver and me. I had never seen that amount of money before in my life.

After I had handed over the money, the Chief excused himself into the inner room, with the promise of coming back with the £3,000 for the purchase of one hundred bags of fertilizer, while myself and his driver, now my impromptu friend and partner in crime, waited for him to reappear. After thirty minutes waiting in vain, his driver, now made an excuse, promising to hurry him up, to bring the money and he left to get his boss.

I waited again for over an hour, without seeing either of them come back. When I couldn't take it any longer, I went out of the room to the street. Luckily enough, I bumped into an old friend who was known as 'Barclays' from the Biafra Air Force. I related my sorry story to him, how two men had taken my money and simply disappeared. I pleaded with him to help me recover my money from them.

Barclays immediately warned me as a friend to find my way out of there, if I loved my life. He said I was a 'mugu' He said that in life, if a 'mugu' falls and 'guys wacks' which means that if anyone is foolish or stupid enough to part with their money, the crafty recipient will be happy to laugh all the way to the bank. He said those men were conmen, criminals and fraudsters and that I risked my like if I refused his advice. I quickly jumped into the next available bus back home to lick my wounds. I never told my father about my horrendous ordeal, and I thanked my God I did not lose my life. The big question remained, how was I going to get my school fees?

I finally made it back to the village and school and after deep reflection, I promised myself I would never again be so foolish as to fall victim to such a scam. What happened to me was the early form of the present-day Nigeria criminality called '419' frauds, named after section 419 of the Nigerian Criminal code. As usual, I dealt with my misadventure by resorting to the selling of my remaining livestock, to raise funds. I also visited and obtained a paltry sum as assistance, from my junior sister, Pat, who lived in Uwani, Enugu and was teaching at a nursery school.

## HSC AND A' LEVEL GCE EXAMS

The Higher School Certificate, Cambridge Exams was held in November 1971. Months before the exams, there was frenetic swotting and "cockroaching," a term used to depict the act of studying throughout the nights. We heard of "expos" where some invigilators sneaked out question papers and sold them to the students before the exam dates. Fortunately, or unfortunately, we could not get any "Expo." When the HSC results came out the following year, we heard that certain schools' results were withheld or cancelled due to hard evidence of "EXPO" at their schools.

After Rogers had left for his studies in America, he kept his word and got me admission into the University of Minnesota.

The letter came during my last exam week at SAGS, and I was overjoyed. I told my father I had been accepted into the University of Minnesota. My father was shocked and appalled; 'Why have you chosen to take this path? This is like a bad dream! I hope you're not thinking of dragging me into this, I heard it could cost up to $5,000.00 to go there to study. How and where do you intend to raise this amount of money? Have you forgotten how poor we are? We can barely afford to eat in this house and now you drop this bombshell! Well son, you need to be more realistic, don't bite off more than you can chew, and please do not expose us to ridicule!' My mother interjected, addressing my father 'nnayi' our father, let the young man speak his mind. Stop putting him down! If he wants to dream, let him dream; it is better to have a good dream, than no dream at all!' I beseeched them both to calm down, I was totally confident everything would be fine in the long run. I believed if God wanted me to go to the USA, nothing would prevent it.

Everything soon settled down, however, I remained determined 'I have a dream,' as the black American Martin Luther King once said. My mind was racing. I knew what I wanted out of life, now my time had come, and I wanted to 'take the bull by the horns' and not let go, nor let my dream die.

I had heard my father's misgivings, and I knew it would be impossible to raise enough money to travel to America.

However, on the last day of my exams at SAGS, I felt supremely confident and elated. I took pictures with friends and exchanged some mementos and photographs. The future was rosy and bright once more. From being unable to go to secondary school, due to financial reasons in 1961, I had somehow managed, miraculously, to complete secondary school and post- secondary by the end 1971 (excluding 3years of military service in the Biafra Air Force). Most exciting of all at the time was the prospect of my imminent travel to Minnesota, USA for further studies, by early 1972. My fags and friends helped to take my belongings to the main road at Nweke market, from where I boarded a vehicle to my village in Abba. Normally, senior students and prefects had a fag each (fag meant a junior student who served a senior student in return for protection from other students), however in my own case, I had a 'harem of fags' 4 or 5 junior students who served me. These young boys usually competed for my friendship, companionship, and attention. I did not learn from the bitter experience of expulsion from the Seminary, because I continued to have junior students as fags, who obtained favourable treatments from me due to my position. With hindsight, my attachment to 'fags' appeared to have partly sown the seed for my latter life preference for a large family and traditional marital arrangements. It is also possible that I was influenced by my parental upbringing and by paternalistic men, such as my grandfather and father who had large families themselves. Historically, my great grandfather Okoroha had an even larger family, with multiple wives and many children.

On New Year's Day 1972, I left Abba and travelled to the University of Nigeria, Nsukka, Centre for the A Level, Cambridge examinations, for both theoretical and practical (Laboratory) exams in Chemistry, Botany and Zoology. These were completed within a couple of weeks. I sat the exams in high spirits, with confidence and pride. By the fifteenth of January 1972, I was back home, examinations complete. I now looked forward to the prospect of travelling overseas. My admission letter was already 'in the bag' regardless of whether I passed A-level or not, my admission was not contingent on passing them. I had already passed my English language (TOEFL) exam, taken and marked by the Americans at the USEmbassy. The question then remained, how to obtain money to proceed. I was required to pay $5000 for the firstyear school fees, and the transport fare to USA was £150. I did not own a Nigerian international Passport at that point. I had to go to Lagos, to obtain a passport and visa to USA. Overall, I had less than £5 to my name.

I went to Lagos first to obtain a Nigerian International passport. I travelled on one of the new luxurious buses: Osondu, Ekene,

the Young, became a widespread means of travelling within the country, since the end of the war. Before then, such longdistance travel was undertaken by lorries which had rows of wooden benches. The two rows just behind the driver in the lorry were called second class seats, the cost being a little more than the third-class compartment. The conductors of the Lorries did not sit, they hung on the tail board and usually jumped down in a display of acrobatic skill, before the lorry came to a halt. The early jump off the lorries was necessitated by the need for the conductors to put a wedge in front of, or behind, the rear tyres of the lorry, in order to prevent the vehicle rolling backwards or forwards, dangerously. In those days, Passport Agents used to tout around the passport office. I was introduced to an Igbo tout, and he discussed in Igbo language with me. I paid £10 deposit and was told, when I returned on the fourth day to collect my passport, I would pay another £10. I was required to go to the Police headquarters and obtain INTERPOL clearance. I went to Interpol with trepidation, fearing they would discover I was wanted as an exBiafra Air Force Officer, who had never come forward at the end of the war, for clearance, by the Nigerian Military. Luckily, I obtained Interpol clearance without a hitch. I soon collected my first ever Nigerian passport, and submitted it to Odus Global Travel Agents, who agreed for a fee of £100 to get me a visa and a ticket to Switzerland. They informed me that once I arrived in Zurich, I would be easily able to take a train to Hamburg, western Germany. I collected some money from my dad, he had also borrowed £20 from our relation Mr A.
Mbadike to make up the difference. I picked up my passport, visa and plane ticket on April 20th, 1972, this was about a week before my travel date. I was now sure of departing from Nigeria and

knew the course of my life would be changed forever. My change of itinerary, i.e., to travel to western Germany, was due to the painful realisation it was impossible to raise five thousand dollars ($5,000) for the University of Minnesota, to obtain the coveted USA student's visa. I decided since everyone was expecting me to leave the country imminently, and I was unable to go to USA, then I must leave Nigeria for another country. The next best option was to travel to western Germany, via Switzerland, as the cost of a Visa to the United Kingdom, France or Russia was outrageous and well beyond my reach.

Thus, I was bound for West Germany, come 'hell or high water.' At that time there was no strict visa requirement if one had a passport.

I rushed back to the East to organise my send-off parties and to raise money to collect my passport, flight ticket and travellers' cheques. At home, various cynical individuals were frenetic in trying to mock and cajole me. Some said they thought I was already in the United States. Some asked whether a mysterious benefactor had provided me with several thousand dollars to achieve my goal. I remained upbeat, unbothered, and undaunted. I learned early in life, those who are busy developing themselves have no time at all to destroy others, whilst those who are intent on assassinating the character of others, have no time to develop themselves. The scriptures tell us to aspire to whatever is noble and great. Those who hate you for striving can never be greater than you because they do not venture, aspire nor inspire, until they expire. No-one ever wins a lottery unless they have a lottery ticket, nor can anyone's dream come true unless they have had a dream. Jesus spoke of the power of positive thinking when he said that with faith you can move mountains.

## SEND OFF PARTY: FAMILY/ABBA

Knowing full well no one around me had or would ever be able to give me $5,000 to pursue the USA Visa in Nigeria, I skilfully designed a Scholarship Letter with a gold trim and 'send-off' party cards, which read 'The family of Okoroha (Ozigbu) of Ogwuaga Abba invite the company of Mr, Mrs, Dr, Rev, Mazi, to the send-off party on 2nd March 1972, for their son Mr Adolphus Okoroha, who proceeds to USA for further studies. Contributions, however small would be appreciated.' I also bandied around the letter from my friend, Rogers.

I doctored it nicely, saying all I needed was to get to the USA and my school fees would not be a problem. This pleaded my case very well. Secretly, I simply wanted to get out of Nigeria, travel to Germany and I needed £200 to achieve it.

The letter from Rogers congratulated and informed me that due to diligent work, I had been awarded a full tuition and boarding scholarship by the University of Minnesota. All that I was then required to do was to transport myself to the University of Minnesota in the USA. When the letter was read out to the gathering of my entire family, there was instant jubilation. I became a hero, and I quietly announced my only problem was money needed for the flight ticket to the University in the USA. At that time, a round-trip flight ticket to European destinations was about £150 and to New York, USA was roughly £200. The truth was, I needed approximately £200 for my trip to Germany, and I hadn't a penny to my name.

I ignored facts and reality. I printed two hundred invitation cards for my send-off party. The date for the party was Easter day, 1972, chosen to coincide with when Jesus rose from the dead, and the seasonal period, when many people would return to the village from various townships.

If successful, it would be symbolic of my own resurrection from the tomb of poverty. The venue for the party was my Okoroha family compound. The party was attended by everyone, old and young, men and women. There was a second party for students, boys, and girls, at Abba Technical Secondary School, Abba. This was heavily organised by my cousin, Canisius (Nkrumah) and other friends from the ABBA Elite Club which I had started with other Abba students, who were referred to as the "big guys" such Ukadike (Tshombe), Anumneze (Rigogo), Nwachukwu (Elvis), Onuegbu, Oforma, Unaka, Charlie-Whiti and Uzoma, to name a few.

At the family open party, the women tasked themselves with all the edibles, while the men volunteered all the drinks. There were gourds of Palm wine, a carton of beer and crates of soft drink. The meal consisted of assorted delicacies including cassava salad, pounded yam, yam porridges, rice with stew, cocoyam porridge and jollof rice. Late Chief J. O. Ozigbu was the eldest member of the family and therefore the head of the family. He led the opening, after prayers, by asking everyone to dig deep into their pockets, or savings 'to enable this worthy son of ours to attain what forever will bring honour and pride to the family and our community at large'. He praised me robustly and prayed to God for providence and an opportunity to always present itself, to 'send sons like this very son of ours, abroad for studies, not vagabonds and ragamuffins, who often bring a bad name and shame to the family and community'. My uncle, late Engr. Ike H. Ozigbu, opened the floor with a speech and donation. He also made it clear he was supporting my going to the U.SA simply because of the extraordinary circumstances of it all. The truth being, I had out manoeuvred him and everyone else. Thence, he was prepared to pay the school fees for any of our sons or daughters who gained admission to any Nigerian University. He said he did not support people going overseas to study because, having studied in California USA himself, he knew for sure it was expensive and students suffered, working and studying at the same time. In Nigeria at that time, there were no opportunities for university students to work and study at same time. Hence, their full tuitions fee and maintenance allowances were paid by parents or sponsors.

My late uncle, Chief Lawrence Ozigbu stood up and donated some money, stating I had been an exemplary and example to children in the family, I had shown reverence and fear of God and I had taught other children how to love and respect one's mother and father. I had shown respect to the elders and worked hard towards a noble goal.

Late Chief Titus Okoroha also donated and advised me to study 'proper medicine' rather than becoming a tooth doctor (dentist) because our people do not suffer from tooth problems. He cited an example of one Dentist who studied in England and returned to Nigeria as a Dentist, but who had remained 'as poor as a church mouse'. Late Chief Fidelis Okoroha declared what was happening as 'God's miracle' and gave me his own donation. Late Martin said, 'we have a son, and we have sons,' he stated I was 'a son to be proud of,' and he also gave a donation. Everyone gave me something, be it a penny or a pound. It was most touching, especially from such family members as late Igbedie, my grandmother, late Godwin, late Gilbert, late EW Samuel, late Benson, late Louis, late Benedict, late Augustine, late Cyprian, and others. Also, people from other families. donated whatever they could Some gave more than anyone could have imagined, women and children even happily threw in one or two pennies as their 'widows' mite'. By the end of the day, I had received a quarter of what I needed. Feeling emotional, I thanked everyone in a near tearful voice. I somewhat arrogantly, though sincerely, promised that my going overseas would certainly 'open the door overseas to all the sons and daughters of my great family. The door to White man's land which had seemed shut, since one of our brothers last went there in 1948, today has opened once again for all.' There were rousing hand claps and a standing ovation.

Evidently, the interest of the nuclear family rather the community at large, was becoming the norm. The fact that people 'chipped in' at my party, was thus an exception to the prevailing norm at the time.

The Italian Machiavelli once said 'the end justifies the means. Desperate times call for desperate measures.' To experience such a wonderful outpouring of love and affection from my kith and kin was uplifting, knowing it was God's way of paving my way to greater heights and responsibilities. I was deeply moved and shed tears of joy. I solemnly stated I was going to the USA, only by the grace of God, not by my own power, money or wisdom, or classroom prowess. I stated that I was going as a pioneer, a standard bearer, and a door opener. I publicly promised to open doors of overseas studies to the poor and disadvantaged, to whom such opportunity was a very far cry. I promised, indeed boasted I would bring over one of our children every six months.

Later, I was shocked when I realised that somewhere during my speech, I had said that regrettably, some of the people at my send–off party would be dead before I returned home. However, the speech had been so powerful and promised so much, I even received a standing ovation. The day rounded off with the student's party at the school. Two girls followed me home and I vacated my bed for them, while I slept on a mat laid on the floor. Women were the last thing on my mind; perhaps I was not even sure of my own sexuality. According to the Austrian, Sigmund Freud, a psychoanalyst, in his discussion about libido, he postulates that we are each part male and part female, it is therefore a question as to what degree of femininity or masculinity makes us a man, or a woman. Anyway, I was far more focused on attaining my goal of going overseas for further studies and in search of greener pastures, than anything else.

## THE BISHOP AND THE SEMINARY

Everyone knew that priests hardly gave any money to people. They pleaded poverty and would not hand out church or parish money to other people. However, I decided to try the generosity of the servants of God, since the hand of God seemed to be on my shoulders. My past good relationship with clergy must surely count in my favour. I should be seen as a member of the inner circle, not an outsider. Thus, I took a trip to Enugu, to see Late Bishop Okoye at the Bishop's House in Uwani.

His Lordship was happy for me and gave me twenty pounds. Late Rev. Fr. Orji from Ogwu the former diocese secretary and later a parish priest, also helped me out with twenty pounds. I could not be more grateful to him. I crossed over to the Major Seminary for a call on Fr. Ohaeri from Mbaise. He was glad to know I survived the war. That was our first meeting since our days in Port Harcourt, before the civil war. I told him that I had only come to see him before travelling to the USA for further studies. He was incredibly happy for me.

I left Enugu and travelled to Nsukka, the then location of the Sacred Heart Seminary, my Alma matter, where late Rev. Monsignor Mbah, was still in charge, as the Rector. He allowed me to freely mix and chat with the seminarians. We had dinner together and he allowed me to sleep in his guest room. In the morning, he gave me twenty pounds in crisp new banknotes.

He wished me well and a safe journey to America. The fact he was glad for me was so exhilarating. Everyone who had known me from childhood had effectively given me their stamp of approval. I left there and went straight to Abba to bid my people a final goodbye. The night before my departure from the village, to Lagos, was a remarkably busy one. I was chatting and receiving well-wishers and students, who came to ensure I would always remember them and their own personal needs.

# PARTING FOREVER WITH MOTHER: DEPARTING HOME

At 11p.m, I finally had the chance to sit and talk with my mother in her bedroom. We reminisced until midnight. My mother, in a muffled voice, asked again if I was sure of going overseas. I nodded, 'yes.' She was overjoyed at the events happening in and around her. She knew it as 'the hand of God. What God cannot do, does not exist' she said. She continued to touch my hair, my face, and hands. She could hardly believe I was going overseas for further studies and would one day come home and obtain a job as a senior civil servant, as was still customary at that time. She mostly feared and worried over the possibility of our never seeing each other again. She prayed she would still be alive to see me when I returned. I assured her she would and that nothing would happen to her, that everything would be all right. She laughed and cried at the same time. Ironically, she then wished I did not have to go anymore, or that what we were celebrating was my safe return from the trip on which I was about to embark. She gave me more advice, pleading me to write letters home frequently and to always remember to pray to God the Almighty, and to study hard, remain humble and not become a womaniser, or a drunkard. She reminded me to remember the promise I had made to the family and that I should never lose sight of my vision and purpose. She advised I should not steal or take whatever was not my own. I shouldn't eat from strangers, to avoid being poisoned. I should never be envious, greedy, or engage in fights with other men or women. My mother admonished me to try to do whatever is noble, which my friends and age-mates are doing.

On the morning of 23rd April 1972, I left home for Lagos, many relatives escorted me to Isu main road, where I found transport to Onitsha. The men, women and children, and late Mr and Mrs Anele, became hysterical with deafening and unending 'Dey Umazi good-bye', (meaning the big brother of the little one's good-bye). They bade me a safe journey. We trekked on narrow tracks to Isu town, where I boarded a commercial vehicle.

After a while, one by one, everyone else dropped off, but my mother stayed with me. Two vehicles came and as I flagged them to stop, one after another, my dear, sweet mum would not let me go yet. She had not finished lecturing me. She gave advice endlessly, at the same time she gave encouragement, occasionally tearful 'Will I be alive when you return?' she asked repeatedly. I assured her a million times and swore God forbids that anything bad should happen to her. My mother and I had always had a particularly good understanding of one another, she loved me more than she loved her other children. She had in a sense come to call me 'Nnadim' (meaning the father of my husband). She exclaimed my name any time she mistakenly stumbled on something or dropped something by mistake. She had lots of faith and pride in me. She shared my earlier worries and struggles. We were together through thick and thin. We stood by each other in many tough times, and here I was about to leave her and travel to the foreign land of the white man. The land of ocean after ocean, the end of the world where the sound of cannons cannot be heard between two distant places. Truly, our dreams were being fulfilled, but it was painful and agonizing for her. Even as a young student at St Augustine's, my mother would suddenly turn up on the campus with one family problem or another. I gladly offered solutions to such problems, whatever it was, to the best of my ability. She had often relied on me, not just as her son but as her close friend. During my school days, she often sold her wrappers and Jewellery to help me out, whenever I was so skint financially and had nowhere else to go. In times of crisis, I supported her whenever I thought she was right and openly rebuked her when I thought she was in the wrong. She would immediately end any quarrel if I asked her to do so, and I occasionally settled quarrels between her and my father, or with the other wives. I stood for fairness. Most of the time, I was taught to have the Wisdom of Solomon with no favouritism. As a young man, I believed in equal rights. Many mothers prayed openly that their own sons would be like me. My mother felt deep heartache at our parting. Her hope of seeing me become a full-grown man and leave home to live on my own, appeared not to have been a serious thought, so soon. She thought of me as a child of yesterday. On my part, though excited at leaving home, I was a bag of nerves, a myriad of different thoughts racing through my mind. My absence meant my mother's caring role had been disrupted, as she had always wanted to be near me, to protect and care for me directly and to supervise me, above all. She had wanted me to be close enough for her to offer regular advice, and to monitor the type of company I kept with my peers. If she ever felt they might be of bad influence on me, she would be there like a lioness, protecting her cub. I was always her cub. Despite my age, my mother worried about what I would be eating or drinking, who would cook my food in the white man's land, and would it be to her standard? Would I find garri (fufu) over there to eat? In addition, she strongly advised me not to fight with any white man, because 'they are not strong and can die easily'. I should also not be foolish or get carried away with white women, because rumour had it that if a white woman's saliva entered any man's mouth, the man would forget his mother and siblings, and equally forget his purpose in life, or origin.

She also advised that as her first son, she would not want me to become a 'coconut' meaning, a brown or black man on the outside, but pure white on the inside, due to foreign influence. My mother said all women have the ability and inclination to deceive, confuse and distract a man's attention or education. She reminded me to remain steadfast with my 'Chineke' - the creator. Finally, she urged me to return home the very next day after my graduation. Her gravest concern was the fear of us not seeing each other ever again. When maybe the tenth vehicle came along, I took a deep breath, hugged my mom and climbed into the bus. We waved to each other frantically, until the bus disappeared around a bend on the highway. My heart was heavy, a mix of sorrow and joy, as I ventured into the unknown, in search of greener pastures. I was travelling abroad, for the first time in my life and against all odds!

## PARTING WITH MY FATHER

When I arrived in Lagos, I still had a few days and a few final changes to make, before my flight out of Nigeria. I stayed with my first cousin, Edmund, in his room and a parlour apartment at Surulere. He was then a Principal Collector with Nigerian Customs, at the Ikeja International Airport, Lagos. He was a young, fresh Zoology graduate, at the University of Nigeria, Nsukka. He lived at Olatilewa Street, Lawanson, Surulere. Eddy, as I fondly called him, was the only person with whom I finally shared my true plans. I explained I would board the flight on 28 April 1972, but contrary to widely held belief, I was not going directly to the States. I informed him that the Odus Global Agency had secured a Swiss visa for me. I was booked to fly from Lagos to Zurich in Switzerland and my journey would continue by train to Hamburg, West Germany, where I had planned to work for a while to save some money for my eventual education at the University of Minnesota, Minneapolis/St. Paul U.S.A. Eddy initially panicked on hearing of my risky, perilous plan, as it consisted of so much of an uphill struggle. We had both been in the Biafran, Nigeria War, where he was a captain with the Biafran Army. In shock and disbelief, he warned me of the danger in arriving in the cold climate of Europe, with no contact address and no warm overcoat. He was appalled to hear I was travelling with barely a hundred dollars, in traveller's cheques. His shocked face, amused me, as I reassured him, I was going in the company of my Chineke. (God, my Creator) He wondered if I was talking of the same God. Eventually, he gave up and paid for my new suit and arranged a send-off party in his apartment. We wined, dined, danced, and took photographs, for memories.

I spent the next few days in Lagos, my father borrowed more money, to make up any shortfall in my budget. I also dragged my father to a photographer's studio, where we had our photographs taken and an enlargement made. We had left behind all other photographs he had taken, back at the village: a couple of photos whilst in the Biafra Army, and as a Nigerian police constable (otherwise known as Queen Elizabeth's Police Force). I paid for the photographs and hung one in his living room. He also took a photo with me. I already had my mother's photograph and those of other family members.

Later that day, my father called some friends and family and threw a small send-off party for me in his parlour. He proudly informed his friends that his son would be leaving for the United States of America the next day. I beamed with joy, my mom and dad were so proud of me. They would henceforth walk tall among their peers, even among family members, kindred and townspeople. In those days it was a rare thing to send a first son overseas for further studies. It was every parent's dream that they live to celebrate their offspring's success. It was a thing of honour, it ushered in hope and opened doors to the family. It was a sign of success, which promised a brighter future, irrespective of class or position of the family. My parents believed my actions were dramatically paving the way to a better future for all of us. The fact is my travelling brought hope and a change in their wheel of fortune. Their own stars were about to rise and shine out of what had seemed like a perpetual cycle of poverty. My father repeated the same advice which my mother had given a few days earlier.

They both attributed everything to God's will, because my life had looked so mysterious to them, but from childhood I had remained positive and self-driven. There had been no hope of me ever going to secondary school, even less of going overseas, so soon after the Civil war. Few Igbo men could boast of a hundred pounds in their life savings. My parents were intrigued and fascinated by my life and ways. I used to tease my folks whenever they were astonished at my luck in life. I would explain, with boyish exuberance, that it was all down to being a special child of

God. I also cajoled them, telling them I was 'Christ like' and that is why, I am the first born, son of David (my father's name), son of a carpenter (his trade) not born in a hospital, but in the stable at the back of our house, from humble beginnings, destined for great heights. They would agree and wish me God's continuous blessings and protection. The send-off party at my father's place was quite brief; I thanked him and everyone who attended, in the Amukoko area, Lagos. I told them that when I reached my destination, I intended to function as a representative and a forerunner of underprivileged people. I promised to help disadvantaged children and create opportunities for their growth and success. My father's friends and neighbours and all in attendance seemed incredibly happy on hearing my mission, they cheered and applauded, offering words of wisdom. My father was immensely proud of me; God bless his soul!

## MY COUSIN EDDY

One of the visions of our fathers and forefathers, was that it is beneficial and advantageous to have large families. It is better than being a lone ranger, without the extended family circles. In my experience, I have benefited from a large circle of uncles, aunts, cousins, nieces, and nephews. There is always something one or other members of the extended family may do for you, and you may also impact their lives. Also, you have more people to look up to, or who could assist any member in times of need. Grandpa always said any meal for one can feed two, and a meal for two can feed three and so on. He was fond of the adage: 'having two or more men urinating together, raises an elevated level of foam', meaning there is strength in substantial number. He said he preferred to live in the midst of people, rather than living among trees!

Thus, in line with the above thoughts, yet to my great surprise, as soon as I left my father's house and arrived at my cousin, Eddy's place, another unexpected party awaited me. This catered for the younger generation, overseas hopefuls and young traders with surplus cash and banknotes. Drinks flowed, courtesy of Abela, Benbella, Evidence, Lawrence, and late Cletus Uju. There was plenty of food for everyone.

My cousin Lambert, also an overseas hopeful, told me there was a spiritualist around the corner, who could see a vision of my trips and if she saw any impediments, she would help me surmount them, with strong prayers to clear my way. I was never into issues of spiritualism or soothsayer, but out of curiosity, we both stole away from the party for a few minutes, to consult with her. Lambert had told me the lady was also anxious to see me. She was tall, slim, and light-skinned. I fancied her, the moment I saw her. Her room was dimly lit with a shadowy red bulb, which gave the appearance of a mellow, surreal condominium. Her fluffy bed with white satin bedspread and pillows glittered in a corner of her room. She demanded one shilling from me for candles and after a few minutes' silence, told me I was blessed and that my journey would go smoothly, with no hitches at all. She said I would not spend up to a year in western Germany before crossing over to the USA. She further hinted that in America, my schooling would run smoothly and rapidly too, but she prophesied that at the end of my academic success my life would be made miserable because of two factors.

Firstly, women; I would be entangled with too many women. Secondly, one of my uncles would never be happy with my progress and success. I knew immediately who she meant, but I didn't dwell on it, it didn't bother me,

We rushed back and partied until the early hours, then I managed to get a few hours' sleep, before my flight, scheduled for 9am that day. My cousin Eddy was a Nigerian Customs Officer at the Ikeja international airport. There were a few other friends and townspeople, who bade me farewell and wished me a safe journey. Friends and relatives were there to see me off. Some were already waiting at Ikeja Airport when I arrived. My departure, on 28th April 1972, coincided with the day Nigerian traffic started driving on the left-hand side of the road.

CHAPTER TEN

# Departure from Nigeria

I boarded the Swiss Airline. The doors closed, steps were rolled away and soon the plane taxied to the runway. I had a window seat, as the plane took off, I watched from the window. The buildings got smaller and smaller, until they completely disappeared. All I could see was clouds. It was my first experience of flying. I felt sublimely elated and overcome with joy and hope, for a bright future.
I was not scared. I had the heart and confidence of a lion and my belief in God was my strength. When the plane got to cruising level and passengers were allowed to move around, I walked to the toilet. While there, I looked at myself in the mirror, to be sure I was not dreaming. I gave myself two 'thumbs up' and said 'Adol, Sir Fabro Dudu, against all odds you are leaving the shores of Africa as the first among equals. I wondered how many of those

persons in all the schools I had attended, or people I met in the Biafra Air force could boast of being where I was at that time. With confidence, I muttered.

'Adol, you have made it, don't be afraid, your God is with you.' Afterwards, I returned to my seat, the hostesses served me food and drink, some of which I had neither seen nor tasted before, but I continued, notwithstanding and with clasped hands I silently prayed 'My Lord and my God, not my will, but yours' I remembered Jesus said, 'with faith you can move mountains.' From no hope, to being hopeful!

There is a fine line between genius and madness. I concluded, either I am a madman, or a genius, or both, because I seemed too often able to succeed, against all odds. The situations I got myself into and often wriggled out of unscathed, would sink many people. Few men would contemplate the risks I took. In all honesty, in my moments of quietness, these things baffle me.

## ARRIVAL IN ZURICH, SWITZERLAND

The pilot announced our crossing of the Sahara Desert, which I had studied in geography, and the crossing of the Mediterranean and the Red Sea. We stopped over in Vienna for an hour. I was amazed as I looked down from the aeroplane, how the roofs of most of the houses in Europe were red in colour. The red roofs were not rusty. However, the zinc roofs on the houses in Lagos were mostly rusty. The farmlands were so neatly defined. There was a marked difference to the roofs and farms that I saw, when I looked down from the plane as it took off from Lagos. We took off from Vienna and it was not long before we reached our destination of Zurich, Switzerland. Most passengers were white Europeans. I identified three other Nigerians on the plane, also heading to the Federal Republic of Germany, so we agreed to check into the same hotel and travel together. A bus took us from the airport to a big hotel. In my whole life, I had never seen so many white people.

The hotel had a bar downstairs. The women dancers were almost naked by Nigerian standards. The other three Black Africans were equally surprised, at what we were seeing before us. We surmised that no Nigerian woman, no matter how poor, would expose herself like that, for any amount of money. Even Nigerian prostitutes cover themselves fully, they would even turn off the lights before removing their clothes.

The other three boys were Yorubas, I was the only Ibo. I asked what they intended to study. Their responses were somewhat surprising: watch repairs, mechanics, and photography, respectively. I told them that I wanted to be a medical doctor. The boys had not completed secondary school education. One could say that they were semi-illiterate. I realised, because we the Ibos lived in the hinterland, far from Lagos, we were still 'in the dark' as to how easy it was to leave Nigeria and travel to Europe. In those days, why was I heading to Hamburg? The answer was not so far-fetched, atthat time, firstly, German visa was easy to get, secondly a friend told me that he had a brother, John Obi who was living in Hamburg. So, when the Travel Agent told me they were sending me to Germany, I decided to look up for John Obi. He might be the one to help me in Germany. I became determined to find him. Unfortunately, I hadn't noted the address from his young brother, as while I was at SAGS I did not envisage going to Germany. My hope was to go straight to USA.

I had to work magic to find him. I had never met the man before and he was ignorant of my existence. I began to plan what I would tell him. My plan was ridiculous, bizarre, even though I had noted in my mind, Dr Obi from Nkwerre, who lives somewhere in Hamburg. However ludicrous, when I arrived in Hamburg, I intended to seek him out. The train journey was so smooth and enjoyable, I wished such comfort had been built to link up to Nigeria, so my people could also enjoy the good life and maybe no one would need planes to travel anymore. My mind would intermittently flash back to Nigeria, my family, my friends. Whenever I regarded my reflection in a mirror, I looked more handsome, I considered even if I returned immediately, I would still be classified as a 'been to,' a returnee from Europe, or overseas.

## HAMBURG (GERMANY) MAY DAY 1972

I alighted from the train at Hauptbahnhoff, Hamburg. Everyone but me seemed to know where they were going and appeared to be in a hurry. I sat on a bench, thinking what to do next, now I had arrived. I had less than fifty dollars in my pocket, in the form of a traveller's cheque. I had to be careful not to lose it. The Hauptbahnhoff (Grand Central Station) was the major final station for trains. There seemed to be a swarm of white faces. It was May Day, a public holiday for workers, so train stations were packed with people, holiday makers and fun seekers. They moved along, mostly in twos, hugging and kissing in the full glare of the public. Some pushed their hands into their partners' trousers. I felt ashamed to see such promiscuity before my very eyes. I snapped my fingers at the foreboding abomination, in the classical Ibo gesture of a horrific and shocking sight.

I was measuring everyone with the Nigerian cultural and moral standard and yardstick. What greeted my eyes was a massive culture shock. I saw some couples stick their tongues into each other's mouth. I remembered the warning I was given at home. I concluded with my existing moral compass that what I was seeing was plain abominable, hedonism.

I was contemplating what I should do next, when a German lady walked towards me, perhaps assuming I was an American (GI) She asked me in English where I was going? I quickly replied I had come to look for my brother and had forgotten where I scribbled down his address. She asked me if I had enough money for hotel accommodation and I told her I had only fifty dollars in a traveller's cheque. She advised me not to spend it on hotel accommodation, then proposed we should go to her place, so I could spend the night there. She said it was too late now to look for my brother, I could do that the next day. Although I jumped at the offer, at the back of my mind I could hear the echo of my parent's and uncle's warning, against getting involved with any European woman, and her spitting into my mouth. I dismissed that thought, because, for me at that moment, the name of the game was 'survival.'

I had been 'pressed by nature' from the time I alighted from the train, trying not to embarrass myself by asking anyone where the toilet was. As soon as we arrived at her flat, I asked to be shown the toilet. She generously obliged me. I opened a small door, to observe a beautiful white seat, sitting on top of an enamel bowl, a small amount of water lying in the bottom. I quickly sat on it to do my business and as soon as I finished, I wondered how to make the waste disappear. I looked for a long chain, like the ones used at our Rev Fathers' house in Port Harcourt, Nigeria. There was no chain to pull. I looked everywhere, without success. She came in and flushed the toilet, by pushing a lever. 'Thank you, Madam,' I said, and she muttered 'my name is Inga' I repeated 'Thank you Inga,' she replied, 'you're welcome' We ate and drank and talked until late. At bedtime, she led me to her spare room and offered me a large duvet, I was used to sleeping covered in my small wrapper, at home. That night I slept well, as though I had no worries. The next day she escorted me to the same train station. She was going to work and wrote me her name, address, and telephone number. I was rather afraid of getting too close to her and was careful not to hang around much longer. I don't know if she had sex on her mind, and I was afraid to ask a white woman for sex. I didn't know how to start a conversation with her, when she put her night gown away, I thought she would rape me. In any event I was not desperate, perhaps I was pre-occupied with more serious thoughts battling my mind. Where should I go from here!

I became a wanderer in a foreign land, with no money, no proper contact address and nowhere to keep my belongings. Indeed, I had nowhere to lay my head, or pass the night, yet I was not bothered in the slightest. I stood gazing at the wonders of the civilized world, particularly the massive buildings and beautiful cars. It seemed that everywhere was either tarred or cemented, beautiful concrete slabs, pavements and pathways, with no expense spared. There were attractive lights of different shades and colours everywhere you turned. The speed and ordered movement of automobiles was amazing. I had never witnessed anything like it in my life. I was constantly dazed by the new discoveries. My world was expanding. Everything I had seen was starting to satisfy my inner hunger for adventure. At that point I felt that even coming here to see these wonders was money well spent. I realised seeing novel places was what vacation was all about. Back home, people who travelled overseas did so purely to receive a better education. Our workers and businesspeople hardly travelled far for holidays in those days. Having enjoyed the pleasant weather conditions in Hamburg, I went back into the Bahnhoff to sit on a bench and reflect and listen to God, to instruct me on what next step to take. As I was thinking, two teenagers came and sat at the other end of my table. I ignored their acts of puppy love, kissing, necking and giggling. I was more concerned about what to do with myself, than I cared to bother about useless teenagers. They were speaking German, which at times sounded like Hebrew or Greek to me. Language apart, their acts of shamelessly flaunting their love so boldly and in public view, was to me 'the mother of all shameful practices'. In fact, such acts were taboo in Africa.

More trains kept arriving and departing from the station, in a well-organised sequence. The whole thing seemed like a carnival. People in all types of dress trooped up and down, in and out. It certainly didn't seem the station would close for the night or would ever be plunged into darkness. I wasn't panicking or at all perturbed about where to go. I was happy with my progress so far, and confident that in time, God would provide directions. I bought postcards of Hamburg scribbled my safe arrival and sent them home to Nigeria, via Luftpost (airmail) with no reply address, yet. I bought a hot dog, covered in mustard and a glass of good German beer. Occasionally, a Black person would emerge and pass by. We acknowledged each other as a race, with mutual nodded greetings.

I travelled light, I had left all my clothes for my younger brothers, in the belief that a reasonable person does not take from scarcity to plentiful. I had only a small portmanteau, the size of a briefcase, no extra shoes or shirts. I had just a couple of items of underwear, and as much as could squeeze into my little box. One would have thought I had loads of clothing, neatly ironed, somewhere in Hamburg waiting to be worn. I had a few singlets, the rest of my belongings were mere papers and school documents, which I clung to with my life. It was almost two in the afternoon, and I was beginning to regret my cowardly parting with Inga. However, I was happy I could still telephone her later if needed. The worst she could do was shove her tongue in my mouth, but I would never allow her to spit in my mouth. That would be to disrespect my mother and let her down.

## ADENIJI – SENT BY GOD

Half the battle of this life is won if you have self-confidence and good fortune is with you, as 'fortune favours the brave'. I have always believed this, and it works for me. I am rarely afraid of anyone or any situation, and circumstances in which I find myself. The first thing I say to myself when faced with a dilemma, is to adopt Christ's saying: Ask and you will receive' and 'with faith, you can move a mountain' At worst, the person from whom one requests a favour may say no. Failure, in fact boosts my drive and gives me more impetus to strive and persevere. I love to win of course, but I see failure as a challenge which I must overcome. It makes me better and not bitter.

After about an hour and a half, a bright looking Black man in a trench coat came by and I knew instinctively that he was my man. I got up, signalled him to come to me. I asked him if he was from Nigeria, and he said 'yes.' 'Igbo'? I enquired. 'No" he said, 'but could speak some Igbo language." He was Mr Anayo Ade Adeniji, a Yoruba child, with an Igbo mother and a Yoruba father. I narrated my ordeal to Ade, that I had just arrived from Nigeria yesterday, but I was heading to Minneapolis in the USA. And that I had been trying to contact an old family friend that had lived here in Hamburg for donkey's years. I had his name, but no address. 'That's no problem' Ade reassured me.

He said we could find his address in the telephone directory. We went to a nearby phone booth and looked up Dr Obi. There it was, in the directory: 17th Hochard Street, with his phone number. We dialled the number repeatedly, the phone was not functioning, so we couldn't get through. I felt relieved in a way, had we had spoken to him on the phone, it could have ended my prospects of meeting him. He never knew me, had never heard of me, and would probably have hung up on us with a stern warning not to call back. Ade said that Hochrad was on the other side of the town, after Altona. He was about to resume his part-time evening job, however, he decided that I could go to his flat, where I could wait, and after work he would take me over to Obi's house. It was fine with me. Some may call it luck, or coincidence. I saw it as the omnipresence God at work once again. The first man I called for help was a simple man and happened to be a Nigerian, who was by birth half- Igbo and half -Yoruba parentage. He was a Christian Yoruba Tribesman.

Anayo had been in Germany for three years. He had arrived during the civil war. He was quite knowledgeable and sympathetic about the Biafra case and the Igbo cause. He took me in as a brother, with absolute trust and confidence. He lived alone. He quickly heated chicken stew and boiled some brown rice, which we ate for dinner. At first, I crunched the chicken bones, to suck out all the bone marrow, but when I realised, I still had a lot of meat on my plate, I ate only the flesh, then discarded the bones, suddenly conscious of my table manners. Anayo explained I would soon tire with chicken and eggs; however, this was the cheapest food to buy in Europe. He then advised me to relax, have a shower and get some rest; he left for work, to be back in five hours. At 8 pm, I was surprised, it was still quite bright outside. It felt as if 4pm in Nigeria. I could not help but conclude that providence also gave the white people longer days. We had studied the longer days and shorter nights at school, but here was the laboratory and practical experience. I related the climate to the biblical revelation of heaven, where there would be no more darkness.

Anayo returned home, and decided it was too late to go to Hochard, if I didn't mind, we could go the next day. I said I had no objections; the next day would be fine. I was alright so far, and I was no longer too eager to meet my 'so-called' long-lost relative Dr. Obi. He may not even welcome me, to say the least.

Ade told me there were thousands of Nigerians here in Hamburg wishing to go to USA. It had become almost impossible for a Nigerian to get a USA visa from Hamburg. The US embassy told applicants, who were not settled in Germany, to return to Nigeria and apply from there. I told him I was different and would succeed. His curiosity about me was heightened, he told me I would soon be aware of a harsh reality.

In short, he candidly advised me to forget about going to USA and instead, to start thinking in terms of studying in western Germany, since I was already there. I secretly smiled in my heart, USA, or Germany, made no difference to me, but USA was my preference.

The next morning, he got ready for school. He was studying engineering in an Engineering School. He said I could wait at the flat or follow him to school, to see the town and the school. I chose to go with him. I had my briefcase with me. While he was in his class, I went over to the engineering school administration office. I filled out the application forms and they made photocopies of my credentials and typed out an admission letter for me to study mechanical engineering. I was to do six months of German language school, before the main courses.

Anayo was surprised at my speed and how quickly all this had happened. We went back to his flat, after school, and cooked soup with greens, shaky, oxtails, beef, and chicken, and mixed semovita, a substitute for our dough (garri), He went back to his evening part time job and gave me a door key, in case I wanted to go out and about. I did and felt like I was floating along the beautiful European streets. Curiosity got the better part of me, and I strayed further, to see more things for myself. I saw some white youths, students and as soon as they saw me, they shouted "Nigger! Nigger! Nigger! Nigger!!! The more I ignored them, the louder they screamed. I realised it was me they were focused on. I turned and fled, turned a corner and disappeared. I found my way back to Anayo's flat to await his return, so we could go to find my adopted uncle, Dr Obi.

## HOCHRAD STRASSE, HAMBURG

Ade returned around 8 pm, and we set out to meet Dr Obi at Hochard Strasse. We took the train to Altona, where Ade showed me a huge Statue of Chancellor Bismarck, whose name I recalled from History lessons. We then took the long bus to our destination. We walked up the driveway and rang the doorbell. My heart skipped a beat and began to pound, on what the outcome would be, yet I still had confidence that things would work out fine. By then it was 9pm, twilight, the outside light was turned on to show our faces, before the door was opened.

I thought maybe the light was not in my favour but the next thing that happened was quite astounding. Lo and behold, I heard loud shouts from my school days: 'Sir Fabro! Fabro DuDu Lee; Sir Fabro, Fabro oooooooooo!' The different derivatives of my nickname; from when I was in the Biafra Air Force and when I was at St Augustine's Grammar School (SAGS). I started laughing, Ade joined in my happiness. But I had not the slightest idea who had recognised me and was shouting my name. Another miracle was about to happen.

Suddenly, the front door opened and an old friend Innocent Onyejiaka, alias 'Rakas' rushed out and grabbed me, almost pushing me over, in his enthusiasm. It was a hearty embrace, a bear hug.

# INNOCENT ONYEJIAKA

We went into the house and Rakas was hysterical at seeing me, shouting my name, nonstop. He kept asking me 'Do you want to eat? What drink do you want? Gosh! Sir Fabro Dudu!' 'First let me introduce my friend' I said. 'He is a Yoruba man, but his mother is Ibo. Meet Mr Ade Anayo Adeniji. He Lives here in Hamburg and is studying to be an Engineer. I met him yesterday, at Hauptbahnhoff and he generously agreed to bring me here.' I requested Rakas to kindly thank him for me. 'He is a good man, a godsend!' Rakas thanked Ade, rushed to the kitchen, and came back with bottles of beer and a plate of biscuits. He said he had a pot of soup and a pot of stew, so I should choose either eba, garri, semolina or rice. I ate fufu made from semolina. It was wonderful to eat at our home dishes, in Europe, because I had believed I wouldn't be able to find our traditional menu overseas. Psychologically, I felt, albeit prematurely, I had 'made it,' as I had started to live like a 'beento,' consuming chicken and various meats with each meal, and beer, to finish. I knew this type of 'high living' was the exclusive reserve of the rich, in Nigeria. I was becoming 'pumped-up and glowing'.

Over food and drinks, I asked Rakas, what he was doing in Germany? I recalled we had his send-off party in September of the previous year, when it was announced, he was going to Texas, USA, for further studies. He had completed his HSC at the Government College, Owerri. He had an easy life, as his father was a Chief Inspector of Police. Rakas said the reason for his presence in western Germany at the time was 'a long story.' Suffice to say, in Nigeria he couldn't get a student visa to the

USA. So, he travelled to western Germany, where he remained very frustrated, as the USA Embassy in Hamburg twice refused his visa application. As far as he was concerned, he had decided to 'stay put,' remain and study in Germany. He was still attending Sprach Schule, a German language school, before he studied medicine at any German University. I told him, I too, could not obtain a visa in Lagos (though, I knew I hadn't really tried), but I had come to Germany, with the hope of getting a visa soon, and to proceed to the University of Minnesota, Minneapolis, USA. Rakas didn't mince his words, he assured me I was not going anywhere, anytime soon. He said it was next to impossible. In Hamburg, at that time, there were thousands of Nigerian students stranded there, some of them, children and the wards of Nigerian millionaires, who had paid their school fees in full, to various American Universities, but who were nevertheless unable to get a USA visa.

Some had paid $5,000 - $7,000 in school fees yet could not get a visa. He asked if I had transferred my school fees. I said I hadn't. He then asked, 'how much money did you come with?' I responded, 'not a lot.' Laughter broke out, I even laughed at myself. I was either too confident, or woefully naïve. I assured Rakas I would easily get a USA visa, stretching out the palm of my right hand, and asking him if he wanted to place a bet with me? I earnestly hoped to get a visa soon. I told him a white lie, said I was expecting some money soon, to cover my school fees. I said I hoped he didn't mind my staying with him for some time. He replied that he was more than happy. He added that he had been very lonely, he lived alone. He said the doctor who owned the house, left the house for him, and moved to a small town with his German wife, Innocent. (Rakas) thanked Ade for his help in bringing me; it meant he would not be lonely anymore. They concurred, I should just forget about trying to get a visa to America, I should relax and settle in Germany. Like my friend Rakas, everyone at home believed that we were already in USA, as that had been the intention when we left Nigeria. We escorted Ade to the bus stop and waited with him. His bus arrived and we bade him farewell. We walked back to the house, where we reminisced, until daybreak. We caught up on old stories, wondering where our schoolmates might be now. We drank quite a considerable amount, before we fell asleep that night!

During the next couple of days, after I had settled in the house, I asked my friend how one would say 'He's looking for a job' in the German language. 'Ich will abaiten.' He replied. I was quick to memorise the words. On the third day, I left the house early. I went from office to office, from one business premises to another and repeating 'Ich will abaiten'. My good luck prevailed, and within a week, I had a job. Then I had another one! Two jobs at once! I had to shuttle between the two, while many of our friends hadn't been able to secure even one job, throughout the time they had been in Hamburg. Some had been living off money they brought from home, some were fortunate to be sent more money, from Nigeria. I started working full time: 7.30am to 4pm as a horticulture attendant at Janis Park, by the river Elbe; I was also washing plates, part time, for a posh Italian restaurant, from 8-12 pm. I was earning about five hundred Marks per week, the equivalent of $250 to $300 per week. I saved and banked most of my earnings, so that I could pay the $5,000 school fees to the University of Minnesota, before trying for a visa to the USA.

One day, one of my friends called me, and pleaded with him to let him take over one of my jobs. I thought about it and felt sorry for him. He had enjoyed an easy life. He behaved like the son of a rich man and had lost the raw animal instinct to survive. I considered it proper and right to help the less fortunate. Why should I have two jobs while my friend had none? I also needed time to attend Language School in the evenings, to learn the German language and improve my communication skills. Just in case I didn't leave Germany and needed to study at a German University in the future. I took my friend to my second job, and introduced him to my boss, as my brother. I pleaded with him to allow 'my brother' to take over my job, so that I could go back to school. The manager agreed and asked him to start work immediately.

Every day, I felt fascinated at the progress I had made so far. To me it was one miracle after another, I was, indeed, in Hamburg, Germany. In those days, overseas education was the preserve of the sons (not daughters) of the rich. This made my case seem like the proverbial 'Camel going through the eye of a needle'.

Driven by vision and intuition, I was in Europe and doing better than many of our friends, who were sons of rich parents. I had arrived without even a contact name, or address, with barely $100 to my name. No one knew, even Rakas, how I had felt on that bright, fair day, when I arrived, standing alone, in Hamburg, I had not known where to go, or what to do next. I had become one of the 'top dogs' among the Nigerian community, in Hamburg, within four weeks of my arrival, with the help of a Lutheran Church Minister, (Mr Roth) and his wife, I was comfortably settled in a furnished flat, for only a tenth of my monthly wages. The Catholic priests I met, were cold and snobbish, whilst the Lutheran were more than happy to help me, as a former Biafra Officer. The Evangelical pastors had sympathy for the Biafra cause. They were more practical and helpful. They saw the pictures on television, of the pogrom against the Ibos. They saw the starving children of Biafra. They could hardly believe they were talking to a real Biafran soldier. Pastor Roth and his church members literally offered me everything they had to eat. In some ways, they appeared patronising, in the way they reacted to my consumption of simple food items, drinks, biscuits, bananas and beer. They would excitedly beckon their friends to see me eating, a revelation that an African could eat and enjoy western food.Mostly, I remained a Lutheran throughout my stay in Germany. But in a way, the historical grudge against all Protestants (including Anglicans and Lutherans) which I had acquired as a Catholic, refused to go away, even for my Lutheran benefactors. The Catholic Church is the only church founded by Christ while he was on earth. Led by the Head Apostle, Simon Peter, the Rock, who finally died in Rome and was known as the first Pope.

I worked during the day and attended evening, Pre-medicine, and Language classes, at Hamburg University.

## HANS PETER HAUSCHILD

Two German undergraduates moved into a top room at the house, where I lived with Rakas. Their names were Hans-Peter and Harold, and they quickly became my close friends. We enjoyed each other's company and during most weekends Hans Peter took me everywhere. Once a month, we would drive down together to Ulzen where his parents lived. HansPeter and I were inseparable.

His mother was a retired hospital nursing sister, whom I also called "mutti" (mother) and she was fascinated by me. She took me-in, next to her only child, Hans-peter. When Karen, Hans Peter's girlfriend, gave birth to their first son, Hans Peter named their baby boy Chibuzo Anyiam, after me and these names appeared on the child's birth certificate. I also had other friends: Inga, a casual girlfriend (fraulin), from my first day in Germany. In my neighbourhood I met Brigitte, and before long her whole family, the Pattersons, who also became my friends, including Jens and Karen.

Hans Peter took me to his hometown Ulzen where, within hours, I was granted a resident permit. Most foreigners in the big cities such as Hamburg were finding it exceedingly difficult to change their visitors' visas to a resident permit.

Hans Peter also ate African dishes with me. At first the pepper was unbearable to him, but with time, my German friends didn't mind the pepper anymore when they ate rice and stew with me. Hans Peter took me on various outings. We visited St Pauli, or Riperban, where women, white and black were displayed in glass window "showcases". Old and young men milled around, and if you wanted a woman, you noted her display number, went around to the back door and she would spend private time with you, for twenty German Marks. The equivalent of five dollars in those days.

We visited the Zoo and that was where, for the first time ever, I saw live Elephants, Lions, Zebras, Giraffes, Tigers, Gorillas, Hyenas, Hippopotamus, Bears and many more animals, birds, and reptiles. A great number of people in the western world ignorantly believed Africans were running around naked in the jungle, amongst these animals. In the same vein, when my Church hosts saw me drink beer and smoke cigarettes, they were so excited to see me eat and act like a proper human being. Sometimes, they would give me more, then call their friends and family (kugmal er drinkt beer) to watch me and see what they had never seen before. I noted, they could differentiate between Europeans by their nationalities - Germans, French, Italian, English, Scottish, Irish, Spanish etc., but for Black people, they automatically labelled us Africans, without much care for the country of origin, of the individual. However, as it was not so long before my arrival, Biafra and starving children were so much in the news, most Germans were sympathetic to our cause. Therefore, once I was introduced to a person as a Biafran, I became an instant hero, a momentary superstar. However, I truly hated it when a white person would state 'all black people look alike.'

In my third month in Germany, my sister, Patricia came to join me. For my folks at home, and indeed for me too, my success in bringing my junior sister to Europe, within a brief time, was a monumental achievement, since my arrival in Europe.

My church friends accompanied me to the airport, to meet my sister. They immediately housed Patricia, and gave her every essential item she needed, to settle in. In the sixth month of my arrival in Europe, my cousin Lambert arrived, I picked him up from the Airport, and he lived in the same house as Patricia, and stayed with the Hemuts in Germany.

By the ninth month, my uncle Emmanuel Okoroha arrived. I soon became an undisputed flag bearer and pioneer, for my family back home in Nigeria. as I was boldly fulfilling my promise to open the door of travelling overseas for the entire family.

I wrote to the University of Minnesota (U of M) requesting a change of my matriculation date, from Spring Quarter 1972 enrolment to Spring of 1973. I received a fresh admission letter, form I-20 as I requested. I informed the Registrar that due to unforeseen circumstances beyond my control, my hope of arriving in 1972 was dampened. I could not come for the 1972 start. The new Admission letter came, and it was signed by the Admissions Registrar, Miss Mariletta Wantock. A small handwritten letter was also enclosed. She was happy to let me know she used to be a Nun, a 'Reverend Sister' in Nigeria. She also enclosed a small picture of the Sacred Heart of Jesus and another of the Immaculate Heart of Mary. She related to me as an ex-seminarian, and said she was looking forward to meeting me soon, at U of M. I began corresponding with her, in private letters, until my arrival at the campus.

Within nine months of my stay in Deutschland, I surmounted yet another higher obstacle, by saving up and remitting one year of school and boarding fees, to the U of M. It was an unprecedented success story. The presence of God remained with me, in my life. Five thousand dollars of my own hardearned money saved up and invested in my future. I could not have achieved it, if I had not been restrained and selfdisciplined. From Minnesota, a dated and stamped receipt of payment in full, for the first year of my undergraduate studies, and this enabled me to obtain the coveted U.S. Visa, at first attempt in February 1973. I had to renew my admission, which had lapsed after one year. I collected my payment slip and receipts of confirmation from the bank and took these documents to the American Embassy with my passport, in search of a student visa to study in America.

As soon as I submitted my documents, I sat down to await my fate. After what seemed like forever, I heard my name called by one of the embassy staff. I stood up and rushed to the counter, a member of staff smiled broadly as he said, 'Congratulations Mr Okoroha, here is your visa, welcome to the United States of America'. This was a dream come true. I had been seriously discouraged by my friends 'nobody gets an American visa to study in USA, from Germany' but I had beaten the jinx once again, and against all odds. My friends, when hearing of my success, just could not believe my luck. I have always believed most of life's battles are won if you have self-confidence, and I seemed to have that in tonnes. 'Fortune favours the brave,' a saying which is akin to what Jesus preached, with faith, even as little as a mustard seed, you can move a mountain. I am never afraid of taking chances in life to improve myself. I have always believed God has special plans for me, He has always provided an answer in times of difficulty. As a man of faith, God always sends a guardian angel to rescue me, and builds my faith and confidence in him. I had been in Germany for less than a year, and within one year, I had my own accommodation, a gainful employment, loyal girlfriends, I could speak the German language fluently and now I had secured the coveted American student's visa, to study at the University of Minnesota! There were hundreds of other Nigerians desperate to cross over to America, but their hopes were dashed. My own turned out to be one of those hands of providence. I was over the moon. I saw myself as a legend. Throughout my stay in Germany, I remained, inward and prayerful, as I had in Nigeria. German girls were always around me, yet out of personal conviction, and fear of falling in love, I chose to be a 'distant lover' and made no attempt at marital commitment. I stayed away from marital entrapment. I was determined to secure a university degree, before getting married. So, I held my head high, and walked tall.

There was a night during a weekend, in my early days in Germany, when I had been revelling with some fellow countrymen. We ended up in the red-light district, notoriously called 'Ripparbahn'. I sheepishly went in, like one of the lads. My experience that night was like engaging in a gaming machine, before long, my five 'funf marks' were gone. I regretted it all, and prayed to God, as well as my ancestors, to forgive me for my foolishness. I hoped I had not caught any disease.

## EFFECT OF EUROPE ON MY FAITH

My experience in Germany, Europe and later, my early days in USA, did not stop me questioning the obvious moral decadence in the Western World. It was everywhere you looked. I began to see the West as a classic example of the biblical 'painted sepulchre:' The Western World was good, beautiful, and shiny on the outside, but poor and rotten on the inside. The people appear rich, but with little religious or moral conviction. I came to realise, the very people who brought Christianity to Africa, were no longer practising what they preached. I wondered if I should regret the fact that the Europeans made our forefathers abandon their traditional ways of worshiping the same God. They tamed us with the cross of Christianity. It appeared as if they told our people to close their eyes and pray, while they then pulled up their guns and mercilessly raped and plundered the virgin African continent. They savagely looted Africa of its men, women, and material wealth. As a result, to this day, it has made generations of African people, slaves at home and in Diaspora. Africans remain consigned to second class citizenships all over the world. On the other hand, without Christianity, a person in my situation would not have had the slightest chance to be educated or see the world. The change was too radical and drastic. They could have changed our people as the Asians do: India, China and Japan who continue to retain their ways of worshipping God, yet march on, towards greater civilisation. At times, I wonder if the fault lies with us, it is our misfortune, or do we continue to blame others for our misfortune? Equity does not favour the indolent. With hindsight, I thought we could have done better despite our challenges, we cannot blame others forever for our misfortune, I think it's high time we took a bold step and turned the corner! In the Nigeria of those days, a woman dares not walk around in trousers or pants, dare not be seen in a bikini. Any woman who looked half naked, or left her hair uncovered, would not be permitted to enter the church, let alone receive the blessed Eucharist, in such attire.

She would have been booed out of church before the priest even had a chance to allow her to partake in Holy Communion. Maybe I had been too indoctrinated or naïve, but going to any other church, such as Pastor Roth's Lutheran Church, left me with a sense of guilt and betrayal. I often felt that by so doing I again betrayed my faith, for the second time. 'Christ came to save us', as the bible told us. That Christ established the Church, appointed Peter, one of his apostles to head the church and mentioned that 'the gates of hell will not prevail against it'. In his words he told Peter 'Feed my lambs.' Christ envisaged 'onefold, one Shepherd' and there should be no divisions. Jesus says, 'there is a road to heaven' and 'he who tries to enter the house through the window is a thief'. Christ also states 'whatever sin that you may have committed, and you ask for forgiveness, that it is forgiven already. Christ gave an eternal promise' 'I am with you to the end of time and will send the Holy Spirit to direct and teach you all things' so when the head of the Catholic Church, Pope speaks, he is said to be led by the Holy Spirit. After Christ died, Peter became the head of the church. As evident in the biblical day of the Pentecost, and after the demise of Peter, the rest of the Christians elected a successor, that position became known as the 'El papa' - The Pope. Then after over 1,500 years, for one personal problem, or selfish reason or another, such as marriage scandal, certain people began to question the authority and infallibility of the Pope. They broke away to form various other churches, which are today scattered and proliferate all over the world.

Christians of all denominations believe that Bible is the word of God, the problem is each group translates or interprets the words to suit them. Perhaps having a Pope is ingenious, interpretation would be uniform among all members of Christendom. Many people have been killed on the account of different interpretations, such as the early England, and the Spanish inquisition and in Northern Ireland Christian religious stalemate.

There are no half-truths; things can either be true or false, no mid-way. Christ saw the vision and told his bride, the church, 'there will be many false prophets' but, he equally assured them 'not all that call 'father, father' will enter the kingdom of God'. He told the apostles he was sending them like a lamb among wolves, into the world. So, on this premise, I found it difficult to accept other churches to be in the same breath as the Catholic Church. It is also heart rending, when I see the socalled 'true church' Catholicism, fail to live up to its expectations. Double standard is the same as mediocrity. The European catholic priests I met in Hamburg, were cold, insensitive, and almost faceless. The catholic priests I met in Europe, wore trousers and shirts, a disguise to move round incognito. Parish priests in Nigeria always wore long robes or soutane. In Europe, the Masses were not well attended. The Reverend Fathers had little or no regard for the laity in general. There was evidence of a record number of priests, who were disillusioned, and had abandoned the priesthood altogether. Some fell in love and left the church. There were hundreds of lapsed priests, as well as lapsed and relapsed Catholics. It appears this trend is a continuing unabated phenomenon. The remaining Catholics, who still attended services in Europe, especially women and minorities, were justifiably frustrated.

Onlookers, who felt belittled, talentless and without a calling, at the tail end of the salvation ladder, with little or no role in the divine organisation, in which they belonged. I observed these people became happy when they found a church that made them feel appreciated and allowed them to participate in the church program. Sadly, this gave opportunity to charlatans, who paraded as pastors, then milked the vulnerable dry. They operated these latter-day churches as a personal family business.

A human being has feet of clay and is ever searching for hope.

I am opposed to the notion of celibacy; it is one of the reasons I recanted my vocation to the priesthood. Christ never said only those who had no spouses were holy. Indeed, some of the apostles had wives, and all the great prophets, and men of God, who heard God and saw God's wonders had a wife or wives, such as Abraham, David, Moses, Joshua, Solomon, Eli, Samuel, and Peter. St. Paul said it was better to marry than to burn with lust. How can a priest know how another person feels about his or her spouse or children; his or her rebellion, anger, or hunger, when the priest is comfortably cut off from these realities of life?

Having weighed up all the confusion, I have chosen to be like most modern-day Christians. If am completing a form, I always indicate I am a Catholic. But on Sundays, I attend any church that suits me for that week or stay at home and pray in the privacy of my inner self, to God the Almighty. Christ said that the time is coming and has already come when you need no longer go to Jerusalem to worship God. God is Spirit and those who worship Him must worship in spirit.

## PASTOR ROTH AND THE UHLIG FAMILY

While in Germany, I attended church in the company of my landlady, Mrs Uhlig, as I acquired the room (Zimmer) through her Pastor, Rev Roth, within hours of my telling him I was looking for a place to rent. This was a practical example of helping people here and now. As St Paul said, 'faith without works is dead' The protestant pastors were more eager to assist me. They were more sympathetic to my plight and displayed more humanity. They understood when a breadwinner was scraping to make ends meet, what it meant to be out of work, or in a foreign land, or in need a shelter. Man is God to man, as God shows his Majesty through other human beings. After all, He is God of surprises. God the Surprise!

Pastor Roth recommended me to the Uhligs. The couple had two grown up daughters who were 15 and 17 years old, respectively. They were unmarried university students. They were intrigued by me, and my deep brown colour. They loved to touch me. They had seen black people, Negros, in American films, and then they had first-hand opportunity to live in the same house with one. I lived in one room and shared the parlour, kitchen, and bathroom with them. I lived with the family until 10th of March 1973, when I left West Germany, for the USA. Our people say, 'the dog does not eat the bones that are hung on its neck'. To say those girls were a temptation would be an understatement. They walked around the house in skimpy underwear, they were all over me, however, I managed to supress my animal instincts to pursue them. I had a more burning ambition, to which I gave top priority: to get to the USA and study in English, my second language, and to obtain a University Degree, otherwise known as a meal ticket.

After paying my school fees, I was short of money and Pastor Roth and his church paid for my Trans World Airlines (TWA) plane ticket to the USA. The Nigerian community in Hamburg gave me a send-off party. The main organisers were Innocent, and Jegede who claimed to have been repatriated to Germany from London and had decided to make a living in Ripperban as a stud, a gigolo, a pimp. At my send-off party also, were my main German family friends, namely the Hauschilds, Petersen, Uhligs and the Roths.

*My Lawfirm, Graceland Solicitors, at Woolwich, Arsenal in London.*

*This is Graceland Solicitors office front in Lewisham, London.*

*On holiday in China with my wife, Ling. A visit to Buddhist Temple.*

*The University I Attended at Central Lancashire United Kingdom, where I studied Law in 1999.*

*MYSELF at Stonehenge in United Kingdom.*

*Myself in USA, 1977.*

*With my youngest son, Amara, in Cape Town, South Africa.*

**CHAPTER ELEVEN**

------------------------

# Arriving In USA – St. Paul/ Minneapolis: Twin Cities

## TERRY ROBINSON

The flight from Hamburg to New York, via London, on 10th March 1973, was a memorable day, one I will always cherish. In New York we changed flights, Midwestern Airlines to Twin Cities Minneapolis/St Paul international Airport. As soon as I disembarked and made my way to the baggage carousel, I experienced another miracle. Mr. Terry Robinson, a lanky, Black American seven-footer, who worked as a Trolley Porter, saw me, then took to me as though I was his long-lost ancestral cousin. He was only too glad and proud, to see an African come to enroll at the premier University of Minnesota.

He took me and my luggage to a corner and told me to wait there until he finished his shift, an hour later. He bought snacks and beverages to sustain me while I waited. He clocked out at 10 pm, and drove me through the campus, indicating everywhere was closed. I would have to attend the University the next day to enrol. That night, I was mesmerized by lights beaming on the huge University buildings on the campus. Terry took me to his home. We drove from the East bank to the West bank of the University; the two sections of the University are separated by the Mississippi river. We crossed the river into Hennepin County, to Terry's house on the north side of Minneapolis.

When we arrived, his wife, a schoolteacher, ten-year-old son and seven-year-old daughter were already asleep. We tiptoed around, spoke in hushed tones, and ate a sandwich for dinner. He gave me a pillow and blanket and I slept on a long couch in the living room. Early next morning, Terry was first up and prepared a lavish breakfast of fried bacon strips, scrambled egg, tomatoes, mushrooms and sausages. It was followed by toast and jam, honey, orange juice, a pot of tea and a pot of roasted coffee. His family and I enjoyed breakfast together, before his wife drove off to work. His wife and children seemed to like me; it was as though we had known each other for ages. Terry put my things in the boot of his Cadillac, the two kids jumped in, and we dropped them off where they caught the school buses. The children were being 'bussed,' a term used to describe a phenomenon: pupils from predominantly black or poorer neighbourhoods, were driven on school busses across town, to attend school in more affluent, predominantly white neighbourhoods. Terry and I then headed to the University, where the admissions Secretary, Miss Mariletta Wantock was eagerly awaiting my arrival. Terry left me in her care and promised to telephone her later to find out where I was staying.

## MISS MARILETA WANTOCK

I enrolled without delay. Miss Wantock took me to where I was duly registered, the school fee was paid from my remitted money, and a student photo-Id issued. She walked with me to the International Students Centre, and she introduced me to Mr Moore, the Director of International Students Welfare. Within hours, I was shown my own exclusive room, at the Manche International House, a student hostel. Locking my door behind me, I unpacked and calmly thanked providence for the grace shown to me. My life in America had taken off, beyond all my expectations, yet again, and Against All Odds!

Miss Wantock came to see me on her way home from work, bringing me some edibles, apples, oranges etc. Terry called me early the next morning and told me he was bringing his wife's younger sister along, to see whether I would like her for a girlfriend.

Tanya was a sophomore, a second-year undergraduate student, at St. Catherine's Catholic Girls College, in St Paul. Minnesota. One look at her and I concluded 'Nope!'- she was simply not my type. She was tall, a half-caste, very fair complexion, a big Afro hairdo and plump. She was big breasted and equally well endowed on the backside, but I found these features intimidating. Terry believed all African men love big women. Unfortunately, I was different and certainly not like a typical African man in that area, I am attracted only to skinny women. I could not embarrass either of them by saying no; so, I pretended to be happy about the situation. It took about two months of trying, without success, before Tanya and I agreed that it would not happen, we were not an item.

I moved on with my social life and continued to make new friends, expanding my circle with other people, including Miss Wantock, the admission secretary at the University. She was a white lady, tall, slim, not so skinny, and a bit older than me. She would pick me up on alternate Friday evenings, to spend the weekend at her home. She honestly and deeply cared for me. She bought groceries, shirts, sweaters, and jumpers for me. We discussed how and why she left the sisterhood, and my reasons for leaving the priesthood. We agreed that having had such a religious upbringing, training, and conditioning, had been invaluable. We went to her parish church together; every Sunday and we received Holy Communion. Within a week, she gave me a letter addressed to the Personnel Manager at GRACO, a factory at North Minneapolis. I was instantly employed, full time, on night shifts, so I could attend school during the days. As an ex-nun, Miss Wantock wanted us to get to know each other, in fact commit ourselves to one other, before jumping into bed together. Whenever I was at her house, she gave me the red-carpet treatment. I didn't want to commit, didn't even know how to. She lavished hospitality on me, but I ended up sleeping in her spare room. Life is like that sometimes. What you want, you cannot have, and what you have you do not want! My schooling was going well, and I was also earning over $200 per week.

In 1973, I was a first-year, pre-med undergraduate. In that first quarter, in addition to another four courses, I took English 101, in which I scored an 'A' grade. In time, I met up with over a hundred Nigerians on the campus. Among other Ibos, I formed close friends with Oguagha, Okudo, Oyibo Achebe all from Ogidi. Dr Anyawu from Mbaise, Dr Ugboaja from Umuahia, Agbim from Ojoto, Njaka from Arondizogu and others. There were many Nigerians and other African students diligently pursuing bachelors, masters, or Doctorate degrees, in various academic and professional fields. The University of Minnesota was then the largest Land Grant University in America, with a student population of over sixty thousand students.

## MY FIRST CAR

After I secured the night shift job at Graco, I also took a three-hour part time job on campus, as the hospital café's busboy and washing machine operator. At Graco I worked at the Assembly line, coupling some gadgets. The work was so intense that sometimes, I woke with a panic attack, believing hundreds of gadgets had accumulated at my station, slowing the smooth running of the assembly line. I was always relieved it was only a dream.

At the café, I usually wheeled the trays to the washing machine room. Thereafter, I ensured the plates, trays, and cutlery were arranged in the machine, then pushed the green button. Afterwards, I collected all the items at the other end, stacked them up and wheeled them back to the canteen. In 1973-74, the bus boy job paid about $4.60 per hour. Later I left the job and took an 'on campus' four hour per day job as a janitor, which paid $6 per hour. Within a few months of holding two jobs, I bought a second-hand Skylark car for $300. The car was loaded. It was an automatic, with power steering, power window and a sunroof - the top could be rolled back during summer. At the onset, I bought a bicycle to aid my travel to and from the jobs. I started my night shift: Monday to Friday 4pm to 10pm, for $6 per hour. My take home pay every fortnight was well over $300. I was cycling to work one day, when a pink Buick Skylark, caught my eye, on display in a car sales lot. I went to take a closer look, I enquired about the age, running condition and the likelihood of a discount, on the displayed price tag of $300. They told me it was a 1966 model, ran 'like a baby', and had only one owner.

The car was an Automatic Drive; you pressed on the brake pedal and used your hand to move the gear stick: D to drive, P to park, R for reversing. Though I had never driven any car before in my life, I assumed it would be easy to drive an automatic, so I duly paid the agreed sum and was given a receipt. The used cars salesperson, also known as the most untrusted professional in America, drove the car onto the street for me, waved me goodbye and wished me luck! I shot off like a bullet, slammed on the brake at first sight of the red light, and the engine stopped. It was a motorway. All the drivers behind me started honking and hooting their horns, urging me to move, before the green light turned red again. I didn't know how to restart the car, despite fiddling with the ignition keys several times and I was starting to panic. One kind driver left his car, came over to me and asked what was wrong. I told him my car wouldn't start. The guy said that to start the car, I must select P for park, put my right foot on the brake, before turning the key in the ignition. I did as he said, and my car roared into life. I selected the D, pressed the gas pedal and off I went. The next problem for me was how to slow the car down, and not run into the car in front of me.

I tried to overtake by the curb side with little success, and in the frenzy that followed, I crashed the car into a lamp post. Luckily, there was no fatality. My over-confidence could have cost me my life and the lives of others.

Police came to the scene and demanded my name, address and driving licence. I told the police I did not have a US Driving Licence, because I was a Nigerian and not an American. The police officer enquired if I had a Nigerian Driving Licence and how long I had been in the USA. I answered that I used to drive in Nigeria, but I had no driver's licence. The Officers were bemused, mystified, and bewildered to say the least. In the end my car was impounded. I was handcuffed, bundled into a police car and taken to the Hennepen County Jail. I spent the night in custody, to appear before the Judge on the following day. There were four inmates in the cell with me, there were double bunk beds. Fortunately, I was given a top bunk. As I lay there that night, I pondered on how my mother would have reacted to hearing of my unfortunate situation. I shuddered at the realisation I could have killed or injured myself, and other people.

The next day, the learned Judge ordered my release, after I had paid both a fine and court fee. I was also made to sign an undertaking, to undergo a driver learner course, and to pass the State of Minnesota driver's test and obtain a Driving Licence. I went back to the court within the stipulated twenty-eight days, presented my licence and collected my car, after paying the costs of demurrages.

I had arrived in Minnesota in Spring, 1973, the leaves were fresh and green, then Summer arrived, and everything was in bloom and colourful. The children went mad for the season. Guys and Gals lay sunbathing, on grass or sand. Bikinis and skimpy attire, everywhere. One must be literally dead not to feel amorous at seeing these people sunbathing half-naked! September came, and with it the Fall, leaves started changing colour, then withered and died. The grounds were littered with fallen leaves. By December, January it was the dead of winter in Minnesota. The snow on the ground was up to two feet high. Children played in the snow and built different shapes and sizes of the Snowman, but for me and my fellow Africans the winter weather was always bitterly cold, harsh, and atrocious. In my sophomore year, (second year), I moved into a low cost, new CEDAR Housing Development accommodation which was a one-bedroom flat. The toilet had a bathtub, hand basin, a small cabinet with a clear lighted mirror (glass) and the commode (toilet seat). The kitchen was almost part of the sitting room. A double sliding door opened to a Balcony. I bought wall to wall blinds and curtains, used leather suite- threeseater, a two-seater and a single seater, a glass coffee table, a glass dining table with four matching black chairs. My dining table doubled as my study table. I lived alone, working hard to get a first Degree. Classes were either on the East Bank buildings or West Bank buildings of the Mississippi River. A bridge over the river connected the two campuses. In any one year, two to three white students jumped to their death from that bridge. At that time Nigerians shuddered at how easily the Caucasians can despair to the point of taking their own lives. It appears that a high number of individuals with a white background become suicidal at the slightest disappointment of life. My opinion and belief towards suicidal tendencies is that it could be attributed to an individual's in-depth lack of spiritual awareness, and absence of moral fortitude and moral compass.

However, this is entirely my opinion and not a generalisation on the subject matter.

The year 1974 was a horrible year for the Nigerian community in Minnesota, because we lost Dr Anyawu and Mr Agbim through car accidents. My cousin Lambert also arrived in Minnesota from Germany, and he soon went to Dallas to commence his undergraduate studies. His sister Elizabeth also came, and she was also in Dallas. Two years after I left Nigeria and through my vision and effort, six members of my family were now overseas, I was elated and proud of myself.

I make friends easily and have many: students, workers, black, white, boys, and girls. I had no special friend. I love my own company. It gives me a cool head to think and plan. People fail not because they plan to fail, but because they fail to plan. In the winter of 1973, at St Paul Minnesota nightclub, a petit afro American girl by the name of Bertha Brown, came up to me and whispered in my ear she wanted to dance with me. I sprung to my feet and boogied about to four tunes from the jukebox. A dollar paid for four records at the rate of a quarter (25 cents) per tune. She bought us drinks. She drank orange juice on vodka, whilst I drank rum on the rocks. Bertha wanted me to go home with her and I obliged. Our relationship blossomed and went nicely until late spring 1974. She told me she was unwell and that she was going home to her parents in Chicago. I continued to speak to her almost daily over the phone, but sadly Bertha passed away, due to cancer of the breast, in the fall of 1974.

Girlfriends came and went. When it came to girlfriends, I was colour blind, as the colour was not as important to me as the content of character of the person. Miss Jackie of the Filipino extract called me a jerk and left me. Miss Marsha said she suspected I was gay and that in her opinion I did not respect or like women, so she left. What some of these women said about me never ceased to crack me up, because it showed that those gals did not know me well, or at all. Sheryl and Jennifer were happy and proud of me. Both took me home to their respective parents, one at Easter and the other at Christmas. Going to those remote places outside Minneapolis/ St Paul scared me a bit but I came back safe and well. In fact, each time, I was overwhelmed with the warmth, kindness, and generosity which those middle-aged white folks, the parents, showed me, as their precious daughter's boyfriend. Sheryl also took me to visit her ex-boyfriend and we got along so well that when next the former boyfriend, Steve and his new girlfriend came up to Minneapolis from St Cloud, Minnesota, to watch the football game between Minnesota Vikings v Dallas Cowboys, or San Francisco 49ers, the couple spent the weekend with us. They slept in their own sleeping bag in the sitting room of our onebedroom flat. Sheryl told me that she and Steve had been High School sweethearts. They were each other's first love before he started cheating on her and they broke up for good. They were happy to get out of each other's hair when Sheryl got admission to study Physiotherapy at U of M and moved to Minneapolis. Upon her arrival in the big city, she briefly dated Calin, a medical student, and thereafter fell into my hands, when she ended their relationship and moved next door to me. Jenny, on the other hand, had Mathematics as her major ourse of study. She and her parents took me golfing in Duluth, Minnesota, near a public beach. That was the first time I played golf and really managed golf clubs as a player, rather than as a caddie, which I engaged in on a part time basis, as a young man growing up in Port Harcourt.

Every relationship I engaged in was a learning curve and each experience widened my horizon. I kept saying that 'it is better to have loved and lost than not to have loved at all'. Once you know how to fall in love, or how to make money, you can fall in love, or make money again.

Then I met Carolyn Connie Gene Walker in early 1974. She was born in Wayne, Arkansas, in 1950 and moved up North, to the Twin Cities, Minneapolis/St Paul to be close to her two older sisters Charlene and Barbara Walker. Carolyn was tall, skinny, with the same shade of fair complexion as me. She also wore big Afro as was normal in the nineteen seventies Black America.

We hit it off straight away.

In 1974, I received a letter from my cousin Eddy, that my father had passed away, and had been given a befitting burial at his funeral. Dad was only 75 years old, news heard it that he had mistakenly cooked and eaten rice he collected from a ship which was contaminated with rat poison. As if I had a premonition, I had telephoned him a few days before his death and assured him I was doing well and would soon return home, after my graduation in 1975. I promised to build him a storey house and buy him a new car and hire a qualified driver, to be at his beck and call, to drive him anywhere he wished to go, or to visit. This was never meant to be, they say man proposes and God disposes, that was how I lost my sweet gallant father – The Great old War Horse of his time! May his soul continue to rest in peace in the bosom of our Lord Jesus Christ, in accordance with our Christian faith.

I almost had a girlfriend in every location that I related to or involved with, be it as student or as an employee. My next doorneighbour at Cedar flats, Miss Cheryl Loggan was like a common law wife to me for over 6 months. Ms Cathy, my pharmacy student course-mate became inseparable from me, since the first day we had a Pathology class, which involved the dissection of real human male and female cadavers (dead bodies/corpses). Miss Jane was forever indebted to me because my examination answer-papers were left wide open for her to copy, and she passed every exam that I scored a pass mark for, as well.

## GRADUATION IN 1975

I was working full time and schooling at the same time, and this took its toll. I did not make it into medical school, so I settled on getting a degree in pharmacy. Almost halfway through the pharmacy program, I ran into difficulties because I did not have a full grasp of organic Chemistry at the time. As far I was concerned, in life, when one door closes, another door opens.

I sought and was promptly accepted into the School of Business Administration at the same University. I progressed quickly as a Junior (third year) into my Senior (fourth year). In June 1975, two years after my arrival in the USA, I got a Bachelor of Science Degree (B.Sc.) in Business Administration from the University of Minnesota. I had considered going home after graduation in June of that year. I wrote home to announce my plan of returning to Nigeria, but letters came advising that I should not attempt coming home to Nigeria at that time, because things were not well back home. It was rumoured and later confirmed, that General Murtala Mohammed had conducted a coup in July 1975. General Gowon, who led Nigeria through the civil war, had been ousted, and no one knew where the nation was heading. It was later reported that the new leader had sacked thousands of civil servants, including police and military officials, diplomats, and the likes. I heeded the advice from my folks back home and I decided to pursue further studies in America, hoping that things would get better soon. I was convinced that the best way forward was to be a professional such as, a medical doctor, a lawyer or at least a pharmacist. This made me consider returning to school to study pharmacy or law.

## JOHN HANCOCK INSURANCE OF BOSTON, MASS

About two weeks before the graduation ceremonies, in 1975, several firms came to the U of M campus to scout for talent.

Corporate bodies came and interviewed prospective candidates for employment offers. I was interviewed, among others, by IBM and John Hancock Insurance Company of Boston,

Massachusetts. I was hired as an insurance sales Agent at the St Paul MN Agency under Mr Ackerman. I started full time the following Monday after my convocation ceremony. I was started on $18, 000 per annum, guaranteed for 6 months, and thereafter I reverted to about 60% commission of my monthly gross premium production. I did that job with pride, passion, and enthusiasm. I was naturally a people's person, gregarious, sociable, and amiable. I enjoyed working outdoors and meeting people in their homes. With a new job and a new partner in tow, I soon left the Minneapolis flat at Cedar low-cost housing and moved into a condominium with a Penthouse, in St Paul area of Twin Cities.

I bought a brand-new Camaro car and was making the monthly instalment payments. Going to work in several styles of two or three-piece suits, as well as owning a flashy car and living in a condominium, a great neighbourhood at that time, gave me a boost of confidence. In a way, the good times had arrived.

## MY SISTER PAT VISITED USA

News reached me in 1974 that my sister Pat whom I left in Hamburg Germany had fallen in love with my good friend, Mr Innocent. They had married and had a son together. In 1976, I sent money to my sister to come to America and visit me. I drove to the Twin Cities Airport and brought her back to my residence. I treated her lavishly and assured her that if she wanted to remain in America, I would make sure that she was comfortable. But in the end, she chose to return to her husband and son, Karl Chino in Bad Neuham, western Germany. My sister, Patricia met my growing family in America which consisted of a Nigerian born girlfriend Azuka, and my American born wife, Carolyn and daughter, Cynthia Chinyere
(Chichi).

## CAROLYN WALKER

At a party in 1974, I had met a young twenty-four-yearold lady, from Arkansas. She had just come up North to Minnesota, to visit her two elder sisters. Her name was Carolyn Walker. Her sisters, Charlene and Barbara Walker lived at St Paul, Minnesota.

Carolyn was a registered nurse and was an inch or so taller than me. Her hair was curly, and she said that her ancestors were Creole. She suited me immediately and we got along swiftly. She was so funny and jokingly used to tease me as having nappy hair and a pork nose. She was carefree, outgoing, free spirited and down to earth. Carol, as I called her, believed that those of us from Africa who had come to study in America deserved all the credit. At the time many Americans, even educated ones, also believed that lions, tigers and other big animals were roaming freely in the African towns and villages. The belief was that Africa was a very primitive, strange, and ancient place and that Africans did not go to school. Some were even surprised when an African spoke fluent English with a better accent. Ironically, some of these outlandish beliefs were part of the reasons that spurred Carolyn to fall in love with me, without hesitation. She believed I was a good looking and intelligent man.

In mid1974 Carol told me she was pregnant. At first, I was not sure we were ready to have a child together. At the time, I still believed in my ethos of not bringing a child into this world until I had attained a University Degree and obtained employment commensurate with my qualification. I suggested she had an abortion, but she refused firmly and bluntly, over her dead body. I was compelled to accept her decision to keep the baby. In 1975 our baby daughter was born, and we got married at St Paul, Minnesota Town Hall.

Carol and I decided to keep the two separate flats. One in St Paul's and the other in Minneapolis. We stayed mostly at mine during the week and hers over the weekends.

# DAUGHTER CHICHI

Our daughter Cynthia Chichi Okoro was born in April 1975, it was a momentous year for me personally. I was thirty years old at that time. I got married, had my first child and I graduated from the University in that same year. I began to think that any man should be happy to get a woman who is prepared to give him a child, I was thinking that I will always still be a young man and had my life ahead of me. My belief now is that men delude themselves that they control things, but women rule us in very subtle ways. With hindsight, I began to regret that Patience aborted our first child in 1969. I wished she had stubbornly kept the pregnancy and by then I would have had a six-year-old child.

Carol used to tell me that she was a Creole Black American. There was some confusion in those days about what people of darker skin colour wanted to be called. Some did not want to be referred to as Black; others did not want to be called Negro, while some wanted to be called Black Americans. Anytime I was critical about her ways, she would tell me to kiss her black ass, and reminded me that I had nappy hair, and I was a Nigger, just like her. Black people could kill a white person who called them nigger but in our black homes and circles we sometimes, jokingly referred to each other with the N word, such as what's up N? Come here N.

My white neighbour's children went out every night, smashing car windows stealing hub caps, CB radios, and cassette tapes from cars. They then sold their loot for a pittance just to get a nickel or dime worth of marijuana aka reefers. Every Sunday she never failed to cook elaborate Soul food for Sunday lunch. The recipe consisted of black eye peas (beans), chitterlings or intestines of beef or pork, corn bread, roasted or barbequed ribs and chicken, gravy, greens, corn on cobs, black pudding and so on. Her sisters and their husbands would, on good summer weekends, organise picnics for all in the family. We would picnic in a park or go to a beach, sometimes we even went out of the state to as far as neighbouring Wisconsin..

Black neighbourhoods are sometimes simply referred to as the 'Hood' smoking of 'weed' or 'reefers' was rampant. It seemed to be a placebo that helped the masses get over the general poverty and hardship that was palpable all around them. Many were on one type of social welfare benefit or another and did not have to work or take employment. Women with children received the food stamps. Like the former president Bill Clinton, I could never inhale weed because I have always had a light head. Weed or alcohol made me low, drowsy, and sleepy, rather than 'high' I abstained from those two habits, but since the Biafra War, I became a chain smoker of cigarettes. I smoked like a chimney. Johnny Reid, Barbara's husband, who was an ex-service man, then was in receipt of the GI benefits and was always as high as a kite. There were many people of colour who held good posts and earned respectable amounts of money.

Those who had low paid factory jobs lived from hand to mouth. They were paid barely enough to pay their bills and scrape through. In the Hood invariably gun shots rang out over some bullshit or other, such as domestic argument, boyfriend girlfriend issues, debt, drug, gambling, betting, retaliation and so forth. In these circumstances, black men, women, or kids got killed. It was seen as outrageous if a white person killed a person of colour. However, the outrage was subdued if the killing was black on black. The hood boasted of huge, long, and shiny cars such as Cadillac, Eldorado, Lincoln Continentals, and Cougars et cetera. Life with Carol was fun, wonderful at the beginning. She was a nurse and contributed to the household outgoings. She made sure that I obtained my resident card, called a Green card in America. At times, she could not bear my constant studying. I was a total bookworm and a bore. If she wanted both of us to go out and I decided to study, she would sometimes tell me off, by shouting go to hell! She would go out without me regardless, either with her friends, or to spend time with her family in St Paul, whilst our home was in Minneapolis. This caused a strain in our relationship.

In 1976 her father, Johnny Walker died in Little Rock, Arkansas. We drove to Kansas City, collected her niece, Kitty and her brother Pete and drove to Arkansas via Oklahoma for the funeral. I ended up driving back alone, because Carol chose to remain with the baby Cynthia and her mother, Marie Walker. Carol flew back to Minneapolis with our daughter after about a month in Arkansas.

## AZUKA UCHE

At the Nigerian Christmas party, in Minneapolis in 1975, I met a Nigeria Ibo girl called Uche. It was a grand lavish party. I went to the party with Kalu from Ohaofia and Okudo from Ogidi. I was in my black three-piece striped suit. Okudo and I were in the Pharmacy program together and we fondly called each other 'Agu,' the lion! That night, I danced with Uche, and during the dancing and rocking, she told me that she came to Minneapolis from Iowa City, Iowa. I then learnt that she was from Uguta. She was a sister of one of my schoolmates at St Augustine's Grammar School, Nkwerre. Once his name was mentioned, our fates were sealed. We went to my flat that night and thereafter she became my long-distance girlfriend.

From that time, Uche became my girlfriend. As a Nigerian, she was more like my common law wife. She controlled and looked after me like a mother she would say 'eat this, don't wear that' and so on. She graduated Cum Laude, from Morningside college. After her graduation, she moved to Minneapolis/St Paul, Minnesota. She believed in the traditional roles of people in the household. We ate at least a meal a day, which were well prepared as Nigerian dishes.

In early 1976, Uche insisted that we go to meet her older sister who lived in Manhattan, New York. We drove her car to New York from the state of Minnesota, crossing the states of Wisconsin, Illinois, Ohio, Pennsylvania, and New Jersey.

I left her in New York as she was to attend Cyriacus University. I visited a couple friends in Long Island and Bronx, before I flew back to St Paul MN. Four weeks later, she had sold her car and flew back to St Paul and announced that she was pregnant. I advised her she should terminate the pregnancy, until we were well prepared to raise a child together. I was also conscious I was still married to Carol, who was on her sick bed. She considered it and went to the abortion clinic where the pregnancy was sadly aborted.

That year, over five abortion clinic doctors were shot, or petrol bombed by the Pro-Life Groups for killing the voiceless, unborn babies. Prolife Groups believed that they were God's army, ordered by God himself to protect the unborn foetuses. Their motive arguably was right, but the problem was that they sought to impose their own belief on others, and by killing these doctors, the Prolife Groups took the law into their own hands, acting as the lawmakers, the police, the judge, and executioners. Anarchy is when everyone does as they please and take the law into their own hands.

About the same time, I considered going to enrol for a master's degree programme, but chose instead to go back to school and complete the professional Degree in Pharmacy which I had abandoned half-way at the U of M. I applied and I was accepted in the School of Pharmacy, Creighton University in Omaha, Nebraska. Uche and I moved to Omaha in March 1977. We spent our first night with Mr Uwanaka from Isu, Umuozu. He shared the house with Eric from Anara, Mbano. They had Black American girlfriends. We soon rented our own flat in my sole name and moved in. Uche and I then thereafter hired a U-Hall truck, and we went back to twin cities and Iowa and collected our personal effects which we had left behind.

The Nigerian Community in Omaha, Nebraska was somewhat different from my college days in Minneapolis. At Omaha, they were not so academically minded. They partied a lot. People queued up to host weekend parties. There was obvious competition about the make of car you drive, the way your house or flat was furnished, the outfit you wore and how sophisticated your wife or girlfriend appeared. Many guys were driving flashy cars such as Cadillac, Thunderbird (Tbird), Eldorado, Cordoba, Cougar Mercury and so on.

We settled down. I was in the school of Pharmacy at Creighton University, while Uche started a master's degree in biology at

University of Nebraska. She was employed part-time as a Laboratory Assistant. I was employed at the 'Boys Town' as an Administrative Officer. The logo of Boys Town is very touching. It's a home for young boys who were orphaned as babies, it has a logo of one boy carrying another on his back; the letter underneath the picture says, 'He ain't heavy, he's my brother'.

Later, I found another separate flat and went back to Minnesota and brought my legal wife Carol and our daughter Chichi. Effectively, I set up another home, and I was akin to a man with a wife and a mistress and two different homes. I slept on different nights at either place. They knew each other and seemed to find a way of tolerating the arrangement. However, for me it was a mistake, a downward slippery slope. It was hellish trying to juggle two homes and I struggled severely. I began to lag in my Pharmacy degree programme. I guessed my predicament at this initial attempt at establishing multiple homes was difficult, because I was not prepared for the matrimonial set up that I had engineered. I lacked the financial wherewithal, emotional stability and maturity to cope with such huge responsibilities and challenges. My circumstances at that time were further compounded by three main factors. First and foremost, I loved the two women equally for different reasons, secondly, I was waiting and expecting the grant of the US Green Card through my marriage to Carol. Additionally, I had some privileges being married to Carol, a US citizen such as paying the discounted university school fees - the home rate rather than pay as a foreign student, and I qualified to receive student grants and loans. Secondly, my burning desire to qualify as a professional, either in pharmacy, law or medicine was dire and utmost. Thirdly, Uche and I seemed at the time to have crossed the Rubicon and had inextricably accepted each other as husband and wife in the African tradition. I attended American and Jamaican, (Akata) as we nick-named all black Americans parties with Carol whilst I attended African and Nigerian functions with Uche. The two ladies are slim but whilst Carol was 5ft 9inches tall, Uche was only 5ft 4 inches in height.

## ANNUS HORRIBILIS

Early 1977, Carol decided to go back south to Wynn Arkansas to take care of some family matters. After about four days of her arriving in Wynne, my house phone rang; I picked it up and I was told by Carol's sister Charlene that 'mama shot Carolyn' I said: 'say what?' She repeated 'mama shot Carolyn' and that she had been taken to the hospital in Memphis, Tennessee. She said my daughter Cynthia was fine. I was devastated and asked what happened. I was told their mother had started seeing another man, a few months after the death of her husband Johny Walker and Carolyn would not allow such a thing to happen.

Carolyn felt it was disrespectful to her late Dad. Carolyn started preventing the man from entering their home. Her own mother became very irate and shot her own daughter in the head, with a shotgun. She was lucky to still be alive and breathing. Police arrested the 55 years old mother and soon released her to appear in court at a later date.

The next weekend I had to fly to Memphis Tennessee to see how Carolyn was doing. At Memphis General Hospital she had remained unconscious. Fondly called "Kelli" by her family, she was bed-ridden, fed via the drips and tubes. She could not open her eyes or speak. I could not leave that room with dry eyes. She was neither aware of my visit, nor that I brought some flowers. Everyone thought she would not survive. The doctor and nurses were glad that I came at that time for my signature was urgently needed as a husband and next of kin, for them to take her to the operating room for further brain surgery. The operation was needed to remove particles of bullets that had embedded themselves inside her brain. Before returning to

Omaha Nebraska, I went to Wynne Arkansas, at 190 West Morris Street to see the in-laws. I saw Cynthia in Wayne and she was being cared for by her cousin, Kitty, Barbara's daughter who lived with Marie (carol's Mum). To take my mind off the problem at hand, I also took a cab to see 'GRACELAND,' Elvis Presley's compound and shrine. Memphis mansion of the famous musician, late Elvis Presley, the king of rock n' roll. Tourists were everywhere. Some people still say that Elvis is alive.

In June 1977, I met a Calabar man. Mr Ekong who was a graduate student at Creighton University. We had lunch together at the student centre. He intimated he would soon be leaving to attend medical school called St Georges in Grenada, West Indies. He informed me it was a brand-new school and 1977 set was the first intake. I quickly made note of the school's details and I invited him to come and assist my girlfriend Uche, to apply without delay. He came and assisted us. Lo and behold, after some months, Uche obtained a letter of Admission to the St George's Medical School for September 1977. We were both over the moon for the achievement and bright prospects of her becoming a medical doctor in the family.

Uche decided that we drive to Texas to see her relation Chinwe at Austin TX, and my own Cousins Lambert and Elizabeth in Houston TX. We equipped our Mercury Cougar car with a CB radio gadget, which was used in those days to detect and avoid traffic police. I often went on the air and shouted, 'rubber duck, rubber duck, over' When I had finished shouting, I signed off with 'ten-four' From Nebraska, we drove south through the states of St Louis Missouri, Wichita Kansas, Oklahoma City, Oklahoma, Little Rock Arkansas into Austin, and Houston Texas.

After three days in Texas, I left Uche there and drove back on my own. On a Friday night, I filled my tank with gas and headed home. Rather than drive straight north to Nebraska the same way we came from, I took a detour east and headed to Arkansas, to see Carol and our daughter. I bought a roll of cigarettes, three different pints of Bacardi, Rum, Brandy and twelve cans of Budweiser beer, some water bottles, and a carton of pure orange juice. I also picked up some sandwiches. I was intent on driving all day and all night to make it to Omaha by first light on that Monday. My car was loaded with all types of cassette tapes of almost all the top soul music of the day:
Aretha Franklin, Michael Jackson, Marvin Gaye, Otis Reading, Lionel Richie, Earth Wind and Fire, Dianna Ross, Ike, and Tina Turner, to name a few. I also had my favourite tapes of African music such as from Osadebe, Rex Lawson, Celestine Ukwu, Sir Victor Uwaifo, IK Dairo, Ebenezer Obey, Sunny Ade, The Peacocks, Warrior, Bobby Benson, and Victor Olaiya just to name a few. I was drinking and driving. I knew when I drove past Waco Texas, but after that the rest of the drive was a blur. I was awoken by police officers and their flashing blue lights. I had

driven off the road and ended up in a ditch. I fell asleep at the wheel. Luckily, I was alive and not hurt. A wreck recovery truck came and pulled me out of the ditch. My blood and breath were tested for alcohol, and I failed woefully. I was again detained overnight in Waco and subsequently given a ticket and allowed to go with my car. By a stroke of luck, my car was still drivable and roadworthy.

I arrived at Wynne, Arkansas in daylight and saw my wife, daughter, and the mother in-law. I ate rice, greens and pork or lamb chops. Carol had been discharged from the hospital and she was recuperating at her mother's house. I brought drinks from my car and shared with my in-laws, their family, and friends. My family in Arkansas and Texas could not believe what had happened to me near Waco Tx. Everyone thought I had a lucky escape, some said that I cheated death. I continued to brag in faith and confidence that I am a special child of God. We prayed and thanked God for saving Carol's life, even though she was disabled. Carol had been discharged, but she remained severely disabled. Sadly, Carol was bedridden and would be handicapped for the rest of her life. She also lost the sight of the left eye because the gun shot ripped off the eye from the eye socket. Carol, Chichi, and I spent that day and night at a nearby motel before I left that Sunday afternoon and headed to Omaha. I drove past the acclaimed late Evangelist Oral Roberts University in Tulsa Oklahoma (OK).

Having safely arrived in Nebraska, the 'Good Life State', also known as the 'Cornhuskers State,' I was grateful I made it back alive and unhurt, but for a few pains and aches here and there. The pains meant nothing, so long as I had my head, body and limbs in one piece. I was grateful that my black cougar mercury, reliably stood by me through thick and thin, and did not disappoint, nor leave me stranded. I did not collide head on with any car, lorry, or truck. I did not hit a lamp post, nor fall into a ravine or gully. One can only give testimony God is good and faithful. Neither did the trip cause me any hefty expenses during the entire journey. The total mileage covered and added to the milometer from the round trip was nearly a thousand miles in the six days.

I arrived in Omaha Nebraska on late Sunday night, and it was in the early hours of a workday, Monday. I firmly ignored the loneliness in the apartment and snuggled up in my bed to get some sleep before rushing out to work. Not long ago, I had two women to myself, but at that time, one was sick in Arkansas and the other frolicking in Texas, with a view to going to medical school soon. My alarm clock was probably my most reliable possession. It woke me up on time, so I was hardly ever late to work. I was then an administrative officer at the OFFUT Airforce base at Bellevue, Nebraska. Sometimes, I woke before the alarm, and stepped into my office at seven thirty, on the dot. It was such a lousy day, that full day, I felt like I had received a pounding, or terrible beating from the neck down. I fought off persistent sleep that hovered over me all day.

I sought to establish an independent and self-sufficient lifestyle as a grown man, without undue reliance on women. I had a deep reflection and recalled one memorable day in the past, when I had felt that same way. It was the day I dreamt, and I fought with a lion in my dream. In my previous dreams, I usually flew over and above houses, mountains, and valleys. But in that dream, singularly, I just could not lift myself up and off as much as I had tried. I was immobilised as it were. I screamed and screamed out awake. My mate shook me up 'what is it?' she asked, I blinked, shook my head 'Move over fool' I replied, rubbing my palm to confirm it had only been a dream, and there were no deep scratches and pugnacious Lion's claws. The reason for my nightmarish helplessness in that dream was because she had tucked me in with one of her legs and wrapped one of her arms around me. That kind of smothering love or affection which I did not let any woman lavish on me. I was in the habit of making love before I slept, but after that I would prefer to sleep alone, even if it meant on the floor or on the couch, to avoid a situation of being cramped or smothered. In my own experience, bad dreams were, mostly, a premonition of an unpleasant situation, days after.

By the way, talking of dreams, as a kid I was a bed wetter. I would normally dream that I was doing one thing, or another then went to wee in a toilet, or by roadside only to wake and realise that I had peed on myself in my bed. I did not understand why only dreams of urine came true. If I dreamt of fighting a lion or flying or being rich, I did not wake up to those realities. My grandfather used to advise me, that I should eat wall-geckos to cure me of my bed wetting.

The day after the horrible dream, guess what? my friend Zeb, a graduate student from the Democratic Republic of the Congo was mugged and clubbed to death. In fact, he was set up by his American wife of convenience over a fat scholarship cheque, which was remitted to him. In addition to that, it was rumoured and later confirmed that he and the so-called wife had taken out an Insurance Policy, with accidental double indemnity clause and with each other as the sole beneficiary. Mr Zeb as well as Mr Igwe had married nutters - crazy women, just to get the coveted Green

Card. Mr Zeb's wife was nowhere near his looks, his social class or academic standing. Unfortunately for Zeb, the over possessive witch of a woman read his letters which his fiancé wrote from his home country. She totally lost her head, and in cold blood took his life, through an arranged hit man. Our mutual friend, Igwe obtained a Green Card, but died of natural causes shortly thereafter, after a brief illness in Houston, Texas. Anyway, I managed to go to work on that first day after the Houston trip. However, because of my earlier reflections, I resolved to take control henceforth. So, after work that day, I went home, after picking up a takeaway order of Deep-Pan Pizza from Pizza Hut. I braced up with the realities, to grow up and be the man I intended to become. I was determined to have a go at living the life of a single man, getting used to living without a woman all the time. Learning to pick up after myself, do my own laundry, cooking and washing up. Above all to break the jinx of daily sex, even if it was a 'spell' put on me with a 'Voodoo, Obeah, Abracadabra' or witchcraft (juju), to render it invalid and no longer effective on me. The Pizza was juicy and loaded with eight toppings including mushrooms, salami, red peppers, cheese, tomatoes, pineapples, peperoni, and olives. I decided not even to take the initiative of calling Uche at Texas, until she phoned me. After a warm bath, I made up my mind not even to step outside, but rather to watch T.V, evening comedies and the ballgames till I fell asleep. If my memory serves me right, I thought the Houston Rockets were locking horns that night with Los Angeles – L.A. Lakers. And whenever those two teams meet to play Basketball, it never diminishes from being a sort of fireworks! It always went to the wire! I mean to the last whistle! Before I came to America, I deeply believed in the efficacy of prayers, and accumulation of catholic indulgencies, in case I need them after death, to wipe out my sins and enable me to go to straight to Heaven or to enter Paradise after a spell in Purgatory. But apparently, my belief in religious creeds had become very weak. What was wrong with me? I wondered. There is an all-powerful God, the Almighty One. The maker and mover of all things, but I was becoming increasingly Agnostic. This means no human being is able, or capable of expressing, or explaining God and His will. When I came to U.S. at the age of twenty-eight, I was celibate, almost priest like. Where did I go wrong? Has the power I had left me or what, I wondered.? We are all required to conform, or else we could be classed as 'lost'.

'God, Jesus Help me' I prayed, and unconsciously this type of ejaculatory prayer, which I learned during my seminary days, tumbled out from my sub conscious. But it was not to be. After five hours, my willpower failed me. At about twelve midnight, hell! I could never be alone. I had to ring Texas to ask Uche to return with immediate effect. I could not stand it. I had done everything to fall asleep, to no avail. I rang her up at Lambert's house, shouting; 'Put Uche on the phone'.

She took the receiver and cunningly whispered 'Hello, Hello!' I roared 'What the hell do you mean, you never called me all evening?' She went 'honey, we all went out, they took me out, just came in, and I thought it was too late to be calling you up, you know, but honey, sweetheart….' 'Don't you honey and sweetheart me! I want your arse back here, latest six p.m. tomorrow evening' I arrogantly commanded. It is only a myth that men rule the women. She laughed a sinister laugh which seemed to say, 'poor you, I knew you would not be able to manage it' She was still giggling as she said 'Baby, I'll come, but it will be in two days, try baby, you can manage it'. My response was 'no-way girl! If you do not come back home tomorrow, you will be sorry. I am not kidding.' She had a good understanding of me and my nature inside-out, 'O.k. darling' she said. 'I'll definitely be back tomorrow and only for tonight you can go out and mess with some white girls, or you can ring up Tracy' She also knew that I was a shy but unpretentious man. I could not hide what I did and could not keep a secret for long. I consider those who hold such secrets as shallow cowards, living lives of impoverished falsehood. One lie begets another lie, leading to a cyclical life of lies, deceits and mistrusts, ending in irretrievable break down of relationships. She knew all along that Tracy was always my 'bit on the side.'

I yelled back 'I do not want to mess around with nobody, because you know how I am, once and they are hooked and I cannot get them out of my hair again, and that is it!'. She laughed at my hopelessness and plight. Finally, it was settled that she had to return the next day, which meant I spent a night alone.

After I hung up the phone, all further efforts to relax proved abortive. Gaddamm! I went into the kitchen and opened a brand-new bottle of Jack Daniels whisky. I had run out of cigarettes at midnight. Chain smoking in between drinks. I had gone through two packs, forty cigarettes in a day. For more cigs and other reasons, I dressed up casually, went downstairs and drove out into town. A quick stop at the 7-11 Kwick Store, I stocked up on tobacco and orange juice, cheese, soda, and baloney sandwich meat. After a few turns around the Downtown streets, I decided it was not worth it, the risk of getting arrested for kerb-crawling. I was only looking for any honky-tonk bar which was still open late at night, just to sit around folks and listen to white people's music of Country Western Rock 'n' Roll for a change. The kind of music we called 'Sentimental' in Nigeria. But I also could not help glancing occasionally at the ladies of the night who walked the downtown streets. Those 'working ladies' are abhorrent to some men and will totally kill my nature. I could not get into the spirit if I had to pay for sex. I do not mind being generous to a lady afterwards, but the mention of money first, would put me off. Those were the days before the advent of AIDS and its H.I.V. Today, it is a more perilous business for all persons involved. Use of condoms could halve the risk, but not totally obliterate it. It could slip out, fluids could slip in, it could be torn, and both parties would perhaps feel nothing, as the whole business would lack friction and the natural feel of it. Do not get me wrong, those ladies are said to be in the oldest profession since the beginning of life. Many men prefer them for reasons of total lack of inhibition, no commitment, purely business and the fact that without them some men would burn inside or embark on a wanton spree of raping other people's wives, daughters, or mothers.

It is not right for any woman to sell her body for money. First, their safety is compromised. Secondly, they could be spreading incurable diseases. Thirdly, character of that class of women is questionable. Fourthly, in most instances the women in question were not only drug addicts, alcoholic, and thieves themselves, but also moved in packs, with their pimps in tow, who were invariably robbers, perverts and yet another disgusting and ruthless set of human beings. Moreover, at best, sellers and buyers could even be picked up by plain clothes or undercover police as a 'punter' or 'prostitute' respectively. One may then end up with a criminal record of soliciting for prostitution. The irony is that men who pick up girls at shopping malls and clubs or wherever, hardly know when they have picked up 'off- duty' harlots, with all the attended risks. If all women are in same business, then it is best to allow men to have two or more wives if you wish to and can afford it, till death, do them part, that way you can be sure that you have a trusted and dependable partners or customers. It was after 4 a.m. anyway, so I safely went home and slept like an exhausted child that had been crying. Anyway, Uche finally returned to Omaha after about three days, and we began contemplating whether she should go to the medical school. As for me, I lost my battle to overcome my weakness for the females and my quest for independent living. It seemed that in my word the aphorism 'damned with women and damned without them' remains a truism.

## PATRICIA RETURNS TO NIGERIA FROM GERMANY

In Summer 1977, news also reached me that my sister, Patricia had left Germany and returned to Nigeria with her 3year old son Chino. I heard her marriage to my friend Innocent had hit the rocks. I was told parts of the allegations for their irreconcilable differences were that her husband was irresponsible and too laid back. Her husband was at the time chasing illusive admission to study medicine to become a medical doctor. Many years later, he eventually qualified as a medical doctor. My sister arrived in Nigeria safely and she quickly settled in Kano, Northern Nigeria. I was elated to hear that our two younger brothers Damian Iyke Okoroha and Eugene Chinedu Okoroha were with Pat in Kano and attending school and learning trades in Kano. I heard that our mother was jubilant to see her return from overseas alive and well, and with our mother's second grandchild. Pat started work immediately with Duala Hotel as a caterer.

**CHAPTER TWELVE**

------------------------

# Cletus, My Baby Brother Admitted to The University of Nebraska, USA

In the same summer of 1977, I woke up one day and I decided to bring Cletus my junior brother over to USA, from West Germany, where he had been for two past years with my sister Pat and her husband. Within a week, I secured the admission letters, and I paid the $8,000 school fee for his first-year tuition. I posted the admission letter, receipts and sworn sponsorship to him in Hamburg. I expected him to arrive in the USA in September 1977, as Uche would be going overseas to study medicine. I thought it would be nice to have a junior brother around, both for his own good and for my own support. Once it was confirmed he was coming to America that fall, I figured that it would be splendid to cap off my achievement for the year by booking a flight to Nigeria, so I could see my mother, who became a widow in 1974 when my father passed away. It was most regrettable that when my father died, the sad news reached me after about a month. He had already been buried. I did not have the means to travel. I had little or no money and I was desperately waiting to receive my green card from the US Immigration Service. Thus, I booked my flight to Nigeria with a departure date scheduled for the 15 December 1977.

## U.S. OFFUTT AFB BELLEVUE, NEBRASKA

Meanwhile by 1977, I had quit my post at Boys Town for a more glamorous and better paid position at the civilian wing of the Strategic Air Command Base, Bellevue Nebraska. I was an Equal Opportunities and Affirmative Action Officer at the U.S Offutt AFB Bellevue, Nebraska. I had both office and residential telephone numbers, and Mr. Remington was my boss. A genial and indefatigable man. Though 'short cake' a rather busty Black lady typist, who worked with the pay department described him as the type of white man, that any average Black American (Negros) would nickname 'red neck' I found out what she meant after collaborating with him for a month or two. Our bi-weekly reports to the head of department gave me the most uncomfortable concern. We were required to monitor each other, as well as every department and section, to ensure that minority people constituted in at least ten percent of the workforce in the departments. Also, that the civilian supply, service, and maintenance contracts were placed with ten percent minorities and minority small businessmen.

Minority people of America included Afro-Americans, Mexican Americans, and such other Americans that came from or had their backgrounds from the Philippines, Puerto Rico, West Indians, Chinese, Vietnamese, India, Korea, Japan and so on. The fortnightly reports were muddled through. It was a sham, an unrealistic cosmetic window dressing. Figures were inflated after I had submitted my findings to make believe that we were quite close to the 'target' When the actual situations were a mere one or two per cent, vastly different from the stipulated achievement level. The higher authorities were given the erroneous impression that we had seventy to eighty-five percents, accomplishment level. The big shots of the higher echelon accepted the reports, turning a blind eye, and even patted us on the back for seemingly making enormous progress. I choked and frowned hopelessly, often boiling inside. My disposition was influenced by my apparent lack of understanding of the 'system of bureaucratic injustice.' A system set up to cure, but had taken on a life of its own, and was then mostly in business to perpetuate and sustain itself. My job was no longer enriching, nor satisfying. Thus, my own job was put on the line. Though I still went to work daily, somehow, I knew my daily base car sticker and base identity card could be demanded sooner or later, even when I least expected it. I believed I would soon be fired.

Reading between the lines, I came to understand that as a black man, African- American for that matter, I was not an 'equal' nor entirely hired on 'merit,' but by patronage, or as a gap/percent filler. A Black person was only to be 'seen' and not to be 'heard.' Though I had a superior degree from the University of Minnesota, while Mr. Remington graduated from a junior college from down south. I did my absolute best to hold on to the God-given job, for as long as possible.

My roles included ensuring that in recruitment of staff, black people and other minorities were well represented and were not prejudiced at every stage from advertisement, short listing, and interview and selection process. I also investigated complaints of racism and other discriminatory practices at the workplace. After work one day, just before Uche had returned from Texas, God 'buttered my bread' for me. I had a good female company from the Air Force Base, until the following morning. It was so soothing that her primary quest was for fun and an enjoyable time. Money, or no money, was obviously passive or not on her agenda. She was generous and I must admit I was an officer and a gentleman! Angel (short for Angela) got up thirty minutes earlier than me, and in a catlike manner and with poise, she tiptoed around, straightening things, then prepared the great American breakfast of bacon, sausages, fried eggs sunny side up, toast, juice, and coffee. She was a self-professed liberal, one of the roaring twenties, with long brown hair and wearing Levis blue jeans. A twenty-four-year-old daughter of a retired Air Force officer, she was endlessly fascinated about people from other cultures. She was born in Europe whilst her father was stationed in Germany. I spoke a little German, "ein bischen, und ich lieber dich," so she almost thought I was a G.I, or Vietnam Veteran. I said I was a Biafran Air Force Officer. People, including myself, always told her she was gorgeous she said, but she did not believe one bit of it. I guessed out of her humility, to avoid being vain, or to avoid making some other less fortunate girls' bitter. Uche called incredibly early that day; to say she could not make it, because her friend was making a dress for her which wasn't ready. She did not find out the reason for my apparent calmness. 'Thursday for sure, darling, love you' she said. 'Fine, see you then, be good. Ciao! Me too!' Then she said, 'don't do what I would not do' I replied jokingly 'that gives me a lot of scope!'

## UCHE MY FIANCÉ WENT OFF TO MEDICAL SCHOOL

Uche finally returned the day after my escapade with Angel. She arrived aboard a North-western, or Eastern airline, which touched down at 1700 hours. Enthusiastically, I was at the Omaha Eppley Airport early enough to gulp a tall shot before the plane arrived.

My face shone with a broad smile and delight as I caught a glimpse of her, beaming broadly, as she elegantly stepped down the steps of the aircraft. At the baggage collection belt area, we embraced and kissed, she had a way of sticking her tongue in my mouth. We went to the parking lot, got the car, and happily drove off.

Except for a few days' sightseeing, the whole idea of her going away was a totally wasted effort. But, how about her going to the Caribbean for medical school? She had wondered about the feasibility of our being separated for any length of time. 'Well, we just have to think twice about it and try' I calmly responded, though deep down I was having lots of reservations and misgivings about the entire scenario.

It was 18th of August 1977 she returned from Austin Texas. If we agreed on her going on to the medical school at St. George Granada, then she would have to leave again in six days' time, the 24th of August. In that case we had, as it were, just one week to be together, six days in fact, to even make the final decision on her going or not. If she went, she would be gone for three months at a time. To come back mid- December for one month winter holidays, to leave again mid- January till spring or summer the following year. The cycle would then repeat perennially for five or six years, after which, all things being equal, we would then live comfortably thereafter. It was a tough decision to make. Frankly, I was in a fix, and that was an understatement. From the airport, we went to Dodge Street, Taco Bell, where we had red pepper hot Mexican Food for dinner.

We went to bed rather early. I was awoken by what seemed to be a mild panic attack. I left the bed, walked out of the bedroom with a pillow and went into the sitting room in my pyjamas. After switching on the dim table lamp on the side table, the wall clock chimed one. On turning on the television, I clicked on the remote control to the cable all night channel. Debbie Winger was the actress. That is her and that's Linda Lovejoy, they both kill me for some reason, with their romantic roles in those cable home videos. I fixed myself a drink and stretched out on the couch to watch the movie. One drink led to another, so did one cigarette lead to another; my thought wondered up and down and in circles.

Unexpectedly, Uche woke and came looking for me. I was dead drunk, and the time was three o'clock. 'Honey is it well with you?' she asked. I did not reply. I kept mute because I was the last person to admit that I lacked confidence or was insecure. The truth is that all men, even heroes, have feet of clay and even the richest, bravest, and most powerful amongst men, also have their own fears and soft spots. 'What is it baby, why did you come out here, drinking so heavily all by yourself in this dead of the night?' she further demanded. I stroked my head, lit a cig, but hesitated to open up.

Looking back now, I can tell you for a fact I almost squandered my good health in those days, out of ignorance and godless living. I hope some people will learn from some of the errors of my ways.

Suddenly, she jumped to her feet, walked into the bedroom and almost, at the same time, re-appeared with her purse in one hand and some papers on the other. I thought those were her medical school admission letters. I was indeed right. She laid them in front of me and said with such earnestness in her face. 'I know you are worried and thinking too much about my going away to West Indies for the schooling. Here, if you do not want me to go, if you honestly think you cannot be able to stay alone for three months, then just tear up these admission papers and I can still study pharmacy here at Omaha. In short, I do not even want to go anymore, as I see it, it is going to break us up, the only reason for my wanting to be a doctor is to please you.'

I was thinking of so many things at the time, from Carolyn's condition, my little daughter, my dead father, my then living mother, who I had not seen since my father died, my shaky job position, an impending court case and what the outcome might be, and of course, she was clearly and inextricably entangled in the alleged offence. I reflectively decided to lay on her the only aspect of the problems that touched her most. 'Sweetheart' I said 'you know that I want you to go and become a medical Doctor more than I do not want you to go. What is giving me the headaches is this crazy and strange thought, one supposes I personally could not be alone and therefore before you come back another woman ends up living here with me, or worse yet, what if you get over there and from careless convenience dating you fall in love with another medical student and ….'

Now she spat spittle, out of sheer reflex action, shuddered and acted like she had been stung by a bee. I stopped speaking. I must have hit a nerve, a sensitive spot in her heart. She went to the kitchen, speechless, brought back with her a pinch of salt in a teaspoon. She knelt on the other side of the coffee table, direct and opposite me, as if about to perform a ritual, and, near to tears, she made an emotional but powerful speech.

'Darling, both of us are from the same Ibo ethnic group, we both know the meaning and significance of salt. Since you cannot tell ripe maize when you see one' beating her chest with a half - clenched fist she continued:

'You still doubt my total and un-conditional love for you.' Raising the spoon with salt she announced she was going to take an oath and vow never to disappoint me in this world, or ever fool with another man. After which, it would be my turn to also swear to the same oath in like manner. Except that for me as a man 'fooling' and 'messing' were allowed, because such was a man's nature. So long as it only ended with a mere 'hit and run' I was to swear only not to 'disappoint' 'abandon' and 'dump' her to 'marry another woman'.

She continued 'You know... not kidding! you are a nice person but too weak with women, and that is why they fall for you... your problem is that you have messed around with so many American women, to the point that you now think all women are riffraff. I am well bred, from good stock, daughter-of thesoil, not a son-of-a-bitch (SOB), my mother breastfed me, not with animal milk; I grew from the ground up. How can I come here from thousands of miles away to fool around from man to man, to flirt and let my body be destroyed? Or leave my body loose and let men play with it like a football. I know what a shameful thing is. I have been with you for two years now, everybody knows about us and has seen us together. I am not a harlot. I cannot live for anybody else. Instead, I am afraid that it is you who is going to dump me. I can now see it coming. After using me and making me useless, you want to leave me, and get rid of me just like that. Instead of that, I would die. So, we both must take this oath now!'

We did! Frankly, I had to. I wondered why I even doubted her in the first place. I was deeply moved and felt that in fairness I owed her a serious apology for my apparent fastidiousness. Inwardly, somewhere I was however, still tempted to say that all that glitters may not be gold, or that nothing in this world is so guaranteed, or that no one can be sure about tomorrow, for it is pregnant with outcomes. But since I had no more courage to utter any divisive word, I went along with her idea, if only to make her feel good. Moreover, I did not really consider such superstitious naivety to be of any far-reaching significance. Besides, soberly I thought to myself that God would never forgive me, simply because I had to always sleep with somebody therefore, I debar someone from becoming a Medical Doctor, thereby depriving humanity of such a blessing. I had to let go, offering it to God who alone knows the future.

A drop of blood from each person's finger. Mixed with the salt. We leaked it and swore one after another never to leave each other. The karma for reneging was that the culprit was never to get all the expected good things of this world. Come to think of it now, no one gets everything they wish to get in life. Not even the Pope in Rome, if he did get his wishes, the entire world would be Christian, Roman Catholics.

Having vowed, it was like crossing the Rubicon. I gave her my blessing to go to the medical school. It was a good thing and good for our future together. I would be all right. I will wait for her. She smiled at me, I smiled back at her, we switched the lights and gadgets off and went back to sleep.

On the 24th of August 1977, Uche left Omaha for the West Indies. She also left with all our savings, but for two hundred dollars in total, which was left in four different accounts at Omaha, Commercial Federal Savings and Loan Association and the Franklin Federal Credit Union. These were left for the sole purpose of keeping the bank accounts open. My next fortnightly pay cheque was to come in a few days, the coming Friday. Before she left, in all honesty I was again seized by last minute panic, thirty minutes before her departure. The reason to me was incomprehensible and unexplainable. For one thing, I would be making an ass of myself if I began to tell her that I was changing my mind about her going. We had agreed over and over that she was going. She noticed and cheered me up with the fact that one of my junior brothers, Cletus, was to arrive in four days from Germany, where he had been for nearly a year with my sister

Patricia. He would therefore be able to cook for me and do the house chores. She then went a step further to say that if after the first semester, I was still not coping well, she would then drop off for at least one semester. I escorted her to the foremost departures gate, as far as the airport authorities could permit a non-passenger. At that point it was final goodbyes. She was to call me later from any point. I gave her a peck on the cheek, turned and brusquely walked away, without looking back again. I then went to the bar to collect my change, which I did not have enough time to demand when the final boarding announcement was made over the intercom. It was a twenty-dollar bill, and we had drunk drinks of only eight dollars and thirty-five cents. The cashier rang up the cash register and counted out the change into my palm. Saying 'eight dollars and thirty-five cents, you drank, dropping in a nickel, eight- forty; then puts a dime, eight fifty; then two quarters, nine dollars; then a dollar bill, ten dollars; two fives, twenty. Thank you, come again!' she said, as she tore out the receipt and handed it over to me. Not bothering to even glance at it, I rumpled it and threw it into the first available ashtray bin along the hallway. Wondering what happens when people's beliefs are violated in foreign lands. Where I come from it is taboo and indeed in my tribe people do not let others 'count' money directly into their palms. It was said to cause stoppage of more money coming your way in a lifetime. It was funny also how Americans count out change backwards or so it seemed. A Nigerian cashier not only would have counted out the change in his or her own hand first, but would have said you spent $8.35, your change from twenty is £11.65; here is ten; plus, one is eleven; plus 65pence. What difference does it make anyway? Cashiers all over the world make mistakes.

As I faced the exit doors to walk outside from the main lounge of the Airport building, I vividly remembered when I was a kid in 1957, we had gone to Port Harcourt Aerodrome in Nigeria, to see what an airport and planes looked like. I bought biscuits, groundnuts, and minerals from a kiosk inside the lounge, the total of which came to two shillings and six pence and half- penny. I gave the cashier ten shillings note; there were no cash registers then. After racking his mathematical brains, he carefully gave me a whopping seventeen shillings, six pennies and a half penny. That was the good old days when a pound was a pound.

A pound was also twenty shillings. Who talked of returning excess change then? Instead, everyone surmised from local belief, that the incident was one of good omens that my future life was going to be one of a remarkable success. Future apart, there and then, our joy was indescribable as we abandoned the rest of the excursion. It was more than a rebate; it was more like winning a jackpot in one of today's Las Vegas casinos or the lottery.

I heard an aircraft take-off and I thought again of Uche. I walked outside the main building crossed the zebra-walk in front of cabs, cars, and porters with their trolleys. A few minutes' walk on the sidewalk; I turned onto the pedestrian crossing, walked up to the "F" floor ramp. I took my car, paid the ramp or parking lot attendants at the exit gate, put on a Kool and the Gang cassette tape and off I went home straight to my apartment.

It was a mess, because we left in a hurry, to make sure she did not miss the flight. There were dishes to be done, cartons of books to be carried back into the closets, trash, and trash bags to be picked up, or emptied. Even the bed was still unmade. I reluctantly dragged myself to straighten up the bunk, but was squeamish about doing the dishes, pots, and pans. I sat at my study desk with a felt tip pen and paper. I thought I would just take stock of myself as a man. Examine my conscience, assess my life and lifestyle, list my accomplishments and failures, list my liabilities and assets, my net worth, enumerate birth – to – date fortunes and misfortunes, my weaknesses and strength, vices, and virtues. How would I compare? How far and how well have I done in my life goals and aspirations since I left Nigeria five years ago? Indeed, I took a hard look at myself, looked at my image; how I saw myself and how I felt or thought others saw me, stood by the mirror, and asked the man in the mirror what he thought of 'us' thumbs up, or 'boo', observed if I saw eye to eye with the man staring back at me in the mirror. That was my conscience, my best judge.

The reason for taking such an inventory was because something was going seriously wrong in my life, and my way of life. At the age of 32 years, education seemed to have occupied most of my life. Funnily, it appeared that so long as one's life revolved around schooling, one hardly stopped thinking young. At that point and time, I did not know if I was still a boy or a man. In my comportment and in my willpower, in my concentration and in my rationalisation. I did not know what it was, but I felt as if I was losing a grip of myself. Not in physical terms, maybe psychologically, for physically other than having sporadic bouts of appalling headache, blurry vision at times, especially when tipsy, I was evidently healthy and robust. Hardly ever been sick and I hated medication.

I arrived at certain conclusions about my life. Pointedly, I gave myself a pat on the back for being a self-made man. From arid poverty and deprivation, I was driven by innocent ambition, determination, and diligence. I had prayerfully pulled myself by the proverbial shoestrings, left Nigeria with barely a hundred dollars and I have made good thereafter.

All on my own! I had come so far, like a rocket, catapulted and guided by Instinct, Providence, Fate, Destiny, Blind Chances, and Sheer Luck.

I was mindful of the fact that most of my contemporaries, who came to America at the same time as I, were sponsored by the government or their parents or guardians, for their tuition and boarding, and they might have used between forty and fifty thousand dollars in those five years. I had never received a dime or a penny from home or anyone; rather, I had constantly remitted money home for family support, younger siblings' school fees, feeding and at other times, when the proverbial unexpected and unscheduled rains had fallen.

Within five years, I had earned a Bachelor of Science Degree in Business Administration from the University of Minnesota, a foremost tower of learning in America. It was one of the first ten top Grant Ivory Institutions in USA.

I wondered why I had abandoned BSC Pharmacy program at Creighton University, Omaha NE. At the time, I was enrolled on the Doctor of Pharmacy (PharmD) programme at the University of Nebraska, studying to qualify as a Doctor of Pharmacy. However, doubts crept up on me and I began to seriously consider abandoning the Doctorate program. I was then 32years old. I told myself that I was not a kid anymore. I decided to abandon Pharmacy altogether and aimed to complete a Master of Business Administration (MBA) Degree at the University of Nebraska and strove to complete a Ph.D. before returning home to Nigeria. To my mind, I reckoned very few contemporaries had done better, surely some did quite less. A considerable number of my contemporaries had not graduated at all. There were some black sheep of the Nigerian student community, the 'no dope no hopes' group who had completely dropped out of school. Some of these people had joined the circus or the American merry go-round, or joined the underworld, or had gone under, were cut down, dead. I figured that my progress, by and large, was not bad after all.

In my mind I was convinced that as long as I was mandated to become a Medical Doctor when I left Nigeria, anything short of that expectation, to my kith and kin back home, was hardly good enough, in no way praiseworthy. The closest thing to Medicine would have been Pharmacy or law, and I had also studied Pharmacy in the past three years, both at Minnesota and at Creighton University, and at the University of Nebraska. That peculiar situation bothered me and caused me much anxiety. I would bite my lips in distress. My only consolation in this respect rested on whatever became of Uche and her medical career, and then of our future together as Mr and Doctor (Mrs). On my other departure 'promise' to open a 'floodgate' of relations and friends to come abroad for further studies; I had so far outstripped everyone's expectations. I brought seven family relations, four friends and other distant acquaintances overseas. I found out the hard way, maybe as Christ did, that it is impossible to please the World. Although eleven people had come following my footsteps, yet a million others despised me for literally not picking them up from Africa and dropping them on American soil. That seeming failure to please all and sundry also gave me grave concern. It ate at me terribly. That was a fault in my nature too, yes indeed, for I did not know of any other Nigerian in U.S, no matter how rich they and their fathers were, who had more zeal, willingness, and unselfishness to assist and bring so many, even their own very blood relations. It is sad that if you do ninety-nine things for anyone, they will usually forget them and bitterly remember only the one thing you did not do for them. I considered that I still deserved a pat on the back, no matter what view my critics may have taken. Mark you, there is a fine line between selfless virtue and selfishness. Family- wise, my dearly beloved Dad had died two years after I left home, and sweet Mum was alive. I had an invalid American born wife, and a long-distance Nigerian girl friend or fiancée, and a two-year-old daughter. Secretly, I wished she were a boy. Anyway, not bad at all. I named her Chinyere, which means 'God's Gift' I had the U.S. permanent residence status, the coveted Green Card. That was a plus. I took a decision: Positively, un-failingly, I vowed that I must go home that December 1977. Gee! Uche may be disappointed if she came back for holidays and did not see me. Going home to see my widowed mother after 5 years abroad was more important than any other woman, I counselled myself.

I would be dammed if I did not go to see my mother and spend the Christmas with her in Nigeria. She would be so thrilled to see me after five long years. I was equally hungry to see her and was home sick as well.

Not only did I underscore the thing about going home for Christmas that December of 1977; but I also tinkered with the lofty imagination of possibly bringing my mother and the last of my two youngest brothers at home, all to America to live with me. On the other hand, something told me my mother would never agree to abandon our village for U.S.A. Well, maybe she could visit with the boys, then, she could leave them behind with me when she returned to Nigeria. Yes... but alas! Knowing my mother, she would shrug and put her fingers across my mouth to hush me. It would really hurt her to hear I ever contemplated staying in the U.S. a minute longer than necessary, to finish my studies. She would construe such an utterance as if I were lost and wasted, like a prodigal son who had forgotten why he went overseas in the first place.

I recognized the dire need to build a decent modern storey house at home in our village. My folks still lived in my father's house, which was a three-bedroom, L – shape and Zinc roofed. My grandfather and my father lived in that house before their deaths, respectively. It was initially a mud house with raffia palm roof. The raffia thatches and bamboo ceiling were removed before the Biafra war, and it was re- roofed with corrugated iron sheets, otherwise known as Zinc, and the ceiling was made of asbestos. Being the first son of my father, under the Ibo custom, I inherited the house after the death of my father. The house itself was worthless to me, but it was situated on a prime piece of land in the family compound. To replace that house or build a modern storey building was my top priority. For one thing, if my coming to America was to show an iota of success in my life, or have any meaning, then I must erect a modern storey building, the sooner, the better. I cringed with the chilling realisation that if I died, without fathering a boy, then the family lineage and heritage would shift to the next oldest son of my father.

On that note, another concern with the house was that so long as I was the first son of the first son, and the heir in the Ijezie Okoroha dynasty - family lineage, no other son, grandson, brother, or sister could touch, demolish, or rebuild the hut unless I was dead and buried, without a surviving son. It was my exclusive birth right and responsibility to decide what happened to the house. Furthermore, it was the head hut, or the "Obi" otherwise known as "Obokoro" or small obi in the Ijezie Okoroha family compound.

I recalled part of my family history, in about 1800 AD, a man named Okoroha Ezeala begat four sons namely: Ozigbu, Ijezie, Nwaokoro and Ofoha. Since then, all the members of the family accepted and called the dynasty; the OKOROHA Family, since over two hundred years. There are now over two hundred members of this family Dynasty. Mazi Ijezie Okoroha, the second son of Okoroha is my grandfather. My father David Azunnah Okoroha was his first son, and I am my father's first son and in the stool of the number 2 man of the extended Okoroha family. If the Okoroha family heirloom or land was to be shared, I would take immediately after the lineage of Ozigbu Okoroha, the first son of the Okoroha Dynasty. I thought of our beautiful compound in Nigeria. I remembered the copious sunshine, the cool breeze and wind, the whispering leaves, the shrubs, and elephant grass, whistling tall trees, the singing birds, the unspoilt quietness of the village, people, and animals co– existing and each one going about their daily routine with absolute serenity. If I had wings, I would have flown home that very day. I was home sick. I believed that if one does not go home, the purpose of going overseas is a total failure and if one does not have an heir in one's fatherland, it appears also as a massive failure. To me, success without a successor is absolute failure, or an exercise in futility, I vowed not to fall into either two categories.

The decision for me to go home that coming Christmas became necessary – a 'sine qua non.' I planned on my return trip to Nigeria at Christmas. I would secure large, homely accommodation in USA and bring my daughter and her disabled mother back home to Omaha, Nebraska. In essence, this meant I needed to get a duplex, or bungalow.

Personally, I was always quick at making friends. But one dreadful thing about me was that although I tended to love everyone equally, I also had the tendency to forget or ignore anyone equally. I love my own company, yet I am a born extrovert and gregarious in nature. I had no favourites or best friends, neither do I have any enemies. As far as I know everyone I knew, either liked, or loved me. At that time, my partner, Uche, had travelled to St Georges' Medical School in Grenada, and knowing the Course could last four years, meant I could be living alone, this sent me into an emotional tailspin. The situation was compounded by the fact that a long-distance relationship could break down, over a long period, because either one of us might succumb to temptation. I knew myself very well and I was likely to be the one to succumb first. It saddened me that if I did, then the hope held by Uche and I for a future marital family life, after her time in Grenada, would be shattered. My state of mind became clouded with these thoughts. Somehow, I was still hopeful, broadminded, ambitious, and extroverted, but I was also becoming edgy, bored, reclusive, and moody. I began to shun friendships or relationships in general.

Slowly but surely, I was racked by bouts of depressive moods and episodes of insecurity and fear, regarding my goals and ambition. Fear of something I could not pin down; probably about my purpose, vision, and goals, and meeting expectations, based on other peoples assumed, or real expectations of me. These were no longer quite so clear to me. My priorities had changed since I left home, however, I didn't know exactly what they were anymore. My intrinsic priorities as a Nigerian at home, were now different to my priorities in the U.S. In fact, I was judging myself by two separate standards of merit and assessment. Living in two worlds at one time. Dangling like a pendulum, between the real world in Nigeria, and my fantasy, 'pie in the sky', world in America.

Many fellow Nigerians in the city loved me and enjoyed my company. I was clearly the life and soul of our social functions. I was highly respected and feared as well. Feared not that I was evil or mean but was rugged in a unique way. I was that sort of guy; I could fight my own battles and could stand up to anyone, at any time. I didn't let anybody, or any situation ruffle me. Some people were mystified as to how I came to have two loyal dedicated girlfriends, concurrently. Moreover, these ladies knew of each other and to some extent, cooperated with one another. Another thing was the nature of the position I held at the United States Air Force Base. A High Security place to work! Some guys were finding it difficult to find employment, even in a Janitors job, and in finding a loving woman to keep them from loneliness, also keep them attracted. In a nutshell, my actions seemed to baffle some and dazzle others around me. My closest family saw me as an enigma, they saw every selfmade person, as selfish, egocentric, and too ambitious and opportunistic. For me, what mattered was to be a beacon, a springboard, for the generation to come. To bequeath a legacy of light to my wider family. I was energetic, determined, and tireless, but rightly could be said to have been led mostly by intuition and practical common sense, rather than knowledge or expertise. I lived and let others live, rarely yearning for anyone's downfall. I took everyone in, with open arms and I trusted them. Even when they fell short of my expectations it never surprised me, no one is perfect, and it takes all sorts.

UNIVERSITY OF NEBRASKA AT OMAHA
Commencement
August 14, 1982

*Graduation at Law School.*

*My call to Bar in Nigeria Law School in 2016.*

*At my investiture as a Knight of Saint Columba in 2006.*

*With my sister, baby and brother's wife, Chiyere.*

**CHAPTER THIRTEEN**

------------------------

# Abandoning Pharmacy and Law for MBA and PhD.

Again, for the fall of 1977, I decided to transfer to the University of Nebraska (U.N.O.) graduate school, for the Master of Business Administration, evening (MBA) program. I toyed with the idea of following Uche to St Georges, but eventually banished the thought. I would have had to study outside the United States, and I didn't fancy the prospect at all. My Cousin Lambert had decided to follow Uche to Grenada medical school. I naively thought I would benefit doubly, if a future wife and Cousin both qualified as medical doctors. I would never ever go hungry.

Therefore, the hard decision was our ability to endure and manage separation while Uche was at school in the Caribbean.

It was now the first week in August 1977, and the decision for Uche's future was left for me to make. She was indifferent, so long as the decision pleased me. I wrestled with it painfully. To have a medical doctor as a future wife was more tempting than having one that was a pharmacist. But, before she could become an M.D, I would have to live without her for four to five years, I could vividly see her. Deep down, I was doubtful I could last a week without a woman by my-side. However, I made the right and noble decision to allow Uche to pursue her dream, of becoming a medical doctor, come what may be.

UC as I affectionately called Uche, when I was happy, or tipsy. She was short in stature, at five feet five inches, but dynamite, unique and admirable - an African lady to the core. She was busy in the kitchen with a selfless sense of duty, preparing egusi (melons), olugbu (dry bitter leaves) the Nigerian soup with okporoko (dry cod or stockfish). Whenever we cooked our traditional African dish, American tenants talked of how they could smell the rich aroma from their apartments. Some would say it was good and spicy, others would say it was awful.

One man's meat is another man's poison. I did not complain when they (Americans) ate smelly sauerkraut, stilton, or goats' cheese, they even kiss dogs on the mouth! Where I came from, the reasons for owning a dog were for hunting, guarding the compound of its owner and eating leftovers. We enjoyed the relish of our native menu, swallowing balls of semolina mixed with mashed potatoes, the combination was a substitute for the native garri or pounded yam. Chasing it down with icy water straight from the tap, which was as cold as water from the fridge in Nigeria.

Taking an inventory of my spiritual life, my moral standpoint remained based on my Christian upbringing and childhood Seminary training. I became convinced that I had indeed gone astray. I had derailed and was getting lost. As an Ex-seminarian, I should be ashamed to say it. But my belief in God had descended to 'He created the Heaven and Earth' and somehow, I believe that God controls, or pulls the strings from 'up there'. I had lost fellowship, communion, and communication with the Almighty God. Both in the three in One God and in the One in Three.

When I prayed, it was almost by accident, or out of habit. I found no reason to go to church. As far as I was concerned all the churches from A to Z had failed me. I was disillusioned with Christianity and religion. I began to think all religions manipulate and brainwash people to believe without question whatever they are told, without any proof, or evidence. I was under the impression that so long as I didn't mess with people, their wives, children, properties and didn't hurt or take anybody's life, then I was good in God's eyes, and I was 'as clean as a whistle' in God's books. I believed that smoking, drinking and being with any mature consenting woman, in short, promiscuity per se, could not simply make anyone a hell deserving sinner. God is in the heart, and as a spirit, He is everywhere. I never stole from anyone. I did not fight or argue except occasional family bickering and squabbles with my women 'n' stuff. I had no police record other than a couple of traffic offenses. I had a triple "A" credit rating record. I do not mean to sound 'holier than thou' or portray myself as a holy man, I was simply an upstanding average bloke.

In retrospect, I heard the message of the Word, but may have missed the point. True enough, God is in the heart, though some people may have shallow hearts. However, each heart has a God Centred hole, which gives each person the conscience for discerning what is right or wrong.

Financially, it appeared I was up for some challenging times ahead. Suddenly, I had to shoulder the bills alone, which hitherto I had shared, in some proportion, with Uche. For example, the car note, the rent, phone bill, gas bill, light bill, and credit cards bills. These alone amounted to several hundred dollars a month. I began to think I had been too nice to everyone! I built up other people at my own expense! At this point, I decided to become a full-time businessman, rather than an employee. I was under fire that year on many fronts, but I was determined to achieve two most important projects, namely: to send Uche to Medical School, and to bring my junior brother Cletus to USA.

## CLETUS ARRIVES USA

September 1977, two weeks after Uche left for St Georges' Medical School in Grenada, West Indies, my junior brother, Chidex Cletus arrived at Omaha, Nebraska. Cletus arrived with no money of his own, so his upkeep, school fees, books, etc., became my responsibility. I had paid his one-year school fees of $8,000, to secure his admission letter, and to enable him to get an American Student Visa from Germany, where he was residing with my junior sister, Pat. I was still paying some of the money I had borrowed from my credit card accounts. In addition, I had my own school expenses, car maintenance, grocery bills, to mention a few. The arrival of Cletus was a fulfilment of the promises I had made when I departed Nigeria. Since I set the process in motion of fulfilling my promises, bringing relations and friends over to America, these things usually gave me a wonderful sense of accomplishment. My philosophy was Ghandi said " if you give a man a fish you feed him for day, but if you teach how to fish, you feed him for life". Reverend Jesse Jackson, a Black American political activist said to the effect that what we ask for is to give us a hand, not a hand-out. A little kindness to a man can makes a significant difference to his life, and in the end the love and kindness we give in our lifetime is the only love and kindness people will remember about us. Jesse Jackson also said, 'if you think education is expensive, try ignorance'. Prior to Cletus' arrival, a Form I-20 and admission letter were sent out to him in Bad Nauheim, western Germany, where he was staying with our sister Pat and her husband. This followed with a guarantor's affidavit of financial support, which stated my place of work, position, and income. With a powerful cover note from the vice chancellor of the University of Nebraska, it was sent directly to the American Embassy in Frankfurt Germany. From what I heard, the Embassy, after looking over the documents took the initiative to call on the young child to report at the US Embassy and pickup his visa to Nebraska, U.S.A. He was expected to commence his university studies in September 1977. That very year, for no apparent reason, the Nigerian students' community in Nebraska became engulfed in a new craze. Show of big cars, further adorned with new brides -American born women. Some of the fashionable big cars then were Monte Carlos, El Dorados, Mercury Cougars, Thunderbirds, Cordoba, Fleetwoods and Lincoln Continentals. I had always enjoyed compact sports cars, but to be like the 'Joneses' Uche and I jointly bought a heavy, wickedly loaded metallic black Cougar Mercury. It was indeed a prestigious ride. When we did not go to the automatic car wash centre, we spent hours washing, waxing, polishing, before rolling it out for a cruise around town, and especially through downtown, the Lakeside and the Parks in those crazy summer days. With the side windows rolled down, we greeted other drivers and pedestrians, including total strangers, bellowing 'what's up men!' or 'what's up girl! or responding, 'alright am hip!' 'Ride on' or 'not a lot!' etc., Occasionally, we cruised to social functions, speakeasies and house parties, which usually lasted after hours, or to the early mornings. There were barbeque parties, picnicking, and all manner of happenings at the weekend.

I thought, albeit briefly, that it was utterly selfish for Uche to have left me stuck in such a financial tight spot.

Like the Kenny Rogers song in 'Lucille' – which says 'you chose a fine time to leave me' I felt sick to my stomach at my financial situation. I was so perturbed, that after a reckoning exercise, I ripped the paper to shreds, without a second thought. I might as well do the "goddam" dishes, to keep everywhere spic 'n' span before going out, in case I happened to come back with a slick chick, or in case I got a surprise visitor. I plugged the kitchen sink, poured in an appropriate amount of liquid dishwashing soap. After running hot water, it foamed, and I began to wash and wipe the flat plates and the soup bowls. I scrubbed the dishes with soap and rag, rinsed and dried with the dish towel. Having finished and stacked away the plates in the dish cabinet above the cooker. I paused with a can of Adolf's Coors Beer. Then, I resumed with alacrity, to finish off the washing of the wine glasses, tumblers, and cups.

I took a rag, with a half- clenched fist and shoved it into the first submerged fragile wine glass. I may have tried to reach the bottom of it when I heard a shattering or a crack and felt a cut on my index finger. I let go of both glass and rag and eased my hand out. Go- -so! I had a deep laceration to my finger, blood gushing everywhere. I gritted my teeth in pain and frustration, and went to the bathroom basin, washed, and cleaned the open wound. The cut was deep, the finger was nearly severed. I bandaged it with my handkerchief over a couple of Kleenex tissues. I moaned and groaned, as I drove with one hand, and bled all the way to the University of Nebraska Medical Centre, Emergency Unit.

I was rushed into a cubicle by the nurses, within minutes a doctor came to examine me. I was given seven stitches, plus I was given an intravenous ATS injection. My finger was dressed, painkillers prescribed. I was discharged to report back at the Outpatients Department (OPD) in three or four days. I adequately covered with Blue Cross, Blue Shield Insurance, even for major medicals. I handed over my insurance card to the cashier, who copied the card numbers and promptly returned my card to me. I left the building, feeling rather upset about the day so far, only to find out that my car had been clamped at the left rear wheel, by the Campus Police or Security, as I had blocked a fire exit. I had to pay twenty dollars, before my car was released. I thought it was preposterous to ticket an emergency patient's car, because if I had phoned the hospital from my house, they would have had to come with sirens to pick me up. In fact, I was in no mood to argue. I went home and stopped there for the rest of the day.

## TIME WITH JOHN HANCOCK INSURANCE COMPANY

Having left the job at the Air force Base, and dropped out of the Doctor of Pharmacy programme, I obtained admission to study the MBA programme and decided to return to flexible employment, as an Insurance Salesman. I was hired easily by my former employer John Hancock Insurance. The staff of company, John Hancock Insurance take pride in stating that Mr John Hancock was the first American to sign the American Declaration of Independence in 1775.

## SOLACE IN THE UNRAVELLING UPHEAVAL

Despite the difficulties in my way, I took solace in finding relevant texts in the Bible, this gave me consolation. I chose biblical references such as the word 'ABBA' and personalised by referencing to my hometown of Abba. I am an ABBA son, and the bible mentions God as 'ABBA, FATHER.' My middle name is Chibuzor, and the Holy book testifies 'So God created man (Chibuzo), in His own image, in the image of God He created him.' (Genesis 1:27). I have always felt that God refers to me when He said, 'Before I formed you in the womb, I knew you; before you were born, I set you apart' (Jeremiah 1:5) Also, I claimed the biblical reference from God that He chose me because He emphatically states "You did not choose me, I chose you and appointed you" (John 15:16). Further, the Bible states that 'For those, He foreknew He also predestined, to be conformed to the LIKENESS of His son, that he might be the FIRSTBORN among many brothers' (Romans 8:29). I incorporated these to be my personal motto; Nwachinemere – Akaraka meaning that everything that happens to a man is controlled by the unseen hand of destiny. (God Almighty)

## LULAMA CAME ALONG FROM SOUTH AFRICA

In the same week in September 1977, after my baby brother had arrived in the USA, I went to the University of Nebraska Omaha (UNO) Student Centre to invite some of my friends to a small party, which I intended to hold in my flat that evening. I saw two young girls who appeared to be looking at me with keen interest. I went across to them, introduced myself and we chatted a little. I invited them to my party. They gave me their names as Ms Lulu and Ms Pam, and I gave them my home address. They duly arrived and thoroughly enjoyed themselves. I danced with both, and sometimes the three of us danced together, or they took turns to dance with me, one at a time. At the end of the evening, they helped me wash up. At about 4 am, the three of us huddled up on my waterbed. The girls were in their early twenties, and had come from South Africa in same week, to do their master's degree in social work, on Fulbright
Scholarship. Subsequently, the three of us became very friendly and ended up living together, with my brother, in my flat. As time went on, it became clear to Pamela that Luluma and I had become

an item. Pam came home, after a month and announced she was moving out, to live with another Nigerian she met at the campus.

I took her to her new address, and I continued to visit her from time to time, as a friend. By December 1977, Lulu was pregnant with our first child. I left her at the flat with my brother Cletus (Cley) and flew to Nigeria, on the fifteenth December 1977. I had been informed my sister Pat had arrived in Nigeria from Germany with her four-year-old son. I heard also she had obtained good employment in Kano at Magwan Hotel and Dalai Hotel and that our mother was extremely elated to see her first grandchild, Chino Carl. Therefore, I was also in high spirits to see my sister and meet my nephew. My baby brother, Chidex increased my expectation, when he perhaps exaggerated how happy our mother and sister would be to see me in Nigeria. He said that to our mother, it would be a dream come true.

## THE DEATH OF MY MOTHER

I arrived in Nigeria on the 16th of December 1977, my cousins Edmund (Eddy), and Samuel (Sam) and our uncle Emmerson (Emma) came to the Airport to meet me. We all slept at Emmerson's flat at Itire, Lagos. The building itself was in a bad state and one could smell human faeces as we walked up the stairs to the flat. Mosquitoes were in abundance, and it was difficult to sleep. As early as 4.30am, I was woken up by the Muslim's call to prayers of the faithful. The loud blaring speakers from the mosque next door further interrupted my sleep. Early that morning, we loaded up Eddy's 504 Peugeot. Sam, Eddy, Emma, and I left Lagos for our village, Abba, Nkwerre in the Eastern part of Nigeria. Sam, who was then a professional driver, took the wheel. We left Lagos, passed through Shagamu on the route toward Ore and Benin City. On the way, we stopped for me to buy certain special edibles, which I intended to give my mother, giant snails (Congo meat), dried bush meat or grasscutter (nchi), bunches of ugu and ukazi vegetables, and a bag of garri.

When we arrived in Benin, we stopped for lunch at a neat roadside restaurant. I picked up the tab and we continued our journey, whilst discussing, joking, and laughing along the way. We crossed the Onitsha Bridge and Upper Iweka and headed towards Ozubulu and Oba, when we came across a head-on collision, which was a fatal car crash. We saw dead bodies everywhere. I wondered how and why the car and bus ended up in the bush. I prayed that the souls of the dead people would rest in peace (RIP) (ha zuru ike na ndokwa).

We drove past Ihiala, and I remembered my first love, Patience. In fact, I was tempted to make detour to her husband's compound for a quick visit. However, my cotravellers persuaded me to get home first before visiting anywhere else. We continued through Ihioma, Orlu, Nkwerre and at Nkworji, we veered left to Abba town. From Onitsha to my hometown, I could vividly feel, smell, and taste our native Igboland. The red mud houses, occasional zinc houses, the tall palm and raffia palm trees, Iroko trees, banana and plantain trees, the elephant grasses, yam and cocoyam cash crops and the other familiar scenery. As we approached our compound, I was surprised to see so many people in front of our house. I said to others in the car that I told my mother not to tell people I was coming home. I was shocked that so many people were seemingly waiting for my arrival. Our car came to halt right in front of my father's house. All hell broke loose! People were, crying, wailing, or sobbing. My sister Patricia threw herself on me and yelled – "Adol, mama awula oooh" – Adol, our mother has died. My two junior brothers Damian and Chinedu were crying, and they both came and touched me. My mother's senior brother, Christopher Uzoukwu from Ezike, Umuduru, Mbano, accosted me and whispered in my ears 'They have killed her!'

He beckoned me to follow, so he could show me where my mother had been hastily buried the previous day. The crowd of mourners followed us to the grave site. I stood over the red mound and shed tears. I muttered "Mama, Adol is back from USA" and "May your soul rest in perfect peace." I thanked her for her motherly love showered on me as I was growing up. From my mother's grave site, I went over to where my father was buried in 1974, two years after I left Nigeria. I said similar things over his grave, thanked him and prayed for his soul to rest in perfect peace. Thereafter, I returned to the centre of our compound, I looked left, right and centre. People were wailing, howling, crying, shedding tears and one or two might even have been shedding crocodile tears. I looked around. Nothing made sense anymore. Was it a dream or was it real? Any direction I looked, I noticed people in that direction scampered and disappeared, perhaps thinking 'I had lost my marbles'. They all believed that, maybe having come from America, I might start shooting people dead at any moment. One village woman shouted out that I should be restrained, else I might kill myself.

I ignored the rants. My thought at the time was that she was probably trying to incite me to attempt suicide. Physically, I did not cry out as I should, because I could hear my parents saying to me to be strong, to bear the pain with fortitude, to be a man and take over the reins of the family, and not allow others to mock me.

I was told that my mother, late Mrs Elizabeth Fanny Ejimoleke Okoroha had gone to the Nkworji market that eventful day 13/12/77 and bought food stuff for her small restaurant business. She and her staff were cooking rice and stew when she collapsed. She was rushed to the nearby Mrs Vicky's Maternity Home, where she was put on a sugar solution drip, she hadn't known she was diabetic, she had collapsed on the account of diabetic coma.

My brothers told me how happy she was, looking forward to my coming home from overseas. I had sent a thousand dollars ($1000) to her in the same week, to tide her over and to facilitate repairs to our old house. I advised her to also use the money to prepare for my return. I was devastated at her sudden death. She was barely sixty years old. The timing was ironic, harsh, and cruel. Fate and destiny rule the events of our lives, however, I felt this was so unkind.

I knew many people were unhappy about my mother's good fortune. I was also aware many other people envied her, indeed, some didn't like her, for the simple fact that three of her children were overseas, whilst none of theirs were. I could not put a finger on any one person and say, 'you killed my mum.' I asked God for answers but got no response. So, I followed my heart and my instinct. She was a Christian mother; she always wore the Rosary around her neck and attended church every day. She prayed day and night and joked and laughed with everyone. I am like her, with no bitterness whatsoever in the heart, for anyone. My mother would never hurt a fly. People always say that whatever happens is the will of God. That period was an extremely low moment for me. I was tempted to ask God, where was He in all of this, and why did he allow my good mother to die, when so many wicked persons were walking around on the face of the earth? Anyway, that was how it was. My mother's demise finally convinced me for the last time that life is simply vanity upon vanity. I came to accept the words of the acclaimed poet Henry Wandsworth Longfellow, that life is 'but an empty dream.' I was crushed, but I picked myself up and moved on. I told my sister to look after our siblings until I returned from the USA, with the intention of arranging for the young boys to join me in the USA. I instructed my mother's co-wives to look after my mother's farms, cash crops and livestock. I directed my sister to take any of our mother's personal items she wanted. After Christmas 1977 and into New Year 1978, I returned safely to Omaha, Nebraska, USA.

That chilly winter morning, from JFK Airport in New York, I telephoned my home in Nebraska. My brother Chidex broke down and cried uncontrollably, when I told him I didn't see our mother, that she had died two days before I arrived home. With tears in my eyes, I consoled the poor boy and urged him to accept it as the will of God, and to be strong. When Chidex regained some composure, I enquired about the situation at home, particularly whether Uche had come home for Christmas holidays. He told me Uche came home from medical school on 18th December and met the pregnant Miss Lulu at the flat. I understood there followed an altercation, resulting in a physical fight. The two women fought fiercely, exchanging blows and scratches. Lulu, being pregnant, fled the flat for sake of her unborn baby. Chidex told me her whereabouts were unknown, as some good neighbours took her to an undisclosed location, pending my arrival.

During the journey, I reflected on everything that happened to me in the past year, and I was glad to be alive, the annus horribilis was behind me.

When I got to Omaha, my long-term girlfriend and fiancée Uche, was in the flat. She cried over my mother's death and consoled and sympathised with me on my bereavement. Then we discussed Lulu, my new girlfriend, who was pregnant. I confirmed I indeed wanted the baby. Uche hit the roof, she was unhappy, to say the least. She questioned why I encouraged her to have abortion in 1976 and had encouraged her to go to medical school, yet suddenly I developed an appetite for a wife and a baby. I spent the rest of the holiday with her in our flat, until she returned to her school in January, to return in June 1978, for the summer holidays. Whilst I was with Uche, I was able to visit Lulu regularly. at her temporary accommodation. However, as soon as Uche departed Omaha for the West Indies, Lulu returned to the flat. Subsequently, on Lulu's initiative, we found improved accommodation in a posh neighbourhood with her name and mine on the tenancy agreement. Lulu ensured her name appeared on the Tenancy, to prevent Uche from returning, to kick her out. Our new rented accommodation comprised a two bedroom apartment, large living room, spacious kitchen and bathroom, situated in West Omaha, after the Crossroads shopping centre. We moved in together, with my brother Chidex who occupied our spare room and thereby stopped sleeping on the living room sofa.

## BIRTH OF MY SECOND DAUGHTER

The year 1978 started well for my growing family and me. My partner, Lulu advised me we should go to Wayne, Arkansas and bring my wife Carol and daughter Chichi back to Omaha. I thought it was a great idea. Since I was still married to Carole, I had to obtain another flat, in both our names. So, I secured a flat on Military Avenue in Omaha, Near Mutual of Omaha Insurance Company headquarters. Then, Lulu and I drove down to Wayne Arkansas and collected my three-year-old daughter and her mother, then drove back to Omaha, in my Cougar Mercury. My daughter lived with Lulu and my brother. Carol and I lived at the other flat on Military Avenue. After a month, Douglas County Local Authority assessed Carolyn Okoro, and offered her a permanent place at the hospital, also known as Old Folks Home. Chichi and I usually visited her mother every alternate weekend, or at least once a month. Carolyn was always elated to see us. We also took to her a bottle or two of ground snuffs. She had developed a habit of putting snuff in her mouth, in the aftermath of her gunshot incident in Wayn,e and whilst she was in the Memphis Tennessee Hospital. I kept Carol's flat available for Uche, when she returned for the holidays. Uche and I lived at the flat when she came for the summer holiday, in 1978. Uche was still in Omaha when Lulu delivered a baby girl, in July 1978. I was present at the hospital and watched the full delivery of the baby. As soon as the baby was delivered and it cried, Lulu asked what gender the baby was, and the midwife replied it was a girl. Immediately, Lulu held my hand and said 'Chibuzo, I am sorry that it was not a boy.' When I went home that night, and told Uche the news of the baby's birth, Uche couldn't hide her joy, as she blurted out 'Thank God, it was a girl.' I asked Uche the reason for her jubilation, she responded that if it were a boy then Lulu would 'never be out of my life'. I named my beautiful daughter Chioma

(Blessing) Delores Okoro. Delores is shortened to Didi.

Uche left Omaha after that summer and did not come back again. During her 1978 December Holidays, she telephoned me on a few occasions from Burbank, California and Long Island, New York. Years later, I heard she qualified as a Medical Doctor, with speciality in Gynaecology and Obstetrics. I learnt also she had subsequently married a white guy, and was practising medicine in New York, USA.

This crazy thing called love! It is so funny, this mysterious human psychological state of trance, known as being in love. It can blossom like a flower and may flourish like a palm tree by the seashore, or it may wither like autumn leaves. Who would have foreseen, or believed one day Uche and I would be living with different lovers, without any inkling of each other. Yet, at one point, we were inseparable, as if we were joined at the hip, like Siamese twins. It had seemed at the time that we could not exist without each other.

*Myself on holiday in Washington DC, USA.*

*Myself and my staff, Solicitor Fola and Titus, at Graceland Solicitors Woolwich Office in* London.

*At Graceland Solicitors Christmas party in London.*

**CHAPTER FOURTEEN**

# Military Avenue Dry Cleaners and My First Home

In 1978, I was studying for my master's Degree in business administration MBA Programme and working for John Hancock Insurance Company. To assist Lulu, I decided to buy an on-going Laundromat and dry-cleaning outfit, located on the same Military Avenue as Carol's flat. I bought both the business and the building on a land contract. The arrangement was that I made a substantial initial down payment and committed to fixed monthly payments for a specified number of years. It was agreed that upon the expiration of the period, the ownership of the business and the building would be mine, free and clear. The seller was Mr Schaiffer, a white man, who was a renowned tree surgeon and who was at that time tired of juggling his tree trimming business, with running a laundromat. The

Laundromat was next door to an apartment complex of flats. Lulu attended classes for her master's degree lectures and returned daily to run and manage our laundry outfit business. The University of Nebraska (UNO) Lulu and I attended operated four terms in an academic year, namely Winter, Spring, Summer, and Fall, which also represents the four seasons in USA. In winter, December, January and February, the weather is freezing cold, with snow everywhere. There are no leaves on the trees, unless those of some evergreen plants, shrubs, and trees. Many insects and animals hibernate. Everyone, including students, bundled up with many layers of clothes, socks, and overcoats. Days are shorter, as darkness falls early, starting at about 3 pm. The falling snow is pretty and fun, but once on the ground it turns to black ice, which is slippery and treacherous. The student centres and cafeterias are usually full of students eating, drinking, chatting, and socialising. Throughout the year, the campus security police are busy checking unauthorised parking and issuing tickets and/or towing cars away. Some people fall in love easily in winter, people like to share their beds with others to stay warm.

Spring is in March, April, and May. The snow starts melting and the days gets brighter. The daffodils bloom, the flowers, shrubs, and trees start sprouting new green leaves and flowers. It is not as cold, and dressing becomes lighter. Birds start to sing again and there is freshness in the air. Some areas can be flooded and, in some places, melting snow can run like a small stream.

Daisies grow everywhere, and you see young men and women making daisy chains, signifying their love.

Summertime comes usually in June, July, and August, and in my view, these are best times of the year. There is plenty of sunshine and fun, beautiful women everywhere, wearing skimpy bikini bottoms, or shorts. Those who have it, flaunt it boldly and loudly, with no apologies. Some young men and women walk around almost naked. It was usual for people to drive to the lakes or parks for small parties.

Fall is also called autumn in Europe, and it is in September, October, and November. The leaves turn brown, and blossom starts falling from the trees. There are dry leaves and blossom petals everywhere on the ground. The gardeners have a busy time sweeping it up. Fall is usually very windy at times; it is a prelude to winter. It is usually the beginning of a new academic year.

By early 1979, I took a mortgage and bought a three-bedroom house on 42nd Street in North Omaha NE. I gave up the tenancies of the two flats. Lulu and I, together with our two daughters (Chichi and Didi) moved to the new house. Cletus used the opportunity to rent another flat in his sole name and lived separately from us. In the same year, Lulu graduated with a master's degree (MSc.) and we attended her graduation, and I hosted a lavish house party in her honour. I considered my journey so far, since coming to America: Lulu attended graduate school classes, alongside managing our business. I reflected that I had started as a bus boy at University of Minnesota, when I arrived at USA in 1973. Thereafter, I was a janitor as an undergraduate. In my freshman and sophomore years I cleaned classrooms. Later, I worked at Graco in Minneapolis MN, on a factory assembly line, in my Junior and Senior years, before becoming a door-to door Insurance Salesman for John Hancock in St Paul MN after attaining my first degree in Business

Administration. Subsequently, I worked as an administrator at Boys Town, Omaha NE, and at Offutt Air Force Base in Belleview, Nebraska, before I finally had a break, and opened my own Laundry and DryCleaning business in 1978, whilst simultaneously working again for John Hancock in Omaha NE, and at the same time completing an MBA on a part time basis.

In 1979, things continued as normal. Lulu and I had two daughters, lived in our own home, and had two cars. Lulu completed her master's degree in social Welfare and her $400 per month Fulbright scholarship stipend was stopped. The immigration thought she should leave the USA, as per the terms of her scholarship. I was prepared to stand shoulder to shoulder with her and fight the US Immigration Authorities, but my beloved Lulu really wanted to leave. She was also pregnant with our second child. She urged me that we should take our children, leave USA, and return to Nigeria. I told Lulu to go there first and stay with my sister Pat, and her four children in Kano, and that if she could get employment, then I would return home to Nigeria, and we would live there. She was already heavily pregnant, and I was hopeful for a boy this time, after my two girls. My four-year-old daughter Chichi, bluntly refused to go to Nigeria with Lulu without me, preferring to 'stay with Daddy.'

Towards the end of 1980, Lulu left USA to South Africa, from where she intended to travel to Nigeria to live. She had her second child, a baby girl on 2nd January 1981. She named the baby girl Adaeze (Ibo word for Princess) and Wellekezi (Zulu word for second daughter).

Easter 1981, I flew into Zambia, then on to Gaborone in Botswana, where Lulu and her brother's wife Ms Thandi Kray collected me, and we drove to Mabatho, Mafeking and onwards to Tuang, where Lulu's mother lived on a big farm. That area of South Africa was called Bophuthatswana. At the time, in Zambia, President Kenneth Kaunda had been in power for over 20 years. I recollected that during the Biafra war, Kaunda was one the African leaders who recognised Biafra as a Country, in 1968. In the Zambian capital Lusaka, I spent 4 days at the Caledonian Hotel, costing only a few Zambian Kwachas per night, however, the taxi driver who drove me to the Airport on my departure, ran off, disappearing with my super-fly leather Jacket. In those days it was risky and dangerous to travel to South Africa with a Nigerian Passport. The Government in Pretoria felt Nigeria's opposition to Apartheid was a grave concern. That was the state of things before Mr Nelson Mandela was released, after twenty-seven years imprisonment, on February 11th, 1990. My mother-in-law, Lulu's mum, ensured a huge ram was slaughtered to welcome me, and to cement my traditional and customary marriage to Lulama Okoro (nee Qalinge). I spent a week with the family, before briefly visiting Nigeria, from where I returned to the USA. I agreed with Lulu that she and the kids would go to Nigeria before Christmas of that year.

## THE MILITARY AVENUE LAUNDERETTE IN NEBRASKA

'Life is tricky, when one appears to have mastered the tricks of life, then it's time to go, so I reasoned. As mentioned earlier, from my fat weekly wage from John Hancock Insurance and my savings, I was able to purchase a laundrette, in Nebraska. I bought the place, the business and whole building from Mr Schaefer for $50.000 in 1978. It was on a land contract, which meant I paid agreed monthly instalments to the seller. I could pay any extra amount at any time, to reduce or clear the balance owed. It turned out to be a money spinner. Lulu managed it well, until she left at the end of 1980.

In 1981, one American boy, joked that my laundromat could be 'a suitable place in future'. Little did I know that some nutters would, within a few weeks, set the place ablaze and then simply disappeared into thin air. I strongly suspected the young child but could not place his motive for such a criminal act. Moreover, I did not have details, of his whereabouts and I didn't want to compromise my insurance claim. I was at home, when I was called by police and fire services department, to be told my business premises were on fire. I drove down to the spot and watched helplessly, with other onlookers, as the fire brigade tackled the inferno, engulfing my business and property. Later, I had to report the fire incident to my insurers, who asked rigorous and relevant questions, and subsequently paid compensation for my loss. I used the money to pay off the balance owed to Mr Frank Schaefer, and to re-build a bigger premises. When the business re opened I started getting dry cleaning contract offers from major American organisations, such as the Air force. The tragedy became an opportunity of good fortune for me. Good life and good living rolled in; my good luck appeared to have held up at the critical hour.

## SHERRY SMITH AND OUR SON MONSO

In 1981, Lulu was no longer in USA. Uche had disappeared and stopped contacting me, whilst Carol was stuck at an old people's home, as disabled. I started looking for a new lady, at least to help me look after my five-year-old daughter. The first one that came along was simply fine. She was petite, her name was Sherry Smith, a Baptist pastor's daughter, from Missouri city, Missouri. Sherry was visiting her aunt in Omaha and her aunty was a girlfriend to my colleague, on the Doctor of Pharmacy programme (PharmD). His name was Mr Emeka. He had given me a shout inviting me to come and meet a 'pretty young girl'. I went over and it was 'love at first sight' for both of us. She was about 10 years younger than me and already a single parent. She had given birth to her two-yearold daughter when she was seventeen years old. I took her home on the same day, and she quickly settled in.

At the end of the same week, I drove to Missouri with her, where she introduced me to her parents. I slept overnight at a nearby motel with Sherry, and thereafter we collected her things and returned to Omaha. Sherry lived with me for the rest of 1981. She was five months pregnant when she left me and went back to her parents, with the pregnancy. One problem with me is that women despise me when they are heavily pregnant, because my constitution is unable to be intimate with a lady when she is heavily pregnant. I get squeamish or develop a morbid unrealistic fear, that the child in the womb may be harmed in the process. This was one of the reasons for the departure of both Lulu and Sherry whilst they were pregnant. In 1982, I was present when

Sherry delivered our son, and I named him Monso (from the holy spirit) Marc Anthony Okoro.

In December 1981, I went to Nigeria in the company of my daughter Chichi, because I had agreed with Lulu that she would come to reside in Nigeria and get employment, to enable me to finally return to Nigeria. When I got to Nigeria with Chichi, there was no sign of Lulu, or the two kids. I left Chichi with my sister, Patricia and I returned to USA with my other younger brother Damien Iyke. I had obtained admission for him to study engineering at the University of Nebraska. I was able to pay his school fees for one year, which was around $8000.00. I assembled my tax documents and other relevant papers, and I took them with me to Nigeria. Thereafter, whilst I was in Nigeria, I took Iyke to the American Consulate and within an hour, my brother Iyke was issued a US Student Visa for three years.

I had earlier invited him to come to the USA as a visitor, with the aim of trying to change his visa, once he arrived in the USA. The US Immigration in New York stopped him, unfortunately, and he was asked the purpose of his visit. He told them he was visiting his senior brother Mr Adolf Okoro. When they searched his luggage, they discovered a letter that said, 'if you come as a visitor, we could change your visa to a student visa afterwards'. On the account of that letter, he was remanded to appear before an immigration Judge the next day and to show cause why he should not be refused entry into USA. I called around from Nebraska and succeeded in hiring a New York Lawyer, Attorney Brown, to represent my brother, before the Immigration and Nationality Services Tribunal (IMS Tribunal). I flew into Manhattan NY the next day from Omaha. I checked into a holiday inn and took a taxi to the hearing the next morning. We lost the case and my brother was denied entry into the USA. On top of my expenses, I lost the cost of the round-trip tickets which I had bought for him – Nigeria to USA and from USA to Nigeria, under the guise he was coming mainly to visit me in the US. I incurred additional costs of my flight to NY, and the cost of overnight hotel accommodation and legal fees. However, in my frame of mind at that time, I did not consider the costs, expenses and inconvenience as wasteful, because I had an obligation to assist my siblings, my kith and kin. Nowadays, I have observed with great sadness, many people are so self-centred, individualistic, and vainglorious, they refuse to give a helping hand to close family members and relatives. It reflects the corrosion of family values in these modern times.

1982 was also an eventful year in my household. Apart from the birth of my son, Monso, I also obtained a master's degree in public administration, from the University of Nebraska, and immediately commenced an external PhD programme, which I completed in 1984. Lulu eventually went to Nigeria with our two kids in December 1982. They lived with my sister Patricia. After six months, she was employed as a Lecturer, at the Bayero University in Kano. She was given private accommodation, and started demanding I return to Nigeria, as we previously agreed. However, I procrastinated, until April 1984, when I finally mustered enough courage to leave America, 'God's Own Country,' and returned home to Nigeria for good. It seemed that the pull of my homeland, as well as my filial and family obligations, superseded and triumphed over my desire for the American 'good life', or Pie in the Sky. In 1983, I found myself alone again for one week. I met Ms Inez Robinson. She was a skinny and tall, half-caste. Her physique and stature just suited me. Her mother, Ellein, was white and her father was a native Black American man. Inez had known better days. She talked endlessly about her days and experiences as a cheerleader, with various football teams, including Nebraska Cornhusker and Dallas Cowboys. On our first date, Inez stood me up. She simply did not show or offer any reasonable apology. She later explained she had developed cold feet, for two reasons. Firstly, she and her ex-husband used to be my customers at my laundromat. Secondly, she said that she had never dated an African, and was unsure of what she was getting herself into. She had heard African men treat their women as chattels, and women must 'do as they're told'. I told her that was gibberish and untrue. Inez also informed me she also contested in various beauty pageants. When I met her, she was a Dietician at St Joseph's Hospital, in Omaha Nebraska. She was going through a divorce and had two daughters Pat and Michelle, living with her. Inez and her husband finally divorced, sold their house and split the proceeds. She rented a small two-bedroom house for herself and her two kids, in North Omaha. Whenever I went and slept at her house, she would tell her daughters to stay with their grandmother, at the granny's house. Neither the children, nor other family members approved of the arrangement. One of Inez's brothers, Bootsy, decided to take matters into his own hands. I was at Inez's house one evening, waiting for her to come home from work. There was a knock at the door. I tiptoed to the door and looked through the peephole. I saw Bootsy with a double-barrelled sawn-off shot gun aimed at the keyhole. Instinctively, I ducked and dived in a flash. Simultaneously, I heard the exploding gun shot. I hid under the dining table, wondering if the shooter was coming in. The hole in the wooden door was wide enough to slam dunk a basketball. When I looked outside, from behind the window blinds, I couldn't see anyone. I called Inez to come home, explaining her brother had shot at me. Inez quickly responded she wasn't coming. She questioned whether I was out of my mind, since I should have known her brother could equally have killed her, if she'd been at the door. I dialled 911 and called the police. I also called my brother, Damian, to come over. I told him that I had been shot at, and he started crying over the phone. My brother Cletus was in Nigeria at that time. Police took incident reports, my brother helped pack my things into the car and we drove back to my home in West Omaha. I was breathing heavily at my very narrow escape, akin to a cat with nine lives. I had just cheated death. Inez drove straight to my flat later that night and remained with me, stating she would never return to her house, ever again. We lived together happily thenceforth.

By April 1983, I evicted a tenant at my North 42nd Street house, and Inez and I moved into the house, which used to be the residence of Lulu and I. Inez and I lived there until I returned to Nigeria, in April 1984. By the way, no one was ever prosecuted for the attempted murder on me, as Bootsy, the main suspect, denied it was him who shot at me.

When I returned to the US, from Nigeria, to visit in 1985, I sadly discovered Inez had either refused, or failed, to pay the monthly $250 mortgage on the house. Thus, after ten months of arrears, the Mortgage Bank had repossessed the house. I lost all the equity I had built up in the house, for trusting a woman, who betrayed my trust.

Once my brother Cletus heard about the upcoming Nigerian Elections in 1983, as a graduate of Political Science, he left America and returned home to Nigeria. He also lived with our sister Pat and her children in Kano.

I brought Cletus and Damian to USA and very nearly killed both, over their misbehaviour and my overreaction.

## DEATH OF CAROLYN CONNIEGENE WALKER OKOROHA

In December 1983, I was preparing to visit home, Nigeria, for Christmas, when suddenly Carolyn Okoro passed away in her sleep, on 18th December. May her soul rest in peace. The postmortem examination recorded the cause of death as by natural causes. Her two sisters, Charlene Walker and Barbara Reid, came from St Paul Minnesota to Omaha, for Carolyn's funeral and burial, at a West Omaha Cemetery, on a cold January in 1984. My intended home visit for Christmas was cancelled, and I forfeited the ticket. Later, our family life insurance cover with John Hancock Insurance Company paid an insurance benefit of $10,000 to me, as the surviving policy beneficiary.

## LEAVING AMERICA – RETURNING HOME TO NIGERIA

In 1984, I decided to leave America and return to Nigeria for good. I knew this was an uphill task, requiring a great deal of planning and money. I had asked Lulu to go first to Kano and stay with my sister; she later got a job as a lecturer, at Bayero

University in Kano. I sold my dry-cleaning businesses and my other rental properties, loaded my Volvo car and other personal effects, into a container, for onward shipment to Nigeria. I also had with me a treasured black box, containing my savings of $50,000 dollars in cash. The exchange rate at that time was about one dollar to one Nigerian naira.

I had a great deal on my mind, as I prepared to go home to Nigeria. There was great expectation, both within me and outside, to 'measure up' after all my achievements in the USA. I was expected to at least build a modern storey building. Hence, this was a priority. As a first son, in our Ibo culture, it is a 'sine qua non' that I should have male heirs, therefore I needed to have more children. My father used to tell me that success without a successor is failure. In my circumstances with three daughters and a son in America, who will never return to live in Nigeria, I desperately needed male children to bear my family name, in my community and to possibly take over, when God decided my work on earth was done. The Ijezie Osuagwu Okoroha and David Azunnah Osuagwu Okoroha lineage must continue uninterrupted, ad infinitum. I would not permit any act or omission on my part, and on my watch, to break the continuity of my heritage, if I was still alive and kicking. Our elders say one cannot be crying soap is in his eyes, whilst he is still in the stream of waters. No onewill take my rightful position of headship in the family as the first son.

Mrs Igbedie Osuagwu Okoroha, my mother's aunt and second wife of my grandfather, and her sister, my mother Mrs Fanny

Elizabeth Osuagwu Okoroha ensured by fate and good fortune that I am in my current hereditary position in the family tree. I was schooled from childhood in the history of the betrothal of my mother to my father and the personal sacrifice of my mother's aunt, Igbedie. I have the burden of tradition to uphold and maintain the heritage and dynasty of my Osuagwu Okoroha lineage. I did not choose it, but the hand of history was laid on me.

During the weeks leading up to my departure to Africa, I went out daily in Omaha Nebraska with my young girlfriend Miss Sweetie Hughes, to buy items to be shipped in my container, which was to be loaded at Houston Texas. I picked up a fridge, freezer, television, household items such as mirrors, wall clocks, cutlery and crockery. I bought suits, shirts, caps, shoes, and ties. Twenty-one-year-old Miss Sweetie and I had been trying for a baby for over two years, but to no avail. Every time she had her monthly period, she said in disdain 'the stupid mother nature was here again'.

For the two-day journey to Nigeria, I rented a big U-Hall truck, and we loaded it up. My partner Ms Inez Johnson and I took turns to drive the truck and my Volvo 244DL to Houston. In Texas, my cousin, Dr Lambert and Peter and their wives, Amaka Okoro, our sisters, Mrs Elizabeth Okoroafor, and Mrs Ngozi Agenti were present. Also, Mr Eden and Mr Don Nwoke and their wives were present, and they took Inez and I to the harbour, where the container was being loaded for shipment. They also took us to places where we bought more items for shipment, rugs, coffee tables, couches, wall to wall blinds and so on. Our relations in Houston met me, and I took them out for lunch at the Houston Space Centre. Having loaded my container, Inez and I flew back to Omaha. The container was to take about a month for the ship to reach Nigeria. I was already booked to fly out to Nigeria at roughly the time of the container's arrival.

Ms Inez and I felt woozy about our impending separation. I promised her I would return to the USA within six months, and I begged her to please be sure to pay $250 monthly mortgage, to avoid losing our residential house. If I had rented it out, I could have made about $750 per month which was the rent paid by the former tenant. But since Ms Inez didn't want to go elsewhere, I allowed her to continue to live there and just pay the mortgage. We dined at an expensive restaurant the night before I left. I also left a balance of about a thousand dollars in one of my personal Bank Accounts. I gave my brother, Damian the card and the pin number, but warned him to be sure not to touch the money, until I needed it. Alas, about a year later when I returned to visit America, I discovered the hard way that my money had vanished, and my house had been repossessed. So much for my trust in my brother and my partner.
Independently, they both betrayed my trust. But I guess that's life!

## ARRIVING IN NIGERIA 1984

I flew from JFK Airport, New York and arrived safely in Kano, Nigeria, on a sunny day in April 1984. General Muhammad Buhari had seized power on 31st December 1983 and Brigadier Tunde Idiagbon was appointed his second in command.

Political instability in Nigeria was one of the things I had always feared and dreaded, especially whenever I thought of returning home. For one thing, politics in Nigeria can be ruthless, bloody, and deadly. It is usually a 'dog devours dog' scenario. In the aftermath of the military coup, there suddenly emerged military check points everywhere, and no one knew who a friend was, or a foe. It was a terrifying and chilling atmosphere, with soldiers allegedly abusing civilians with impunity. The so-called austerity measure became the norm; prices skyrocketed, fuel shortages, endless queues and so on. It became unlawful to possess any form of foreign currency in Nigeria. A famous musician, Fela Ransome Kuti was jailed for trying to leave Nigeria with sum of £5000 US dollars in his pocket.

Lulu, and our three daughters Chichi Cynthia, Chioma and Didi, and Adaeze Welie came to meet me at the Airport, along with my junior sister, Patricia and her four children Chino, Joy, Uche and Chika. My brothers, Mr Chinedu, our mother's last born and Cletus Chidex who returned from USA and was serving as an (NYSC) Youth Copper, were also present. It was a good feeling to be welcomed home by other family members. We went to my sister's flat off Zoo Road, Kano first, and everyone was fed and watered. I gave out some presents from USA, and later Lulu, our three younger kids and I went to her house near the University.

I remained in Kano for a few days, before heading home to Abba, Imo State. After spending some days at my hometown, I travelled to Lagos, where I sorted papers for the clearing of the container and my imported car, at Port Harcourt Onee wharf. My car was a three-year-old, two door Volvo 244 DL saloon car, with sunroof. Upon obtaining the clearance papers, I flew to Port

Harcourt to pursue the actual clearance of my Container. Five of my relatives were operating as clearing and forwarding Agents at the Port Harcourt/Onee wharfs. I requested the most senior of my cousins, Eddy, in the business, should charge me and do the clearing, but for some undisclosed and inexplicable reason he bluntly refused to assist me in the clearance of my goods. The second most senior cousin, Chike voluntarily offered to clear it, without charging me a penny, other than third party expenses. After about a month, my Car, and the rest of the contents of my Container were at Abba City, my hometown, then in Nkwerre Local Government of Imo
State.

My Abba house, a newly completed four-bedroom bungalow, with a twenty foot by twenty-foot parlour, was ready, except for the installation of the window louvres. I covered the windows with blinds, curtains, and wrappers for a few days, before the louvres, rugs and carpets were fitted. I installed mercury florescent light bulbs. My house gave a vestige of an imported American home, domiciled in a quiet African village, with its veneer of a superbly grand layout and staccato. My shiny Volvo private car parked at the front of my house, complimented the beautiful atmosphere, and pronounced the success and attainment of the owner, as a 'been to' who had really 'arrived'.

My wife Lulu came from Kano to see how I was, and I told her I was trying to bring her down to the East, to possibly live in the village. I remarked that from what I had seen in Kano, I didn't like the thought of living there. If I were to leave America and to live in Nigeria, I wanted to live among my people, my kith and kin, people with the same tongue, same attire and dressing code, the same food, norms and culture, where I would be recognised, respected, and appreciated.

I took Lulu to my school mate Rev. Father Sunny Obiukwu who was a dean and a don at Alvan Ikoku College of
Education, Owerri, Imo State, to find employment for her.

Within a week, Fr. Obiukwu told us Lulu could effectively come and start teaching as a lecturer. I was elated, unfortunately Lulu refused to leave Kano and I refused to move to Kano. There was a stalemate. The next serious conversation we had was my expressed intention to have more children, including male heirs. As a first son, I wanted Lulu to understand and accept I was traditionally and culturally obliged to have more wives, with a view to having more children. My common law wife, Lulu, found it difficult to accept my proposal.

The next time Lulu came down to the East, from the North, she was shocked to see two other ladies cooking, washing, and pottering about in my house. After her short holiday stay, she went to Kano, with no intention of returning. By the end of 1984, Lulu informed me she was going back to South Africa with our youngest child, for a vacation. My sister, Pat insisted - now with hindsight, in error- that Lulu went with her own two daughters. She said she was only going on holiday, but that was over thirty-five years ago.

*My National Youths Service Corps (NYSC) in Owerri Imo State, Nigeria, in 1984-85 at Ministry of Commerce.*

With *Abba Chiefs*

*With my cousin, Johnbosco.*

**CHAPTER FIFTEEN**
---------------------------

# New Wives and Children

By 1985, I was living in my village at Abba with my daughter Chinyere Chichi, and my four common law wives, namely, Mrs Chinyere Okoroha (nee Uzowulu), Mrs Susan Okoroha (nee Egeonu), Mrs Ursulla Okoroha (nee Arimah) and Mrs Eucharia Okoroha (nee Onwuzuruike). At the end of 1985, Mrs Chinyere Okoroha sadly suffered a miscarriage. Mrs Susan Okoroha had a baby boy (Ugonna David) and Mrs Ursulla Okoroha had a baby boy also (Kelechi Kennedy) whilst Mrs Eucharia Okoroha had a baby girl (Akwaugo Emily). Shortly afterwards, Mrs Chinyere Okoroha left me, and I heard she later remarried, within two years. Sadly, I learnt that Chinyere had since passed on. Mrs

Susan Okoroha had two more boys namely Iheanyichukwu Leroy and Nnamdi Derick, respectively. Mrs Ursulla Okoroha also had two more girls namely Amaka Constance and Ginikanwa Stacy. Mrs Eucharia Okoroha did not have any more children and untimely passed away in 2015. In any event, by 1990, six years from when I returned from USA to Nigeria, I had seven children, of which four were boys and three girls, in addition to my other children.

## NYSC

After my arrival in 1984, I went to Lagos and registered to serve as a youth copper, in the compulsory National Youth Service Corps (NYSC) scheme for all University Graduates, before they could be employed in the country. I was forty years old in 1984, but because my first degree was in 1975, I was caught in the scheme. I was one of the last old elephants to serve at such an advanced age. My application for a waiver failed, but I was recompensed by being allowed to serve in Imo State, my home state. I served at the Ministry of Commerce and Industry, Owerri. I commuted daily in my red Volvo 244DL, with open sunmoon roof, from Abba, my hometown, to Owerri, the capital city of Imo State. I met one of my wives at my place of primary assignment. I passed out from NYSC in 1985 with a Certificate
Number 348936. There was an overrated program announcement that those who had passed out from the NYSC, and who had feasible business plans, would be granted an interest free Government loan to start their own businesses. It was a requirement that the business must use local raw material, create

further employment, and the products should benefit the local community, or serve as export produce.

I spent money and commissioned a feasibility study for two different business ventures in manufacturing, or rather the processing of Garri, the local staple food, alternatively going into poultry farming, involving mass production of chickens and eggs, for local sales and consumption. In the end, I was unsuccessful. Again, I realised that to get such a loan, one must know, or be related or connected to the officials at the very top of the program. I was like what was referred to as a 'Johnny just come' JJC, a newcomer without roots. Having just returned from America, I literally knew no one at the top of any government department, or any corporate bodies. Worst of all, I did not even know any person who knew such persons at the top.

## BUSINESS

In 1985, while in Nigeria and serving in the NYSC, I conceived an idea based on my wide experience of insurance brokerage, sales, and marketing in America. I could forage into Insurance brokerage in Nigeria. Consequently, I strove to establish an Insurance Brokerage business in Owerri and later with a branch in Lagos. My Gold Flames Insurance Brokers had its central office, situated at 54 Market Street, Owerri, Imo State. It was on the first floor, with three rooms of office space. I had a Receptionist/Secretary, a landline telephone, and tables and chairs for the Insurance sales Agents, and their clients. A cupboard in my office contained the necessary stationery and forms. There were fitted ceiling fans in all the rooms. However,

I sadly discovered Insurance Business at that level was not lucrative at all in Nigeria. I found out the hard way that the sales Agents were wolves, (thieves) in sheep's clothing. I gave them booklets of fifty insurance covers note in duplicates to sell. However, some of the so-called agents disappeared with the cover notes and went on their own frolics. Most of those who came back, unashamedly told me one unintelligible story after another, in an attempt to explain how the whole booklet had gone, was lost, or stolen, with not a penny realised. I discovered operating an insurance brokerage business in Nigeria was mere tantamount to selling worthless cover-notes, which were to enable drivers to cross the police checkpoints. In case of loss or damage to one's vehicle, one could not claim. Not even for loss of life, or limb. After paying for rents and outgoings, I hardly broke even, let alone made any profit, for two years. I finally took the drastic step of folding the insurance outfit in 1987 and started desperately searching for gainful employment.

Since my return to Nigeria in 1984, I was always on the lookout for well-paid employment, in the private and public sectors, alas, without success. Once again, who you know matters a great deal in Nigeria. Many middle management and top-level managers took advantage of me on several occasions. I was gullible and vulnerable, because living in America or Europe made people lose the aggressive animal instinct, things are structured, easy, and organised. Merit and achievement are usually accorded prominence in employments and appointments, except in cases of racial and other prejudices. It is axiomatic that people would do the right thing - that they would queue up, or that they would give the job to the right, or most qualified person. I know things are not perfect anywhere, but in Nigeria the situation was next to hopelessness. After closing my insurance firm, I desperately intensified my jobhunting activities. In three separate instances, I was told to bring thousands of Naira as bribes, to grease the palms of the recruitment boss - Mr Big, all to no avail. I was systematically ripped off. I was 42yrs old and I was forced, due to my precarious financial circumstances, to retire to my village. I began to use my Volvo coupe as a private taxi to ferry passengers. I commuted between my town, Abba to Anara or Orlu or Okigwe; or to Owerri and from there to Port Harcourt, or Aba or Onitsha or Enugu on different days. Initially, my Volvo was quite reliable but later, the bore headed tyres would burst, while I was driving. On two separate occasions, on the account of burst tyres, I found myself in the bush, and had to call people to help push my car out of ditches and back on to the main road.

At that point, life was hectic, and I began to regret ever returning to Nigeria. I was literally down on my knees, as nothing appeared to work for me in the area of employment or business. It became a herculean task to maintain my evergrowing family. It seemed I had bitten off much more than I could chew, by acquiring four common law wives and having more children. Yet in fairness, my four unemployed customary wives gave me so much love, respect, affection, and admiration, combined with challenges, that I was imbued with the determination to pick myself up and attain a better life with my family, and succeed at all costs. I must emphasise during these profoundly serious and trying times, my wives stood solidly beside me. They clothed me with care, affection, and sympathy. They never slighted me, embarrassed me, or ridiculed me. Collectively and individually, my wives expressed confidence in me and informed me I was down on my luck, because I had no support, or influential connection or network to assist me to secure an excellent job, with my impressive qualifications, or to promote my business.

I observed my wives strove to make me comfortable in these difficult circumstances. They often went without food, to ensure that I was fed. They believed my sojourning in America had softened me, and that I must not be exposed to the extreme hardship of Nigeria. Thus, they ensured I had regular meals, such as fried eggs, fried plantain and yam, bread, milk, beans, rice etc. even when they themselves had nothing to eat. They ensured that they cushioned my hardship with joy, attractiveness, love, and enthusiasm, despite occasional family squabbles between the ladies.I reciprocated their kind gestures, by ensuring that any time I made good takings in my taxi business, I spent money on my family, by purchasing a whole leg of a goat, chicken, and all sorts of condiments and/or new outfits for them. I also spent earnings from my cabbing business, on my partners and kids, as much as I was able to afford.

With reference to my four customary wives, there was no church, religious or court wedding. However, to satisfy the local custom concerning marriage rites, I bought the necessary traditional bride gifts including hot drinks, beers, soft drinks, snuff, kolanuts, packets of cigarettes, and other condiments. On each occasion, I attended and presented these gifts to the family of each of my wives, in the company of my relatives. In each case, I gave my words that when things got better, I should return to pay the requisite bride price, and the parents in each case amicably gave their daughter away to me, to hold, love and cherish!

Had I not carried out the above minimal customary rites, the Ibo custom would have regarded me as a mere boyfriend to each of the girls. A long-established Ibo custom holds that a boyfriend does not have any child born outside the customary wedlock. My wives and their parents urged me to perform at least the limited customary rites, to remove shame and stigma of their daughters living with a man, who had not carried out even minimal marriage rites.My four wives in order of their ranking in my family are as follows: Late Ms Chinyere Okoroha was very fair in complexion, of slim build and of average height of about five feet seven inches. She was a native of Mbano in Imo State. She was introduced to me by the mother of my cousin, who was married into her family. We hitched up and she became my wife. Unfortunately, we divorced later due to her own personal reasons.

Mrs (Lolo) Susan Okoroha is from Irete, Umuwaoha in Imo State. She is very slim with dark complexion and of about five feet ten inches in height. She was my secretary at the Ministry of Trade and Industry, Owerri, when we dated, she subsequently became my wife and remains so.

Mrs (Lolo) Ursula Okoroha was initially an employee at my insurance brokerage firm. She is very petite, with a height of about five feet and four inches. She hails from Emekuku in Owerri, Imo State and has remained my wife, ever since.

Last but not the least, Late Mrs (Lolo) Eucharia Okoroha who was a native of Ndegwu, Umuwaoha in Imo State. She was always allegedly referred to as my most beloved and trophy wife. She was taller than me at five feet and eleven inches and ebonydark and very slim. She remained my wife and passed away peacefully in 2015 in her sleep, after a brief illness, following a diagnosis of cancer.

## VISIT TO USA FROM NIGERIA — SHERRY AND MONSO

Due to the difficulties which I encountered in both business and employment coupled with my family circumstances, I seriously considered jumping ship and returning to USA. Indeed, in 1985, whilst four of my wives were pregnant, I travelled back to the USA with the hopes of restarting my life in USA, where I had left off. My green card was still active, I could come and go at will. In Omaha, Nebraska, my girlfriend, Inez had lost my home on 43rd Street, North Omaha. I had sold my businesses before going home to Nigeria. I had also resigned employment with John Hancock Insurance. Ms Inez Jackson, my girlfriend, told me that she had no place of her own and was living with her mum, a sister and the brother who once aimed and took a shot at me with a sawn-off shot gun. I refused to go and stay with her at her mother's house. I took Inez to my brother (Damian)'s flat for a week. In the end, I felt very humiliated that my junior brother whom I did everything to bring to USA put me up in a box room which was barely 4ft by 5ft with a little single bed. It dawned on me that I could not try to start life afresh in Omaha. I was despondent, so, I left Omaha after a week and caught a bus to St Joseph, Missouri. I went straight to Reverend Joseph Smith's house, in search of her daughter, my ex-girlfriend Ms Sherry and our son Monso Okoro. They were happy to see me, but after few days in a motel with Sherry and our son, I opted to leave town, to Houston Texas. The Reverend knew my past glory and did not hesitate to give us his old Cadillac Eldorado to use for our trip to Texas. Sherry and I packed up, hit the road and headed South to Houston TX. In Oklahoma City, we turned off and visited Franca, my cousin and her husband and children. We were well received. We continued Southward through Kansas, Wichita, Arkansas to Waco, Texas. In Houston Texas, we squatted or slept rough at few of my friends and relatives' homes. After a couple of weeks, it became clear to me I could not maintain Sherry, Monso and myself without any employment or business. I was no longer the comfortable businessperson they knew before I went back to Nigeria. I quickly obtained a Texas driving Licence, but almost immediately, the car broke down, the engine knocked beyond repair, and we sold it as scrap. We slept for few days at my junior brother, Cletus' flat in Dallas, Texas, until he gave me notice to please move on with my family, so he could return to the master bedroom. To avoid any embarrassment or face off, I promptly left Dallas with Sherry and Monso. In Houston, my cousin, Lambert gave us a guest room for a few days, after which he reminded me that some of my school mates lived in Houston. I took a hint and promptly moved to one of my friend's home, Mr Sam Igwe after visiting Mr Zobus Ihekwoazu and his family. Mr Igwe was a Wallgreen store manager whilst Mr Ihekwoazu was a pharmacist. I envied the fact that they were stable in the

USA as I had been, and it appeared I had effectively destabilised myself. I had little or no income at the time. Thus, our stay in Houston was slippery and precarious. Sherry genuinely suggested that we should go to the welfare department with our four-year-old son and apply for income support, but I declined, as I considered I had not really become so destitute as to rely on government handouts. I used the money from the sale of the car to buy a one-way ticket and put Sherry and our son on a Greyhound Bus from Houston to St Joseph, Missouri. That was the last I saw of them, even to this day. A few years later, whilst I was in Nigeria, I received sad news, my friends Sam and Zobus were dead in Houston, in separate circumstances. In the case of Sam, there was a mix up and the wrong body was airlifted to Nigeria, for burial.

**CHAPTER SIXTEEN**
------------------------

# Diagnosed with Diabetes in Houston, Texas

The circumstances in which I found myself, in Houston in that summer of 1985, was indescribable. Only two years before, I was a homeowner and a buoyant business owner, with a few girlfriends around me. I was driving two posh cars. However, I voluntarily decided to return home to Nigeria in what I saw as a call of duty, to return to my homeland, to occupy my father's and grandfather's seat. I went also as an exemplary

Nigerian, to serve my country and contribute to nation building in Nigeria. Alas, my entire world appeared to have crumbled, and I was in Houston, deflated, down and almost out. I reflected that I went home to Nigeria to be with Lulu and our daughters, but they had left me in Nigeria and returned to South Africa. It occurred to me that before my impromptu relocation to Nigeria, I was living with the very elegant Ms Inez Jackson, who as a dietician was gainfully employed. Unfortunately, on my return to USA, she was unable to assist or house me.

I should have been angry at the fact all the people I had helped along the way had, at that point in time, abandoned me to my fate. Uche was somewhere in New York practising as a medical doctor. I had her number even whilst I was in Nigeria. However, when I arrived in Houston and heard that she was living with another man, I decided not to contact her. Primarily, I chose not to disturb her new relationship, also because of my pride and integrity. Sherry had just left me in Houston, and she was gone with our son. I was squatting with a friend, Mr Sam, in his two-bedroom house. He had no wife and brought no girlfriends. I had no money and had no means of income.

At the age of forty-two, I was becoming too weak, old, or tired to start any menial jobs, such as janitorial, as a means of livelihood, as I had when I first arrived in America, in 1972. Looking back to Nigeria, three unemployed ladies were pregnant by me at that time, and they were all anxiously waiting for me to come back with some money, at least. For the first time in my sojourn overseas, I became frightened and restless. I couldn't sleep. I didn't have a woman to comfort me. I could not go clubbing without money, or car. I spent many sleepless nights worrying about things I had previously taken for granted. It was difficult for a person such as me to pretend that all was well when I was down to my last dollar and no help whatsoever was in sight. I was usually a brash, broadminded, outgoing, and confident and outspoken personality; hence pretence was never on my card. I considered that the best way forward was, perhaps to return home to Nigeria and to take life easy with the three ladies. As the saying goes, if you move, you lose.

In August 1985, on one extremely hot Sunday afternoon, in Houston, I decided to treat myself to a tub of ice cream. A couple of hours later I needed a wee, and I did pass an ample quantity of urine. As soon as I sat back down to watch television, I felt pressed again to go and urinate. I felt tired and thirsty. This repeated and again, almost all night long. Mr Sam agreed I must go to the Hospital, first thing in the morning. At the Methodist hospital, the next morning, after they took blood, stool, and urine samples from me, they told me to wait to be called. I took the opportunity to go out to smoke. I was so nervous; I smoked several cigarettes in a relatively short time. I heard my name called over the intercom, and I went inside. The nurses grabbed me, sat me down in a wheelchair and I was transferred to a stretcher. I was put in a single hospital room, a doctor, and two nurses surrounded me. I undressed, down to my underwear, and was told to put on a hospital gown, back to front, and to lie down. Eventually, they told me they suspected I had an extremely dangerous level of glucose (sugar) in my system. They finally diagnosed me with diabetes, a life changing condition. I was advised that, henceforth, I could only eat a single slice of toast for breakfast, a few spoons of rice for lunch, and half an egg on a potato for dinner. However, if I could inject insulin into my body by myself, upon my discharge from hospital, then I could eat a little more. I was advised diabetes is caused by a shortage of insulin, which is produced by the pancreas. When the insulin producing cells of the pancreas are damaged, then little or no insulin is produced. When food is eaten, it is broken down in the stomach, into glucose; insulin is like a vehicle that carries the glucose to different body cells. Where there is little or no insulin, then the glucose, or sugar, is left floating in the blood stream and the person is said to be suffering from Type 2 diabetes – mellitus- too much sugar/glucose in the blood and in such an event the body tries to get rid of the excess sugar through the urine. This is glycosuria. Diabetes can be hereditary and may also be brought about by a person's lifestyle. I suspected it was latently in my genes, propelled by the combination of my gargantuan worries, sleeplessness and by my carelessly eating a tub of ice cream, during the week of my affliction.

I tried every day for a week to inject myself, without success. I was given an orange to practise on, piercing it with a needle. However, pushing a needle into an orange, was entirely different to plunging a two-inch needle into my thigh, stomach, or upper arm. After a week, I was discharged and my weight had plummeted from two hundred and three pounds, to just eighty pounds. At five feet nine inches in height. During that week in hospital, I was almost starved to death. Diabetes, they said, was incurable. It is a lifelong illness. They told me if it is professionally managed with little food, lots of exercise and proper medication, one could still live a full life, but if any of the stipulated factors is neglected, the person's life expectancy could be shortened drastically.

When I was diagnosed, I was forty years old. I reckoned in all honesty, at best, I had just a few years left to live. What terrible news. My entire world came crashing down and I acknowledged my life was now in a state of emergency. I had to do all in my power to have some male children and re-populate my traditional homestead in Nigeria. Time was running out, I must return to ensure the safe delivery of my pregnant ladies, in Nigeria. I must ensure I didn't perish in America; I didn't wish to be buried anywhere outside my ancestral compound, in Nigeria. I also reckoned financially my brothers Cletus and Damian, could not and would not be able to shoulder the burden of taking my body, by cargo, to Nigeria. My perception of them at the time was that they were behaving like selfish ingrate- brats. I decided to do whatever was necessary to return alive to Nigeria. Once home, I would be happy to die and be buried in my ancestral compound. Thus, I booked my return flight to Nigeria. I had some fleeting thoughts, I could die in flight, like another professor friend of mine, who was going to Nigeria, everyone thought he was sleeping, he was not. In my own case, I had lost weight from two hundred and three pounds to now, just fifty-five pounds. I was a shadow of myself, a 'walking dead' and I prayed for God to preserve me, until I got home to my compound, and could go to my respective family homes, with my four pregnant ladies. And to officially announce my return, reconfirm my marital commitments, and take them back to my compound. Time was of the essence. It was like injury time in a football match, and I chose to do things my own way, by not letting anyone decide or dictate to me. Drastic situations demand drastic solutions. I did not regret anything, and I owed no one any apologies for my way of life and my decisions.

As soon as I arrived safely home, I summoned my family elders and informed them to accompany me on my new mission as 'I am going to marry three more wives, all on the same day.' I announced, without waiting to hear what anyone had to say. I continued, 'we are going to make short visits to their families, drop off all the traditional marriage requirements at each bride's family home, and move on to the next, until all three are fulfilled.'

Within a month of my customary marriage ceremonial activities, my three wives had three babies, in the space of one month.
The births in 1985 solidified the succession in my linage in the Okoroha family. We welcomed two boys and a girl, born between October and November 1985. By the end of seventh year with the ladies, miraculously, I was still alive, and I had had seven children with the three ladies. My boys were born in Nigeria, and I told myself, 'Well done!Now my lineage is intact and safeguarded, even if I died thereafter, I would die a happy man, as my linage was safe and secure.' My thoughts were akin to the reason my father and grandfather named me ANYIAM, meaning that by my birth their lineage is secured. Thus, I had fulfilled my destiny and lived up to my ancestral hope and expectations!

People were talking; some said I was possessed, or that I was the biggest womaniser. A few acknowledged I had down to earth common sense. I was not the type to be perturbed by such diversion. Some spoke from their level of understanding, and knowledge of life. Others expressed their shallow level of spiritual or religious perspectives. For example, there are people who believe a person will certainly go to hell if an individual divorces a spouse, or marries a divorcee, or marries two persons, or lives with a partner, without marriage in (Catholic) church. These beliefs are unimportant. People try to speak for God. My family home at the time could be likened to a local baby nursery. There were no more quiet nights in the house. I told myself that 'God is at work; God is in charge, and he will make everything good in the fullness of time.'

My diabetes was worsening. Most of the medication I was buying in Nigeria, turned out to be fake, an adulterated imitation, containing coloured water. Ignorantly, I continued to inject myself with them, in the false belief they were potent insulin. My health condition was worsening, other ailments started appearing. In Nigeria, wicked, heartless persons floated fake, adulterated, or imitation drugs, which had no medicinal potency, with no care for those taking them and who could so easily die. One of the problems in Nigeria is that no one could successfully sue anybody for a bad drug, medical negligence, or unprofessional diagnosis or treatment. Most of these fake medicines were made locally, such as at Nnewi or Aba but given the appearance to look like the real thing and were clearly labelled 'made in China' or 'made in India' or any other foreign country. The scenario to me is the average Nigerian prefers foreign products, even though they are usually more expensive, for several reasons. Firstly, local products tend to be inferior to the foreign products, in terms of quality, aesthetic, efficacy, and efficiency. Secondly, the local industries appear to lack the skills and equipment in the production of some desired products. Finally, the absurd mental state of mind of an average Nigerian, is that anything foreign is better than any locally sourced product, regardless of the relative performance of such competing products. This colonial mentality is further exhibited in the general belief by Nigerians, that foreigners, especially the white folks, are more knowledgeable and reliable, than the average black person.

## RELOCATION TO LAGOS

In 1987, two of my younger cousins, Nathaniel, and Paul dropped off some kind of financial assistance to me, on a few occasions. My brothers and cousins, whom I had assisted or brought to the USA, did not care much about me, and they did not want to know. Our family could at that time boast of two wealthy and prominent men. At the time, neither of them had any agenda to bail out a struggling, drowning brother, such as me. Some people were of the opinion my hardship was self-induced, I made my bed, I should lie on it. Some assumed I was well off anyway, since I was in a better position than most people. There were few of those who could have helped me, in one way or another. There were also so many who were disappointed, because they had looked up to me as their financial saviour, and to no avail.

One day, Nath said to me 'my elder brother (Deedee Dudu) please leave the village and come to the city of Lagos.' I left for Lagos, not really expecting much. I slept in his living room at Ajao Estate, Mofuluku, behind the Stop over Hotel, for a week or two. Then our uncle, Chief Emerson connected me with one Chief Anumnu, who ran an insurance brokerage firm at Breadfruit Street, Lagos Island. He employed me without much ado. He placed me on a fixed pay of five hundred Nigerian Naira, per month, for six months. Thereafter, the fixed payment stopped, and I was to be on a sixty per cent commission, based on my production. I subsequently rented a flat in the Itire, Lawanson area of Lagos. I travelled East and collected my Volvo and one of my wives. I decreed that my wives would take turns to be in Lagos, for a month each. Unfortunately, I did not produce, or generate, much new business. However, as fate would have it, a wealthy businessman, Chief Nnanna, who I had approached to persuade him to transfer, or insure, all his multi holdings business through our insurance brokerage, persuaded me to work for him. He offered me one thousand Naira per month, to join him, as a member of his staff. He wanted me to register a new Insurance firm, African Insurance Company, for him. In those days, to float an insurance firm, one was required to deposit five hundred thousand naira (half a million Naira) with the Ministry of Commerce and Industry. My fixed six months agreement with Chief Anumnu's insurance brokerage was coming to an end in a month's time, so I gave notice that I was resigning. Then, I gave notice to my new employer, that I was joining his company, as senior permanent staff. An Ibo adage says that life turns round and round like a snake, meaning one minute you may be down, in the second, you may be up. The sun was shining on me again. Chief Nnanna bought a brand-new station wagon Peugeot, for my new department. I was given a full-time driver, and I was chauffeured wherever I went in Lagos City, former capital of Nigeria.

I moved into a more solid and comfortable two-bedroom flat in Adeboyega Street, Ijesha Tedo, near Aguda, Surulere, Lagos. Despite my crowded marital life, one of my boss's sisters proposed to marry me as well, after our secret tryst. She appeared dead serious, but fortunately I was able to shake her off, and eventually her infatuation withered. In 1987, I was conferred with a chieftaincy title by the king (Eze Oguoke) of our neighbouring town, Agbaje Mbano. I took the title of Akaraka 1 – meaning, what we become, or what happens to our lives, in most cases, is ninety nine percent pre-ordained and predestined. Even the Bible in Romans, chapters 8 and 9 talks about predestination in our lives. The Holy Book states that those he chose and predestined to be the children of God. This is one of the mysteries of religions which no human being can decipher. My thoughts are that I try to do my best, which is probably one per cent, and my God does ninety-nine per cent for me. I have no other way of explaining the travails and the fortunes of my life.

Two years into my new lucrative job, I hired a young professional insurance agent, to assist me in the task of running a new insurance firm. His name was Mr Isiuba, and he was one of my distant brothers in law, as he was related to one of my wives. Within three months of hiring him, he went behind my back, and convinced Chief Nnanna he was more capable of heading the department. He told tales of how I was using my employer's sisters for personal gratification. He alleged my position was obsolete and wasteful. Thus, one morning, I was summoned to a meeting with my boss, who presented all the allegations before me, which I vehemently refuted. However, I was asked to take garden leave. Subsequently, in 1990, my employment contract was terminated. Alas, I was unemployed once again. I reverted to doing what most unemployed men do in Nigeria, contract chasing and supply business. On a few occasions, I travelled overseas to buy goods to sell in Nigerian local markets. Additionally, I engaged in part time insurance brokerage and fortunately, I had two wives in Lagos, who were engaged in trading.

Meanwhile, my diabetes continued to worsen. I was literally going as blind as a bat, and I had two ulcers in my left leg and toes. The boils on my toes were popped, pressed, and drained of yellow pus. However, by the following morning, they were as bad as ever. My father-in-law (Ursulla's Dad), Mr Arimah, a former primary school headmaster, looked me in the eye and told me bluntly that 'as an educated man, with overseas connections' it would be shameful for me to die of a simple illness like diabetes, which could be easily managed abroad.

Eventually, in 1994, at the age of fifty, I took a daring, risky and bold step to leave my growing family in my beloved Nigeria, once again, and I migrated to London, United Kingdom.
Primarily, this was for health reasons, but also, to search for fresh, more stable, greener pastures. This was like my own Second Missionary Journey. I was determined to start life all over again, in the United Kingdom.

*With my older uncles, Michael, and Emma Okoroha.*

Top: *At my daughter, Amaka's, wedding with her mother.*

Below: *At my chieftaincy title serenaded by Ikprikpe Dance Group from Ohaofia.*

*My chieftaincy title in 1979 at Abaje Mbano Eze Ogoeke*

*With my cousins at my birthday where they honoured me with a gift of a Gavel as a birthday present.*

*My send-off party in 1972 by family elders.*

*With Four of my daughters, L-R: Chiyere, Akwaugo, Ginikawan and Amaka*

**CHAPTER SEVENTEEN**
-------------------------

# Migration To London, United Kingdom (UK)

In 1994, I telephoned a medical specialist, Dr Bloom, at Harley Street London, and booked an appointment for specialist treatment of my diabetes. With the letter of appointment, I obtained a UK visa, valid for six months. I arrived in London in February 1994, as a visitor with a visiting visa. Unfortunately, as cruel fate would have it, I ignorantly fell afoul of the law. I resisted the forced to return to Nigeria and was detained until the final decision on my claim. I could appeal any unfavourable decision, but the Home Office retained the right to detain me, while my appeals were ongoing.

After I was granted a temporary release from detention, I continued to report monthly at a stipulated police station, whilst my application to remain in UK indefinitely, continued to be processed. My application, refusals and appeals became protracted, lasting a long time. Initially, I could not work legally. I resorted to taking on several voluntary jobs to get by, whilst receiving stipends and allowances from charitable organisations and well-wishers. I was not deterred in starting life all over again. Sometimes, I did two minor jobs and was paid 'in kind' or 'under the table'. In those days, persons with pending applications, you were entitled to housing, free medical care, and free part time education. Though I could not engage in any commensurate or meaningful employment without a National Insurance Number, I still made the most of my situation. I did whatever I could to survive, earn a little money to look after myself, also send money home for the women to feed and pay school fees for the children. I reckoned it was better to be a servant in paradise, than to be a king in hell. I lived in a decent one-bedroom flat, which the UK government paid for, under the Housing benefit system. My diabetes was now under proper control, and I was in good health again. When I looked back, I could pat myself on the back: I had three University degrees, eleven children, at the time and I had built my home in Nigeria. In fact, I was no longer under pressure to achieve anything. I was, for the first time in a long while, peaceful and content. I made sure I took daily walks in the park, for an hour,

Additionally, there were adequate sexercises, since I had a couple of girlfriends. One of my lady friends, Ms Merlene, was working at the Preston Job Centre. Eventually, I was invited to the Job Centre and issued with a National Insurance (NI) Number, which is the equivalent of the Social Security Number (SSN) in the USA.

The NI number is required, before anyone can be employed and paid salary or wages in the UK.

In September 1994, after my fiftieth birthday, I mustered the courage to study law. Thus, I enrolled at the University of Central Lancashire, Preston, in a three-year law degree programme. I had decided to study law, considering I could not get a proper job, with my qualifications, age, and immigration status. My frustration rose, because of the negative attitudes of employers. Some said I did not have sufficient experience in particular areas, whilst others said I was overqualified. I decided to go back to school for more education, it improves your mind, and keeps you young. I chose to study Law, because I wanted a profession I could carry out from my own parlour, sitting room or basement, if necessary. A job I could do even if no one wanted to employ me. It is so honourable to assist people to obtain justice and redress, for any injustice they have suffered. As Martin Luther King Jnr says, "Injustice anywhere is a threat to justice everywhere ... and whatever affects one directly, affects all indirectly."

While studying law, I did some volunteer work for charities, and odd jobs, here and there, to survive.

A few of my friends, family members and colleagues tried to talk me out of going back to school. Some people argued that since I have a B.Sc, M.Sc. and a PhD already, they were exasperated by my desire for another degree, it appeared superfluous. But I knew what I wanted. I needed something intellectually liberating and professionally fulfilling. I told myself I would be just as contented to have the LLB (Hons) prefix attached to my name, even if I did not work with it. Therefore, in 1997, I successfully and proudly gained a degree in Law, LLB (Hons). One of my beliefs in life is 'Do what you can do, when you can do it, half of this life's battle is won if you have confidence in yourself.'

## PATRICIA, MY EX - WIFE

In 1996, a year before my graduation, I met a beautiful British lady, named Patricia. We met in Preston; she came from Blackpool. I saw her in a Morrisons Supermarket, and I approached her, as she was selecting a bottle of wine. I complimented her on her slim figure and beauty. She giggled shyly. I knew immediately I was in luck. I pressed her for her phone number, she insisted that she would rather take my number, and she promised to ring me. Anyway, the rest is history. Eventually, after six months of dating, Patricia and I married at the Preston Registry in September 1996.

There was a long delay before my immigration status was regularised. In any event, I obtained my UK residence papers with the attendant rights of ingress and egress from the country, as well as the right to work legitimately in UK. After the completion of my law degree, Patricia insisted we leave Preston and relocate to London. For me, it was a hard pill to swallow, because I was so comfortable in Preston. I dreaded London, it is a highly populous city, with a high crime rate and large concentration of ethnic minorities. However, I agreed, and we rented a self-drive truck and headed to Woolwich, London SE.

Prior to our arrival, we had negotiated rental on a three-bedroom house off Eglington Road, in Woolwich. Also, my wife had secured a job transfer from Premier bond, to being an Executive Officer at the Treasury (Government) Solicitors in London. Within one week after our arrival, I signed up as a volunteer at the Plumstead Law Centre, to assist people with their legal problems. It also gave me the opportunity to gain work experience and I had a place to go daily.

While Patricia and I were waiting for my status documents, I made progress wherever possible. I returned home one day and told Patricia I wanted to buy a house in Woolwich. I reasoned there is no profit in being a tenant, paying off another person's mortgage. In tenancy, there is no equity, paying rent is just money going to waste. She turned around and gave me one of the most awful looks, sternly rebuking me. Patricia warned me I should never mention her name in this crazy plan of mine. She raised concern such as 'what happens if the roof of the new house caves in?' What happens if the boiler breaks down?' She concluded by saying 'Now you don't have a job, how do you intend to pay the mortgage? And where would you get the deposit?' I told her I had been putting some money aside. 'How much?' she asked, 'three thousand pounds' I replied. She was shocked at this 'I was the only one working in this house and now you are going to buy a house, in your name?' Patricia subsequently insisted I must add her name in the purchase. Thus, within a few months of arriving in London, we bought our first home in joint names. The property was a three-bedroom terraced house in St Mary's Street, Woolwich London SE18. Having bought our first property, it became the way to acquire five houses, within seven years of our marriage, the rest is history. When I arrived in Woolwich, I discussed buying a house and securing a mortgage with some of my Nigerian friends, but most of them did everything to discourage me, by telling me It's a no go area', and 'it's a typical rip-off' and they emphasised once you missed a payment, the bank could repossess your property, and all the money you've ever invested would have gone down the drain.

Today, I've proved them all wrong, and they marvel at my wisdom and business acumen. Some say the secret of my success in UK, was my previous experience and exposure to financial dealing and wheeling and dealing in USA. Deep down, I believe that once beaten by a bee, you dread a house fly – meaning my experience in Nigeria imbued me with the passion, zeal, energy, and determination to succeed. I had learnt in the harshest conceivable way that poverty is not an option, but stable and enduring success is the key to life.

## GREENWICH, LONDON BOROUGH

In 1998, I was finally fortunate to obtain secure employment with the London Borough of Greenwich (Greenwich Council) now known as Royal Borough of Greenwich. It became a Royal Borough because King Henry VIII once lived in the borough. This gave Greenwich Council a royal connection. My first job with the Council was as a regeneration project secretary. It paid £1000.00 a month. I was 'over the moon' at securing a job with such a good level of pay, considering for several years I had been toiling as a volunteer, at the Law Centre and Citizens Advice Bureau (CAB). My working hours were 9.30 am to 5.00pm with an hour lunch break, when I often used to walk in the nearby park. The work hours suited my class attendance, since I was attending the BPP Law School, Holborn, London for the Legal Practice Course (LPC) in the evenings, three times a week.

After six months, I applied for and got a new position with the Council as a housing officer and my salary increased to £20,000.00 per annum. Six months later, I became a temporary accommodations officer, and was promoted to Senior Officer Grade II (SO2) with an increase in salary to £26,000.00 per annum. Patricia was also working as an Executive Officer at the Home Office, and with the double income in our household, I managed to acquire six rental properties, in our joint names, in London Southeast area. Concerning my ambition to become a lawyer, my Legal Practice Course (LPC) programme was scheduled from 1997 to 1999. However, at the end I failed to achieve the required grades, in six legal courses at a sitting. I went back to BPP after two years absence and presented myself to re-sit the six courses, including business law, Conveyancing, family law, civil litigation, criminal litigation, accounting for solicitors and legal writing. The LPC Course Advisor Mr Chantry was concerned I appeared to be seeking to unduly punish myself, at my relatively advanced age of sixty years, I had been away from law school for two years. I persisted, prepared, and sat for all the examinations, within five days. It was incredible, yet fulfilling, I passed all the papers at a sitting, with flying colours. Mr Chantry, my course advisor, gave me an extraordinarily strong reference, in addition to my LPC certificate.

I juggled work, school, the property business and my extended family responsibilities, both at home and abroad and it seemed I was doing well and had good luck. The good life continued until

2004, when suddenly there were shocks in my ordered life. One day, I was alleged to have referred a Council Tenant to my Solicitor friend Mr Abbott, who was running a nearby law firm, in order that he may sue the council on behalf of the tenant, for disrepair in the tenant's council flat. Subsequently, I was summoned to a disciplinary hearing for alleged conflict of interest, as a senior officer of the Council.

From a temporary suspension, I was eventually dismissed. I filed an action at the employment tribunal against the Council.

Mr Ozuzu declined, saying he did not want to get involved. My friend, Mr Fasuyi attended with me as a litigation friend. However, on the day of the hearing, we were able to settle at the Tribunal's doorsteps. I received a small compensation; my pension was protected, and I was given a good reference. Shakespeare once said that 'when it rains, it pours' and so it was for me. Immediately on my suspension, my wife, Patricia, commenced divorce proceedings against me. Patricia stopped her pay cheques going into our joint accounts and evicted a tenant, and moved into one of our rental properties, in an act of separation. Our marriage of eight years 'went up in smoke'. Her solicitors' letter arrived, they proposed signing a consent order, transferring fifty percent of our assets to her. Though I did not wish for the divorce, I consoled myself: not long ago I had nothing in the UK, however after the divorce I became the proud sole owner of my home, and two additional rental properties.

# LYNN OKORO

In a twist of fate, within a week of my separation from Patricia, I met a beautiful young lady of Chinese origin. Her name is Shoaling, and I call her Lynn for short. We hit it off straight away and became inseparable. On our second date, we decided to live together for the near future. I discovered the Chinese are a very hardworking, honest, meticulous, dedicated, energetic and upright people. Initially, I bought a business centre in Lewisham for Lynn to run, and she turned the place into a goldmine. When I qualified as a solicitor, Lynn became the manager of one of our two law firm offices. She could have a good relationship with people, take the initiative, and function as a computer expert and an accountant, to boot.

Meanwhile, I parted ways with Greenwich Council in 2004. Within a week, a friend, Mr Fasuyi who had a run-in with the same Council, referred me to an employment agency, which he had also used to get a locum (temporary) job. I went to the agency's office, near Blackfriars Station, London. As soon as I attended the interview at the agency, I was immediately referred to the London Borough of Croydon, for a job interview, for a position as a housing officer. Fortunately, the position with Croydon Council was similar in every respect to my last job with Greenwich Council. At the conclusion of a brief interview, I was offered an immediate appointment for the post. I started the following Monday. I had been on the post for barely three weeks, when one day a letter landed on my desk from a local law firm, requesting that the Council should provide local authority accommodation, for the firm's client. After reading the letter, I noticed the principal solicitor of the law firm was Mr Anyiam. His last name was the same as my middle name, Anyiam. He was a caseworker at the Plumstead Law Centre, where I worked as a volunteer when I initially arrived in London in 1997. I put a call to him, his secretary answered and transferred my call to Mr Anyiam. Once I spoke his first name, he recollected my voice and shouted "chief, chief Okoro." I told him his letter to Croydon Council was in front of me. He enquired if I had qualified as a solicitor, and I responded in the negative. He curiously asked why not, and I told him that though I had successfully completed the LPC, I had not been able to secure the requisite two years training contract, in order to qualify as a solicitor in England and Wales. Mr Anyiam sympathised with my plight and invited me for an interview as a trainee solicitor in his law firm. I promptly visited the firm on the next day, for the interview, after which I was offered a training position. I informed him I would need to give Croydon Council; a two week notice of resignation from my position as a housing officer. Salary wise, I told him I was earning £26,000.00 per annum and he immediately told me that he could not pay me that much. We negotiated and I voluntarily accepted a reduced salary of £18,000.00 per annum. I reckoned it was worth it, if only I could qualify as a solicitor. I was given credit for six months, for all my previous work experience at different law firms, and I was then required to do only eighteen months training contract. After twelve months with Mr Anyiam, he called me to his office and informed me he could no longer pay me, and that he would cancel my training contract. I pleaded, to no avail, and thus my training contract was cancelled, when I had only six months to complete training.

*My Law Degree Graduation at The University of Central Lancashire Preston Uk in 1997*

*With the Director of Nigeria Law School in Abuja*

*Visit to Law Society in 2006*

**CHAPTER EIGHTEEN**
-------------------------

# Becoming a London Lawyer in England

I believe in a God of surprises; He works in miraculous ways. He fights fire with fire to ensure progress. I was so unhappy and bitterly disappointed at the shenanigans concerning my training contract. As always, when a door closed, I wasted no time in seeking another open door. On the night of the cancellation of my training contract, I was unable to sleep. I weighed up all options. Eventually, I decided to muster courage, swallow my pride, and contact Mr Ozuzu again for assistance. This time around, he was very sympathetic and agreed for me to come to his firm, to complete the remaining six months of my training contract. I welcomed his magnanimity, and we completed all the Law Society's formalities and documentation.

Thereafter, upon completion of my further six months training, I applied to be admitted to the Roll of Solicitors of the Supreme

Court of England and Wales (now known as the Superior Court of England and Wales).

Further to my application, the Law Society wrote to me stating I had disclosed a previous infraction of the law and that the London Borough of Greenwich (as it was then known) had drafted a report to the Law Society, informing them I had been dismissed from the Council's employment. The law Society felt these issues affected my fitness and propriety to be admitted as a Solicitor. Hence, I was requested to provide four-character references in further support of my application. I was also invited to attend two separate screening interviews before different panels. Eventually, I was approved for my suitability to be a Solicitor. I felt joyous and fulfilled. Consequently, in 2006 at the age of sixty-two years young, I became enrolled as a Solicitor of the Supreme Court of England and Wales.

I wasted no time and immediately applied for an exemption to be allowed to open and run my own law firm, without the requisite three years post qualification experience. Again, I was summoned to appear and make my case for exemption before a panel at the Society. I attended, and persuasively presented my arguments, citing my age, previous legal business, and administrative experiences, extensive education, financial security, family commitments, social and religious positions and my passion, vision and quest for justice, and desire for legal practice. Several of my friends gave me references. Amongst whom are Mrs Elizabeth Randell, Dr Sope Adeeko, Late Mr Tony Maduagwu, Mrs Mary Forrest and Rev.

Gibbard. In the end, my application was refused. I was so desirous of establishing a law firm, I paid over one thousand pounds to put an advertisement in the Law Society Gazette, seeking a solicitor with three years post qualification experience (3-year PQE). I shortlisted and interviewed about five solicitors. At the end of the process, I employed Mr Vatawinge, a gentleman of Sri Lankan origin. Upon the employment of a qualified solicitor, I was able to establish a law firm – GRACELAND SOLICITORS, in partnership with the qualified solicitor. When Mr Batabinge left the firm, the firm employed Mr Christopher Athersych, an English gentleman with over 20 years PQE. After three years of working with these lawyers, as the beneficial owner of the firm, I became fully qualified to be the sole principal and supervisor of the firm.

## ESTABLISHING AND MANAGING A LAW FIRM

I qualified as a solicitor in February 2006, at the age of sixty two, and opened my first law firm in November 2006, at Woolwich London SE18. The firm's branch office was opened at Lewisham London SE13 in March 2007 the Law profession gave me the good life I had craved since childhood. Solicitors Regulation Authority (SRA). This is a body set up to regulate the Law Society members and protect members of the public. The SRA enunciate rule which guides the conduct of solicitors. Invariably, lawyers find these rules cumbersome and onerous, so much so, at times one wonders on which side the SRA is. Every Solicitor fears the SRA because of its powers to undertake an intervention in a law firm or commence an investigation into the law firm's affairs at the drop of a hat, with short notice, or none. Black people generally feel they are more at the receiving end of the SRA stick, than their white counterpart.

Charging and income – One of the good things about running a law firm is that you can set your own prices, so long it's within the reasonable limit, or as prescribed by the regulatory authorities. I am usually on the low end, but that also has its merits and demerits. More clients come to me because of my reasonable rates, but some of the high charging and brave colleagues charge higher fees from a single client, which will be more than I received from a couple of clients, to undertake similar professional work. Overall, as an elderly lawyer, I am easily contented and I derive enormous joy and fulfilment from helping people to obtain justice, whilst I am earning a decent living at same time. I have sometime observed that fellow Black people and ethnic minorities who are well off, would rather patronise European and English firms at all costs. Managing the staff – Though not by choice, in London people assemble law firms according to their ethnic and social backgrounds. Hence, a lawyer of African background tends to work in African owned law firms, and Asians tend to work in Asian owned law firm. Even the whites, Chinese, and Jews congregate in firms reflecting their backgrounds. Thus, my firm has been populated mainly by lawyers of Nigerian background, a mix of Ibos, Yoruba, Benin and others, with very few English and Asian lawyers. Many of my staff from Nigeria are hardworking, diligent, and honest. Occasionally, one rotten egg comes on board and makes my life miserable, as the proprietor, until they are relieved of their engagement. At any point in time, we have a staff of over a dozen legal and paralegal workers.

Clients – I have noted earlier that our clients are mostly of the African and Caribbean backgrounds. They are mostly of substantial earning capacity. Their areas of legal work generally fall within immigration, housing, family, and criminal matters. Thus, we have Legal Aid franchise in these areas, this has been both beneficial to my firm, and to our clients. I must confess our clients in my experience are mild mannered, cooperative, appreciative, and grateful for our efforts. They often haggle, to further beat down our already low prices. We seek to accommodate everybody and generally, arrive at a mutually agreed fixed fees. I have had the occasional taciturn and difficult clients who have been rather unpleasant to deal with. There have also been out and out rogues, fraudsters and con men and women who tried to exploit the firm for unfair advantage, and for monetary compensation. A couple had lodged complaints that threatened our professional existence. However, at such times we have been vindicated by God's grace.

As many of our clients are upwardly mobile and becoming prosperous, their demand for expanded legal works have increased. Hence the firm engages in companies' formation, trusts and probate maters and in major property transactions such as residential and business leases, property transfers, acquisition and disposition of landed properties and other commercial transactions within our competence.

Additionally, every solicitor with a practicing certificate in England and Wales is invariably a Commissioner for Oaths, thus administration of Oaths, certification and witnessing of legal documents form core part of our firm's legal work.

Training Contract – Reflecting on the difficulty I had, obtaining, and completing my Training contract at two different law firms, HIACE and Abbots Solicitors respectively, I made it a point at every two intervals I would train one prospective lawyer to qualify as a solicitor. And so far, I have trained four solicitors. I am delighted to state that some of my previous trainees who later worked for me as solicitors, have gone ahead to establish their own firms and train more lawyers.

Work Experience Opportunity – Graceland Solicitors Limited is proud that since its inception, it has provided experience to over a hundred secondary school and A-levels students who are interested in pursuing law and related courses at the University level. In similar vein we have afforded opportunities to budding law scholars, foreign lawyer and students who wanted to have a first experience of law and practice in England.

Professional development and training - Every year, lawyers in England and Wales are required to have acquired about sixteen hours of professional development training. I have used the requirement to broaden my knowledge and skills in Legal Practice. Over and above these general requirements, I acquired extensive specialised core knowledge and training in some key practice arrears. I am an accredited Police Station and Criminal law Supervisor. I am also an accredited Supervisor in Family Law, Prison Law and Immigration and Asylum Laws.

I started the firm Graceland Solicitors in 2006 as a partnership, with myself being sole equity owner and after three years the firm restructured and became my sole Practice. In March 2015, the firm became incorporated as Graceland Solicitors Limited, a UK registered private Limited Liability Company, with myself and my wife Lynn Okoro as Directors. Subsequently, in December 2015, the firm became a Licenced Body, with authorisation from SRA to undertake the specified reserved legal activities and other related legal activities. It is noteworthy that Graceland's has attained the coveted LEXCEL - Legal Practice Quality Mark, which is the Law Society Excellency mark, in Legal Practice Management and Client Care.

My firm keeps a list of associates, consultants, non-practicing barristers and related experts, who have associated with the firm over the years. I presume it is inorder to mention a few, namely: Honourable Barr Samuel Ekenna, Dr, Barr Adesope Adeeko, Barr Colin Ikoku, Barr Emeka Emekaesili, Femi Sodola Esq, Tony Serdorf Dike Esq, Pastor Titus Ojo, Ms Sholape Ali, Ms Tianne Fadayomi, Fola Ajala Esq, Chris Athersych Esq, Wimal Patabendige Esq, Aniere Ebuzoeme Esq. Peter Ibhagbemien Esq, Kelechi Kennedy Okoroha Esq, Mrs Lynn Zhang Okoro, Godwill Agbakwue Esq, Ms Daniela Johnson, Jean Pierre Jacobs Esq, Adewale Babatunde Shoroye Esq, John Jenkins Esq, Leonard Alakija Ogilvy Esq, Pius Opong Esq, Kingsley Onyekwuluje Esq, late Alex Oringa Esq, Dr Cosmas Ikegwuruka, Ms Nnenna Ndirika, Kenny Shoye Esq, Pastor Grace BabalolaOjo, Chief Boniface Uzoma Esq, Ms Eva Kofi, Barr Kunle Omojuwa Esq, Noah Ogunniyi Esq, Ayo Onikosi Esq,

Ikemfuna Onyia Esq, Michael Ukwuoma Esq, David Ugonna Okoroha Esq, Emmanuel Okoroji Esq. Ms Lauren
Amako, Alex Owusu Esq, Ms Helen Kugbe, Ms Florence Egbuaba Duval, Barr Kojo Smith. Barr Emmanuel Ogbu, Bar Esther Udoh, Ms Winnie and Ms Adaora Dr Gladys Mbamalu, Femi Oluade Esq, Ms Kendra Williams, Barr Innocent Ugwuoke, Ms Patience Ani, Samson Mirikwe Esq (RIP), Victor Duru Esq, Ms Uju Okoli, Patrick Osemota Esq, Ms Risicat Isiaka, Raphael Eze Esq, Barr Julius Omisore, Barr Obinna
Baranta, Barr Austin Ajuzie, Mr Bennard Ikeri, Mr Chukwuka Ozigbu, Ms Sarah Hellier, Joe Ndanga Koroma Esq, Barr Bentley Igbunu, Mr Bamidele Oguyenum, Mr Raphael Onyewotu, Barr Anastasia Mushi. Don Sama Wickermabandu Esq, Philip Membu Esq, Patrick Fadoju Esq, Ms Enoh Agege,
Mr Clyde Baker, Barr John Aziba, Ross Monioro Esq, Barr Tom Adhikari, Barr Esther Udoh, Ms Tycia Riley, Ms Michelle
Mattis, late Mr. Kanu Bassey Onugen (RIP), Ms Pauline Osuagwu Iwuagwu, Dr Jesse Mashatte, Barr Elizabeth Lanlehin, Mr Ezekiel Atawojaye, Barr Tom Bhaja, Barr Dibugwu
Ogbonna, late Ms Nike Akinwande (RIP), Augustine Machi Esq, Ms Rebecca Hazelwood, Ms Yetunde Ojo, Denis
Okezuruonye Esq, Violeta Ranisaul Jevio. Barr Stanley Igbudu, Barr Angela Igbudu Chilaka, Mr Oyejide Adebowale, Barr Myke Osuji, Barr Ugonna Nwachukwu, Ms Susan Jeno, Mr Ibrahim Bangura, Mr Felix Anyiam, and Ms Mbila Muela. Late Alexander Oringa. (RIP) Lucy Achala, Adaorao Kobote esq, Ayo, Winifred Ezera

# LING ZHANG AND OUR SON, AMARA, GUAI GUAI

After my divorce from Ms Patricia Parkin Okoro in 2003, I almost immediately formed a new relationship with a beautiful young Chinese lady, Shoaling Zhang (Lynn) and we married in 2004. I was 60 years old; our marriage was blessed with a bouncing baby boy - Amarachukwu Okoro (Guai Guai) – meaning 'a good boy', in Chinese Mandarin language. The first name is usually shortened to AMARA,

I was elated, with the addition of a young family, my growing law firm, three of my children who were born in Nigeria, had also joined me in England. Two of my sons, David and Kennedy, are studying to qualify as lawyers and my daughter Emyline, Amaka, and Ginika have joined me in the UK and are studying and working. Amara Guai Guai the youngest of my children, now 15 Years old, is making substantial progress in his studies, music (piano), and sports (Tennis and football). After a brilliant completion of primary school at St Joseph's Catholic School in Crayford Kent, he has proceeded to a private secondary school, Kings in Canterbury, Kent, England.

When I met and married my girlfriend, who I affectionately called Lynn, she had newly arrived in the UK. She was studying English Language and spoke little English. She was slim, petit young, a beautiful woman, of course she was much younger than me. I was enchanted by her, and we hit it off. We immediately became fond of each other, she moved with me into a 3-bedroom terraced house at Woolwich, southeast London and we started cohabiting. Later Lynn and I upgraded and moved into a 4-bedroom House in Bexleyheath Kent.

Before we moved to Kent, I had purchased a Business Centre in Lewisham Town Centre, to keep Lynn engaged in some business activities. To my unexpected but welcome surprise, within a noticeably brief time, Lynn displayed such incredible business acumen, skills, ingenuity, honesty, diligence, and entrepreneurial abilities, that the lugubrious business became a money spinner. I was earning my living by working as a trainee solicitor at the time and had a sizeable income rental property. However, immediately I established the law firm in Woolwich, I had hesitation in converting the Lewisham Business into a branch of the firm. Quite understandably, I appointed Lynn as the manager of the branch office. The appointment was an inspired decision by me. Though, qualified solicitors always supervised the branch namely: Mr Athersych, Mr Owusu, Mr Sodola and Mr Agbakwue respectively, but Lynn remains the nerve centre of the entire operation. Lynn is an Accountant by profession, with previous experience in China, before coming to the UK. She has incredible management and personal interrelationship (PR) skills which have enabled her to manage over ten lawyers, as well as the office staff and operations, in a peaceful, harmonious, and profitable manner. Lynn is our bookkeeper and in-house Accountant, and she is deeply knowledgeable in most aspects of computer and E-commerce matters. She is so versatile with the SRA rules and the Rules governing the Legal Aid regime, that quite often practitioners seek her guidance and advice. In the event, Lynn became the manager of the whole firm, and she is a director of Graceland Solicitors Limited. She and I are the official managers of the firm, and we are co-signatories to the firm's Bank Accounts. I am the firm's SRA recognised Complaint Officer and the Compliance Officer for Legal Practice (COLP), whilst Lynn is the firm's SRA recognised Compliance Officer for the Financial Affairs (COFA) of the firm. Due the volume and intensity of legal Aid work done in the Lewisham branch Office, in the areas of crime and care proceedings, the branch produces more income than the turnover realised from the Woolwich Head Office, which deals mostly with private paying clients.

## VISITS TO NIGERIA AND OPENING OF MYANCESTRAL HOME AT ABBA

In April 2005, I visited my homeland. Upon arrival, I was informed that David, the eldest of my children born in Nigeria, was matriculating at the Imo State University, Imo state, Nigeria. I attended with my wives and other children, when I observed that his younger stepbrother Kennedy of same age was not among the students matriculating. I took an immediate decision, that he must study in London. Upon my return to UK, I obtained admission for him at the Greenwich School of Management in London, paid one year's school fees, approximately six thousand pounds, and I signed the sponsorship letters, as a Lawyer. Within two months Kennedy arrived in London and commenced his studies, with the intention of qualifying as a Lawyer.

Thenceforth, I visited Nigeria annually, especially at Christmas and Easter festival periods. In 2011, I visited Nigeria, specifically to officially open my ancestral home, a three-storey mansion building, consisting of twenty-nine bedrooms, two large parlours on the ground and first floors. I deliberately constructed a large house, due to my already large and expanding family. All my children from USA and South Africa came home to Nigeria, it was a grand occasion. The catholic priest of our Christ the King Church (CKC) parish came, blessed the house by sprinkling holy water throughout the house. The Reverend father subsequently prayed, then cut the ribbon to formally declare the house open. As custom dictates, the priest was given special presents. The traditional Kings or Ezes of our town also attended, poured libations, and customarily prayed for safety, security, happiness, good health and longevity of all occupants, visitors, and entrants of the house. The rest was a funfair of feasting and merry making, in the company of family, friends, in-laws, and well-wishers.  In summer 2011, my mother-in-law Mrs Xiu Lan from Tianjin. China visited Ling, her son and I, in London. She appeared to thoroughly enjoy many aspects of the western life, that London and United Kingdom offered. Among other attractions, we took her London Eye, Madame Tussaud, Buckingham Palace, Greenwich Park. We also visited the beaches at South End-on-Sea and Brighton.

# LUNG CANCER IN 2012

On 5th January 2012, Lyn, Amara and I flew back from Nigeria, into London Heathrow, with Air France. My Mercedes Jeep 270 ML had been parked at Heathrow Airport parking lot, while we spent two weeks of the Christmas Break in Nigeria. My sons, Kennedy, and David, both 27 years of age at the time, were at the arrivals section in Terminal 4 when we touched down and came through the Immigration and Customs checkouts. We collected our luggage, which was now lighter than when we had travelled out to Nigeria. I collected my Jeep, and in less than an hour along the M25 motorway, we were back in our home, sweet home, in Bexleyheath, Kent. I drove and smoked my cigarettes throughout the short journey. My passengers continued to complain and protest at my smoking, imploring me to stop smoking for my own good, and indeed for their own safety, as passive smokers.

My four-year-old son, Amara Adolph Okoro Jr. became the most vociferous. He kept saying 'Daddy, stop smoking here, now!' On that day, I promised him that once I finished the open pack of twenty cigarettes, I would get a patch to help me, and I promised to stop smoking for good. Period. The next day, I went to my local General Practitioner (GP) at Ferry view Health Centre, on John Wilson Street, Woolwich London S18 6PZ and booked an appointment to see Dr Brown, or a nurse, to assist me to quit smoking. I was booked to see Nurse Paula in a couple of days. She gave me a gadget to blow into, a reading of ten indicated the amount of carbon dioxide ($CO_2$) in my breath and system. A reading of ten, she said was not too bad for a start, but in the next couple of months the reading should go down to 4, 2, and zero. The Nurse gave me a prescription signed by the doctor, for Nicorette Nicotine Patches and NiQuitin, 4 Milligrams (mg) and Nicotine lozenges mini mints. These prescriptions were meant to give my body some nicotine, other than from smoking. It was believed that gradually I would wean off smoking cigarettes or craving for nicotine in my body.

I quickly and enthusiastically did as I was told, and in February 2012, my breath $CO_2$ was dropped from the reading of 10 to 6. The following month, March 2012, I was almost a nonsmoker and my $CO_2$ level from breath was 2. The Nurse patted me on the back, complimented my effort and I was determination to quit smoking. She said that I was doing very well, and that no one gets zero reading, as there are always loads of $CO_2$ in the air around us.

In April 2012, the reading was still two, but I began to experience relapsing fevers in the evenings, and I started coughing considerably. The Nurses, Doctors and Pharmacists all told me that it was normal to cough when you have stopped smoking. It is said to be the body's way of getting rid of all the muck which builds up in the chest over many years of smoking. Considering that I started smoking at 20 years of age in 1964, I figured that must be quite a load to get rid of.

I had booked and paid about £700 for my ticket to spend Easter in Nigeria. Consequently, at the onset of my evening fevers and coughing, I cancelled my travel arrangements. I forfeited the ticket money, but for a minute fraction of the full amount. Health to me is wealth. I sought medical help at once.

In May 2012, I was still coughing and observed blood in my phlegm. I left my Law Chambers at 3pm on Saturday 2nd June, and decided to go straight to the Queen Mary Hospital in Sidcup, Kent. I waited there for almost an hour, before being examined by a doctor, from one of the Eastern European countries. These Eastern Europeans became European (EU) citizens under EU Laws, and they enjoy free movement of persons and goods, as enshrined in the EU Law. Indeed, doctors, and nurses along with their counterparts from the commonwealth countries, are the bedrock of the renowned British National Health Service (NHS), which is free at the point of service to qualified persons.

The young doctor was very thorough. First, he sent for an x-ray. On examining the x-ray, he stated that from what I had told him about coughing and spitting blood, and my other symptoms, and his having had sight of my x-ray, he was sure that I had a bronchial infection, coupled with either a collapsed or pneumatic lung. Or, at worst, I had tumour in the lung. None of these observations sounded pleasing or good news to me.

The mention of tumour and collapsed lung made me ask if he suspected cancer, and he retorted 'likely' I said, 'God forbid'. I said that cancer will not be my portion, in Jesus' name. The doctor prescribed strong antibiotics, Penicillin, Co-Amoxicillin 500mg tablets. He also advised me to try and obtain a second opinion from another hospital. I arrived home, considerably shaken, and told Lynn about the extraordinary events of the day.

Lynn decided that from then on, she would attend all the appointments with me, because not only was the news distressing but we needed to be sure of what we were hearing.

We hoped for the best outcome yet prepared ourselves for the worst.

On Monday 4th June 2012, we went to Queen Elizabeth Hospital, Woolwich, London SE18, Accident and Emergency I had a blood test, Electrocardiogram (ECG) and X-ray and they informed me I was fine, save for chest infection. When I told the Doctor at QEH, my earlier diagnoses by the doctor at QMH Sidcup, he said in that case he would refer me to a specialist, Dr Sawicka at Princess Royal University Hospital (PRUH) in Farnborough, Orpington, Kent BR6 8ND.

In the months of June and July 2012, I anxiously underwent various tests under the auspices of Dr Sawicka, who is of Polish extraction. I had blood tests, CT scans, X-Rays, Urine tests, Bronchoscopy, Endoscopy and Lung function tests.

I chose Sedation, rather than general anaesthetic, for the Endoscopy and Bronchoscopy procedures. I was required to sign the consent form, so no one else could be blamed if I died during the process. I lay half naked on a trolley, and a nurse put clips to the top of the palm of my hand, one on a finger, to monitor my oxygen levels, and another to monitor my pulse. A tube was then guided through my nose to give me oxygen.

Once I was mildly sedated, the doctor sprayed my throat and nostrils with a local anaesthetic numbing gel, enabling the doctor to pass a bronchoscope through the nasal passage, throat and into the lung. Salt water, saline, is used to wash the lung and sucked back, for lab tests. A tiny piece of my lung was clipped - a biopsy, which was sent to the laboratory for analysis.

At my next appointment, a week later, Dr Sawicka said she had both good and sad news for me. I was with Lynn. The doctor enquired which news I wanted to be given first. I asked for the bad news, she replied that I had cancer. I wondered what the good news could be. She said the cancer was still at the initial stage and may be curable. I was shown a crab-shaped X-ray, and it all became clear. I had been diagnosed with a benign tumour, meaning that the cells had not spread to other parts of the body, but may continue to grow at the original site. This is known as 'non-small cell' lung cancer. It was a squamous cell carcinoma, in the upper lobe of my left lung. Luckily, this was the less dangerous than 'small cell' cancer, which is often fast growing and spreads quickly to other parts of the body. I was devastated and temporarily numbed by the news. I told myself that life is a lottery. I soliloquised that each one of us is going down, one way or another, so if is not this, it is another. I rhetorically asked, 'why me?' and 'who is next?'

By now, my trips to the hospitals made me realise there were many, many people suffering like me, and there were those before me, and there will be those after me. Types of cancer include cancers of the lung, skin, breast, bowel, brain, myeloid leukaemia, womb, cervical, head and neck, prostate, testicular, women's cancer, melanoma, mesothelioma and so on, and so on.

I thanked God at least I was fortunate to be living in Britain, where NHS provides free, prompt, first class and effective health care. In America, the cost of equivalent treatment would have been prohibitive. In Africa, the exact condition may not be detected. As the sickness progresses, the patient is taken from hospital to the native doctor and voodoo-men, then to the Pentecostal church pastors, where he is likely to die. Each of the three healers take turns and try their luck with patients. And the situations are exploited to the fullest, with the milking of the patient and their family. Each patient is warned that his/her faith is very crucial to his/her recovery. Quite often there is a disclaimer by the faith healer, that there is no Guaranty.

As far as I was concerned, the end was near, it was time to make my peace and prepare to die. Death is a debt which we all must pay, one after another, in seemingly random order. I told myself to be strong. I comforted myself, I had run a good race, my family and twelve children were proud of me for my achievement and my legacy. I considered it pointless to be angry or bitter. In fact, the whole thing was so funny, life itself is so funny, the things we take to be so important, end up being of little, or no significance, let alone important in the overall scheme of things. I experienced mood swings. Sometimes, I felt a high sense of elation, at my achievements so far, demonstrable in my large nuclear family, my academic and professional attainment and accolades, foreign and domestic real properties, cars, cash and other worldly endearments. I took pride in the family and friends whom I helped, one way or another, to improve their lives.

However, at other times I was despondent and vacuous, upon realising the futility and vanity of human life and endeavours.

Overall, I remained optimistic, whatever happened, I should be happy and proud to have lived, enjoyed life, and left a legacy and footprints, both nationally, internationally, and transnationally.

As some consolation, Dr Sawicka and her team, Staff Nurses Nicky, and Debbie, told me my ailment was operable. If it had been inoperable, I would have been doomed. Inoperable Cancer, the worst type, would most probably have spread all over my body, to stage three or four. I was advised my cancer was stage two. I was considered lucky that the tumour was the type that doesn't spread quickly, or indeed at all. I was also regarded as fortunate; the tumour was the type that grows bigger but does not spread easily; it was discovered at stage one or two. I was also lucky it was found in the left lung, which has two lobes, rather than the right lung, which has three. The medical personnel advised me that with three or four functioning lobes out of five lobes, I should be able to still lead a near normal life in the future.

I was then sent to St Thomas Hospital at Westminster Bridge Road, London SE1 7EH to present myself for Magnetic Resonance Imaging (MRI), a Position Emission Tomography (PET) -scan and Computerised Tomography (CT) Scan at the Hospital's Imaging Centre. PET (Position Emission Tomography) and CT (Computerised Tomography) Scans allow healthcare team to see how various organs in body are working and identify any organs that are not functioning as they should. The scans were also undertaken to see if there were any tumours detected in the rest of my body. It was important to know this, before doctors could decide whether there was any use, or substantial benefit, for operating on me at all. I was able to consider myself lucky, there were no other tumours, and I was permitted to undergo an operation.

In early August 2012, at Guy Hospital London Bridge, I met my Surgeon, a Frenchman, Mr Loic Lang – Lazdunski MD, PhD FRCS. The surgeon is popular, and affectionately known as 'aka LLL'. I told him Dr Sawicka had told me if I were lucky, the famous Surgeon "LLL" would conduct my surgery. He laughed and assured me he had successfully carried out hundreds of such surgeries, and I should not worry at all. He noted I was an insulin dependent diabetic, and my lung function was incredibly good, with no significant cardiac history. He commended me, that since January 2012, I had drastically reduced my forty cigarettes a day, to five to ten a day, and as a result my body would be more able to undergo a major operation.

I was to be admitted on the 8 of August 2012 and the operation was scheduled for the 9th of August 2012, under general anaesthetic.

Meanwhile, I had earlier in the year developed a trigger finger in my left-hand ring finger. I was scheduled to have an operation to correct it. The operation was performed under local anaesthetic on 18th July 2012 at Lewisham NHS, University Hospital, Lewisham, London SE13 6NL. I told myself I could die from the upcoming major surgery. That was the hard truth. An operation would require that I be put into unusual sleep, which is very different to normal sleeping. In ordinary sleep, a noise can wake you and you can dream, but surgery sleep is next to death, you will be unconscious. You are cut open, flipped over and around, without any pain. Some people never wake up, it could be me. I began to prepare myself for departing this world. Long ago, women in my village sang a song: 'We are not afraid that we will die someday, what we are really afraid of, is how we will die' Some people would choose to die instantly. Others would say it's better to live a little longer, even if means incontinence, to be fed, washed and so on, by others. Personally, I would like to live a little longer, if possible, but with my dignity still intact.

In a situation like this you wonder, 'Where is God in this? Is it his making?' No, I concluded that God or who, or whatever, brought us here to live and die, one-way or another, and for ninety-nine per-cent of us, that happens before we reach a hundred years of age. Death can occur in any number of ways, and at any time.

I went to church that weekend. I thanked God for his many blessings and was grateful for numerous things he had done for me, in my lifetime. I prayed for my children and their mothers, and for family and friends. I prayed in a way like our Lord Jesus Christ's prayer at the garden of Gethsemane. Prayed 'God if it be your will do not let me die from this lung surgery' I prayed that should there be a place called heaven, that I should be forgiven, and found worthy of earning a place there. I figured if I made peace with God now, I would be hedging my bets. That is, if I should die, and there is no God or heaven, I would have lost nothing. But if there is God and heaven, I would reap the reward of eternal life, which all religions teach.

On a practical basis, I began to make my peace with kith and kin. I amended my will and signed my last testament. I distributed my assets in London and Nigeria to my six sons, six daughters and their living mothers. I have a pair of ancestral story buildings in my "Akaraka Compound" in my hometown, including plots of fenced land and plots of undeveloped land. Ancestral properties in Igbo land cannot be distributed or willed out. They belong to all the children of the family, but the first is in charge as a hereditary caretaker.

I said to myself that life's struggles and material acquisitions are 'but vanity upon vanity,' as the bible says. When you think of the risks we take and things we do to ourselves and/or to others, the leisure, and pleasures we deny ourselves. The 'rat race' which we embark on, to achieve and to acquire in this materialistic world. You can't help but shudder, when you realise life, itself can end in a moment and you cannot take anything to the grave with you. The Holy Bible says it: 'We came from clay with nothing and to clay we return with nothing.' At times, it makes life appear pointless and meaningless.

During those dark periods of 2012, I regretted so many things I never had time to do. I surmised the problem with life is when we are young, we are full of energy, and have plenty of time ahead of us, but not enough brain. As we get older however, it appears we develop larger brains, good and great ideas, and sometimes have more money. Unfortunately, we don't have enough energy, or time left, to do much of anything. I thought it would have been great if we were created to live the first fifty years as a test run, and then come back to live the real life. The problem is, we spend the first forty or fifty years learning the ropes and tricks of this life and the world, and just when we have almost mastered it, where life could become plain sailing, it is time to go. When you have done your college degrees, trained your children, your home is almost paid for, then you become ill, you virtually see death staring you in the face, and you cannot duck or dive to escape its cold grip.

I thought, maybe our fear of death is irrational. It is mostly fear of the unknown. Maybe we get too comfortable on this earth, that we do not want to move on to the next level of existence. Our Creator may be moving us on, once our respective missions on earth are finished. The bible says we are given 'three score years and ten,' which is seventy years to live. In that case, if I lived for a further two years, I could say that I had spent my prescribed biblical seventy years on earth. But nothing makes any satisfactory sense. It is all speculations and conjectures, No one is sure of anything, except that we live and must surely die.

On another day, I woke up again and reasoned I have enjoyed life. Life is so brilliant, with beautiful things and people. Life is so sweet, especially now that I was making good success as a lawyer, with my own outfit, and I was able to do and get things that I wanted or needed. Girls half my age still pursued me and fell for me. Life was sweet and I did not wish to die yet. I was lucky and happy to have achieved and acquired things that made me feel good about myself and made my children and family proud of me. In life, we are all in this boat together and none of us is getting out alive. Both the 'haves and have-nots' are going down, turn by turn. I am blessed to be able to bequeath my offspring, a bit of a head start: money, houses, and businesses. On that note, I vowed I would smile as I died. I remained thankful to God for His mercies and blessings.

On 7th August 2012, I called my two grown up sons in London. I telephoned my daughters in America and South Africa, my sons and my granddaughter in the USA, and informed them all my major surgery, which was scheduled the next day. My daughters started crying, as I told them that if I did not come round from the operating table, they should take care, and live in peace and harmony. No fighting, I said. Within a few minutes, my first daughter telephoned my junior brothers in America and told them 'Daddy is talking funny' Thus, throughout the night, and early morning of the next day, my phones were ringing constantly, with calls from family members in Nigeria, South Africa, UK, and USA.

On 8th August 2012, I checked into the Dorcas wing of the famous Guys and St Thomas Hospital for the operation to remove the tumour in the upper part of my left lung, a Left Pneumonectomy. I had been instructed not to eat or drink from twelve midnight, until after the surgery. It was difficult to sleep that night. I considered all possibilities, outcomes, best case, worst-case scenarios.

On the 9th of August, I was woken early, and I took a shower. I recalled speaking to various members of the medical theatre team that morning, doctors, nurses, anaesthesiologists.

It was explained to me again that surgery would be to remove part (Lobectomy) or if necessary, the whole pneumonectomy) of the left lung. The process would be thoracotomy, where the surgeon makes a cut on the side below the shoulder blade and from there reaches the lung, through the ribs. The surgery would not be by median sternotomy - a cut /incision.

At 9am I was put on the cart, and the trolley moved through corridors and elevators into the operating theatre. I was asked to confirm my name and date of birth and my understanding of why I was in the operating theatre that morning. I remember being plugged into certain tubes and lines, suddenly, like magic, the team leapt into action, and I was a goner, unconscious for the next five hours.

At about 6 pm that evening, I opened my eyes, I was in a hospital bed, in intensive care. There were tubes everywhere. A tube feeding me nourishment, an oxygen mask to help me breath. A tube administering pain relief, and yet another providing antibiotics. I was strapped tight to the bed. I was unable to move, but surprisingly I did not feel any pain. I began to wonder if the operation had been performed. Two beautiful nurses on opposite sides of my bed, were assigned to look after me. They cheered me up, I even starting flirting with them. I remained in Intensive care until the next day, when I was wheeled to the hospital ward, where I stayed for the next two weeks.

Whilst in the hospital ward, my four-year-old son, Amara and his mother visited daily. My children in the UK, my office staff, colleagues, friends, and well-wishers also paid several visits to my hospital ward. Visitors expressed shocked surprise and wonderment on hearing I had cancer and had undergone major surgery. At that point, the success or otherwise of the operation was any bodies guess. The doctors suggested I should be followed up with adjuvant therapy, Chemotherapy and/or radiation therapy. I attended discussion groups, where I learned any of those therapies could have adverse effects on the general health of the individual. In the end I boldly opted not to have any adjuvant Chemotherapy follow up. My decision was based on fear and faith, or confidence. There are so many possible side effects from Chemotherapy, such as loss of hair, going deaf, or blind. My doctor, LLL reiterated that if he or his father was in my position, he would not recommend Adjuvant Chemotherapy. My Surgeon and consultant were so confident, I had to believe them. We just had to pray, and hope the cancer never come back. My doctors recommended I be monitored every six months, for five years, at the Princess Royal University Hospital Orpington, Kent. Hoping to stay in remission for as long as possible, I followed the regimen given to me by my doctors. At each of my six-monthly appointments, X-ray of my thorax and lungs were taken and compared with first and previous ones. Luckily, the specialist doctors always said that there had been no change and sent me home a happy guy. Upon my release from hospital in 2012, I was referred to Queen Elizabeth Hospital in Woolwich London, for two months of Oral Anti-coagulants, Warfarin, which is a post operation treatment, to prevent blood clots. I was also advised to eat foods rich in vitamin K such as green leafy vegetables, chickpeas, liver, egg yolks, cereals containing wheat bran and oats, mature cheese, blue cheese, avocados, and olive oil. They recommended obtaining the disabled badge, I was severely short of breath, and could not walk for long without stopping. To this day I enjoy use of the disabled badge, which allows me to park my car in the disabled car bay, which is usually closer to the entrance of any public offices, the badge is clearly displayed on the dashboard of the vehicle.

While recovering from surgery, I felt that having survived a major health scare and uncertainty about my future, I should in any event visit home, and give thanks to my God and ancestors. Before my planned travel, one of my friends Dr Nwosu, recommended a book called Hallelujah Diet. The most inspiring thing from that book is, to this day, a glass of freshly produced juice, containing lime, lemon, cucumber, carrots etc. This helps in building up immunity in the body.

My plan to visit home in December 2012, also coincided with the inaugural celebration of my larger family gatherings annual meeting. In the age-old Ibo tradition of traveling home to celebrate Christmas, the OKOROHA family decided to seize the opportunity of gathering numerous members of the family, to celebrate our common ancestry, on a day we set aside as the

Okoroha Day. Our family of over 200 members consists of children, grandchildren, great grandchildren and all are the descendants of Mazi Okoroha . The four sons of Okoroha as earlier stated, were Ozigbu, Osuagwu, Nwokoro, Ofoha. It is part of our history that some members have their last names as Ozigbu rather than Okoroha. The maiden edition of the Okoroha day celebration took place on 30th December 2012. The occasion which was hosted at our "Isi-Obi" was well attended by dignitaries and sundries. The then Eze of Ogwuaga, Eze Ojiako was in attendance, publicly restating the Okoroha Family remains the head of the Umudim Agu kindred, and thus the head in the entire Ogwuaga Autonomous Community. He confirmed Okoroha Family holds the Ofo Ukwu Ogwuaga (staff of Office). Eze Ojiako also stated the mother of Okoroha hailed from Mr Adam's family in Ezimoha Mbano, and the same Adam's family is the same family where his own wife hails from. The day was something of a carnival, with masquerades, clowns, glisters, men and women drummers and dancers. It was quite a memorable occasion.

Incidentally, I was among those given the task of writing our family history. I was perhaps too forthright that some members became irate and protested. I was pleased that what I wrote was a mere draft to be edited and reviewed, however my defence fell on deaf ears. I took the hint and apologised unreservedly and donated one million naira to family funds. Thus, the hullabaloo meant the comprehensive Okoroha Family history project, remains in abeyance.

Sadly, in June 2013, I had a personal bereavement, my beloved Eucharia passed away. She suffered from cancer of the uterus and battled for about six months, sadly without success. I had an unexpected experience following her death. My late wife's family sent a stern warning to me and my family, that we dare not bury, their daughter, unless they were present at the graveside. And that they would not attend the funeral. unless I personally come and marry her, in line with full tradition and custom, while she lay in the Mortuary. They alleged that when I took Eucharia, their daughter as wife in 1984 without proper customary marriage, I had merely 'borrowed' a wife. In resolving the issue, I proceeded to comply with their demand in full. Afterwards the family appeared satisfied, shook my hand, and accepted me as a full and bonafide in-law.

Upon the lessons I learned from the above incident, concerning my late wife, I decide to 'take the bull by the horns' and immediately regularize my customary marriages to my other consorts. I sent emissaries to visit each of my in-laws and obtain lists of their demands. I subsequently fulfilled the demands and rights for both living women.

In December 2013, I had my coronation of a second chieftaincy title, bestowed upon me by my people. The title and Chieftaincy cap was placed on my head by our town's king, Eze, Hon. Justice, Dim Ohamadike Ojiako (Rtd). He was a former Chief Judge (CJ) of Imo State. Often, I wondered why our traditional rights regarding the chieftaincy ceremony have been based on almost rigid precepts. One would have thought that the sweeping wave of modern-day civilization would have impacted on the archaic tradition but surprisingly it remained resilient, and every process is still embedded in the old beliefs and tradition. Thus, with full pomp and pageantry, I was accompanied by an entourage to the king's palace, with the support of traditional talking drums. Additionally, my entourage had in retinue the old Bende war dancers, otherwise known as Ikperikpe dancers. The dancers consisted of twelve heavily built men, with each carrying a basket of four imitation human skulls, which symbolised the long-standing tradition of displaying conquered and slaughtered soldiers from the enemy's camp. Though, folklore has it that those human skulls were also skulls of natives who had committed heinous or abominable crimes such as murder, rape, incest, patricide, matricide, and treason. The men dancers had their faces painted in red cam wood, mud, and white chalk. They wore feathered arm band and leg cowries. They were big chested muscular men who were girded in Loins with colourful head bands. They were serenaded by war beat drummers. When music reaches its' frenzy, the dancers spurn round and round and different directions with their shinny and threatening machete.

On the day of the ceremony, I was kitted in full traditional Igbo Chieftaincy attire with colourful large beads, anklets, bangles, red cap with eagle's feathers. My attire was complimented by the ever-present titular hand-fan, with my title name carefully hand knitted circular form on it – Chief Akaraka 1. I also had an imposing titular staff, a big metal walking stick, similar in shape and height to a papal ferula or bishop's crosier, and an elephant tusk as parts of my ceremonial paraphernalia. They ended with an elaborate feast and communal party at my palace, where two cows were slaughtered as custom demanded for the great occasion. I entertained family members both nuclear and extended, including my mother's kinsmen, women, and children, and friend from far and wide, in-laws and well-wishers.

**CHAPTER NINETEEN**

# Visit to USA in 2014

In 2014, my wife Lynn and our son Adolph (Jr), travelled to the United States of America for three weeks' vacation. We flew with British Airways, a Jumbo Jet, Boeing 747 with wide body and four engines, from London Heathrow, across the Atlantic Ocean into the New York's John F Kennedy (JFK) Airport. The pilots and the first-class seating are located on the upper level of the aircraft. From JFK we flew a small internal flight to Thurgood Marshall, Baltimore Washington International (BWI) Airport.

My first daughter, Chief Cynthia Chinyere Okoro (RN) (Adadiohonma1) and her teenage daughter, Rochelle, and my two brothers, Chief Dr. Chidex Okoro and Chief Engineer Iyke Okoro, along with their respective wives Lolo Stella Okoro (RN) and Lolo Dr Calista Okoro and all their children, three each, namely two Juniors, during our time in Maryland USA, we went for a meal at my cousin's house Mr and Mrs Moses Okoroha's house, in Green Belt area of Baltimore.

We spent a week in a hotel in Baltimore, visited my brothers' houses in various parts of Largo, Baltimore, and my daughter's house in Mount Rainier, Baltimore, and my son Nnamdi Derick Okoroha's flat in Hyattsville. We also went to factory outlet shops in Virginia and spent a full day in Washington, visiting the White House, Capitol Hill, Washington Memorial Monument, and many other attractions.

In 2014, at the age of 70 years, I was called to the Nigerian Bar by the Body of Benchers and the Council of Legal Education. As a UK practicing solicitor, I had recommended many Nigerians to the Nigerian Law School in Abuja and Lagos. Finally, in 2013 I decide to go to Abuja and seek to qualify as a Nigerian Barrister. It was a difficult experience from food, security, amenities and even dealing with other human beings. Eventually, after hustling and bustling, and burning the midnight oil, combining lecture with private lessons, I succeeded in passing the Bar Finals. I was aware of how difficult the Bar final was, and many who had repeatedly fallen by the wayside. I noted there were more women than men at the Nigerian Law School during my studentship.

Many of my classmates called to the Barr at same time as me, continue to complain at the lack of employment and suitable remuneration. Yet, every year Nigeria Law School produces over three thousand new lawyers. It seems that the appetite to qualify as a Barrister or lawyer among Nigerians is insatiable, just like all over the world. I lived off campus in an executive suite at a nearby hotel. I participated fully in student life at the Law School. I had my fair share of the social life and a collegiate of female friends and admirers. I was open minded, gregarious, knowledge seeking and loaded. Indeed, I might have promised marriage to a few suitors. In the end, long distance dating is for the birds. On and off Campus, one must be careful not to fall prey to dupers. Some will promise good grades and some Pentecostal Pastors claim that if you sow a sizeable seed in cash, they will pray and decree success in your final Bar exams.

In December 2014, I celebrated my 70th Birthday. This was another fun filled activity in my household. My children, led by the eldest, Chief Cynthia Chioma Okoro (RN) organised and sponsored the 70th Birthday party in my honour. The party cost over four million Naira at the time. All my children, their mothers and my brother's returned to Nigeria from various places, including Europe, USA, and South Africa. Brochures and Banners were made to commemorate the occasion. Tents and Canopies were set in my compound whilst part chairs and tables were beautified and decorated. A live band was on stage for the day. Professional caterers were hired and supplied a variety of dishes and cool or chilled wines, beer, mineral or soft drinks and other beverages. Our family women and our married sisters were dressed in separate clothes, which were paid for by my children.

I took the microphone and gave personal testimonies and reminiscences about how grateful to God I was, for his mercy and grace, that he had brought me thus far. I danced with my children and all my wives. I requested that the birthday brochure contained all family members, including my grandfather, grandmother, brothers, sisters, wives, children, and grandchildren. I also ensured that a prominent place in the brochure was reserved for my memorable poem "DESIDERATA" by Max Ehrmann.

Whilst at home in Nigeria, I learnt two or more new lessons; practically everyone you meet expects something from you because you have arrived from overseas. This demand is often seen as their birthright by some of the people, as if you owe them the favour. Some make impossible demands, without thinking whether you can afford it or not. It appears that as far as they are concerned, you have just arrived from overseas "Alabekee" be it Europe or Americas, and must presumably be rich, so they intend to fleece you of every penny they can get, by hook or by crook. On one occasion, I sent a young boy of about 12 years old, to buy me a packet of cigarettes. He returned without any change, I asked him about my change, because he could not have spent a whole £5 equivalent of Naira at the time, on just one packet of cigarettes. He simply told me they asked him to come back for the change, but I believe the fact was the boy had collected the change, and simply converted it to his personal use, permanently. The boy appeared to have taken his own benefit off me. He thenceforth avoided any contact with me, I never saw him again till I left for UK. Any mature and reasonable person should bear in mind, the person you are pestering to help you, is also looking for anyone who may give or help him, or her. Almost, everyone has needs and wants until the day they die. Whatever is happening in Nigeria today is the same thing happening all over the developing nations, we can only pray that things get better in the future. That is the hope against hope. Things get worse and worse. Crime increases everywhere. Children get increased freedom, they also get bolder and bolder, and increasingly rebellious. People want more money, wealth, and materialism. The socalled freedom once attained or given, cannot be taken back.

Once the Genie has left the bottle, you cannot put it back.

# DESIDERATA

GO PLACIDLY amid the noise and the haste, and remember what peace there may be in silence. As far as possible, without surrender, be on good terms with all persons.

Speak your truth quietly and clearly; and listen to others, even to the dull and the ignorant; they too have their story.

Avoid loud and aggressive persons; they are vexatious to the spirit. If you compare yourself with others, you may become vain or bitter, for always there will be greater and lesser persons than yourself.

Enjoy your achievements as well as your plans. Keep interested in your own career, however humble; it is a real possession in the changing fortunes of time.

Exercise caution in your business affairs, for the world is full of trickery. But let this not blind you to what virtue there is; many persons strive for high ideals, and everywhere life is full of heroism.

Be yourself. Especially do not feign affection. Neither be cynical about love; for in the face of all aridity and disenchantment, it is as perennial as the grass.

Take kindly the counsel of the years, gracefully surrendering the things of youth.

Nurture strength of spirit to shield you in sudden misfortune. But do not distress yourself with dark imaginings. Many fears are born of fatigue and loneliness.

Beyond a wholesome discipline, be gentle with yourself. You are a child of the universe no less than the trees and the stars; you have a right to be here.

And whether or not it is clear to you, no doubt the universe is unfolding as it should. Therefore be at peace with God, whatever you conceive Him to be. And whatever your labors and aspirations, in the noisy confusion of life, keep peace in your soul. With all its sham, drudgery and broken dreams, it is still a beautiful world.

Be cheerful. Strive to be happy.

MAX EHRMANN

# VISITING BEIJING, CHINA

In 2015 After a period of procrastination, Ling and I applied successfully for Chinese visas for me and our son Amara (Guai Guai). We flew Air China from London, in a twelve-hour nonstop flight to Beijing, China. Ling's mother Mrs Xiu Lan, her sister, brother, their spouses, and children were at the Airport to receive us. I was treated like African Royalty. Indeed, on occasion, I was dressed like an Ancient Chinese Emperor, and my wife dressed like a Chinese empress. We kicked it off by going for a meal with the family members. During the two weeks we were in China, we visited the popular Tiananmen Square, the famous China Wall, and the popular Terracotta Soldiers in Xian. Subsequently, we flew to Shanghai for a couple of days and then to Hong Kong, from where we flew 10 hours, non-stop, back to UK.

It appeared my desire to travel around the world became more compelling, having a regard to the universality of my family. Indeed, my family spread around the globe, thus in 2016 Lynn and I agreed to take our son Amara, Guai Guai, to visit our family living in South Africa. I made arrangements and booked our flight to South Africa, my first daughter in Maryland USA, Chichi Cynthia, decided it would be a reunion for all of us, to be in South Africa at that time. In fact, she and her nineteen years daughter arrived at Johannesburg some few days ahead of us. Upon our arrival, Lulu, our three daughters namely, Didi Chioma, Wellie Adaeze, and Ayanda Ngozi and their respective families, as well Cynthia and Rochelle were at the Oliver R.

Tambo International Airport to welcome us. I was particularly elated to meet my grandchildren in South Africa, namely: Didi Chioma's Kayla; Adaeze Wellie's Children; Jaden (7), and Eva (5) and Ngozi Ayanda's children Naima (11), Santiago (1)

There was a convoy of several cars to our hotel in Pretoria. I observed that the hotel overlooked Nelson Mandela Square, where the legend's bronze statue is located. My family residing in South Africa, lavished love, and affection on us. There wasn't a dull moment. We visited the home of Nelson Mandela in Soweto, the Sun City Park, and several safari ranches, where we saw many colourful, captivating, and beautiful animals with their unique characters. On Christmas day 2016, there was a large family gathering at Professor Lulu Okoro's main residence in Pretoria. The entire family, including our in-laws and extended relations congregated and shared Christmas dinner. Incidentally, my cousins Casmir Okoroha, Ethelbert Okoroha and Odinaka Okoroha who live in South Africa, were also present. Casmir attended with his Caucasian South African born wife and three children.

There were assorted dishes, including native South African dishes, Nigerian delicatessen, Chinese menu, and continental delicacies. I felt deep down it was wrong, I had not visited South Africa more regularly. The realisation made me remorseful and reflective. I was so emotionally moved by the love shown to me by my nearest and dearest ten people. On the spur of the moment, after dinner, I doled out one thousand pounds, in five hundred-pound notes, to each member of my family. I felt they had missed out, I also had certainly missed out. It seemed they were elated to present to their South African families, the man "Okoro", whose name they bear. Lynn was basking in happiness and the glory of the moment. She was radiated by the felicitation and outpouring of deep joy, in midst of my South African family.

Additionally, she proved herself a worthy woman, by facilitating the family visit wholeheartedly.

Although we had previous meetings and visits, as family in London, this visit to South African soil was unique. However, this book depicts wholeheartedly, the clinical and canonical reminiscence of an alpha male, undeterred by the turbulence of life. Indeed, a candid and beautiful human story that is rich in anecdotes, proverbs, biblical injunctions, logic, philosophy, and simple common sense. The writing is pungent, no holding back, truthful, and unusually insightful. It is an admixture of the clash of two or more different civilisations, and the challenges of inhabiting a global village, varied, diverse and verse in time, space, culture, and age. This book is a testimony to the 'never say die' spirit of a progenitor, and the acknowledgement of the uncommon grace the creator bestows on everyone, despite the vicissitudes of their life.

A good friend of mine Dr. Chikezie Okoronkwo, an Estate surveyor and an agent, informed me of the availability of certain three plots of land at Toronto junction, Owalu, Uratta,
Owerri. The asking price was three million naira per plot. He also told me the three plots were contiguous, and adjacent to a School.

I considered the prospects of the land and location and decided to purchase. Thus in 2017, I bought the land and I had it fenced with a large gate, mounted at the entrance. Upon purchase, I pondered as to what type of project it might be suitable for. One of my ladies, suggested the building of an hotel, whilst another proposed the erection a couple of apartment complexes. We were still debating the options, the owners of the plots proximate to my three plots, offered their land for purchase also. I considered myself fortunate to have five plots of land together, at the same location. On purchasing the additional two plots of land, Mazi Chike my estate agent called, stating the owner of the uncompleted school and land adjacent to my property, had put the school up for sale. The land situates on three plots, consisted of two uncompleted buildings and a vacant field. In my usual appreciation of nature and providence, I concluded God had favoured me with a benevolent opportunity to build a legacy.

I determined to purchase the uncompleted School and land. Subsequently, I decided to invest in the education sector, spending over N130 million naira on the completion of a group of school buildings and putting a befitting citadel in place. I gave the schools the eponymous name of OKOROHA ROYAL ACEDEMY in honour of my ancestry, and remembrance of my Great Grandfather, Okoroha whose four sons are the forebears of my great family. The Okoroha Royal Academy is fully functional educational establishment, for Nursery, Primary and Secondary education. In 2019, the school was registered with Imo State Ministry of Education and Corporate Affairs Commission (CAC) at Abuja, Nigeria. The management of ORA is currently vested in two of my wives, Susan and Ursula Okoroha, and the management structure will be improved and segregated with the introduction of external and independent educational experts. Mrs (Lolo) Susan Okoroha fiercely contends, since she has a B.Ed. degree and is currently proprietor of her own primary and secondary at

Umuora, Awo omamma she should therefore rightly be appointed as the Principal of ORA.

However, Mrs (Lolo) Ursula Okoro, who holds a BA degree in international Relations, is of the strong view the school management should be split into two, in order that she could manage the nursery section, whilst her co-wife should oversee the Primary and Secondary sections.

My older second wife, Professor (Lolo) Lulu Okoro, opined an independent professional staff would better manage the ORA to maintain a high standard, and ensure stability, viability, continuity, and merit. This is concurred by my younger brother Chief (Engr) Iyke Okoro's wife, Dr (Lolo) Calista Okoro.

I am deeply grateful for the opportunity God has bestowed on me, to be able to accomplish my dream of building a school. I was elated and gratified on the completion and opening of the school. It gives me profound pride and immense joy, as well as honour to bequeath Okoroha Royal Academy (ORA) as a legacy. It is a testament to my belief in educational attainments, achievements, scholarship, scholastic accolades, and the pursuit of education as a life changing eternal tool. ORA is one of the things my pursuit of education has done for me. It is my personal testimony of the product of high educational and professional accomplishment. I must express my sincere gratitude to Mazi

(Dr) Chikezie Okoronkwo for his foresight in affording me the opportunity to acquire the land and school when they became available. Also, for his honesty in managing the financial and human resources for erection of the buildings, structures, landscaping and as well as official inspection and registration of the educational establishment.

Between 2011 and 2014 I suffered what is medically known as trigger finger. Twice a finger on each of my hands, at different consecutive times, would become stuck or locked. It was not painful, but the finger would either be slow to release, or wouldn't release at all. This makes me recollect that as a child, I saw some people at home in Nigeria with fingers that looked like jack-knives or crab legs. The people struggled and grappled to hold a drinking cup and tumblers. I was fortunately referred to orthopaedics, Lewisham Hospital and Queen Mary Hospital respectively, and simple operations and or injections were performed, and my fingers were restored to normalcy.

In 2014 and in 2019, I was hit from behind, twice, when driving. The first time, I was driving my Mercedes Benz Jeep, on a bright day, along Long Lane in Bexleyheath, Kent. I was looking dapper, in a three-piece suit, heading to my law chambers, in Woolwich Arsenal, London. I stopped behind a stationary car, with blinking lights, signalling a right turn. into a Shell petrol station. There was sudden impact "gbowaa" behind me. From my rear-view mirror, I observed a large food delivery truck had hit me. I had no visible or apparent injuries, but could have had an internal injury, or possible concussion, and/or whiplash, I didn't know. I calmly stepped out of my car and went behind to investigate. Damage to my car was mostly to the bumper and left rear light casing. Mr Raj, the offending driver. He must have said "I am sorry" over ten times. He must have been driving over the alcohol limit, or so I thought, or maybe he suffered temporary memory loss, or something? I hadn't stopped suddenly. Why hadn't he seen the stationary cars ahead? I demanded to see his Identity, he handed me his UK Driver Licence, and a photocopy of his Comprehensive Insurance. He printed his full name, address, and phone number, also the name of the company he worked for as a delivery driver. He telephoned his boss and passed the phone to me, to have a word with him. His supervisor at work told me to make sure my car and I were looked after. I then drove off and visited my GP clinic, where I was examined, and given a prescription of Paracetamol. The insurance sent me to their chosen medical doctor, who conducted physical and medical examinations. For medical damages I was paid about £3,000. Later, the insurance wrote off my car, it would cost more to fix it than pay me off. The Insurance Company then made me another offer, with options. I could be paid £4000, and they would take my car, or £3,000 and I could keep the car. I choose to keep the Jeep, and eventually fixed it up and shipped it to Nigeria.

In the second case in April 2019, I stopped at a Zebra crossing to enable an old man and his grandchildren to walk across the road. Again, as in the first accident, I was rammed from behind, this time a small Vauxhall car. The entire process all over again. This time, I was driving my new Range Rover sport, 2018 plate Registration. Again, I was wearing a striped suit, as a lawyer, heading to work in Woolwich, London SE18. This time the culprit was a white middle-aged woman. She promptly apologised, admitted liability, and handed over to me all relevant details, which I required to make a claim from her insurers. Damage was also caused to my car bumper, and I was shaken up. The Insurance sent me to the physical therapy contact, for ten sessions. I took the cash payment of £2,500 to fix my car by myself. I was also compensated £3,000 for personal injury. It's noteworthy, things like this would not happen in Nigeria, there the outcome would have been totally different. This shows the great difference, an organised society, where law and order are respected, and justice prevails.

In 2015, I literally escaped death, whilst involved in an accident. I had driven to a location near Heathrow Airport, in Middlesex. Sadly, it was the funeral of my friend's thirty-year-old son, he died of cancer. My friend, Dee Cosmas is also from my hometown, Abba. He is older than me and married a lady from our town. The couple had three children together. Unfortunately, the marriage broke down and the children lived with their mother. Every effort made to reconcile, was futile, Dee Cosmas then married a young lady, who bore him two more children, a boy, and a girl. It is possible the children of the first wife began to listen more to their mother. And sadly, these children became estranged from their dad. The father went to visit his son, who was on his death bed, and his son told him to leave, he did not want to see his father. We still went to the funeral, together with the weeping and mourning father. Mothers should never poison their children's mind against their father, the children should be neutral and not take sides between two parents.

After the burial, there was socialising and light refreshments. For Nigerians, light refreshment includes plates of jollof rice, fufu (pounded yam) and beer, such as Irish imported Guinness, star, 33, Guilder and Malt, Coco Cola, and other soft drinks. After eating, drinking and a little socialising, I took my leave and set off for home, entering the London freeway, M25, heading east toward Dartford Crossing. After about thirty minutes, I needed to answer a call of nature. I continued to drive until I saw a hard shoulder. I pulled completely into the bay, got out of my car, and went to the passenger side, to be private. I was halfway through urinating, when I heard an almighty sound to the rear, right side of my car. The impact literally shoved the vehicle about a foot forward. I quickly 'zipped up' and ran behind my car, to see what had happened. It was a huge eighteen-wheel truck from Germany. The Driver spoke little or no English and luckily, I speak and understand some German (Deutsch). The driver Herr Shule had fallen asleep, momentarily and veered out of control. The fact he didn't demolish me, and my car, was a miraculous act of God. He was an honest young man. He apologised and admitted liability. He gave his details and details of his insurance and employer company, based in Hanover Germany. The rear of my car was irreparably damaged, but I had no injury, and my car was still drivable. I was shaking, as I drove home slowly. The next day, I contacted the Company in Germany, and they confirmed they were aware of the incident. They instructed me to send two repair estimates to them by email, and within a couple of weeks my UK account was credited with £4,000 to repair my car. They paid the lower of the two estimates.

*With my wife, Ling Okoro.*

*With Ling after the birth of our son, 2008. At our back garden in London.*

*Wedding ceremony with my wife*

*Ling Okoro after the birth of our son, Amara. Ling at Sidcup in England in 2008.*

*My former wife, Patricia, and my wife, Prof. Dr. Lulu Okoro.*

My son, Amara, walking barefoot in my village in Abba in Nigeria.

*My Chinese chieftaincy title as Ogaramba Karamba*

*Myself and my wife, Ling, on holiday in China.*

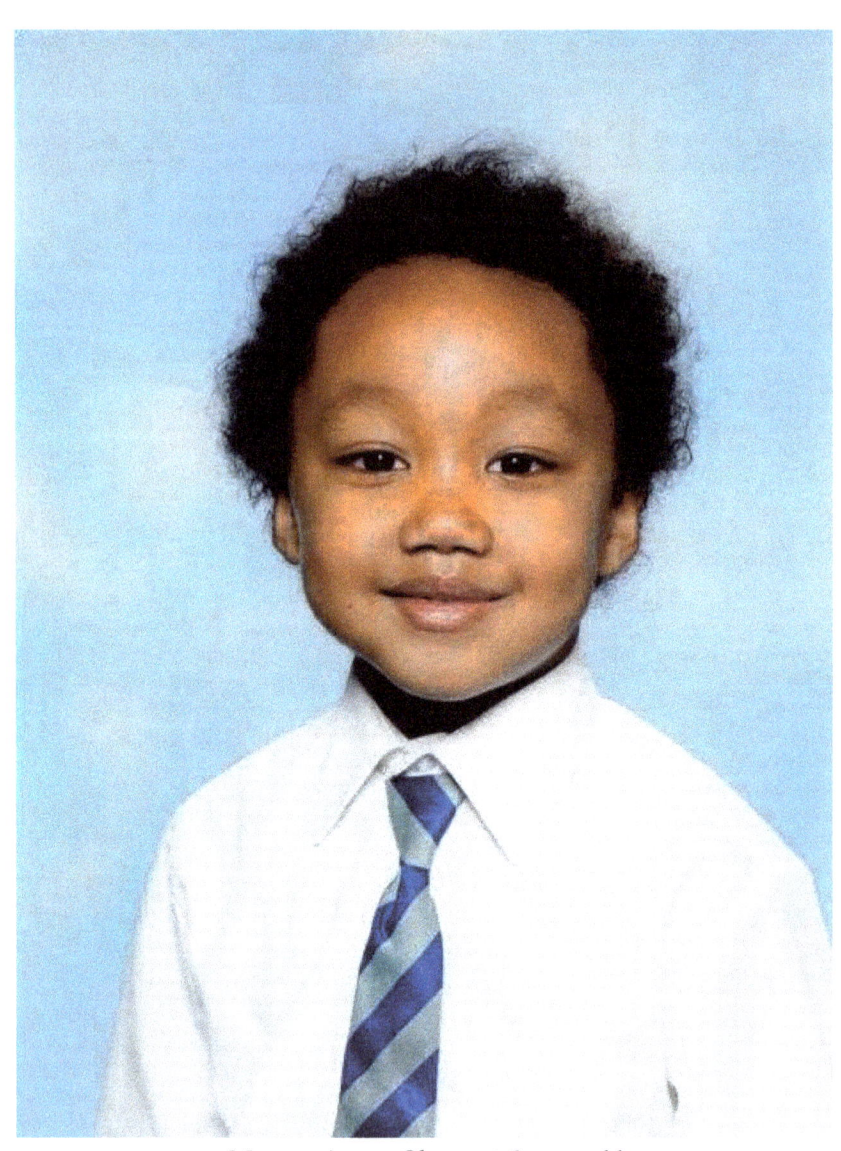

My son, Amara Okoro, at 6 years old

*My second wife, Prof. Lulu Okoro, the mother of Chioma and Barrister Adaeze Okoro.*

*First: My 8th wife, Ukeria, Akwaugo's Mom.*
*Second: My grandfather, Bikkubikku—The 1st Osuagwu Okoroha Third:*
*My granddaughter, Rochelle.*
*Fourth: With my wife, Ursla, Kelechi's Mom*

*My Wives, Kelechi's mom , Ursla, and Susan, Ugonna's mom in 1989.*

*Myself and my wife, Ling Okoro and my youngest son Amara on holiday in China.*

*Myself with my 7th Ex White -wife, Patricia Martins-Okoro.*

**CHAPTER TWENTY**

---

# Acute Or Chronic Sinusitis, (Rhinosinusitis)

In a way, we are our own best doctors. If you are not aware of your body, the doctors may give you the wrong diagnoses, and due to your own ignorance, you may accept it to your detriment. I have been lucky that in all my ailments, I tried to actively contribute to the medical doctors' assessment. Sometimes, doctors have given me a diagnoses or medication which I considered not suitable for me, and I refused to take it. A case in point, in 2018, I experienced an inexplicable pain in my jaw, on the right side. The pain then migrated between my eyes, my right ear, and my cheek bone. I went to see the Doctor at my local Surgery. She was a black Somalian doctor and she asked me if I chew bones? I was very embarrassed when I answered in the affirmative, that yes sometimes I do chew chicken-wing bones. She said that was the cause of my problem, right there and advised me to stop. She confidently and authoritatively explained I was suffering from what in the medical field, is called Temporomandibular Joint Disorder. She printed from the internet to show me, where the jaw is hinged to the skull, and this is near the ear. After two weeks, I went back to the Surgery and saw a white middle-aged English doctor, and reported I had not chewed any bones, but the right side of my face and ear remained sore and painful. The Doctor asked me if I wear dentures, I said yes. The doctor said my dentures may not be properly aligned and that is what was causing me pain. He prescribed painkillers.

Based on this last medical opinion, I went to see two dentists. One was free on NHS and the other was private and I paid £60 consultation. The NHS Dentist was fully booked for six months. The private Dentist, a white eastern European male, agreed my dentures were not properly aligned, and he gave me an estimate of £1,800. I thought the price a total rip off. I wasn't satisfied, so on a Sunday morning, I went to the Accident and Emergency, at Queen Elizabeth Hospital. I claimed I couldn't eat and hadn't slept all night. A short dark Nigerian Doctor examined me, ran some tests, and gave a physical examination of my mouth and ears. He concluded I had an ear infection, that was cause of the pain. He gave me some urgent medication, including eardrops and a prescription, for more medication. After a week, I still didn't feel any improvement. Meanwhile, I went to Croydon, to see the private denture works, who built my dentures over six years before. He tested the dentures and told me they were well aligned and shouldn't be causing me any pain. He said he wouldn't want to take my money to make new dentures, no dentist should. I was confused and 'back to square one'. The next day I booked and saw yet another doctor, at the same local Clinic. I complained bitterly to Dr Chumber, that many doctors just play a guessing game with peoples' lives. I asked why it was that none of the past three doctors who had examined me, knew what was wrong with me. He was a young doctor, he sincerely apologised on behalf all doctors, telling me he would get to the bottom of it. He said he would book an MRI scan of my head, immediately. Within a couple of days, I received a phone call from a private number. A lady's voice asked, are you Mr Okoro? please confirm your date of birth and home address? After this routine modality, she asked if I could attend next Sunday morning for an MRI scan, at Queen Mary Hospital in Sidcup, Kent. I promptly attended. I lay flat, and the noisy scanning machine completed the scan of my head and neck, it took only thirty minutes, or so. Within a week, I received a text message for an appointment with the doctor.

The doctor was eager to tell me he had found the cause of my problems. He said the scan showed that I had Sinusitis, which is when the sinus is infected by a virus, bacteria, or a rare fungus. He said this type of infection causes all the symptoms I mentioned, including facial, jaw and ear pain. He gave me a prescription for two weeks amoxicillin antibiotic 500mg tablets, to be taken three times a day. I was incredibly grateful, and went straight to St James Pharmacy in Woolwich, waited for about ten minutes, and picked up my medication. Before two weeks had elapsed, I had no more signs or symptoms of any infection or pains behind my nose, jaws, and ear. I completed the course and the pain disappeared for good. I had been proactive, finally getting the results I needed.

# EYE PROBLEM

In 2017-18, I developed eye problems. Firstly Cataracts, an operation to both eyes, a month apart. Cataracts or lens replacement surgery is the removal of the natural lens of the eye, that has become opaque, or developed opacification and it is replaced with an artificial, or plastic intraocular lens. I was a little fearful, I hated the thought of someone 'playing God' with my eyeballs. I knew an uncle and two aunties who had Cataracts and went blind because of the surgery. Fortunately, my operations and recovery went very well, and I began to see clearly again. In fact, the world became almost too bright for a while, and I had to wear sunglasses. My vision returned to 20/20 and I could read, watch television, and drive, without glasses. It is funny, that due to habit, I feel naked without my glasses, so quite often, I wear them, even though I don't need them.

In 2018-2019, I was diagnosed with a spot behind my left eye. This is called mild diabetic macular oedema. The treatment was two monthly injections into the eye. The intravitreal injections of Eylea were also a nerve-wracking experience. EYLEA is used to treat Nonvascular (wet) age related Macular Degeneration (AMD). After three injections I was discharged, as my eye was cured. Each time I laid on my back with an eye wide open, waiting for an injection, I kept blinking and shaking.
The nurse or doctor would say 'If you don't stop blinking and shaking, I cannot inject you, and the appointment may have to be rebooked'. Then I would freeze, and in one minute it was done,

'it is over'! she announced, 'you can get up and go'. I was so relieved. After about three, two monthly appointments, on the fourth and fifth appointment, I was cleared by the Ophthalmologist. The assistant Optometrist declared upon examination of both my eyes, no neovascularization could be detected in either eye, and confirmed there was a stable macula in both eyes and good vision bilaterally. Again, 'by Jove!' I was totally elated!

## PROSTATE CANCER

In December 2019, I was diagnosed with Prostate Adenocarcinoma Cancer: PSA 18.4, T2, NO MO with

Gleason score of 9 (4+5). Damn! It was like being struck twice by a bolt of lightning. Once again, I had been hit by 'a ton of bricks.

Anyway, after my initial shock and bewilderment, I began to read up on the disease. Prostate cancer is said to be the second most common type of cancer found in men, after lung cancer. Prostate cancer is said to affect over 40,000 men in a year and kills over 12,000 men every year in the UK. Lung Cancer accounts for 21% cancer deaths whilst bowel cancer kills 10%, Prostate Cancer 7% and breast cancer 7%. It is said that most deaths occur due to late discovery and detection. If detected and diagnosed early enough there can be a remedy. Where the cancer is not detected in the initial stages, it spreads, grows slowly, or extremely fast, from the prostate to other parts of the body: bones, liver, lymph nodes and lung. When it spreads from the prostate, it is said to have metastasised, and becomes deadly. Even at the advanced stage, it is potluck, as some people die sooner, while many live with it for many more years before they die.

In the initial stages of the disease, there are hardly any signs or symptoms, so by the time one starts noticing symptoms, it has probably spread to other organs of the body. At that stage one may have problems with urination, difficulty starting urination, difficulty maintaining urination, or urine leakage. Other symptoms include pain during urination, pain during ejaculation, blood in urine or semen, and erectile dysfunction. Urinary incontinence is mostly related to problems with the bladder, rather than problems with the Prostate.

The prostate is located between the penis and the bladder. It is a small gland, usually the size of a walnut or "ukpa" nut located under the urinary bladder, around the urethra, - the tube which runs down and through the penis, and through which urine and sperm leave the body. The key role of the Prostate is to produced semen, which is a lubricating fluid which carries the sperm, which is produced in the testicles.

No one knows why, but the prostate usually starts to grow bigger as men get older, from 50 years age. Sometimes it can become so big, that it interferes and constricts the urethra making urination slow, or difficult. The condition of enlarged prostate is not cancer. Normally, cells in any part of the body divide and grow in a normal, predictable manner. But where cells start dividing and growing in an abnormal and uncontrolled way, it is said to be cancerous. This is sometimes called a tumour. Thus, it can be cancer of lungs, throat, breast, stomach, liver, ovary, etc., etc. Prostate cancer (PC) is simply where cells of prostate gland are growing abnormally. One in eight men will suffer pc. Generally, prostate cancer discovered in the initial stages, does not shorten a man life. The Prostate gland produces a certain Protein, and from a blood test if the Prostate Specific Antigen (PSA) is 0-6.5 this is normal. Raised PSA, of over 6.5 to 20 is an early sign of prostate cancer. PSA of over twenty is a likely indication the cancer has spread, or metastasised, to other parts of the body, and/or the bones and lymph nodes. Most men ignore health matters until it is too late. This risk is doubled in developing nations, where there are no free medical tests, or treatment available.

Luckily, I have been eleven years in remission from lung cancer. One of the lessons I learned from being diagnosed in 2012, is to regularly submit to tests and investigations, to know what is happening in my body, before it is too late. I survived that cancer because it was discovered at early stage 2 and was operable. Afterwards, I signed up with a private Health Group called Bluecrest. They gave me a health MOT every summer. For the previous 7 years my PSA was under 6.5 but in 2018 it rose slightly to seven. I should have gone to my doctor (GP) at that point, but I recklessly ignored it. I didn't have any physical problems with urination, erection, and ejaculation. I thought the rise in PSA was a bleep and I could change things here and there and I would certainly be fine again.

However, the blue crest test carried out in summer 2019 showed my PSA to be ten. I quickly booked to see my GP, Dr Ascot Berber of Albion Clinic, Bexleyheath Kent DA7. He sent me for another test and the PSA result had risen to fourteen. I was immediately sent to the Urology Clinical Oncology / cancer department, at Queen Elizabeth Hospital (QEH), Stadium Road in Woolwich London SE18, where I was attended to by a young Italian lady, Dr Ella, and an elderly Indian Dr Sarangi, a Pakistan lady, Dr Sindu and a Zimbabwean male Nurse, Mr

Lance. Within a week, Dr Ella conducted a stinking Physical Rectal Examination of my prostate. She told me to pull down my pants and crawl facing the wall like a foetus. In front of a nurse, she put on gloves, put cold gel-lubricant into my anus and stuck two or more fingers into my ass. I could feel her finger rummaging inside there, fiddling with the prostate gland.

I attended the hospital appointment with my fourth daughter, Emilyn Akwugo Okoro, my daughter was told to stay outside the room, whilst the doctor carried out the examination. Following this Dr Ella initially said it was clearly an enlarged prostate, as was felt. She did not feel any hardness, or lump. She said I could be lucky, and it was merely a benign enlarged prostate, which is medically called Benign Prostate Hyperplasia (BPH). She said all men develop a harmless enlarged prostate as they get older. Then she cautioned that more tests must be done to confirm diagnoses. She gave me a follow up appointment for following week. I met Dr Ella the following week, and she examined my rectum again. This time she conducted the Digital Rectal Examination (DRE) She took twenty 'pinches' as Biopsies of my prostate, to be sent to the laboratory for testing. The results came back at the next appointment. It was the turn of Dr Sarangi to give the awful result. He spoke plainly. He said you have cancer, and it is the aggressive type which is spreading fast: A Gleason score of 9 (4+5). I later learned that Prostate cells seen under microscope have patterns, depending on how quickly they are likely to grow. Gleason pattern grades range from 1 to 5. The grade 1-2 are normal, 3, 4 and 5 are cancer cells. The higher the grade the more likely it is to grow and spread. At the DRE 20 biopsies were taken, of which ten samples showed cancer. Of those ten, some were grade 4 and others were grade 5. So, this meant a whopping score of 9. Dr Sarangi said we needed to know if the cancer had metastasised or spread to other parts of my body. I was given appointments for a Magnetic Resonance Imaging (MRI) scan, a Bone scan, Position Emission tomography (PET) scan, Computerised Tomography (CT) Scan. The medical team collated all the results, and a team of doctors agreed a future plan for my treatment.

Once again, as in 2012, I was given the bad news and the good news. The bad news, it was confirmed, I had Prostate Cancer. The good news, it was discovered early. It had not spread to any other part of my body, and it could be cured within three years. There was no need for any operation, to remove the prostate or testicles. This was a relief. I was told not to worry about the prostate. They said that because it was found early, it could be treated and managed and I could live to be a hundred. They said that I might die of something else, but not prostate cancer! The treatment would involve drugs to reduce the PSA to below one, to shrink the prostate itself, and stop cancer growth in its tracks, using twenty shots of radiotherapy to kill off the cancer cells. They started me on hormone implant Zoladex 10.8mg every three months. Zoladex implant is an LHRH Agonist; (Luteinizing Hormone-releasing hormone agonists). This is an alternative to removing the testicles, since they block the message from the brain, telling the testicles to produce testosterone. The idea is that when testosterone is taken out of the equation, the prostate cancer cells will shrink and bring the PSA down. Radiation therapy can then, if you prefer, be used to kill off the shrunk cancer cells, thereby achieving a cure of the cancer. Before the LHRH Agonist implant, I was given 3 weeks of anti-androgen tablets (Bicalutamide) to cushion the effects. This drug is said to be capable of reducing libido and production of testosterone and may cause erectile dysfunction. I took Zoladex for the first three months of treatment. They are also supposed to have several side effects such as hot flushes, fatigue, weight gain, strength and muscles loss, breast tenderness, hair loss, but luckily, I did not notice any of these side effects. But having libido and erectile functionality were important to me.

When I bitterly complained that because I have young wives, I needed to be able to maintain my libido and good erection function, Dr Sindu quickly adjusted my prescription. She took off the Zoladex 3.6 mg implants and changed it to Bicalutamide 50mg tablets, once per day.

Bicalutamide is an Anti-Androgen, which is less likely to cause sexual problems. They are not effective if one has advanced or metastasis of the cancer, or if the patient has any type of liver problems.

The medical team held that there was no need for surgery to remove my prostate. Normal Radiotherapy to kill the cancer cells would suffice. The radiation treatment was due to start in April 2020, but the ghastly Corona Virus (Covid 19) pandemic started ravaging the entire world. My waterworks still works like clockwork! My mojo can still 'get up and go!' My team of doctors agreed that it was best to postpone the treatment, rather going to hospital, and taking the risk of being infected with the Corona Virus.

This evil Corona is an enigma, it has killed thousands of people, all over the world, especially China, Italy, Spain, USA, Britain.

This was reviewed on 1/7/20 at Guys hospital, London Bridge, doctors advised not to wait any further. The cancer had shrunk, and PSA result was now 0.1, which was low. Going forward, I attended Guys Hospital on 10th September, for a second opinion. They again confirmed it was right and safe to proceed with treatment. I was given the option to be treated at Guys hospital which has eight Machines, or Sidcup Guys cancer Centre which has two machines. Each machine treats an average of twenty cancer patients per day. I chose to attend the Sidcup Kent centre, as it is located just fifteen minutes from my home, in Bexleyheath, Kent. I wouldn't have to take public transport, and I drove to and from the hospital in the luxury and comfort of my Range Rover Sports Jeep. I met again with Dr Sindu, and she reconfirmed I could proceed, after I consented to enumerate short- and long-term possible side effects.

I read up on some cancer terminologies. Curing the cancer is the aim of Radiotherapy. Some people may need surgery and radiotherapy to kill any remaining cancer cells. Adjuvant Radiotherapy is given after surgery. Neo-adjuvant radiotherapy is given to reduce the size of the cancer before surgery. In some case radiotherapy and chemotherapy are used in combination. The word 'Remission' is used to describe the five-year period after treatment, because the doctors believe the patient is cured of cancer but are not certain it won't come back, so they say one is 'in remission', rather than cured.

On 7/10/20 I attended Queen Mary Hospital, Sidcup, and the Guys Cancer Centre, for CT scan in preparation for Radiotherapy. The scan captures the position of the prostrate in relation to bladder, testicles and the intestines and pelvis. Measurements and permanent marks like tattoos on my body, were made, to indicate how and where the high rays or beam would concentrate on killing the cancer cells. Before treatment, on daily basis, the patient's rectum must be clear, with neither gas, nor faeces, in the rectum. The bladder must be full, or near full capacity. My bladder capacity was measured to be three hundred cl, so at least 30 minutes before my treatment, I drank water to attain 200 to 300 level. If there is no bowel movement on the day, then one must use a suppository, to purge and clear. The treatment would start on 28/10/20 for 20 days, sessions of about 20 minutes each. The treatment ended on 24th November 2020.

A gentleman from Nigeria told me to avoid western treatment, because they miss-manage simple ailments and make your situation worse. He said that the cost of these sorts of treatments are prohibitive in Nigeria. He said the poor and average Nigerians cannot afford it, so they die eventually of the prostate cancer or disease. He advised me to cure it with daily eating loads of tomatoes and sour-sop fruits. He said I should just avoid sugar, carbohydrates, and starchy foods. He said that all types of cancer relish, feed, grow and multiply if you supply them with sugar. Thus, the remedy is to stifle and starve it with no supply of sugar. I thought there were some truths in what he said, but I would prefer to get some treatment now, with some predictable degree of a good result.

I signed, confirming the Doctor had explained to me the name of the procedure, as Prostate Radiotherapy (external Beam) aimed to cure the disease. The benefits which outweigh the risks. Possible, significant, unavoidable, or frequently occurring risks were enumerated to me. Possible early side effects are tiredness/fatigue, painful urination, urinary frequency, Diarrhoea, sore rectum. Possible late side effects include impotence, minor bowel changes, prolonged mucus discharge, prolonged diarrhoea, rectal bleeding. Uncommon late side effects include inflammation of the rectum or rectal ulcer, narrowing of the urethra, and damage to bones. You must sign that you give authority for your picture to be taken, and your personal data could be used for service development, audit, and teaching, but collected data will have all personal information and identification removed. The Image-guided radiotherapy treatment (IGRT) which allows accurate targeting of radiotherapy to cancer was said to have gone well, without hitches. Though, to be honest, after two weeks you feel as though your ass is on fire. Holding water was 'touch and go' as it was contrary to frequent urination. If the balance is not right, the Radiologist normally refuses to proceed, because the high beam can damage unintended organs or tissues. The Diarrhoea was upsetting, and frequent urination was a pain.

Every patient who comes to the centre with a vehicle was given a code to free parking at the centre. When you arrive fifteen minutes before your appointment, receptionists first make you sanitise your hands. Then you remove your face mask and are given a new mask to wear. Your temperature is measured, if you have an elevated temperature, it could be a sign of covid-19. If ok, you are checked-in and told when to come for your next treatment, and you are given a hospital gown. You are then allowed to go to the Radiotherapy area.

On arrival, two, three or more patients with masks, social distancing and waiting to be treated. I always made conversation with the other patients. We compared notes and cracked jokes, as we waited. When it's your turn, you are taken to a side room, to measure the water level of your bladder. If the bladder is not at least 60% or satisfactorily full, you are given one or two cups of water to drink and wait further to be measured again. Invariably, one could be told to go to the loo and urinate, to remove surplus water. The radiotherapy machine itself works to precision, it will stop if too much, or too little, gas, faeces, or water is detected. When they are happy with your bladder water level, then you are told which changing room to go into and change into a hospital gown which doesn't cover your backside.

Before you get on the table, you are asked to confirm your name, date of birth and home address. These must match your picture and data which is visually display on the screen in the room. Once done, you lie on the table, half naked, save for a light covering of your private parts. The diligent radiologists confirm your details. You are then elevated, as you lay on your back, hands akimbo on your chest.

The radiologists leave the room and watch from their cubicle. The machines kick off with a buzzing, the wheels start to turn, and first a scan is done to confirm your original recorded data and positions. Then, about a five-minute wait, and if everything is in order the actual machine goes around the patient twice, and in ten minutes the radiologist comes out, calls your name, and announces that you have been treated. They lower the bed and help you up. You take your mat from the table, grab your little bag of clothes and shoes, and shuffle off outside, to one of the changing rooms, put on your clothes and go home.

On the last day of my treatment, I attended in my blue threepiece suit. I was in perfect mood: bladder seventy five percent full, gas in my intestine, normal, there was no crap in my rear end, I was in and out. I was given a sort of certificate of completion of treatment. The Radiotherapy treatment summary stated that site of treatment was prostate and base of seminal vesicles. Treatment was from 28/10/20 to 24/11/20. The daily dose was 3Gray, number of treatments was 20 and total dose was 60 Gray. There was a list of side effects which I may experience, such as tiredness.

Two weeks after the treatment, I had a Review with my Consultant Oncologist, Miss Sindu.

I am still alive. Thanks to God. And to the British National Health Service (NHS), all the superb treatment and medications are free. Collectively and indirectly, we pay for what we get, via the taxes we pay. To get this sort of treatment in the developing nations, would cost a lot. Again, this second brush with cancer was my second time lucky, in the sense that both were caught early, before it could spread to other areas of my body. Touch wood! Many people, live longer, due to the good medical treatment they receive.

I remain grateful to the doctors and nurses at the Chartwell Oncology Department, of Princess Royal University (PRUH) Hospital where my lung cancer was diagnosed and managed since 2012. They see me every six months, to monitor my condition, and to be sure that lung cancer is kept at bay, or that I am still in remission. I have been in remission for twelve years now, X-ray imaging of my lungs are taken and compared and studied at every appointment, to see if there are any changes. When I attended a check-up in January 2020, my Oncology doctor, Dr Elizabeth Hadley, of Thoracic medicine, told me that we are no changes, and everything still looked fine. I was elated, and when I told her that a month ago, I was diagnosed with prostate cancer, she was shocked, and immediately developed a new investigative strategy for me.

Within a couple of weeks, in March 2020, while Corona Virus was still rampant, I was asked to attend PRUH in Orpington for a Blood Test. Within a couple of weeks, I was asked to attend PRUH for Magnetic Resonance Imaging (MRI) scans. Later, on April 1st, I received another telephone call, to attend this time for a Pet-Ct scan. The procedure is usually expensive to NHS, but greatly beneficial to the recipient, because it provides full internal pictures of the entire body, organs, and glands in the body. I was offered the choice of having this at St Thomas Hospital, London where the Prime Minister, Boris Johnson was in an intensive care Unit, following his Covid 19 attack, or to attend Queen Mary's Hospital (QMH), Sidcup Kent. I choose the QMH it's only few miles from my home. I attended all my appointments wearing gloves and face masks, to avoid or minimise any chance of being infected with Covid 19, by the NHS frontline staff or other patients. On 15th April 2020 the Pet Scan was carried out in a Mobile Trailer, parked at the OMH ground. The procedure was carried out by Alliance Medical, a National PET-CT contractor to the NHS. The PET/ CT scan was a new NM whole body FDG, which combines PET and CT imaging together.

Usually, PET (Positron Emission Tomography) uses ridiculously insignificant amounts of radioactive tracer – injected into body at a vein in the arm, an hour before the scan starts. The radioactive tracer can then be seen on the scan, and it shows how parts of the body. CT (computerised Tomography) used X-rays to produce images of the different density or thickness of organs in the body. By combining these two images, you get a detailed and accurate internal picture, which a referring specialist can use to help diagnose and if necessary, decide on the effective treatment. I was given a list of side effects, then a Patient Satisfaction Survey, which they use to improve their services to patients. I did not hesitate in scoring the process as satisfactory. I could not have been more elated, when I received a phone call, followed by a letter, in May 2020, confirming the result of my tests, including EBUS Bronchoscopy. They were all incredibly good, and I have nothing to worry about.

Life's a lottery, it's nobody's power but Almighty God's, if you are inclined to such a belief system.

## CORONA VIRUS (COVID 19)

This mysterious disease is said to have started in Wuhan City, China, around November 2019. It was alleged at the time that the virus had come from bats and snakes, which the Chinese sold at the wet market in Wuhan. China purportedly concealed the outbreak from the rest of the world, until after the country had signed a trade deal with USA on 15th December 2019. It appeared because of the alleged concealment, human traffic in and out of Wuhan continued unabated. Prior to this, the Chinese had been aggressively buying homes and businesses in Europe, USA, Canada, and Australia. The 1.4 billion Chinese have also been taking advantage of Western liberal immigration law, and many Chinese have been attaining residence and citizenship in Europe and the Americas.

By the time we were shown pictures of the deserted streets of Wuhan, many carriers of the virus had travelled to Italy and Europe. It was claimed that over three thousand people had died before the virus halted in Wuhan. The rumour was that the virus came because of the Chinese people's (colloquially called Chin chin Chon in USA) habit of eating bats, rats, snakes and the likes, and anything that crawls or moves. I wondered why eating bats and snakes would suddenly cause the rise of a deadly virus. The Chinese have been eating these animals for over two hundred years, so why now? Personally, I grew up in Africa and we hunted, caught, and ate these animals also, and continue to eat ants, birds, and reptiles such as bats, owls, and snakes, without such a virus. The virus became an Epidemic, it has spread to every country in the world. Thus, it is now a pandemic. I cannot get my head around the history and origin of this disease. Why did the virus attack Wuhan, and not spread to other Chinese cities such as Beijing and Shanghai or even to neighbouring cities such as Tokyo and Hong Kong? How and why did the virus go straight to Italy, Spain, France, United Kingdom, and New York? By the first week in April 2020, on
Easter Sunday, 12th April 2020, the virus had killed nearly two million people worldwide. Notably, there were more dead people in Europe and America, than the virus had killed in China. At the time of writing, it has taken the lives of 22,000 Americans (Yankees), 19,000 Italians, 17,000 Spanish, 14,000 French, 10,500 Brits, 4,500 Iranians, 3,000 Germans, 2,700 Dutch/ Netherland,

one thousand Brazilians, one hundred Swiss, 1000 Swedish, seven hundred Canadians, 500 Portuguese all the way to 25 in South Africa and 6 in Nigeria.

In desperation, many countries are fumigating their streets. The purpose of fumigation is not clear to me. I guess the authorities must have their own reasons. Some schools of thought is that malaria medication called Chloroquine and hydroxychloroquine are an effective treatment for corona virus. However, the evidence of the efficacy of these medicines is yet inconclusive, and the virus was still ravaging humanity with no end in sight, I was scared stiff!

There is so much, that I and many others, do not understand about the pandemic. I have noticed that WhatsApp messenger, a free media, carries both indistinguishably genuine and fake news. I have thought about the proposition that USA invented the virus. China and USA blame each other for masterminding this bio-chemical weapon attack, to gain economic supremacy, but no one has any tangible evidence for, or against, any of the propositions. Some say that 5G Technologies telephone providers introduced the virus. Whilst others say the Virus was introduced to wipe out Africans. We are told to wear the face mask to prevent contracting and spreading the virus. Some say the face mask is useless. People who return from overseas are quarantined for 14 days, in most countries. We are told to selfdistance, quarantine and self-isolate.

The UK Government on 23 March 2020, introduced a Lockdown, instructing us to stay at home, and if we must go out, it must be for physical exercise or to obtain medicine, food or engage in essential works, which cannot be done from home. We must maintain social safe distances of about two meters (6 feet) from one another. Over 99% of UK local shops, pubs, cafes, betting shops, car washers, restaurants, churches, dry cleaners, leisure centres (GYM) were shut down to the public. Supermarkets were scantly open. Popular fast-food establishments were shut, including coffee shops, pubs and restaurants, these were all closed to the public, some offered takeaway-away and delivery services only. Many workers in the UK were on furlough. There were long queues of people trying to go into shops. People must wear face masks, maintain safe social distances and only a limited number of people were permitted to enter a shop, or any public place, at any given time. Additionally, there was rationing, in that people were allowed to purchase a limited number of essential household items, regardless of how many items your household needed. I do not know why pasta, toilet rolls, and paracetamol were hard to obtain. Some petrol /gas stations were open, and prices were comparatively low. But cars were parked, because there was nowhere to go, and even those who owned private jets were grounded, like everyone else. Visits to friend, neighbours and family was prohibited. Cities, town centres, villages, public transport, all were deserted. There were no cars or people in the streets. Families were not allowed to visit each other. Children were no longer allowed to visit their grandparents. Boots and many other pharmacy/drug stores were open because they dispensed essential medical items including face masks, thermometers, paracetamols, and sanitizers. Local Rubbish tips were closed and were not accepting rubbish. Many frontline workers, medical doctors, nurses, and bus drivers died from Covid-19. Government maintained lockdown and associated rules, cessation of movement, physical and social distancing, and a ban on any sort of gathering. Effective and efficient measures, to reduce both contracting and spreading the virus. Germany had a low mortality rate, because of its robust testing. The UK should have been testing more people to establish who tested positive and quarantined, or hospitalised, to obviate passing it to other people.

We must wash our hands every ten minutes if we have been out of our home. This ghastly and invisible virus, a universal enemy is purportedly not air borne, but drops to the ground, or on other objects, and thereafter dies within few hours. However, where the virus droplets reach a person, such person may become a likely carrier, only if the virus gets into the persons throat and lungs. We are told that if the virus enters a person, it will first remain in his or her throat for about four days. The virus might only be deadly if it reaches the lungs. If the lungs are attacked, a ventilator may help. We are told to drink lots of hot, alkaline water, beverages, and to eat lime, lemon, ginger, and garlic. We are told to aim to wash the virus down from our throats to the intestine, where the virus is neutralised, killed instantly, before it can reach the lungs. The wearing of face masks helps to prevent both getting the virus and spreading it.

It was advised that the elderly, those over 60yrs of age, and people with pre-existing medical conditions, such as diabetes, asthma, heart, lungs, liver, or kidney problems are at the highest risk exposure. The virus has killed more people in this group. I was shaking like a leaf. My family, my friends and I are living one day at a time. I am now more appreciative of so many pleasant things in life, that we took for granted. Some Africans friends have called me and recommended that I eat lots of pepper soup, tomatoes, and bitter leaf, and to boil hot water with herbs, mentholated ointment, Robb, or Vicks Vapour Rub, Aboniki and put my face over steaming hot water, with a towel over the head. The steam goes through the throat and nostril and gets rid of any virus thereabout. We are told that the virus cannot withstand heat. I have heard that the few cases in Africa are brought there by people returning or visiting from China, Europe, or USA. It has been asserted Covid 19 cannot survive in African Heat. Also, that it is inimical to feverish temperature. Many developing nations citizens call this pandemic, a great leveller, because their leaders and minister cannot fly out of their countries to get better medical treatment overseas.

I have heard the Nigeria Government has introduced a lockdown; no one is allowed to go out of their house or travel outside where they live. No sellers, no markets, no buyers, no church, no mosque, no travelling even to the nearest town, no gathering of any sort. Police and Army are policing the streets.
The masses are cooped-up and lamenting because there is no steady light, no running water, and no money. It is now feared many will die, not of covid-19 but of starvation, hunger and frustration.

My wife, Lynn had a cough and temperature for few days, and then our son had it for a few days. I have had some temperature also for about two days. Luckily, I have packets of paracetamol 500 mg tablets in my medicine cabinet and that was all we took to recover. We were soon well and healthy. We were worried when we had not been tested or vaccinated, and we did not know if we have had bouts of Corona Virus or not. In July 2020, we were tested at a location near the O2, Millennium Dome in Greenwich, and we were notified the next day that we all tested negative. Maybe the fever we had enabled us to build immunity. We may now have an inbuilt antidote or antigen against the virus, but we do not know. There are no reliable scientific advisers, pundits, prophets, religious leaders, national presidents, and prime minister regarding the pandemic. No one knows anything, period. St Peter's Basilica Square, in Rome, Notre Dame Cathedral in Paris are shut down, even for Easter 2020 festivities, marking the resurrection of Jesus Christ from the dead after three days. Mosques and Muslim holy places in Makah and Medina were equally shut down. Prophets and healers of all religions are waiting for this pandemic to be over before they resume their healing work!

Countries and economies are paralysed and at standstill. No commodity is selling or in demand. There are travel bans everywhere, and virtually all airlines are grounded. Governments are guaranteeing salaries, bailing out companies, yet the end is not in sight, nor predictable. Toilet rolls have become scarce and an essential commodity. Everything has been turned upside down.

President Trump wanted to build a wall to stop Mexicans coming to USA, but America now has the highest death toll from Covid 19, and Mexico has banned any Yankee from coming to their country. Corona Virus has proven to be no respecter of persons, as it kills indiscriminately, old and young, rich and poor. It knows no bounds, border, or nationalities. It treats all persons with equality. It is teaching humanity that life is vanity upon vanity, that we inextricably interlinked, and interdependent. No matter who you are, how high or low on the social ladder, or your wealth or esteem, with the present global lockdown, all you need is basic food and toilet rolls for survival. Everyone was humbled, as the unseen enemy has forced everyone to stay in their homes and strengthen the family unit. Unfortunately, domestic violence has risen, partly due to frustration. On the other hand, some are finding out that it is so peaceful staying idly at home, and to hell with rat race, because nothing else seems to really matter.

Some people say the world has experienced similar pandemics such as the Spanish Influenza, HIV, the plague, Ebola, and Lassa fever, and this is a phase that will soon go away, and humanity will forget it and continue, as if nothing had happened. We will never walk alone. Some religious fanatics have proclaimed this is the real 'end of times' of the world as we know it. Is this world ending? I very much doubt it. I decided that since prevention is better than cure, the best protection from "Covid 19" is your Front Door. Stay inside in your home or bedroom. If you unavoidably venture outside your house, then maintain clear and appreciable social distancing from other people around you. Every Thursday evening at 8pm we step out in the front of our homes and clap and make noise in support of our front-line NHS workers, who are putting their lives in the harm's way to serve and save others. Though many doctors, nurses and bus drivers have died, yet these essential professionals are still going to work. Hospitals are open, GP surgeries are closed, few buses and trains are still running. Most hospital cafeterias are closed. Some people are considering class actions for several trillion dollars against China for starting the corona virus. Sadly I lost a young 47 year old cousin, Emeka Okoroha who worked at the Hospital.

**CHAPTER TWENTY-ONE**

# Government Palliative Schemes to Assist UK Residents

Due to the lockdown, and requirements for every person to stay at home, the UK government has promised billions and billions of pound sterling of various schemes and initiatives, to assist individuals and businesses. We benefited from a few of these schemes, and we locked up our offices, since 23rd March 2020 and stayed at home. Our offices only opened for essential and priority services. There is only occasional going out of the house, for physical exercise, or to grab some grocery and food. Luckily, my semi-detached house in Kent has a big back and front garden, which allows a good space for exercising and social distancing.

We obtained three Government assistance schemes: 1) Coronavirus Job Retention Scheme for "furloughed workers" This scheme continued to pay me and my wife up to 80% of our normal monthly salaries up to £2,500 per month. Both of us are Directors of my Law firm: Graceland Solicitors Limited. I used to be a sole trader and I incorporated in 2016 and put myself and my wife as employees. The disadvantage of doing so is that we make various payments as taxes to the government HMRC. 2) We could not benefit from the free ten-thousand-pound (£10,000) Corona Virus Business Interruption grant to small businesses. This is a non-refundable £10, 000 payment to all businesses in UK who paid council tax in the last three years and have partial relief on the annual business rate bill. We were disqualified for having two offices. (3) We were also able to obtain a hundred thousand pounds (£100,000.00) Coronavirus Business Interruption Loan Scheme (CBILS) from Barclays Bank PLC. 4) We were also able to obtain the Twenty thousand (£20,000) Business Bounce back Loan scheme. These loans will eventually be repaid unless you do not recover from the pandemic.

The good thing about the loans is that they are guaranteed by the Government, and the Government pays the interest rate on the loan for a year in advance. Our mortgages, business leasehold quarter rents and council tax bills are suspended for three months respectively, as payment holidays. We are housebound, waiting to see how long this lockdown goes on, and how and when the war on coronavirus will be won. I consider it lucky that we have a four-bedroom, house with a thirty-foot living room and a loft conversion. Our rear garden is sixty feet by twenty feet and impeccably well kept. We have garden and deck chairs and trampoline jumble jumping for our twelve-year-old son, Amara. My mother-in-law, Mrs Xiulan Liu came from China to visit us in the UK in January 2020, and is now stuck with us, because of the coronavirus lockdown. My wife's mother was born in 1938, thus she is 82, and therefore older than me by six years. My grandmother Igbedie, when she was alive said that life may continue to roll her up and down, so long as it did not kill her. In times like this, she would say happiness, serenity and contentment would easily see anybody through seven years of incarceration. Her wise words in the current situation are useful and beneficial. I keep saying in my serenity prayer:

*God grant me the Serenity to accept the things I cannot change; Courage to change the things I can; and Wisdom to know the difference.*

## AKARAKA

One of my sisters in law went through my photo albums and commented 'Chief Akaraka you have really enjoyed this life'. A successful man is one who falls and gets up again.

You may say so, but it was not easy doing the things I had to do. And I always say that I tried my best, but God did the rest. In life, one must learn to believe in oneself. Believe that it is not over, until it is over. Do not sell yourself short. Do not quit before the last whistle is blown. Dr Norman Vincent Peals states in 'The Power of Positive Thinking' that having problems is part of life. Everyone has problems, the difference is how we choose to handle our problems. Successful people choose to live above their problems, others let their problems overwhelm them, and indeed sink them. Being an Akaraka does not mean that, every morning God drops manna from heaven to Mr Akaraka. No, it simply signifies that on the average, Mr Akaraka made the right choices and decisions. These decisions in life include schools or parties you attend, wife or wives you married, the type of books you read, films you watch, type of clothes, shoes, cars you bought, food you eat, friends you make, business or employment, with which you are involved. It is the totality of life choices and decision. It does not mean that Akaraka is always right, but even when he takes a wrong turn, he is able to make the most of any and everywhere he finds himself. I agree some education and average intelligence is helpful, in making such life decisions.

When I look back at my life, I see I had a few misfortunes, and I had made some mistakes of my own volition, but overall, either by sheer luck or design, I always managed to take each disadvantage and turn it into opportunity for growth and advancement. Like the proverbial cat with nine lives, I always landed on my feet and came up smelling of roses. I am so blessed that, though I know a few rich, wealthy and or powerful individuals, as well as many poor and struggling people, I envy no person. I try my utmost to be neither vain, nor bitter. I do not despise, look down or begrudge anyone. I simply, live and let live. I do not have many talents, skills, friends, or enemies, except being me, an optimistic, cheerful, contented extrovert, led by intuition and some luck. My life is a paradox, because some authors agree that having lots of skills, talents and valuable relationships are proportional to one's success. From my childhood, I realised that no one is an island. We need someone to give us hand. I just have sufficient of each class of people for my needs. When I am alone, without distractions, I do produce brilliant thoughts, work, and strategies.

There is no one best way or blueprint to a successful life, but each person is encouraged to find what helps, rather than hinders, their life. If, for example, being proud and stubborn is not improving your lot in life, then change your posture. Life is not static, life is dynamic! As Richard Shell stated in his book, learn and change as you go on your life journey, remain open to the insights you gain. Being successful does not mean that you become the wealthiest man or woman on earth, it is relative, and for me it means in most parts meeting my promises in life, to my past and present family and friends, being happy and contented. Being over seventy years of age is part of success. Being relatively healthy is part of success. And even the ability to calmly accept that you will one day depart this earth, and plan in a small way, for what happens to the family you leave behind. Ability to feel that yes, you have done most of what you, as a child, wished to do in life, and the ability to feel you have left a legacy, which you intend to bequeath to your heirs, it is all part of success in life. I have this feeling, once God has chosen you and blessed you, He has blessed you. Thus, come rain or shine, your blessings and destiny (Akaraka) are set, just as the sun; moon and stars are set by the God, the Almighty. No one, friend or foe, can wipe away your God-given destiny. It appears to me, even one's mistakes are part of the bigger plan, since God works in mysterious ways. In the end, as someone once stated, 'do not blame others in this life, because the good people you meet will give you happiness, the bad people will give you experiences, worst people will give your life lessons, and the best people will give you eternal memories.'

**CHAPTER TWENTY-TWO**

# Use of WhatsApp During The Corona Virus Pandemic

About Corona Virus, a Ventilator ward nurse wrote: Why people who are sixty plus must stay at home, and not take any risks at all; For those people who do not understand what it means to be on a ventilator, but want to take the chance of going back to work and walk into crowded places, such as a mall, or on public transport, such as trains, or buses. For a start: a Ventilator is not an Oxygen mask put over the mouth, while the patient is comfortably lying down and reading a magazine.

Ventilation for Covid-19 is a painful intubation that goes down your throat and stays there until you live, or you die. It is done under anaesthesia for 2 to 3 weeks without moving, often upside down, with a tube inserted from the mouth up to the trachea and allows you to breathe to the rhythm of the lung machine. The patient cannot talk or eat or do anything naturally the machine keeps you alive. The discomfort and pain they feel from this, means medical experts must administer sedatives and painkillers to ensure tube tolerance, for as long as the machine is needed. It is like being in an artificial coma. After twenty days of this treatment, a young patient loses forty percent muscle mass, and gets mouth or vocal cord trauma, as well as possible pulmonary or heart complications.

It is for this reason, old or weak people cannot withstand the treatment, and they may likely die. Many of us are in this boat so stay safe, unless you want to take the chance of ending up there. This is not flu. A tube is put into the stomach, through your nose, for liquid food. A sticky bag around your butt collects diarrhoea, a foley collects urine, an IV for fluids and medicines, an A-line to monitor your BP, that is completely dependent upon finely calculated medicine doses. Teams of nurses, CRNA's and MAs reposition your limbs every two hours, and you lie on a mat, circulating ice cold fluid, to help reduce your temperature, of one hundred and four.

In the light of the above, I thought all my fellow senior citizen friends, should not go out during lockdown, until a cure, or vaccine, was found.

As the saying goes, every situation has another side. Every advantage has a disadvantage and vice versa. I have learned a lot from posts floating about, regarding covid-19, on WhatsApp. Some of the things I read were inspiring, and/or so funny, I have decided to share some of them here. Most of these are wise, confirming my own naturally held understanding or philosophies of life. New ones are internalised. The posts did not indicate the names of the original writers. I have therefore copied them as written, or modified them, as I see fit to convey my intended messages.

1. Bob Marley said that some people are so poor, all they have is money.

2. The sad paradox of a duck with seven chicks. One fell into a hole, whilst the mother duck and six ducklings walked past the hole successfully. The duck goes back to look for her lost chick, and the six chicks vanished into the same hole. The punch line said, 'If you focus on what you have lost, you might lose everything!'

3. We are born without bringing anything. We die without taking anything. Absolutely nothing. And the sad thing is, that in between life and death, we fight for what we did not bring and what we will not take.

4. OVER 60s: A post stated as follows, those who are sixty years old and over; should start using their savings and enjoy their money. Do not keep it for those who may not have a clue about what you sacrificed, to make your money. There is nothing worse than leaving your savings to those who have a big plan for what you have or grandchildren; in due course they will make their own money. Do not be shy to spend your money on yourself. You deserve it. Having supported the children for many years, you have taught them a lot and you gave them shelter. Now it is their turn to start earning money.

Lead a healthy lifestyle, make sure you exercise physically, but do not overload yourself. It is easy to get sick; it is much harder to stay healthy. Stay in shape, visit doctors, and learn how to stay healthy. Do not worry about nonsense. You have lived so long in your life; you can remember all that is good or bad.

Do not let the burden of the past stand in your way today and in the future. Feel the beauty of the present. Regardless of your age, feel young and love life. Be proud of yourself - both internally and externally. Look good, feel good, this increases self-esteem and strength. Always keep up to date with latest developments. Read and watch news programs. Stay in touch with old friends, it is important at your age.

Life is too short to spend time communicating with those who depress you. Spend life in the company of positive cheerful people, and life will be more enjoyable. Do not be tempted to live with children or grandchildren, it is good to be surround by loving relatives, but each of us has the right to our own personal space. Do not give up on your interests, adopt new habits. For whatever reason, remember that you are just so lucky. You have managed to live a long time. Many simply do not reach this age. And so it happened, so have fun! Try to see the fun, and the funny side of each situation.

Do not pay attention to what is being said about you, even less about what people might think about you. It will always be this way, and you are proud of yourself and your life. Let them tell you, this should not bother you. They do not know what you went through; they do not know what you know. This is your time to enjoy peace and happiness.
Remember life is too short to worry or drink bad wine!!

Do not stop looking your best, from top to toe. Visit your doctor, dentist, hairdresser, or barber, always dress your best, as life is a giant camera. Wear your best perfume and eau de toilette (Mine is Kouros by Yves Saint Laurent). Be content and happy on the inside and outside, then uphold your self-esteem and strength inside.

Always be up to date with latest developments. Read, watch news programs, but laugh a lot. It is good medicine.
Always see the bright or funny side of life and the fun side of every situation. For whatever reason, remember at fifty plus, you are already incredibly lucky indeed. You have managed to get this far, and you take it for granted, forgetting that many simply do not reach this age. So have fun. Be happy.

Do not pay attention to what is being gossiped or said about you. You are miles ahead and better than many of them. Many of them envy you and would like to pull you down. It will always be this way, remain happy and proud of your life. Hold your head up high. Do not get in the gutter with any fool. They do not know what you know, and they do not know what you went through, to get to where you are.

**CHARACTER:** The 3rd US President, Thomas Jefferson said: A man's character is his fate. Nothing can stop the man with the right mental attitude from achieving his goal. Nothing on earth can help the man with the wrong mental attitude to achieve his goal. As a clergyman, I have watched pitiably how people self-sabotage themselves, by seeking a spiritual solution to character-deficit issues. They look at everybody, as suspects for their own failure, or predicament, when their greatest demon lurks within them- their character.

5. Is Prayer Everything? Prayer helps because, prayer is a fervent wish. Success is ninety nine percent inspiration and one percent perspiration. What common sense cannot achieve; no amount of prayer can achieve it. What we often call our destiny (Akaraka) is truly our character, and since character can change, then destiny can also be altered. Your Character is your Destiny. Many people believe we can pray, fast, do penance in order to get rich, healed, get employment, visas or qualifications etc. There is no amount of prayer or spiritual penance that can substitute for character. A Dutch Priest said: Prayer is not a check request asking from God; it is a deposit slip – a way of depositing God's character into our bankrupt souls. You can speak in public and maintain a holy appearance, but it is your behaviour and character that will trigger the manifestation of all that God has for you.

6. A British writer Thomas Macaulay said, of the measure of man's character. 'What destroys a successful man is not enemies waiting for him, but his character even

after he has succeeded. A man's character can be defined by how he treats those that cannot help, harm, or hurt him'. Learn to respect yourself and treat people with courtesy. Your character can cause you to miss a lucrative opportunity and a critical miracle. Do not look down on anyone, because God can use anyone to change your story. Many people pray, and fast and try binding demons that do not exist, when our real demons are just our greatly flawed character.

7. The Great Wall of China was constructed by Emperor Qin Shi Huang (259-210 BC), aimed to prevent incursion from Mongolians and Barbarians nomad into Chinese empire. UNESCO designated it as world heritage, and the Chinese greatest military defence project. It is the only man-made project that can be seen from space. They had believed that no enemy could climb, or scale over the high walls. In spite the wall, China was successfully invaded three times. Each time, the enemy did not have to climb over the high walls; the enemy bribed the guards and came in.

8. While Chinese Emperor built the high walls, he forgot to build the character of the citizens and the guards. How many people and homes have been invaded, looted, and devastated by the enemy through the bribery of ego, self-indulgences, insincerity, and unfaithfulness within? William Shakespeare captured it succinctly when he said: 'the fault is not in our stars, but in ourselves'. Peter Schultz Porsche said: 'we hire Character; and we train Skills'. When Germany was divided by a huge wall into poor communist East and rich capitalist West, one day East Berliners dumped a truck load of rubbish and garbage in the West Berlin side. The people of West Berlin took a truck load of canned foods, bread, milk, and other provisions, and neatly stacked them on the East Berlin side with a note 'Each Gives what he has So what do you have inside you? Hate or love? Violence or peace? Capacity to build, or capacity to destroy? Team spirit, or divineness? Former US President Barack Obama said – when I think about the depth of the grave and the kilos of sands that are going to be thrown at us, there is no need

to harm my brother. When I think of the darkness that pervades the tomb after it has closed, there is no need to hurt my sister. When I think of the heat driven back by the ground, and the amount of water that will drown me during the rains in this grave, I cannot make my neighbour suffer! When I think I will be alone, abandoned by all, I prefer to enjoy communion while I am alive. When my relationships are cut off by my past, I want to perfect my future. If I could be reborn and start all over again, I would no longer make mistakes in my actions. After long meditations, I understood that all is vanity on earth. May I cultivate humility and love of my neighbour, because vanity gives vanity, everything will be vanity. Be happy and make someone happy. End of all.

9. Grapes must be crushed to make wine. Diamonds and gold form under pressure. Olives are pressed to release oil. Seeds grow in the darkness of the soil. Whenever you feel crushed, under pressure, pressed, or in darkness, you are in a powerful place of transformation and transmutation.

Trust the process. When in the Bible, he said 'I am Joseph.' His brothers, who had sold him, were shocked. May God the Almighty, repackage you and reintroduce you to those who wrote you off. So long as you are alive, you are an unfinished work, God is not done with you, even when others think you are through.

10. Peace of mind is a beautiful gift, which only we can give to our self, just by expecting nothing from anyone.

11. Order In Court: A man and his wife were in court for being drunk and disorderly. When the Usher announced "Order, Order" the man shouted, "half cup of whisky". The honourable Judge sent both down.

12. False Prophets: There was a priest who prophesied that a big tree in a town centre should be cut down. According to him, the tree was responsible for all the woes and drawbacks facing the people of the town: car accidents, early deaths,

unemployment, and sickness generally. I personally attribute this to ignorance.

13. Lion: I like the one written under a picture of a Lion. It says fear has two meanings. Either you forget everything and run, or you face everything and rise. A lion does not bother himself with little animals talking about him behind his back.
14. The turtle makes progress only when it's sticks out its neck. Yet another says, do it, if it makes you feel good, so long as no one is harmed. I found it funny when I picked up a book titled 'Everything Men Know about Women;' when I opened the book, it was completely blank. I concluded men know nothing about women.

15. I beamed with pride and joy, as I read this WhatsApp announcement by the President of my Town Union, presently called Abba Autonomous Communities Development Union (AACDU): In commemoration of his upcoming seventy sixth birthday Celebrations, and as a way of showing gratitude to the God Almighty for his benevolence, and other

numerous mercies and blessings to him and the entire Ezeala (Okoroha/Ozigbu) family. High Chief, Dr, Barr Adolph Okoroha; Akaraka Gburugburu; Bikku Bikku 3rd of Abba, has graciously provided a grandiose Palliative to be given and shared to the entire Umu Abba Ama Ano People through the AACDU. The President General (PGs) of all respective Abba autonomous communities or their Representative, are advised to come to the Abba Central School field on Wednesday 19th August 2020 to collect their shares of the Palliative, for their respective communities. Time was 12.00 noon prompt. The leaders of AACDU- Chief Paul Ozigbu (President), Sir Joe Asole (Secretary) and Barr (Mrs) Nkechi Oguamanam were present They also sent on behalf of Abba, sincere appreciation to Chief Adolph Okoro for his kind provision of Palliatives, at the challenging time of Covid 19 pandemic and lockdowns, to the people of Abba Ama Ano.

16. Lolo Barrister Nkechi Oguamanam wrote: Thanks so much, Chief Dr Barr,

Bikku Bikku 111. These Palliatives came at the most auspicious time, when our people at home were prayerfully expecting mana from heaven. And lo and behold, God sent the mana, using you as his instrument. You will never have expected the kind and interesting part of that day was the announcement made by AACDU President, while letting our people know who sent them these palliatives materials, to the effect the Donor specifically requested that the items were NOT for politics, nor interest in any office, nor in any official nature. Rather they were to be shared to everyone on equal basis, especially the hungry and needy. Dee Akaraka, "igaghi anwuchuru umu Abba." (You will live long for Abba)

17. HRM Ugoeze Benadette Nkechi Uzoka wrote: My darling Bikku Bikku 111, Akaraka Gburugburu Chief Dr Sir Barrister Adolph Okoroha. My youthful darling. Happy birthday in advance. Long life and good health are your portion in Jesus'name. Di oma Nwanyi, what you do for us "na Ala Abba" (Abba town) is beyond comprehension. You

give and give without let. May God bless you and bless the works of your hand in the mighty name of Jesus (IMNJ) We love you.

18. Chief Nze Obinna Akwiwu, Nwachinemere 1, Ukeje 11, Odokaraomee 11, Oshimiri 111, wrote: Bikku Bikku well done. Congrats again on the accession of your upcoming seventy-six birthday.

19. Chief Engineer Paul Ozigbu, Nnayereugo 1, Ekwueme11, the Chairman of Abba Amano Community Development Union (AACDU) wrote: Our elderly political leader, Dee, Your magnanimity is immeasurable. The indigent, the downtrodden and even the rich and noble recognised, acknowledged and appreciated your kindness and generosity to humanity. God will continue to bless you and replenish your purse in great folds. Lots of love.

20. Chief Dr Frank Ojiako the acting President General (PG) of Ogwuaga Abba, wrote: Unbelievable. The consistency with which our big brother, High Chief Barr, Dr Adolph Okoroha, the Bikku Bikku 111 and Akaraka Gburugburu, relates to needs of our people without conceivable returns. It does seem that Chief Akaraka, a highly erudite, articulate and very sociable, humanitarian cannot feel good without extending his goodwill to his people. He has modern Nursery, Primary and Secondary school, The Okoroha Royal Academy situate in Owerri, which aims at inculcating the best education in our greater tomorrow. To date, he bemoans the fact that he could not get enough space to locate that edifice in Abba Clan. On Behalf of Umu Ogwuaga, I Dr Frank Ojiako APG (Acting President General), I thank you Bikku Bikku for always thinking about home. May God Almighty bless you; grant you many more beautiful years in good health and all-encompassing fruitfulness. Happy 76th Birthday Sir.

21. My Junior brother Chief Cletus Chidex Okoro wrote; I appreciate my senior brother, Chief Dr Barr AAC I generosity to Abba Ama Ano and to our great Ezeala family. God will continue to bless him.

22. The family Chairman Chief Raphael Okoroha wrote Dee Umuashi, may the Good Lord continue to grant you good health, long life, and prosperity. Well done, Sir.

23. One of my sons, Pastor Ifeanyi Okoroha wrote: I celebrate you Daddy, Bikku Bikku of Abba. A man of unrelenting faith. A man who proves he cannot be restricted with limited achievement of good successes of meritorious honours because of age. Even at 76, you are still experiencing and expressing the ancestral blessings of Nnanyi St OKOROHA of blessed memory and of insurmountable blessings of justice.

24. My baby brother Chief Omereoha, Engineer Dem Iyke Okoro wrote; The Emperor Himself. Ogaramba kara mba. The Wash of Washington. The Lon of London. The Sa of South Africa. The Dim of Dimagu. The Hou of Houston and the Ogwu of Ogwuaga. Akaraka Gburugburu, Bikku Bikku 111, I join the entire people of Abba and Ogwuaga in thanking you for your giving spirit. May the Lord Almigthy continue to bless you abundantly with good health and sound mind. Remain blessed and keep fit. Amen. Much love from me to you. Omereoha/ Ugodiohamma.

25. Lolo Susan Okoroha (B. Ed) stated: I really thank the Almighty God for the life of my husband, Chief Sir Barrister Dr Adolph Anyiam Okoroha. Akaraka Gburugburu, Bikku Bikku 111, I write to show my appreciation and gratitude for what you did for the entire of Abba and Ezeala (Okoroha/Ozigbu) family. May you live long, my King. You have showed nothing but love for your people and your family. May the Almighty God reward all your efforts and love towards your family. Amen You are indeed my

mentor and teacher as I continue to learn wisdom, knowledge, humility arduous work to achieve goals after goals on my own, without depending on others. You taught me humility diligence and love for family etc. I am indeed humbled to be by your side as your wife. In all I say, a big thank you my dear husband –Lolo Bikku Bikku.

26. My response: "I sincerely thank everyone who appreciated and or voiced appreciations and gratitude toward my humble provision of Palliatives to our noble people of Abba Ama Ana and the entire Ezeala Okoroha/ Ozigbu Dynasty. To God be all the glory for His mercies, grace, and blessings. "E no bi (it's not by) any man's power." I also thank you all sincerely for your greetings and felicitations with respect to my upcoming 76th birthday. May you all stay safe and remain blessed. Okoroha AA.

27. Kindness is a language which the deaf can hear and the blind can see. Luck is when preparation meets opportunity. Be always thankful for whatever you have, you will end up having more. Whilst if

you concentrate on what you do not have, you can never have enough.

28. Salt or Insult: Are you a salt or an insult to the world? Salt has no need to look like other ingredients. It does not send out any aroma like other seasonings, but without it the soup is tasteless. Men of true value do not fight for position or visibility; their results speak for them, not their propaganda. You do not need to shout to be heard. A salt maintains its integrity amidst pollution. No one demands to taste salt before paying for it. Do you have to swear before others can believe you? One funny man said that a silent man is a wise man; a silent woman is an incredibly angry woman.

29. The Pope: I like the one attributed to Pope Francis: Rivers do not drink their own water; trees do not eat their own fruits; the sun does not shine on itself, and flowers do not spread their fragrance for themselves. Living for others is a rule of nature. We are all born to help each other. No matter how difficult it is ... Life is good when you are happy; but

much better when others are happy because of you.

30. Life Examination: Life is the most difficult exam to take. Many fail, because they try to copy others, not realising everyone has a different question paper. Three people exceedingly difficult to advise in life are: A woman in love, A man with money and an African woman following a religious prophet. Before a man can eat a woman's money, he is either a pastor or a native doctor.

31. Nelson Mandela said that our world is not divided by race, colour, gender, or religion. Our world is divided into wise people and fools. And the fools divide themselves by race, colour, gender, or religion.

32. These are sad, but true – I realised no matter what you say and how you say it, some people will never 'get it'. No matter how pure your motives are, somebody will still accuse you of ill intentions. No matter how humble you are, somebody

will still consider you proud or arrogant. No matter how generous you are, somebody will still call you selfish. Sometimes, some of your greatest disappointments will come from those you love most, or to who you gave your best appointments, or commitments. Sometimes, some of the worst things you will hear about yourself may come from those you speak the best of. Sometimes, good people may be poor and/or die young. Sometimes, not everyone in your ship is paddling in the same direction as your dreamed destination. Sometimes, loving people means feeling you ends up making you look a fool. Tough as it seems, any evil done against you can become a seed for your promotion … it depends on your response. No matter what wrongs are done to you, you will be better off when you forgive freely, quickly, and wholly. Pain makes you tougher than pleasure does to you. Many people will celebrate you, only if your advancement does not exceed their expectation of you. Hating those who hate you makes them your leaders, because you are following their footsteps. Success is not where you got to, but where you started. Success is the belief in the best, even when you are going through the worst. How you respond to any situation is more important than the situation itself. A big heart is the ability to overlook offence. Broadmindedness accommodates other people. Kindness makes you the most beautiful person in the world, no matter what you look like. Great men think of legacies, shallow souls think of self.

33. Abraham Lincoln: I am personally inspired by Lincoln's failures. He was born in 1809 into poverty. In 1816, aged seven, his parents were evicted, and they became homeless. He started working at seven to help his parents. In 1818 aged nine, his mother suddenly died. In 1831, his business failed, he then took a job, and he was fired in 1832. He ran for state legislature and lost. He applied to attend law school and was rejected. In 1833 he borrowed money and before the end of the year the business failed, the money he had borrowed from his friend. In 1834 he ran, and won, and was elected to State legislature. In 1835, his sweetheart, whom he was engaged to marry, suddenly died. In 1836 he suffered a

nervous breakdown and was hospitalised for six months. In 1838, he ran to become speaker of state legislature, and lost. In 1839, he was admitted to practice law in the state of Illinois. In 1840, he was defeated in his bid to become an elector. In 1843 he ran for congress and lost. In 1844, he opened his own law firm. In 1846 he ran for congress and won and went to Washington. In 1848, he ran to be re-elected, and was defeated. In 1849, he applied for a job of land officer, and was rejected. In 1854 he ran for US senate and lost. In 1856, he was defeated in his bid for his party's nomination as vice president. In 1858, he ran for US senate, and lost. In 1860, he ran and was elected the 16th US President. He was one of the greatest US presidents. The Moral of it is, that no amount of failure stopped Lincoln from trying. He is attributed to have said 'if you want to test a man's character, give him power, that the true test of a man's character is give him power'.

34. Helping other people: Nothing makes life sweeter than making other people happy. The people you help today

become your soldiers in the battle of life tomorrow. Investment in properties is good, but to invest in people is far better. Try to make money but try also to make away from people's faces, not the things you acquire. Your greatest achievement should be raising achievers.

People will defend, stand by you, and honour you when they realise you value them. Do not let an ingrate stop you from making others great. Be kind and compassionate with people, because someday, somewhere, you may need them. Even great business leaders know that investment in people far outweighs investment in equipment. It is one life, make it count.

35. The cost of a cup of hatred: I wanted to know the cost of hatred, so I went to a makebelieve shop that sells hatred, to find out. The shop keeper asked how he could help me. I told him I wanted just a cup of hatred. The wise elderly man smiled, and asked if I could afford it. I smiled back at him and asked, 'how much is it?' He took a deep breath: 'This is the cost: It will take away your inner peace. It will cost you incurable worries. It will eat up your heart. It will be deeply

bitter, whenever you set your eyes on the person you hate. When others are celebrating him or her, you will always be looking for why he or she is not dead or does not deserve it. You will become so weak and tired of seeing the person. When the person you hate laughs, you will cry. While others are busy planning their lives and future, you will be busy looking for how to pull him or her down. You will become unhappy, angry, and bad tempered. You will have deep grudges, bitterness, health issues: high blood pressure, diabetes, heart, kidney, liver diseases, stroke, cancer, etc. You are likely to die before your time'. I realised I could not afford even an ounce of hatred. I left in a hurry remaining as I am, happy, free spirited and open-minded. Why pay such high price for hatred when I can love others easily, freely, and cheaply. Positive thinking leads to positive living.

36. Are your children ready to inherit you? A certain son of a wealthy man wanted to inherit his father's business. The old man gave him one condition to fulfil, or else he would give away his fortune whilst alive, or by means of his Will. The father

told his son 'Go and earn $10,000 dollars, show me the money and my multimillion-dollar business are yours'. Not long after, his son brought the money. He had collected it from his mother, claiming he worked for it. His father took the cash and threw it into the burning oven. The two watched the oven, until all the money was burnt to ashes. The father told his son to go and work to earn the money and bring it to him. The father wanted to be sure the son knew how hard it is to make money, so the son could appreciate and value any money left for him. The overzealous and protective mother gave her son another $10,000 and told the boy to wait for some time, so he could disguise, and look worn out, before seeing his father. When he eventually met Once more, he told his son to go to work, save $10,000 dollars and show it to him, and the inheritance would all be his. The young man was furious, knowing that his father was determined and stringent with the condition of working and saving up $10,000 before he could have access to his inheritance. The boy again met with his mother who had been giving her son money, to deceive her husband. She was thinking of another way out, but her son told his mother not to worry, he would go out and look for real employment, work and save the money for his father. He went to a far place, did menial, hard, and odd jobs. He spent years denying himself, making sacrifices, forgot his previous lifestyle, no more pleasure, no good accommodation, no expensive women, or the designer wear he was accustomed to, to save up money for his father. When he eventually came back his mother wept, she hardly recognised her thin, emaciated, and wretched son. In this desperate condition, he presented the money to his father. He narrated how he made the money, with pain and hardship. He gave his father the money and once again his father threw it into the fire. The boy immediately rushed to the fire and retrieved the money, exclaiming 'Father! You absolutely cannot burn my sweat!' The father replied, 'You have indeed worked for this money my son, nobody will stand looking, seeing his efforts going up in flames, as has happened previously, when your mother gave you money to bring to me'. The father was convinced his son now appreciated the hard work involved in earning money, and would prudently manage his inheritance, he then willed all his wealth to his son.

37. The Moral of the above story is that people put value on things that cost them most. Wealth gotten through effortless ways, will soon end up in the oven, or be wasted. Fools are soon parted with their money. Before you hand over your business to your child or children, first hand over wisdom to them. It is good not to over-pamper your children, saying you do not want them to go through what you went through, as an indigent child. Overpampering takes away the animal instinct in every human being, without which, the child cannot survive. I am convinced that success in life, without a successor, is failure. Sometimes, it is good to create artificial scarcity to harden-up your children for tomorrow. Share your difficult childhood stories with your children to teach them life's problem solving. Wisdom (ako na uche) and a good name are best inheritance you can bequeath

your children. Huge wealth handed over to unwise and spoilt children, without character and morals, will end up in other hands. Common sense is not common. Success and wisdom are not taught in schools, but in the streets, through challenging work, dedication, courage, focus, determination, resilience, diligence, honesty, perseverance, comradeship, character, prudence etc. Knowledge is taught in schools. Experience is the best teacher.

38. The Mock: The bloke asked me how far mate? I said Great. Thank God. So far, so good. He enquired why: I replied that I am happy, contented and not doing so badly at all. He laughed at me with scorn. He wondered why I should be happy and grateful to God. He showed me mates my age, who are living in mansions, or running countries, or huge organisations. I said yes, but there are also many mates of my age, who are buried and rotting inside dirty old graves. Why them? He then showed me fat bank accounts of some of my mates; I showed him the hospital bills of some others, who are terribly sick, who cannot eat, cannot

drink, and cannot go to toilet on their own. He took me to boutiques and showed me the most expensive designer clothes, worn by some of my mates. I told him as we speak there could be many of my mates in prison, having lost their freedom. Some have been there for years. Some are there for alleged crimes they did not commit, or they were too ill, ignorant, or unintelligent to know what they were doing at the time. I told him that as we speak, some of my mates are naked and lying in a mortuary. I said you find your own reason to be happy. No one has it all. Learn to be happy and contented. Why did you say, why me? Try also saying why not me? Do not let any situation stress or depress your life. You are not a mistake. You are yet an unfinished work, of Mother Nature. You may not have everything, but you certainly have many things to be grateful for, one of which is you are alive now, and reading this. If only you know how much evil and shame God has spared you, from the time you were born, you would be incredibly grateful. A living dog is better than a dead lion. What goes around comes around. We are all in this boat of life together, and none of us is getting out of here alive. It is better to say that is through where the legend escaped, than to say that is where the corpse of the legend was found.

39. Why is it when you call a man a Lion, he is incredibly happy, but call him an animal he will be truly angry, is a lion not an animal?

40. God why is it that in Japan a seventeen-year-old is a doctor. In Brazil, a seventeen-year-old is a footballer. In India, a seventeen-year-old is a shop owner. In China, a seventeen-year-old is an engineer. In Iraq, a seventeen-year-old is a soldier. In the USA, a seventeen-year-old is a celebrity. In Israel, a seventeen-year-old is a priest. In the UK, seventeen-year-olds are yobs and hoodlums.

41. In Africa, thirty-five-year-olds are WhatsApp group admin.

42. Once you are married to a bad wife, the devil will leave you alone, because he has settled you for life, never to know peace.

My neighbour just finished authoring a book on 'How to Make Money' Now he needs money to publish it. I told him to read the book.

43. FAITH: Faith is not going to church, mosque, or other religious places every day. To me, faith is all about trusting and believing the invisible. You do not know how it will happen, but you know it will happen. To me faith is seeing the invisible, believing the unbelievable, which leads to receiving the impossible, after the unbelievable. You must be tested, before you can have a testimony.

44. Do not give in and do not give up so easily. Success may be just a step away. It is not the size of the dog in a fight, but the size of the fight in a dog. It is not how many punches one throws, but how many punches one can take, and remain on his feet. Better to say how the hero escaped, than to say where his lifeless body was found. Do not regret growing older, it is a privilege denied to many. Note, that time is a great healer.

45. A post states that if you are seventy-five years old and you work eight hours per

day, and sleep eight hours, at this age you would have slept for twenty-five years, worked for twenty-five years and enjoyed for twenty-five years. As early as you can, try to own an investment that earns money while you are sleeping, and/or enjoying life.

46. How do you convince the upcoming generation that education is the key to success, when poor university graduates and rich criminals surround us?

47. Many people do not know the pain, challenges, and disappointments you had to go through to get to where you are today. Indeed, you went through hell, and pulled yourself up by your bootstraps, like the proverbial green "Ugu" vegetables, that provide the water with which it is cooked, but that does not mean that others coming behind you should go through the same ordeal. Accept and thank providence that you have paid to make it easier for the next generation.

48. Life is too short to try to have peace with people who do not want to have peace with you. Some of your relatives, you

love them, but you must love them from a distance. Do not frustrate yourself trying to make things happen, that they do not want to happen. It is not being disrespectful, but being responsible with the gifts God has given you. I am a peacemaker and try to be at

peace with others. Some people have their own issues, if they do not like who they are, how are they going to love who you are? If they do not have a good relationship with themselves, how are they going to have a good relationship with you? No matter what you do, it is never going to be enough, because they will always find faults and be critical, and try to make you feel guilty. There are people who do not like about you, but about the blessings on you. They make all the taking, but they give nothing. You are not made to be controlled by them. There are people who like to make the most withdrawals, but they make the least deposits. Quit swimming across the ocean to help people who will not cross a pond to help you. Make a change if the relationship is one-sided, and they do all the taking. Breakaway from people like that, who get offended because you do not meet their every expectation, they are not loyal friends.

49. Year 2021 has arrived with two new strains of virus in the UK and other parts of the world. The new strains, though they have the same symptoms as the first, spread faster in the populace. I have received the sad news that one of my cousins living in northeast London, is admitted to hospital, having contracted a strain of covid 19. The Southeast London and Kent as well as some other parts of UK have again been placed under tier 4/5 lockdown. This means the complete closure of almost every business and school. I believe if there was no religion, faiths, and beliefs, then there would be much evil and crime about. The poor would murder the rich. Pretty women could not walk the streets alone. Life would be brutish; primitive and it would be survival of the strongest.

I heard the one about a woman who was asked a question thus: Are you a working woman, or a housewife? She stated, and I quote; I am a full-time working housewife. I work 24 hours a day. I am a mum, wife, daughter, and daughter-in-law. I am an alarm clock, a cook, a maid, teacher, waitress, nanny, nurse, and a handy woman and much more. I am a security officer, counsellor, and a comforter. I do not get breaks or holidays. I do not get sick leave or take day off. I work all day and all night. I am on call all hours and yet I get asked 'what do you do all day?' They say that a woman is the most unique character, like salt, in that her presence is never acknowledged, but her absence makes it all so tasteless. They say that when a woman is quiet, millions of things are running through her mind. She wonders why she is taken for granted, made to be a second-class citizen, and is there only to serve others. It is said that a woman is usually a multiplier. If you give her sperm, she gives a baby. If you give her a house, she will give you a home. If you give grocery, she gives you a meal, and if you give her a headache, she will give you hell. As the owner and Director of two law firms or chambers, in London, England, United Kingdom, the experience is extremely rewarding. The headache can also be double.

We are lucky in that we have Legal Aid franchises in Criminal, matrimonial and housing matters. It is so gratifying to be able to aid those without enough money to be able to obtain justice. The rates we earn are much lower than we earn in private or cash matters. The advantage over cash matters is also substantial. The income is guaranteed because it comes from an arm of the government. When you are paid, it comes in bulky amounts.

We accept instructions in other areas of law such as Immigration, civil and company laws. Solicitors are free to set their own prices. I advise my lawyers and professional colleagues it is better to eat in small bites for a long time, than to eat big chunks for a noticeably fleeting time. It is better to charge moderately, and not to be greedy. They should charge according to need and one's ability to pay. To provide best services at reasonable rates. The law of averages is positively on our side.

For any Nigerian businessman or women, the biggest challenge is getting honest and reliable staff. Many people nowadays who pretend to be looking for work and offer to help you, are looking for an opportunity to steal as much as possible. Even in politics, most seek public office as a gateway to line their own pockets. No one goes into politics seeking an opportunity to serve. They are all seeking the opportunity to 'loot and steal big'. All Pentecostal churches pray for their members for a financial 'breakthrough,' regardless of their level of education, social class, marital status, business, and employment status. And, to stay abroad and set up any business in Nigeria is a total waste of time, unless I have plainly decided to set it as a legacy, but not as a profit-making venture. Nigerians at home do not give account, and when they do, it is not worth the paper it is written on. I know friends who started poultries, transportation, and hotels, but saw no accounts, let alone profit. They build their own mini business, under your own, and then use your resources to run their own profitable businesses.

Because Nigerians do not trust each other, we end up having small law firms and other forms of business. Indian's whites, even Lebanese, can pull resources together and build big firms and companies.

It is funny how an average Nigerian will accuse the Nigerian politicians, police, and other civil servants of incompetence and thievery, whilst they will surely do the same thing, or worse, if they are given half the chance. Arguably, the only reason any Nigerian has not stolen billions of government money, is simply because they have not had the opportunity.

## THE YEAR 2022

The year 2022 has been a great year for me and ended with a bang. Health wise, I was fine, home front and office are in great shape. My wife, Lynn came up with a surprise Caribbean cruise holiday. We flew out of Gatwick on the 14th of December 2022 and after nearly nine hours non-stop flight, we landed at Grantley Adams International Airport, Barbados.

We checked into the Radisson Hotel. The next day, we went to the capital city, Bridgetown for sightseeing. Later, we hired a taxi and had an all-round tour of the entire beautiful island. On the third day, we boarded the large cruise ship, Rhapsody of the Seas, and sailed off to other Caribbean islands. The ship is about half a mile long and ten storeys high. It has cabins, restaurants, casinos, swimming pool, Gym room, running tracks. Food and beverages are buffet.

We stopped at Trinidad, Tobago, Grenada, and St Vincent, where I personally visited St Georges University medical School. One of my ex-partners, and my cousins Dr. Okoroha and Dr. Ozigbu graduated from the medical school.

We sailed to St Lucia, Dominica, St Kitts and St. Maartens. In every country, my wife, son and I chose to leave the ship and take an organised tour, of four to six hours. There are tales of how mostly the English, and French fought over dominance and control of these islands, and the English always prevailed. All the indigenous black population were brought to these islands, as slaves from Africa. Apart from Barbados, other islands are very hilly. It was an exquisite, exotic experience to say the least. On 27th December, we returned to London. The flight back, across the Atlantic Ocean, was very stormy and we had to keep our seat belts on for over two hours. Four hours later, on same day, I was on another British Airways (BA) flight to Nigeria, for Christmas and for the coveted Nze and Ozo full induction Ceremonies scheduled for the 30th of December 2022.

I arrived at the Nnamdi Azikiwe International Airport, Abuja, Nigeria in early hours of 28th December 2022. I was impressed to see how neat and modernised the airport looked. Nigeria is demonstrably far ahead of any of the Caribbean little Islands in my estimation.

Surprisingly the Abuja Airport immigration and customs officials, appeared to have waned off the bribe begging attitudes of the past. I went to local side of airport where, after two hours haggle, I successfully took a United Nigeria airline flight to Sam Mbakwe Airport Owerri, Imo state Nigeria. I had a few hiccups at the Abuja airport, as only one piece of luggage is allowed with booking, anything additional is extra, which had to be weighed and paid for in Nigerian Naira.

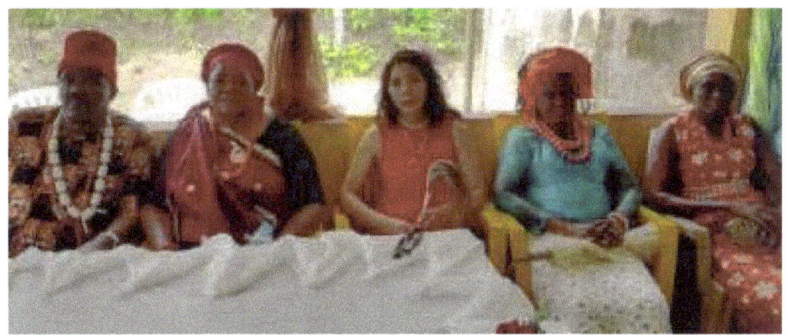

*Four of my wives at another chieftaincy title at Omuduru Mbano*

*Top: Patricia my Ex-white wife.*
*Below: Myself with Dr. Sope Adeeko, Our Lead Property Law Department.*

*In Law School classroom in Abuja Nigeria*

*My chieftaincy title by Eze Justice Ojiako*

*My beautiful house in Abba, my ancestral hometown, in Nigeria*

*At The Buckingham Palace Gate in United Kingdom.*

*Myself and my two younger brothers, Cletus and Damian, at my Master's Degree Graduation at University of Nebraska.*

*My daughter, Cynthia Chiyere Okoro, as a Titled Chief In Nigeria. She lives in Maryland USA*

Myself at a funeral ceremony in Nigeria

*With kingsley Onyekwuluje a multi-award winning Author/Lawyer*

*Myself and my 2nd wife, Prof. Lulu Chief Adolph Okoro in S/Africa Safari.*

*My first chieftaincy title in 1989 at Abba my ancestral home in Nigeria*

*Myself and three of my wives and my youngest son, Amara, in Nigeria*

*Our family married daughters, called ' 'Umuada' in our family compound at Abba in 2014*

*Myself with John Jenkins, one of my Legal Staff, at Graceland Solicitors*

*Lulu in USA with my two daughters, Chioma and Chiyere at Omaha Nebraska, USA.*

*My 1st house built in 1984 when I returned from USA*

*My son, Amara.*

*With my two daughters, Chiyere and Chioma in the USA.*

*Myself with my cousin Philo.*

*Myself and my beautiful wife, Lolo Lynn Okoro*

**CHAPTER TWENTY-THREE**

---

# Our Surprise Caribbean Cruise Holidays booked by My Wife, Lynn Okoro

From UK, one could take alcohol in the checked-in luggage, but in Nigeria, I had to negotiate and beg, before I was allowed to fly with bottles of alcoholic beverages from London.

Before going to Nigeria on this occasion, I was very fearful and nervous. My concerns emanated from the fact that in recent times, stories from home continued to tell a tale of woe: wanton, random and reckless killing of people in Igboland, the former Biafra-land of Nigeria. Some of the known, or unknown gunmen are allegedly from either of these groups: Bibeau who claim to be protecting Igbos from indiscriminate killings of nefarious Government agents, and bokoharam and Fulani herdsmen oppressors; the Indigenous People of Biafra (IPOB) who are protesting against the continued detention of their Leader, Mazi Nnamdi Kanu. Then there are also the Fulanis, herdsmen and other mafia men who have AK47s and are surreptitiously eliminating the Igbos. Unfortunately, when any person is killed there is no way of arresting or identifying the culprit, among the contesting groups. Everywhere in Nigeria there seems to be a general breakdown of security, there are Bandits, even unemployed graduates, who kidnap people, disappearing into the bush with their victims, and demanding huge ransoms.

I put my trust in providence and went anyway. My family picked me up from the airport in my Jeep, and in less than 30 minutes, I was safely home in my ancestral compound, in Abba. One of my junior brothers, Chief, (Engineer) Dem Omereoha Okoroha and his son, Mr Chijioke were also home from Maryland, USA and waiting for me. but his wife Dr Juliet Chiwendu Okoro could not come home. My brother Chief (Dr) Chidex Dikeoha Okoroha's wife Lolo Stella and my cousin Dr (Chief) Lambert Owelle Okoroha and his wife, Lolo Amaka were also at home from Houston, Texas waiting for my arrival. My Cousin, the family Prince, Chief Kingsley Idejimba Ozigbu had bought and delivered a large Cow to my compound, as a gift to support my induction into the

Abba Ama Ano, Oha Nze na Ozo forum. My nephew, Mr Chinoye, the only son of my late beloved baby brother, Mr Chinedu Eugene Okoroha also delivered a huge goat, as a gift to me. My niece Ms Joy Adeleke- Okoro, the first daughter of my only sister, late Mrs Patricia Onyejiaka, nee Okoroha also came home from Kaduna and presented me with hot drinks. Ifeanyi Leroy is my only son in Nigeria, Amaka, is my only daughter in Nigeria. My other children are overseas with their partners and children, namely, Didi and Adaeze Okoro are in Johannesburg, South Africa. Mark Anthony Munso and Chichi Cynthia Okoro, and Derek Okoroha are in MD USA. My children in London are David Ugonna, Akwaugo Emyline, Kelechi Keneedy, Ginika Constance Okoroha and the youngest Amara Adolph Okoro and his mother, Mrs Lolo Lynn Zhang Okoro.

I went through all the plans and preparations for the big day. My Obi, parlours and entire houses were renovated and re-painted. Some chieftaincy seats were bought. There were decorations and canopies and new chairs. Chief Omereoha kicked off the event on the 29th, the eve of the main day. There was a sevencanon gun salute and sumptuous meal and party, with live band, at his own ancestral compound.

On 30th December 2022, my cousin Mazi Cosmas Ozigbu and one of my daughters, Mrs Amaka Okoro Ndukwe had ensured everything was in place for the smooth running of the ceremonies. The day started with another seven rounds of cannon guns shots salute, slaughtering of the cow, six goats and several chickens. The married women of the family cooked food almost all night. Some caterers were also paid to provide special dishes: pounded yam, soup, ugba with stockfish, ukwa (breadfruit)

Approximately thirty Nze na Ozo title holders and two kings (Ezes) assembled at my cousin, Chief (Engineer) Paul Ozigbu's house, and from there they dramatically entered my compound, with music, pomp, and pageantry. All the Nzes were wearing Leaf Green Ishiagwu, red wrapper, red customised caps and red mourfla. They sat in order of seniority and ranking.

In attendance were His Royal Highness (HRH) Eze
Ononenyi, Boniface Uzoma, The Ekiti 11 of EkitiAfor Abba, and His royal Highness (HRH), Eze Nduwueze Maduawuchukwu, Eze Nwauruogu, Uburu 11 of Abba Ancient Kingdom.; Nze Nkem Obialo, Onye Ishi, Nze Dr C. K. C.
Anyanjo, Nze Nnanna Azubuike,Nze Uzoma, Nze Nwaotike Nze Obinna Akwiwu, Nze Bonny Duru, Nze Victor Uzoma, Nze Ifeanyi Ekwueme, Nze Chinedu Ohiaeri, Nze Bonny Maranzu and so on. However, Nze Goddy Ihegboro was absent, as he travelled to USA.

Present were also my uncles Chief Michael Okoroha and Sir Emmanuel Okoroha both of whom I knew from when I was born, as they were 10 years and 5 years old respectively, at the time of my birth. Some of my younger cousins were also present, including Chief
Okey Mmiri Okoroha, Chief Ralph Omeudo Okoroha, Dr. Nnamdi Ozigbu, Chief Barr Aham Ozigbu, Chief Uke Okey Okoroha and Engineer Ken Ozigbu and Dr Prince Dubem Ojiako. Absent with notice included Chief (DR) Eddy Okoroha, Chief (Dr) Bosco Ozigbu, Chief Paul Ozigbu and Bishop Peter Ozigbu,

I presented four Igbo Kola nuts to our visitors. The Nzes washed their hands and began induction. The Ezes prayed for everyone with libation and hot alcoholic drinks (Schnapps). Then they applied Nzu (white chalk) for purifications. Additionally, they prayed with Odo (red chalk) and Nchara for purification. Nze (Dr) Akogu read out full list of items, and the Rules and Regulations of the Nze na Ozo forum. My Elders confirmed my qualifications and entitlement to be inducted into Abba town Nze na Ozo titled men. The Secretary confirmed I provided everything required of me in the list, including fees, material items and dues.

Further pouring of libations and prayers and praying with the traditional Nzu and Odo. With the purification of the Inductee completed, the kings (Ezes) and senior Nzes then officially carried out the investiture by placing the wrist beads and neck beads on me, and gave me the Odu staff of office, the hand fan, and the walking stick. The Chairman and Ezes placed the seal of induction - a cap, (Okpu nwagoro) on my head. Subsequently, I performed the same rituals on my Lolos Susan, and Ursula. I was reminded of my past indiscretions and offences, forgiven, and henceforth I must live a life of total uprightness, purity, and a stain less behaviour. I was admonished to always stand on the path of the truth, fairness, and justice. I must not commit crime, evil or abomination, and I am required to speak no evil or falsehood, to always help the needy, the poor and widows, and to live an exemplary life, worthy of emulation. An Nze title holder should not eat in public, nor have an altercation, quarrel, or fight with anyone, except if it's the last option to defend one's life.

There was another six-canon gunshot salute to mark the completion of my induction. Myself and all the Nzes and Ezes danced in nobility and majesty to live traditional music. The Nzes washed their hands and went upstairs for feasting, eating. drinking and merry making. The pictures were taken, and 4 slaughtered goats were shared among the 4 Nzes of Abba Ama Ano kindreds.

Before Leaving Nze Okoroha's Compound, the Nzes paid courtesy visits to my junior brothers, before going home. Three live bands played late into the night.

For the completion of the Induction ceremonies, on the next day the Nzes met at HRH Uzoma's house, from there we led a procession of Ipu Ahia (going to the 4 Abba Markets: namely Afo Abba at Ekitiafo Abba, Afo Udo at Ogwuaga Abba, Orie Abba at Umudurunna Abba, and Nkwo Ebu at Umuokwara Abba. Finally, we went to Okpu Nwabana, the official origins of Abba. There were Okonkos and Nwaokorogboo dance bands. The day ended with entertainment at HRH Eze Maduabuchukwu's house. Ehi Ozo (native cow) 2022 would be slaughtered later in the new year.

Our Surprise Caribbean cruise holidays booked by my wife, Lynn Okoro

**CHAPTER TWENTY-FOUR**
-------------------------

# What Is Nze Na Ozo Title?

Nze na Ozo is an age old traditional and cultural institution. It is an ancient and honourable, oldest, and highest title in the whole of Igbo land, even before the coming of the White man, with his so-called western civilisation. The cult/ organisation stands firmly to uphold the ancestral heritage, culture, and tradition of the Ibos. It recognises life is not static, it therefore continues to evolve and modernize its customs, traditions, rules, and ethos. The purpose of Nze na Ozo forum of any town is to preserve the tradition and culture of the community.

To become Ozo implies being an NZE, becoming a living spirit and ancestor. You become a sacred representation of ancestors in human form. Nze refers to avoidance; one who avoids bad things that depress conscience, life and social value, an Nze represents the ideal of a good person in morals and character. Nze na Ozo is all about Integrity and Honour. For example, before the arrival of Christianity, Nze na Ozo members were obviously not Christians nor Muslims, but today one can belong to any religious or non-religious calling, and still hold a Nze na Ozo title. Today, many native catholic non-Catholic priests, pastors and Imams are also Nze na Ozo title holders. Nze na Ozo title has become more open, transparent and with sincere and honest purposes. In meeting, all glory and honour are given to Chukwuokike Abiama, that is, the one and only God the creator and the Almighty. The Igbos revere four market days. Eke, Orie, Afo and Nkwo. All the activities of Nze title holders are communal and for the betterment of humanity and the community.

Nze na Oze is not a chieftaincy title. One can hold several chieftaincy titles from several communities, but one can only be a Nze na Ozo in one's own hometown, and only once in a lifetime. After the arrival of the White man and his colonisation, for ease of administration, Lord Lugard appointed the District Officers (DO) who in turn appointed local warrant chiefs to collect taxes, among other things. These Chiefs were respected and feared in those days. Today, to be called a Chief is still prestigious and an honour, but only ceremonial.

A person has to go to an Eze's house to be made a Chief, but the Eze(s) and Nzes go to the inductee's home to be conferred with an Nze na Ozo title. Women, non-natives and strangers can be given Chieftaincy titles, but women, non-natives and strangers can never be made Nze na Ozo in Igboland.

A Nze na Ozo person is prohibited from lying, cheating, stealing, or committing any crime or abomination. He must be a married man, an indigen with a son, and a role model of visible financial means and transparent honesty. He must not have sex with another man, a child, an underage, or his own blood relative, such is incest.

Personally, I have lived in the west for over fifty years, an educated and learned gentleman, a practising Barrister and solicitor of the Supreme Courts of Federal Republic of Nigeria, and solicitor of the higher courts of England and Wales. I am an Officer of the courts in two jurisdictions, an ex-seminarian and a Knight (sir) in the Catholic Church. I find it befitting and honourable to identify myself with my culture and my kith and kin, who are striving to maintain and uphold the Ibo and African traditional pride, culture, values and heritage.

I was elated to have safely travelled and accomplished these events. I left the Imo state on 14th January and spent a few days at Abuja Transcorp Hilton Hotel, before I returned to the United Kingdom in January 2023.

In 2023, I luckily managed to attain more legacies to name. I built three one storey houses for three widows in our family. I built a one storey hall for Ogwuaga Abba Community at the compound of Ogwuaga Health Centre. Mrs Chiwendu Okoroha and Mrs Ella Okoroha.. I rebuilt my Bikku Bikku Palace or Obokoro

Osuagwu Okoroha. At 79, and fairly in good health. I have 12 children and 20 grandchildren. One of my sons, Kelechi started building his own home within the family compound at Abba. My law Chambers are thriving.

## THE LAST LEG OF LIFE!!!

Most of us are now in the last quarter of our lives and should read this interesting piece of advice. This is one of the nicest and most gentle articles I've read in a while:

No politics, no religion and no racial issues - just food for thought.

You know, time has a way of moving quickly and catching you unaware of the passing years. It seems just yesterday that I was young and embarking on my new life. Yet, in a way, it seems like years ago, and I wonder where all the years went. I know that I lived them all. I have glimpses of how it was back then and of all my hopes and dreams. However, here it is, the last quarter of my life and it catches me by surprise!!! How did I get here so fast?

Where did the years go and where did my youth go?
I remember well, seeing older people through the years and thinking those older people were years away from me, and I was only on the first quarter, and the fourth quarter was so far off, that I could not visualise it, or imagine fully what it would be like.

Yet here it is!! My friends are retired and getting grey, they move slower, and I see an older person now. Some are in better shape and some in worse shape than me, but I see the great change. They're not like the ones I remember who were young and vibrant. But, like me, their age is beginning to show, and we are now those older folks that we used to see and never thought we'd become.

Each day now, I find that just getting a shower is a real target for the day and taking a nap is not a treat anymore!! It's mandatory, because if I don't do it of my own free will, I fall asleep where I sit. And so now, I enter this new season of my life, unprepared for all the aches and pains and the loss of strength and ability, to go and do things I wish I had done, but never did. At least now I know that, though I'm on the last quarter and I'm not sure how long it will last, when it's over on this earth, it's all over. A new adventure will begin, I feel! Yes, I have regrets. There are things I wish I hadn't done; things I should have done, but truly there are many things I'm happy to have done. It's all in a lifetime.

So, if you're not on the last quarter yet, let me remind you that it will be here faster than you think. So, whatever you would like to accomplish in your life, do it quickly. Don't put things off too long. Life goes by so quickly. So, do what you can today, as you can never be sure whether you're on the last quarter or not.
You have no promise that you will see all the seasons of life. So, live for today and say all the things you want your loved ones to remember - and hope they appreciate and love you, for all the things you have done for them, in all the past years.

Remember, it is health that is real wealth, and not pieces of gold, silver, or printed notes, or even property. Life' is a gift to you. Be Happy! Have a great day!

## YOU MAY THINK:

Going out is good - but coming back home is much better!!! You forget names - but it's okay because some people forgot they even knew you!!! You realize, you are never going to be good at anything like golf - but you like the outdoors. So, do it. The things you used to care to do, you aren't as interested in anymore - but you really don't care that you aren't as interested.

- You sleep better on a lounge chair with the TV on than in bed – you call it 'pre- sleep'! If you enjoy it, just do it.

- You miss the days when everything worked with just an 'On' and 'Off' switch!!!

- You tend to use more four-letter words – 'what' and 'when'?

- You have lots of clothes in your wardrobe, more than half of which you will never wear – but just in case!!

## OLD IS GOOD

- Old is comfortable.
- Old is safe.
- Old songs.
- Old movies. and - best of all,
- Friends of old!!!

So, stay well, 'Old friend.'
Have a fantastic day. Have an awesome Quarter, whichever one you're in!!!

TAKE CARE.

SEND THIS ON TO OTHER "OLD FRIENDS" AND LET THEM BE SMILING IN AGREEMENT.

IT'S NOT WHAT YOU GATHER, BUT WHAT YOU SOW!

Myself in my Chieftaincy Regalia

*With Auntie Diana, December 2022.*

*The house I built for my grandfather's wife, and her children.*

*With lolo Stella Okoroha, wife of my baby brother, Chief Sir Dr. Chidex* Okoroha.

With Chief Cozy Ozigbu at the Nze na Ozi *induction*
*2022*

*With Chief Sir Dr. Lambert and his lolo, Amaka Okoroha. At the Nze Na Ozo induction 2022.*

*With my two uncles, Chief Michael and Chief Emma Okoroha,*

*With the Abba traditional chiefs.*

*With Okoroha/Ezeala Family Chairman, Chattered Accountant, Chief Ralph Okoroha.*

*With Chief Sir Engr Dem Okoroha.*

*With Nze Dr Anyanjo and Nze Dr Akogu at my my induction as an Nze, December, 2022.*

*Confirmation as an Nze na Ozo by HRH B. Uzoma and HRH N. Maduabuchukwu.*

*My conferring Lolo of an Nze na Ozo Akaraugo, Chief, Sir, Dr, Barr Okoroha A A.*

*With Nze Obinna Akwiwu at my induction as an Nze na Ozo Abba 2023.*

*With lolo Susan, lolo Ursula and lolo Juliet at the induction.*

*With lolo Ling and Son Amara Okoroha in London, January, 2023.*

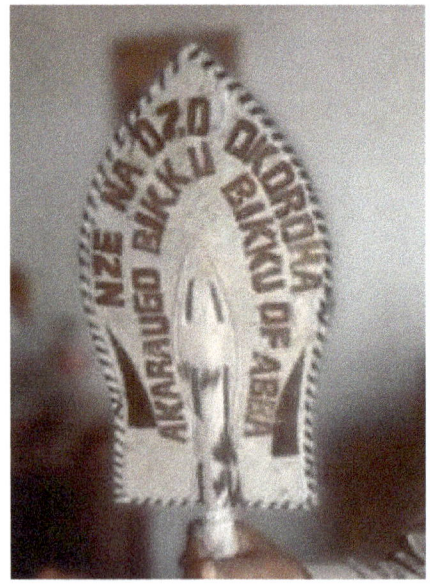
*One of My Chieftaincy Memorabilia (Taking my Grandfather's Title:'BIKKU BIKKU OF ABBA) Destiny Fulfilled!*

*My Amara A. Okoro*

*Nze Osuagwu Ijezie Okoroha BikkuBikku 1 (1860 – 1962)*

*Son: David Ugonna*

*Sons: David Ugonna and Kelechi Kennedy Okoroha*

*Son: Amara*

HRM Benedth Uzoka

With HRM Benedth Uzoka

*With my lovely wife Lynn Okoro*

*My Father: Azunnah David Osuagwu*

*Presenting the Kolanuts*

*My baby brother: Dr Okoro*

Myself and My Young Family

Kenndy and Wife

*Receiving My Chieftaincy Title*

**WAKE UP CALL!!**

*At 79-years old, Nze, Chief Barr Adolph Anyiam Okoroha, Akaraugo, Bikku Bikku III has donated a 2-level building, for health Centre facility, to his kindred, people of Ogwuaga Abba.*

*ALA OGWUAGA DOWA ONWEYA*
*Chief Engr Paul Ozigbu*
*Nnanyereugo 1*
*Ekwueme Abba 11*

**MY RESPONSE:**

*Our Engr Paul Ozigbu -Nnanyereugo, our Ebere Achuonye, our Dr Frank Ojiako -Ochuariri and others:*

*I am humbled and grateful for your kind words with respect to my philanthropic gestures, buildings and legacy to my own people - Ogwuaga mumnu.*

*To God be all the Glory.*
*Together we can make Ogwuaga Greater.*

*Nze, Barrister Adolph Anyiam Okoroha.*
*Chief Akaraka Gburugburu*
*Nze Bikku Bikku 111 Abba Nile*

*Dede Sir Fabro Dudu*
*London 2024*

www.ingramcontent.com/pod-product-compliance
Lightning Source LLC
Chambersburg PA
CBHW061250230426
43664CB00024B/2906